# THE WORLD ALMANAC® FOR KIDS 2014

WORLD ALMANAC® BOOKS
An Imprint of Infobase Learning

# THE WORLD ALMANAC® FOR KIDS 2014

**Project Management:** Robert Famighetti
**New Content:** RJF PUBLISHING

**Contributors:** Emily Dolbear, Jacqueline Laks Gorman, Richard Hantula, Lisa M. Herrington, Amanda Hudson, William A. McGeveran
**Photo Research:** Edward A. Thomas
**Index Editor:** Nan Badgett

**Design: Q2A/BILL SMITH**
**Chief Creative Officer:** Brian Kobberger
**Project Manager:** Paul Blake
**Design:** Brock Waldron, Shanin Glenn, Jackson Blount, Nidhi Sharma, Dalbir Singh
**Production:** Robergeau Duverger, Deb Sarkar, Ronald Ottaviano, Julia Edwards, Christina Mazza, Raina Accardi, Liana Weinstein, Luke Zeigler

**INFOBASE LEARNING**
**Editorial Director:** Laurie E. Likoff
**Senior Editor:** Sarah Janssen
**Project Editor:** Edward A. Thomas



**World Almanac® Books**
An imprint of Infobase Learning
132 West 31st Street
New York NY 10001

Hardcover
ISBN-13: 978-1-60057-176-3
ISBN-10: 1-60057-176-X

Paperback
ISBN-13: 978-1-60057-177-0
ISBN-10: 1-60057-177-8

International Standard Serial Number
1087-1764

*The World Almanac® for Kids* is distributed to the trade by Simon & Schuster, and to schools and libraries at special discounts by Infobase Learning. For more information, contact (800) 322-8755 or visit www.InfobaseLearning.com.

You can find *The World Almanac® for Kids* online at www.worldalmanac.com

Book printed and bound by RR Donnelley, Crawfordsville, IN
Date printed: July 2013
Printed in the United States of America

RRD BSG 10 9 8 7 6 5 4 3 2 1

# CONTENTS

# FACES & PLACES IN THE NEWS

## NEW POPE

Pope Francis, elected by the College of Cardinals on March 13, 2013, spoke to people gathered in Vatican City on Easter Sunday.

## FLEEING FROM WAR

These children, outside a refugee camp in Lebanon, were among more than 1 million Syrians who fled to other countries by early 2013 to escape the dangers of civil war.

## THREAT TO PEACE

North Korea launched a long-range rocket in December 2012, stepped up its nuclear program, and made threats against other countries, despite penalties by the United Nations.

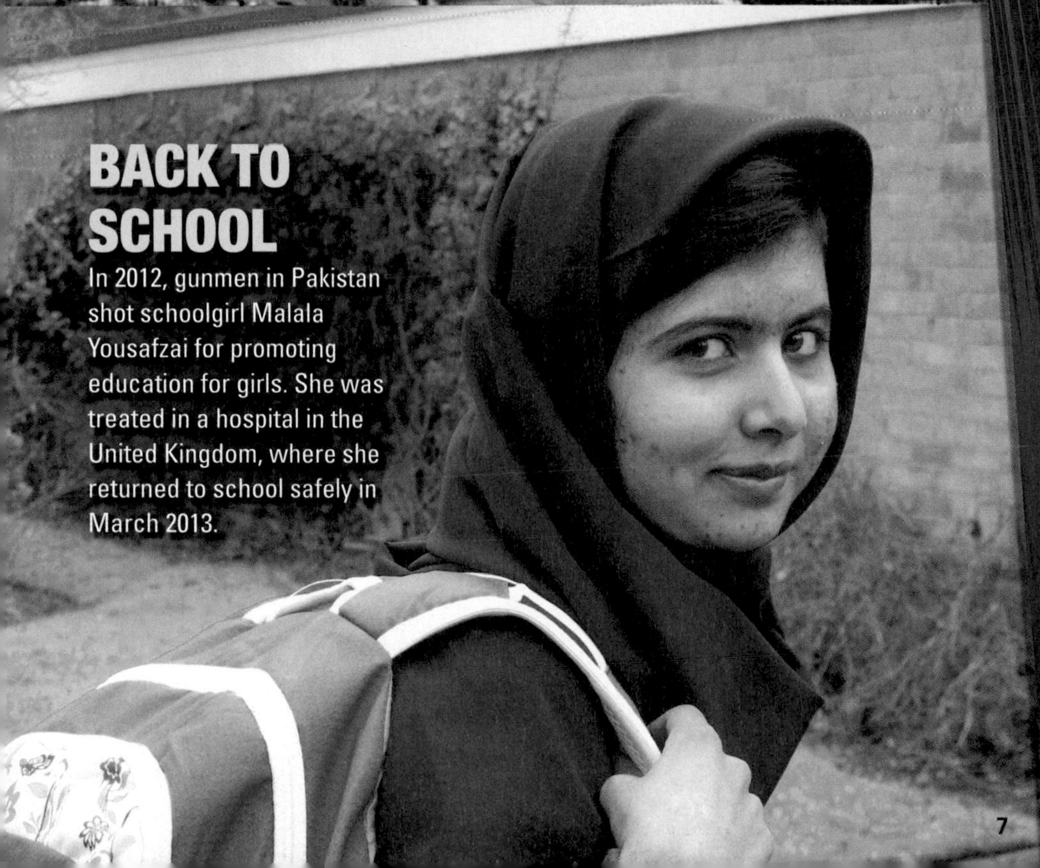

## BACK TO SCHOOL

In 2012, gunmen in Pakistan shot schoolgirl Malala Yousafzai for promoting education for girls. She was treated in a hospital in the United Kingdom, where she returned to school safely in March 2013.

# IN THE NEWS

## INAUGURATION DAY

President Barack Obama was sworn in for a second term on January 21, 2013, at the U.S. Capitol.

## DEADLY TWISTER

On May 20, 2013, a huge tornado leveled homes and killed more than 20 people in and around Moore, Oklahoma.

## TRIBUTE

Running shoes were hung from a barrier near the finish line of the Boston Marathon, as a memorial to victims of bombings on April 15, 2013.

## THE DREAM LIVES ON

Fifty years ago, on August 28, 1963, Martin Luther King inspired the nation with his "I Have a Dream" speech at the Lincoln Memorial in Washington, DC. Today, the King Memorial, in the nation's capital, honors his words and achievements.

# TELEVISION

## FUTURISTIC FICTION

Viewers tuned in to the science-fiction drama *Revolution* to imagine a future world without electricity.

## *BIG* HUMOR

Leonard, Penny, Amy, and Sheldon returned for more laughs in the sixth season of *The Big Bang Theory*.

## NEIGHBORHOOD WATCH

A suburban family discovered they were surrounded by extraterrestrials in the hit show *The Neighbors.*

## *ONCE* AGAIN

The second season of *Once Upon a Time* featured more fairy-tale drama between Rumplestiltskin and the evil queen.

# MOVIES

## STYLISH STARK

Viewers lined up to see Robert Downey Jr. return as billionaire Tony Stark in *Iron Man 3*.

## MORE *MONSTERS*

The beloved characters from *Monsters, Inc.* went to college and learned how to scare in *Monsters University*.

## SUMMER FUN

Liam James and AnnaSophia Robb starred in the quirky coming-of-age comedy *The Way, Way Back.*

## *OZ* ORIGINS

*Oz: The Great and Powerful* imagined what might have happened to the Wizard of Oz and Glinda the Good Witch before Dorothy arrived in town.

## *GATSBY* GLAMOUR

*The Great Gatsby*, based on the novel by F. Scott Fitzgerald, starred Tobey Maguire, Leonardo DiCaprio, and Carey Mulligan.

# MOVIES

## *STAR* SEQUEL

Zachary Quinto and Chris Pine returned to play Spock and Kirk in *Star Trek Into Darkness*, a sequel to 2009's *Star Trek*.

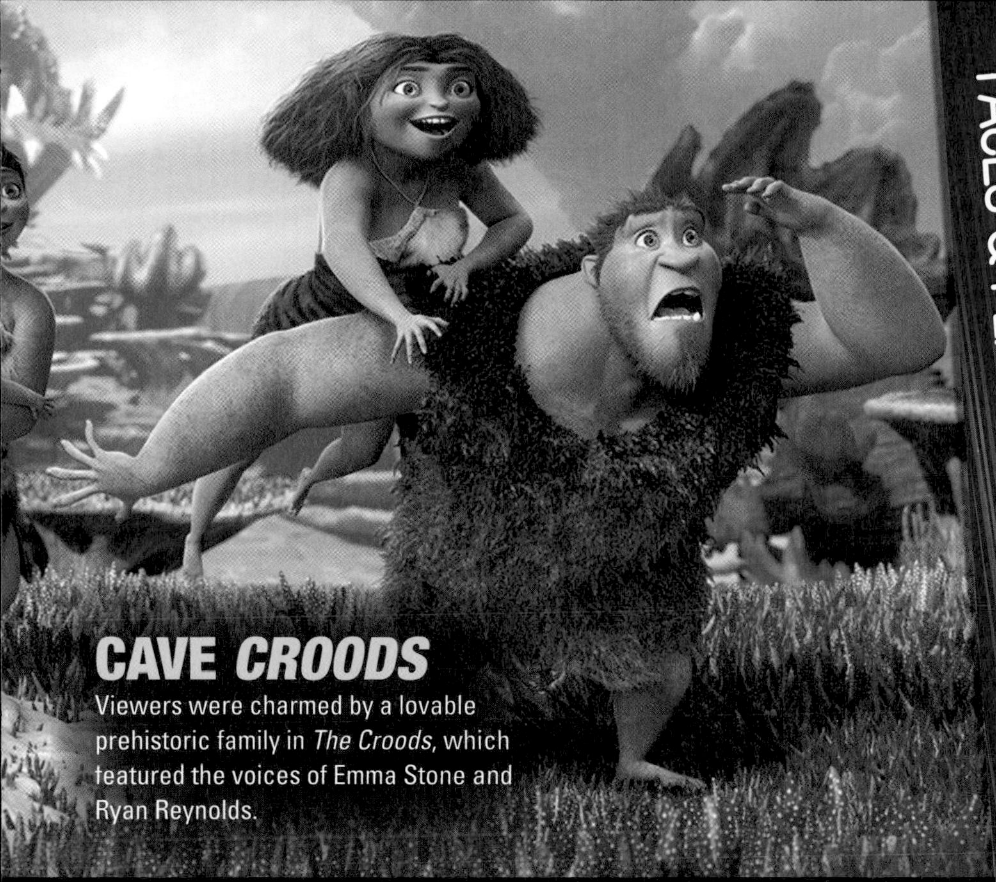

## CAVE *CROODS*

Viewers were charmed by a lovable prehistoric family in *The Croods*, which featured the voices of Emma Stone and Ryan Reynolds.

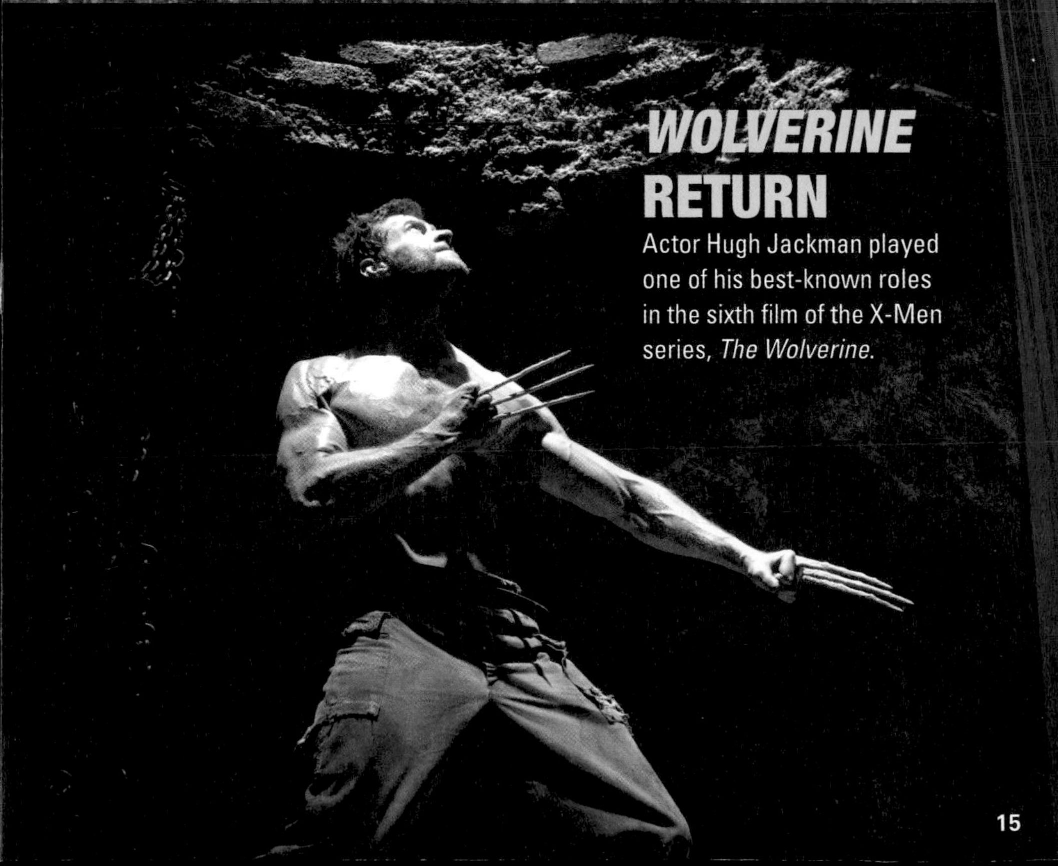

## *WOLVERINE* RETURN

Actor Hugh Jackman played one of his best-known roles in the sixth film of the X-Men series, *The Wolverine*.

## MRS. CARTER

After a powerful performance at the Super Bowl halftime show in 2013, Beyoncé toured the globe on her Mrs. Carter Show World Tour.

# MUSIC

## JUSTIN TIME

Justin Timberlake's third solo album, *The 20/20 Experience*, sped to the top of the charts as soon as it was released.

## YOUNG AND FUN

The band fun. took home two Grammy Awards in 2013, including Song of the Year for "We Are Young," featuring Janelle Monáe .

## TOURING TAYLOR

Taylor Swift performed in sold-out venues all over North America as she promoted her album *Red*. She also sang at the 2013 Grammy Awards.

## GO, JOE!

Quarterback Joe Flacco (5) threw three touchdown passes in the Baltimore Ravens' 34-31 victory over the San Francisco 49ers in Super Bowl XLVII on February 3, 2013.

# SPORTS

## FRESHMAN ON FIRE

Unstoppable UConn freshman Breanna Stewart was named the Most Outstanding Player of the Final Four. Her team beat Louisville, 93-60, in the 2013 NCAA championship game.

## SCORING MACHINE

On January 16, 2013, LeBron James became the youngest NBA player to score 20,000 career points.

## TWO'S A CHARM

In his 400th career Cup start, Jimmie Johnson won the 2013 Daytona 500 in February. It was his second Daytona win.

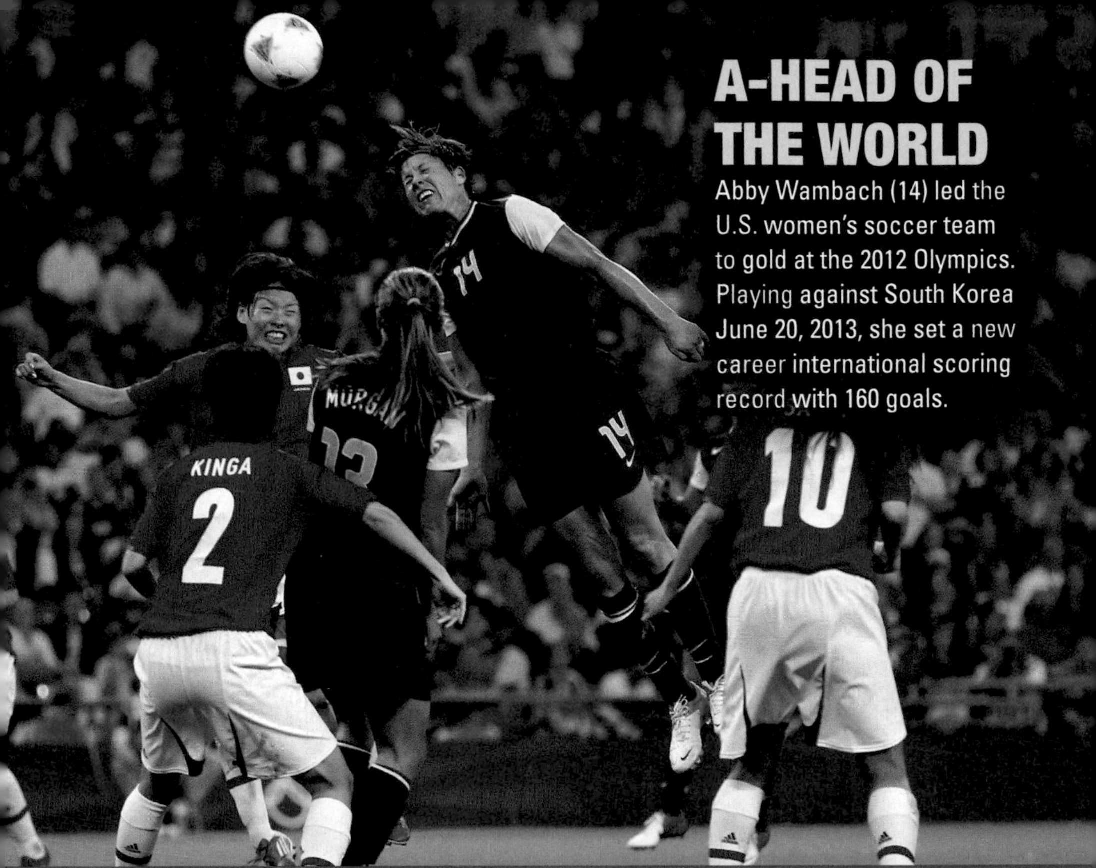

# SPORTS

## A-HEAD OF THE WORLD

Abby Wambach (14) led the U.S. women's soccer team to gold at the 2012 Olympics. Playing against South Korea June 20, 2013, she set a new career international scoring record with 160 goals.

## BIG WIN

Alabama beat Notre Dame, 41-14, in the BCS title game in January 2013. Alabama running back Eddie Lacy was named the game's Offensive MVP.

# UNLIKELY STAR

Louisville's Luke Hancock became the first reserve player to be named the Most Outstanding Player of the Final Four after his team defeated Michigan, 82-76, in the 2013 NCAA championship game.

# HISTORIC DAY

On March 31, 2013, the Texas Rangers played the Houston Astros as members of the same league (AL) for the first time in the teams' history. The Rangers won, 8-2.

→Which breed of dog is the most popular? PAGE 28

# Weird Animal Facts

Furry or scaly, creepy or crawly, schoolbus-sized or microscopic—animals can often surprise us. Here are some facts about the Animal Kingdom.

## Flying Frogs

A new species of frog has been discovered in the forests near Ho Chi Minh City, Vietnam. The animal is a type of "flying" frog, which means it can glide between trees. The scientist who found the species nicknamed it "Helen's Flying Frog" (after her mother). There are actually hundreds of frog species that glide. Helen's Flying Frogs have huge webbed hands and feet, and females have flappy forearms to help them parachute among the trees. Scientists say that the frogs went undiscovered for so long because they spend most of their time high up in trees, blending in with green leaves.

## Koala Fingerprints

At first glance, humans and koalas may not look like they have a lot in common. Koalas spend most of their lives in trees and sleep for up to 20 hours a day. But humans and koalas share one unusual characteristic. Koalas have fingerprints that are very similar to human ones and are unique to each animal. Even under a microscope, it is almost impossible to tell human and koala fingerprints apart! Scientists are not sure why koalas have fingerprints when most of their close relatives do not, but they think that the grooves on koalas' fingers may help them pick and grasp eucalyptus leaves, which make up most of a koala's diet.

# LIFE ON EARTH

This timeline shows how life developed on Earth. The earliest life forms are at the top of the chart. The most recent are at the bottom. All numbers are years before the present.

|  |  |  |
|---|---|---|
| Precambrian | 4.6 billion | Formation of Earth |
| Precambrian | 3.8 billion–542 million | First evidence of life on Earth. All life is in water. Early single-celled bacteria and achaea appear, followed by multi-celled organisms, including early animals. |
| Paleozoic | 542–443 million | Animals with shells (called trilobites) and some mollusks form. Primitive fish and corals develop. Evidence of the first primitive land plants. |
| Paleozoic | 443–417 million | Coral reefs form. Other animals, such as the first known freshwater fish, develop. → Relatives of spiders and centipedes develop. |
| Paleozoic | 417–354 million | The first trees and forests appear. The first land-living vertebrates, amphibians, and wingless insects appear. Many new sea creatures also appear. |
| Paleozoic | 354–290 million | Reptiles develop. Much of the land is covered → by swamps. |
| Paleozoic | 290–248 million | A mass extinction wipes out 95 percent of all marine life. |
| Mesozoic | 248–206 million | In the Triassic period, marine life develops again. Reptiles also move into the water. Reptiles begin to dominate the land areas. Dinosaurs and mammals develop. |
| Mesozoic | 206–144 million | The Jurassic is dominated by giant dinosaurs. In the late Jurassic, birds evolve. |
| Mesozoic | 144–65 million | In the Cretaceous period, new dinosaurs appear. Many insect groups, modern mammal and bird groups also develop. A global extinction of most dinosaurs occurs at the end of this period. → |
| Cenozoic | 65–1.8 million | Ancestors of modern-day horses, zebras, rhinos, sheep, goats, camels, pigs, cows, deer, giraffes, elephants, cats, dogs, and primates begin to develop. |
| Cenozoic | 1.8 million–10,000 | Large mammals such as mammoths, saber-toothed cats, and giant → ground sloths develop. Modern human beings evolve. |
| Cenozoic | 10,000–present | Human civilization develops. |

# ANIMAL KINGDOM

The world has so many animals that scientists looked for a way to organize them into groups. A Swedish scientist named Carolus Linnaeus (1707–1778) worked out a system for classifying both animals and plants. We still use it today.

The Animal Kingdom is separated into two large groups—animals with backbones, called **vertebrates**, and animals without backbones, called **invertebrates**.

These large groups are divided into smaller groups called **phyla**. And phyla are divided into even smaller groups called **classes**. The animals in each group are classified together when their bodies are similar in certain ways.

## VERTEBRATES

### Animals with Backbones

|  |  |
|---|---|
| **FISH** | Swordfish, tuna, salmon, trout, halibut, goldfish |
| **AMPHIBIANS** | Frogs, toads, mud puppies |
| **REPTILES** | Turtles, alligators, crocodiles, lizards |
| **BIRDS** | Sparrows, owls, turkeys, hawks |
| **MAMMALS** | Kangaroos, opossums, dogs, cats, bears, seals, rats, squirrels, rabbits, chipmunks, porcupines, horses, pigs, cows, deer, bats, whales, dolphins, monkeys, apes, humans |

## INVERTEBRATES

### Animals without Backbones

|  |  |
|---|---|
| **PROTOZOA** | The simplest form of animals |
| **COELENTERATES** | Jellyfish, hydra, sea anemones, coral |
| **MOLLUSKS** | Clams, snails, squid, oysters |
| **ANNELIDS** | Earthworms |
| **ARTHOPODS** | |
| Crustaceans | Lobsters, crayfish |
| Centipedes and Millipedes | |
| Arachnids | Spiders, scorpions |
| Insects | Butterflies, grasshoppers, bees, termites, cockroaches |
| **ECHINODERMS** | Starfish, sea urchins, sea cucumbers |

**HOMEWORK TIP**

How can you remember the animal classifications from most general to most specific? Try this sentence:

**K**ing **P**hilip **C**ame **O**ver **F**rom **G**reat **S**pain.

**K** = Kingdom; **P** = Phylum; **C** = Class; **O** = Order; **F** = Family; **G** = Genus; **S** = Species

# IT'S A ZOO OUT THERE!

Throughout history, humans have been curious about wild animals. Zoos have given people a way to safely observe these animals up close. Fossils found in Egypt suggest the first zoo dates back to 3500 B.C.

For many years, zoos were very different from the ones we know today. Animals were often kept in small cages and given only the most basic care. As time went by and people became more knowledgeable about animals, zoos began to change. In today's zoos, animals live in open areas designed to be like their native habitats.

Modern zoos also do much more than just house animals. Through breeding programs, zoos work to increase the populations of endangered species that are at risk of becoming extinct. Some animals raised in zoos may later be released into the wild. And zoos are sometimes the only homes for types of animals that have already become extinct in nature.

**Here's a look at just a few of today's major zoos.**

## SAN DIEGO ZOO

More than 3,700 animals can be found in the San Diego Zoo, which opened in 1916. It is home to four giant pandas—the largest population of giant pandas in North America. The zoo has been at the forefront of conservation efforts and captive breeding programs for these critically endangered animals. The San Diego Zoo was a pioneer in "cage free" exhibits—its first, for lions, was opened in 1922.

## HENRY DOORLY ZOO

The Henry Doorly Zoo and Aquarium in Omaha is Nebraska's most popular tourist attraction. The zoo is home to the largest indoor desert in the world, the Desert Dome. Visitors to the Desert Dome can see plant and animal life from three different deserts around the world. The zoo offers many educational programs for kids, including opportunities to camp overnight at the zoo and learn more about its conservation efforts.

## TORONTO ZOO

The largest zoo in Canada, the Toronto Zoo has been in operation since 1974. It now holds more than 5,000 animals and covers more than 700 acres. The zoo has been closely involved with conservation efforts for the black-footed ferret. Scientists at the zoo have bred and released hundreds of these endangered animals into the wild.

# BIGGEST, SMALLEST, *FASTEST* IN THE WORLD

## WORLD'S BIGGEST ANIMALS

**Marine mammal:** Blue whale (100 feet long, 200 tons)

**Heaviest land mammal:** African bush elephant (12 feet high, 4-7 tons)
**Tallest land mammal:** Giraffe (18 feet tall)

**Reptile:** Saltwater crocodile (20-23 feet long, 1,150 pounds)

**Heaviest snake:** Green anaconda (16-30 feet, 550 pounds)
**Longest snake:** Reticulated python (26-32 feet long)

**Fish:** Whale shark (40-60 feet long, 10-20 tons)

**Bird:** Ostrich (9 feet tall, 345 pounds)

**Insect:** Stick insect (15 inches long)

## WORLD'S FASTEST ANIMALS

**Marine mammal:** Killer whale and Dall's porpoise (35 miles per hour)

**Land mammal:** Cheetah (70 miles per hour)

**Fish:** Sailfish (68 miles per hour, leaping)

**Bird:** Peregrine falcon (200 miles per hour)

**Insect:** Dragonfly (35 miles per hour)

**Snake:** Black mamba (14 miles per hour)

## WORLD'S SMALLEST ANIMALS

**Mammal:** Bumblebee bat (1.1-1.3 inches)

**Fish:** *Paedocypris progenetica* or stout infantfish (0.31-0.33 inches)

**Bird:** Bee hummingbird (1-2 inches)

**Snake:** Thread snake and brahminy blind snake (4.25 inches)

**Lizard:** Jaragua sphaero and Virgin Islands dwarf sphaero (0.63 inch)

**Insect:** Fairyfly (0.01 inch)

## HOW FAST DO ANIMALS RUN?

This table shows how fast some animals can move on land. A snail can take more than 30 hours just to go 1 mile. But humans at their fastest are still slower than many animals. The human record for fastest speed for a recognized race distance is held by Usain Bolt, who set a world record in 2009 in the 100-meter dash of 9.58 seconds, for an average speed of about 23 miles per hour.

| SPEED (miles per hour) | ANIMAL |
|---|---|
| 70 | Cheetah |
| 60 | Pronghorn |
| 45 | Elk |
| 40 | Ostrich |
| 35 | Rabbit |
| 32 | Giraffe |
| 30 | Grizzly bear |
| 25 | Elephant |
| 15 | Wild turkey |
| 10 | Crocodile |
| 5.5 | Tiger beetle |
| 0.03 | Snail |

# How Long Do Animals LIVE?

Most animals do not live as long as humans do. A monkey that's 14 years old is thought to be old, while a person at that age is still considered young. The average life spans of some animals in the wild are shown here. An average 10-year-old girl in the U.S. can expect to live to be about 86.

| ANIMAL | AVERAGE LIFE SPAN |
|---|---|
| Galapagos tortoise | 100+ years |
| Blue whale | 80 years |
| Alligator | 50 years |
| Chimpanzee | 50 years |
| African elephant | 35 years |
| Bottlenose dolphin | 30 years |
| Horse | 20 years |
| Tiger | 16 years |
| Lobster | 15 years |
| Cat (domestic) | 15 years |
| Tarantula | 15 years |

| ANIMAL | AVERAGE LIFE SPAN |
|---|---|
| Dog (domestic) | 13 years |
| Camel (bactrian) | 12 years |
| Pig | 10 years |
| Deer (white-tailed) | 8 years |
| Kangaroo | 7 years |
| Chipmunk | 6 years |
| Guinea pig | 4 years |
| Mouse | 3 years |
| Opossum | 1 year |
| Worker bee | 6 weeks |
| Adult housefly | 1-3 weeks |

# MARSUPIALS: FACT OR FICTION?

Many people are fascinated by marsupials. These animals (including koalas and kangaroos) have some special characteristics and are not found in all parts of the world. Learn the facts about these unusual animals.

**FACT OR FICTION? Marsupials Have Pouches.**

**FACT.** Marsupials are often called "pouched mammals." Like almost all mammals, they give birth to live young. But newborn marsupials are helpless and need further development. After birth, a marsupial baby makes its way into the mother's pouch. The baby stays there, drinking its mother's milk, until it is large and strong enough to survive in the outside world.

**FACT OR FICTION? Marsupials are not found in the United States.**

**FICTION.** Though marsupials are much more common in Australia and South America, there is one naturally occurring marsupial in the United States—the opossum!

**FACT OR FICTION? All marsupials are nocturnal.**

**FICTION.** Most marsupials are nocturnal, meaning they sleep or rest during the day and are most active at night. But one exception is the numbat, or banded anteater, which is fully active during the day in its native home of Australia.

# WHAT ARE GROUPS OF ANIMALS CALLED?

Here are some (often odd) names for animal groups.

**BEARS**: ***sleuth*** of bears
**CATS**: ***clowder*** of cats
**CATTLE**: ***drove*** of cattle
**CROCODILES**: ***bask*** of crocodiles
**CROWS**: ***murder*** of crows
**FISH**: ***school*** or ***shoal*** of fish
**FLIES**: ***swarm*** or ***cloud*** of flies
**FOXES**: ***skulk*** of foxes
**GIRAFFES**: ***tower*** of giraffes
**HARES**: ***down*** of hares
**HAWKS**: ***cast*** of hawks
**HYENAS**: ***cackle*** of hyenas
**JELLYFISH**: ***smack*** of jellyfish
**KITTENS**: ***kindle*** or ***kendle*** of kittens
**LEOPARDS**: ***leap*** of leopards
**MONKEYS**: ***troop*** of monkeys
**MULES**: ***span*** of mules
**NIGHTINGALES**: ***watch*** of nightingales
**OWLS**: ***parliament*** of owls
**OYSTERS**: ***bed*** of oysters
**PEACOCKS**: ***muster*** of peacocks
**RAVENS**: ***unkindness*** of ravens
**SHARKS**: ***shiver*** of sharks
**SQUIRRELS**: ***dray*** or ***scurry*** of squirrels
**TURTLES**: ***bale*** of turtles
**WHALES**: ***pod*** of whales

## DOGS at the Top

**Here are the most popular dog breeds in the United States.**

1. Labrador Retriever
2. German Shepherd
3. Golden Retriever
4. Beagle
5. Bulldog
6. Yorkshire Terrier
7. Boxer
8. Poodle
9. Rottweiler
10. Dachshund

Source: American Kennel Club, 2012

## PETS Q&A

**Which breed of dog is the smallest?**
The smallest dog breed is the Chihuahua, which generally grows only 6 to 9 inches tall and weighs less than 6 pounds.

**True or false? Some dogs have webbed feet.**
**True.** Many water-loving breeds, such as Newfoundlands and Labrador retrievers, have webbed feet to help them swim. Mixed-breed dogs may also inherit this trait.

**True or false? A guinea pig's teeth never stop growing.**
**True.** Guinea pigs need healthful things to chew on, like crunchy fruits and vegetables, to help keep their teeth filed down.

# TIPS FOR CHOOSING A PET

**Some of the most popular pets in the United States are cats, dogs, and birds. If your family is getting a pet, how can you decide which type will be the best fit for you?**

## Birds

**Birds** can be an excellent option for people who live in small apartments or homes. Some people think that a pet bird requires very little work and care, but this is not the case. Birds do not need to be walked, but responsible bird owners keep the living space very clean and research which type of bird is the best fit for their lifestyle. Some types of birds can be an even larger commitment than a dog or cat—a large parrot can live for up to 100 years!

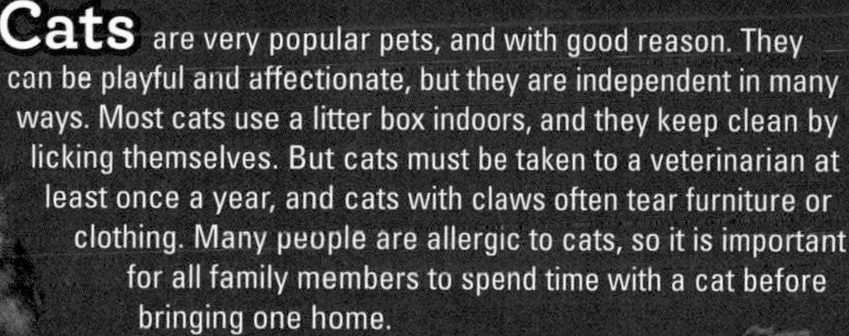

## Cats

**Cats** are very popular pets, and with good reason. They can be playful and affectionate, but they are independent in many ways. Most cats use a litter box indoors, and they keep clean by licking themselves. But cats must be taken to a veterinarian at least once a year, and cats with claws often tear furniture or clothing. Many people are allergic to cats, so it is important for all family members to spend time with a cat before bringing one home.

## Dogs

**Dogs** are well-known for being loyal and loving to their owners. But of all the popular pets, dogs may require the most work. Puppies often take many months to be housebroken, or trained to relieve themselves only outside. Adult dogs need daily exercise, and many breeds require regular grooming. Dogs are often given to animal shelters by owners who are overwhelmed by the need to care for them. Once your family has decided to get a dog, animal shelters are a great place to start your search!

# ENDANGERED SPECIES

When a species becomes extinct, the variety of life on Earth is reduced. In the world today, many thousands of known species of animals and plants are in danger of becoming extinct. Humans have been able to save some endangered animals and are working to save more.

## SOME ENDANGERED ANIMALS

**CHIMPANZEE** The closest living relative to humans, chimpanzees are highly social and take care of their young for years. Millions of chimpanzees used to live throughout Africa. Today, that number has been reduced to fewer than 250,000.

**Reasons for population decline:**
- Hunting by humans
- Loss of habitat due to increased development

**LEATHERBACK SEA TURTLE**

The leatherback sea turtle is the largest turtle in the world. It can grow up to seven feet long and weigh 2,000 pounds. The turtles spend their enitre life at sea, except when females leave the water to lay their eggs on beaches. Once common in every ocean except in polar regions, these turtles are now critically endangered. It is estimated that only one in 1,000 leatherback turtle eggs produces a turtle that survives to adulthood.

**Reasons for population decline:**
- Choking on plastic trash, which the turtles confuse with their favorite food, jellyfish
- Theft of eggs from their nests by humans, and loss of nesting areas because of beachfront development
- Fishing methods, including use of nets and hooks, that indirectly harm turtles

**AMUR LEOPARD** The Amur leopard, native to southeastern Russia, is one of the most critically endangered big cats. These solitary animals are strong and athletic—they can jump more than 19 feet high. It is estimated that fewer than 30 Amur leopards remain in the wild.
**Reasons for population decline:** • Hunting by humans • Habitat loss

# POACHING: A Threat to Animal Survival

**Wildlife experts say poaching, or illegal hunting, is the single greatest threat to several endangered species—including some of the world's most beloved animals.**

## TIGER

In the past, tigers were primarily hunted for their fur or for their heads, which were displayed as trophies. In recent years, large numbers of tigers have been poached so that ground tiger bone and other body parts could be used in traditional medicines. Despite laws banning the sale and trade of tiger parts, more than 1,000 tigers have been killed in the past ten years. Fewer than 3,200 tigers remain in the wild today.

## RHINOCEROS

Of all the species currently threatened by poaching, experts may be most concerned about the African black rhinoceros and white rhino. In early 2013, the World Wildlife Fund announced that the poaching of rhinos in South Africa had reached a new peak—up by 5,000 percent since 2007. The animals are illegally hunted for their horns. Ground rhino horn is used in traditional medicines, and some rhino horns are carved to make knife handles or other decorative items.

## AFRICAN ELEPHANT

Elephants are poached for their tusks, which are made of ivory. The ivory is usually carved and used to make many kinds of decorative objects. International trading in ivory has been illegal since 1989, but a demand for ivory still exists—and is growing in some parts of Asia. Experts estimate that every year poachers kill 25,000 African elephants for their tusks. Police try to stop illegal ivory shipments.

## Animals Word Scramble

**Unscramble these words to find the names of some of the animals you've read about in this chapter.**

**oaalk**

**chortis**

**musopso**

**uingae ipg**

**mezhpancie**

**kncihump**

**ANSWERS ON PAGES 334-336.**

# Working Animals

**People and animals have worked together for thousands of years. The first animals to become domesticated, or comfortable with humans, were wolves. Wolves are the ancestors of the dogs that people live with—and sometimes work with—today. Many types of animals have been trained by people to do important jobs. Here are just a few examples.**

## Elephants

Elephants have long been put to work by humans. They have been called "the tanks of the ancient world" for their role in early wars, carrying supplies or charging enemy lines. Over the centuries, elephants were trained to carry many types of heavy loads—and some still do. It is estimated that 15,000 elephants are at work in Asia today. These elephants may transport tourists, lead religious ceremonies, or lift logs onto trucks.

## Horses

Horses have played an important part in human history. Before the invention of cars, people traveled on horseback or in horse-drawn vehicles. Horses were also used to pull plows on farms, to herd cattle on ranches, to move goods in horse-drawn wagons, and to carry soldiers into battle. Today, police officers work on horseback to see above crowds and get into areas where cars can't travel. Horses are also used in search-and-rescue missions, because they can travel faster than people over rugged terrain. Some farmers still use horses to herd livestock and plow fields.

## Dogs

Dogs work at more jobs than any other domesticated animal. They work with law enforcement officers to help find people who are lost or to sniff out bombs and other chemicals. Dogs who work with military personnel have been trained to spot snipers or find buried explosives. Service dogs may guide people who cannot see, alert hearing-impaired people to things they cannot hear, or give warnings when a person is about to have a seizure. Dogs protect and herd livestock on farms, and they have been trained to find bedbugs, termites, or other pests.

→ON THE JOB←

# Veterinarian

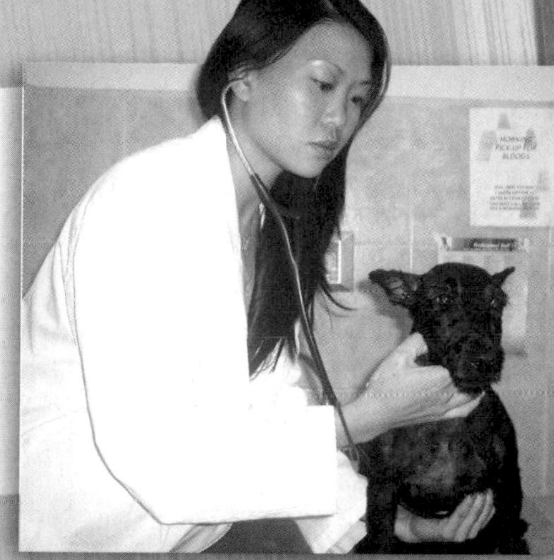

Veterinarians are doctors who take care of animals. Some work mostly with small animals, such as dogs and cats, in vet clinics. Some specialize in one type of illness or work with large animals on farms or in zoos. **Vivian Ng**, a veterinarian who works in a clinic, agreed to talk to *The World Almanac for Kids* about her work.

**What do you do in a typical day?**

I see patients, perform surgeries, and interact with people. I am a small animal vet, which means I primarily work with cats and dogs. It's important for me to communicate with owners about how to give the best care for their pet. When a pet is sick, my biggest challenge is figuring out what is wrong. Animals can't tell us why they're sick or how they are feeling. Another important part of my job is performing spay and neuter surgeries. These surgeries help prevent overpopulation of dogs and cats.

**What interests and strengths of yours make this job right for you?**

I have always been interested in animals—my pets are like family to me. This connection makes me more compassionate in my work. I think compassion and clear-headedness are extremely important in this career. There are many emergency situations that require vets to stay calm and think clearly.

**What kind of education or training did you need to get in order to do your job?**

I have a doctor of veterinary medicine degree from the Atlantic Veterinary College of the University of Prince Edward Island.

**What do you like best about your job? What is most challenging?**

I love the diversity. You can choose to interact with large animals, small animals, exotics (like hedgehogs and snakes), marine animals, or zoo animals. You might try different career paths—such as private practice, research, public health, or teaching. Not all veterinarians take care of pets. What I find most rewarding is to be able to help animals feel better and to help to comfort their worried owners. There are many days that are long and stressful, and that is challenging—but knowing that I made a difference in an animal's life makes it worthwhile.

# ART

→What are complementary colors? PAGE 37

# All About ART

## WHAT is art?

The answer is up for debate. Usually art is something about life or about the world that an artist interprets for an audience.

## WHY do we need art?

Sometimes art simply gives us pleasure, as when we look at a painting of a beautiful scene. Art can also make us think. Works of art sometimes get us to rethink ideas we take for granted. Sometimes they give us insights into the character of people.

Artists express their ideas in their art, and their work can help the rest of us understand our world and ourselves better.

## WHEN I see a work of art in a museum, what should I look for?

Look at the artwork without thinking too hard about it. How does it make you feel? Happy, sad, confused, silly? Study the work, and try to discover the colors, shapes, or textures that create those feelings in you. The information card next to the work will usually tell you who created it and when it was made. You can compare it to other works of art by the same artist or from the same time.

## HOW old is art?

Art goes back to our earliest records of human life. Researchers recently found painted stencils of hands that date back 40,000 years on the walls of caves in southern Spain. Other caves in Europe have paintings of animals that are tens of thousands of years old.

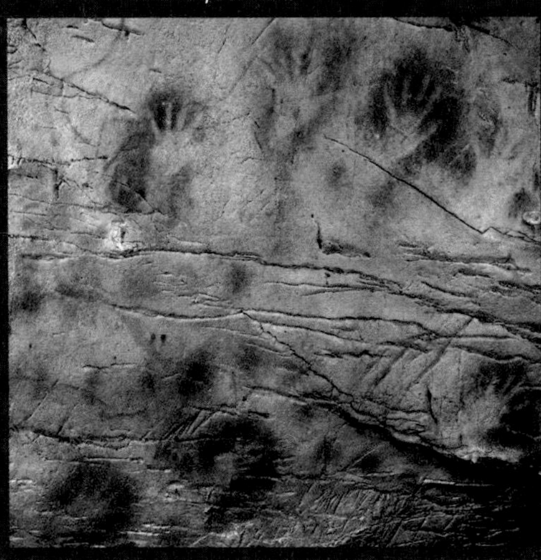

# DIFFERENT KINDS OF ART

Through history, artists have painted pictures of nature (**landscapes**), pictures of people (**portraits**), and pictures of flowers in vases, food, and other objects (**still lifes**). Today many artists create pictures that do not look like anything in the real world. These are examples of **abstract** art.

**Photography**, too, is a form of art. Photos record both the commonplace and the exotic. They help us look at events in new ways.

**Sculpture** is a three-dimensional form made from clay, stone, metal, or other material. Sculptures can be large, like the Statue of Liberty. Some are realistic. Others have no form you can recognize.

Artists work with many materials. Some artists today use computers and video screens to create their art.

# SOME FAMOUS ARTISTS

## BERENICE ABBOTT (1898–1991)

*Blossom Restaurant* (1935)

Born in Ohio, Berenice Abbott became one of America's foremost photographers. She is particularly known for her series of photos called *Changing New York*, which captured the city as it rapidly modernized in the 1930s.

## JOHANNES VERMEER (1632–1675)

*Young Woman With a Water Pitcher* (1660s)

Vermeer lived and worked in the Dutch city of Delft. He painted small canvases, usually of beautifully lit interiors. His work seems to capture a moment in time, and peace and calm fill his pictures of people doing everyday things.

## MARY CASSATT (1844–1926)

*Summertime* (1894)

Cassatt was an American painter who lived most of her life in France. She was part of the Impressionist movement, using color and brush strokes to give an "impression" of a scene. Many of her paintings are tender images of the daily lives of mothers and their children.

## LEO VILLAREAL (1967– )

*Cylinder* (2011)

Leo Villareal is an American artist who uses LED lights and computers to create large sculptures. In *Cylinder*, he attached LEDs to long steel strips. A computer controls when the lights go on and off, creating constantly changing patterns.

# Art Around the World

Throughout history, all cultures have created their own art forms. This art reflects each culture's traditions and beliefs. Here are a few of the different artistic traditions that are found around the globe.

## Miniature Paintings from India

During the Mughal Empire, which controlled India from the 16th to the 19th centuries, artists who worked for India's rulers created beautiful miniature paintings. Some of these small works of art were used to illustrate books. Others were simply painted to be enjoyed. Despite their small size—some paintings were just a few inches high and wide—these artworks are incredibly detailed. They usually show life at court, battle scenes, portraits, or hunting parties.

## African Masks

Many African peoples have created masks for use in religious ceremonies. The wooden masks are beautifully carved and sometimes elaborately decorated. They can represent people from earlier generations or such things as good and evil spirits. Sometimes they have a mix of human and animal features, which is meant to represent the close relationship between people and nature. African masks have influenced the work of many Western artists, including the painter Pablo Picasso.

## Australian Aboriginal Art

For Australian Aborigines, traditional art is connected to what they call the "Dreamtime." This is a sacred time that began in the past, during which people developed ways of living and creating art. "Dreaming" is the total of everything that is known and understood. This idea is expressed in Aboriginal art through symbols that represent important aspects of life, including animals, human activities, and natural phenomena such as rain.

# The Color WHEEL

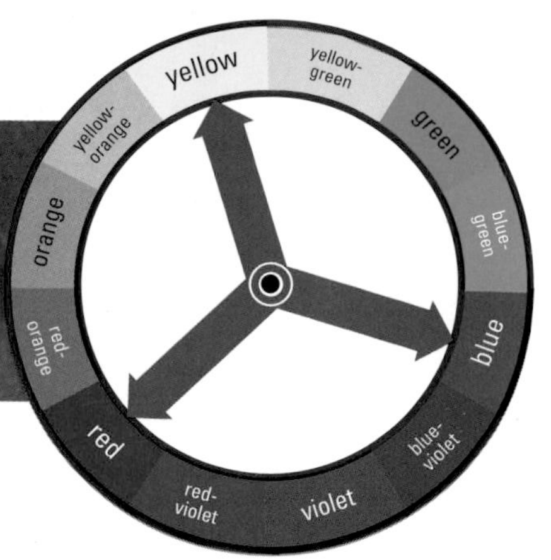


A color wheel shows how colors are related to each other.

## PRIMARY COLORS

The most basic colors are **RED**, **YELLOW**, and **BLUE**. They're called primary because you can't get them by mixing any other colors. In fact, the other colors are made by mixing red, blue, or yellow. Arrows on this wheel show the primary colors.

## SECONDARY COLORS

**ORANGE**, **GREEN**, and **VIOLET** are the secondary colors. They are made by mixing two primary colors. You make orange by mixing yellow and red, or green by mixing yellow and blue. On the color wheel, **GREEN** appears between **BLUE** and **YELLOW**.

## TERTIARY COLORS

When you mix a primary and a secondary color, you get a tertiary, or intermediate, color. **BLUE-GREEN**, **YELLOW-GREEN**, **YELLOW-ORANGE**, and **ORANGE-RED** are all examples of tertiary colors.

# MORE COLOR TERMS

**VALUES** The lightness or darkness of a color is its value.
Tints are light values made by mixing a color with white. **PINK** is a tint of **RED**. Shades are dark values made by mixing a color with black. **MAROON** is a shade of **RED**.

## COMPLEMENTARY COLORS

Contrasting colors that please the eye when used together are called complementary colors. These colors appear opposite each other on the wheel and don't have any colors in common. **RED** is a complement to **GREEN**, which is made by mixing **YELLOW** and **BLUE**.

**COOL COLORS** Cool colors are mostly **GREEN**, **BLUE**, and **PURPLE**. They make you think of cool things like water and can even make you feel cooler.

**WARM COLORS** Warm colors are mostly **RED**, **ORANGE**, and **YELLOW**. These colors suggest heat, and they can actually make you feel warmer.

**ANALOGOUS COLORS** The colors next to each other on the wheel are from the same "family." **BLUE**, **BLUE-GREEN**, and **GREEN** all have **BLUE** in them and are analogous colors.

# BIRTHDAYS

→What symbol represents a Taurus? PAGE 42

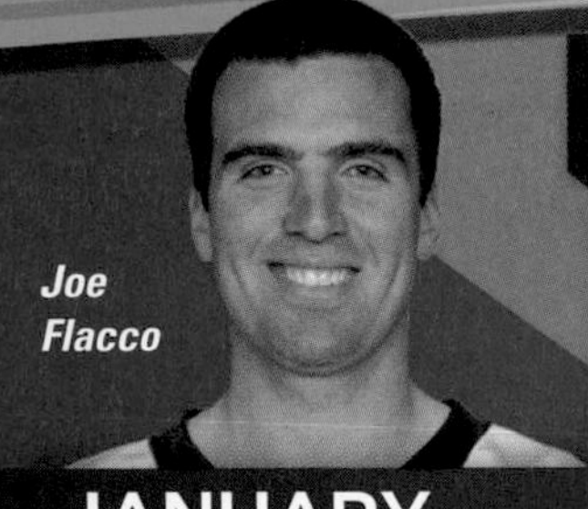

*Joe Flacco*

## JANUARY
### BIRTHSTONE: GARNET

**1** J. D. Salinger, author, 1919
**2** Dax Shepard, actor, 1975
**3** Eli Manning, football player, 1981
**4** Isaac Newton, scientist, 1643
**5** Bradley Cooper, actor, 1975
**6** Carl Sandburg, poet, 1878
**7** Katie Couric, journalist, 1957
**8** Stephen Hawking, physicist, 1942
**9** Catherine (Kate Middleton), Duchess of Cambridge, 1982
**10** George Foreman, boxer, 1948
**11** Mary J. Blige, singer, 1971
**12** Naya Rivera, actress, 1987
**13** Liam Hemsworth, actor, 1990
**14** LL Cool J, rapper/actor, 1968
**15** Rev. Martin Luther King Jr., civil rights leader, 1929
**16** Joe Flacco, football player, 1985
**17** Michelle Obama, first lady, 1964
**18** A. A. Milne, author, 1882
**19** Paul Cézanne, artist, 1839
**20** Buzz Aldrin, astronaut, 1930
**21** Ashton Eaton, decathlon gold medalist, 1988
**22** Ubaldo Jiménez, baseball player, 1984
**23** John Hancock, patriot, 1737
**24** Edith Wharton, author, 1862
**25** Etta James, singer, 1938
**26** Ellen DeGeneres, TV personality, 1958
**27** Lewis Carroll, author, 1832
**28** Ariel Winter, actress, 1998
**29** Oprah Winfrey, TV personality, 1954
**30** Christian Bale, actor, 1974
**31** Justin Timberlake, singer, 1981

## FEBRUARY
### BIRTHSTONE: AMETHYST

**1** Harry Styles, singer, 1994
**2** James Joyce, author, 1882
**3** Rebel Wilson, actress, 1986
**4** Rosa Parks, civil rights leader, 1913
**5** Hank Aaron, baseball player, 1934
**6** Ronald Reagan, 40th president, 1911
**7** Laura Ingalls Wilder, author, 1867
**8** John Grisham, author, 1955
**9** Alice Walker, author, 1944
**10** Emma Roberts, actress, 1991
**11** Taylor Lautner, actor, 1992
**12** Abraham Lincoln, 16th president, 1809
**13** Grant Wood, artist, 1891
**14** Drew Bledsoe, football player, 1972
**15** Amber Riley, actress, 1986
**16** John McEnroe, tennis player, 1959
**17** Joseph Gordon-Levitt, actor, 1981
**18** Jillian Michaels, TV personality, 1974
**19** Amy Tan, author, 1952
**20** Ansel Adams, photographer, 1902
**21** Ashley Greene, actress, 1987
**22** Edna St. Vincent Millay, poet, 1892
**23** Dakota Fanning, actress, 1994
**24** Steve Jobs, computer innovator, 1955
**25** Rashida Jones, actress, 1976
**26** Fats Domino, musician, 1928
**27** John Steinbeck, author, 1902
**28** Linus Pauling, scientist, 1901
**29** Herman Hollerith, statistician, 1860

*Amber Riley*

*Johann Sebastian Bach*

## MARCH
### BIRTHSTONE: AQUAMARINE

**1** Justin Bieber, singer, 1994
**2** Reggie Bush, football player, 1985
**3** Alexander Graham Bell, inventor, 1847
**4** Knute Rockne, football coach, 1888
**5** Eva Mendes, actress, 1974
**6** Elizabeth Barrett Browning, poet, 1806
**7** Rachel Weisz, actress, 1970
**8** Kenneth Grahame, author, 1859
**9** Bow Wow, actor/rapper, 1987
**10** Carrie Underwood, singer, 1983
**11** Benji and Joel Madden, musicians, 1979
**12** Christina Grimmie, singer, 1994
**13** Joseph Priestley, chemist, 1733
**14** Albert Einstein, physicist/ Nobel laureate, 1879
**15** Eva Longoria, actress, 1975
**16** Lauren Graham, actress, 1967
**17** Nat King Cole, musician, 1919
**18** Adam Levine, musician, 1979
**19** Philip Roth, author, 1933
**20** Fred Rogers, TV personality, 1928
**21** Johann Sebastian Bach, composer, 1685
**22** James Patterson, author, 1947
**23** Keri Russell, actress, 1976
**24** Peyton Manning, football player, 1976
**25** Danica Patrick, racecar driver, 1982
**26** Keira Knightley, actress, 1985
**27** Mariah Carey, singer, 1970
**28** Lady Gaga, singer, 1986
**29** Megan Hilty, actress, 1981
**30** Eric Clapton, musician, 1945
**31** Cesar Chavez, labor leader, 1927

## APRIL
BIRTHSTONE: DIAMOND

**1** Rachel Maddow, TV host, 1973
**2** Hans Christian Andersen, author, 1805
**3** Jane Goodall, scientist, 1934
**4** Maya Angelou, poet, 1928
**5** Booker T. Washington, educator, 1856
**6** Paul Rudd, actor, 1969
**7** William Wordsworth, poet, 1770
**8** Taylor Kitsch, actor, 1981
**9** Kristen Stewart, actress, 1990
**10** Shay Mitchell, actress, 1987
**11** Mark Teixeira, baseball player, 1980
**12** Claire Danes, actress, 1979
**13** Thomas Jefferson, 3rd president, 1743
**14** Abigail Breslin, actress, 1996
**15** Emma Watson, actress, 1990
**16** Kareem Abdul-Jabbar, basketball player, 1947
**17** Boomer Esiason, football player, 1961
**18** America Ferrera, actress, 1984
**19** James Franco, actor, 1978
**20** Don Mattingly, baseball player, 1961
**21** Charlotte Brontë, author, 1816
**22** Robert J. Oppenheimer, physicist, 1904
**23** Dev Patel, actor, 1990
**24** Kelly Clarkson, singer, 1982
**25** Ella Fitzgerald, singer, 1917
**26** Channing Tatum, actor, 1980
**27** Cory Booker, politician, 1969
**28** Penélope Cruz, actress, 1974
**29** Daniel Day-Lewis, actor, 1957
**30** Dianna Agron, actress, 1986

**Channing Tatum**

**Archie Panjabi**

## MAY
BIRTHSTONE: EMERALD

**1** Wes Anderson, filmmaker, 1969
**2** David Beckham, soccer player, 1975
**3** Sugar Ray Robinson, boxer, 1921
**4** Will Arnett, actor, 1970
**5** Adele, singer, 1988
**6** George Clooney, actor, 1961
**7** Johannes Brahms, composer, 1833
**8** Sonny Liston, boxer, 1932
**9** Prince Fielder, baseball player, 1984
**10** Kenan Thompson, actor, 1978
**11** Cory Monteith, actor, 1982
**12** Tony Hawk, skateboarder, 1968
**13** Robert Pattinson, actor, 1986
**14** Sofia Coppola, director, 1971
**15** Emmitt Smith, football player, 1969
**16** Megan Fox, actress, 1986
**17** Sugar Ray Leonard, boxer, 1956
**18** Tina Fey, actress/comedian, 1970
**19** Malcolm X, militant civil rights activist, 1925
**20** Jimmy Stewart, actor, 1908
**21** John Muir, naturalist, 1838
**22** Ginnifer Goodwin, actress, 1978
**23** Margaret Wise Brown, author, 1910
**24** Bob Dylan, musician, 1941
**25** Mike Myers, actor, 1963
**26** Sally Ride, astronaut, 1951
**27** Chris Colfer, actor, 1990
**28** Jim Thorpe, athlete, 1888
**29** John F. Kennedy, 35th president, 1917
**30** Cee Lo Green, singer, 1974
**31** Archie Panjabi, actress, 1972

## JUNE
BIRTHSTONE: PEARL

**1** Marilyn Monroe, actress, 1926
**2** Zachary Quinto, actor, 1977
**3** Anderson Cooper, journalist, 1967
**4** Angelina Jolie, actress, 1975
**5** Mark Wahlberg, actor, 1971
**6** Natalie Morales, journalist, 1972
**7** Liam Neeson, actor, 1952
**8** Kanye West, musician, 1977
**9** Johnny Depp, actor, 1963
**10** Maurice Sendak, author/illustrator, 1928
**11** Peter Dinklage, actor, 1969
**12** Anne Frank, diary writer, 1929
**13** William Butler Yeats, poet, 1865
**14** Harriet Beecher Stowe, author, 1811
**15** Neil Patrick Harris, actor, 1973
**16** Tupac Shakur, rapper/actor, 1971
**17** Venus Williams, tennis player, 1980
**18** Roger Ebert, film critic, 1942
**19** Zoe Saldana, actress, 1978
**20** Nicole Kidman, actress, 1967
**21** Prince William of Great Britain, Duke of Cambridge, 1982
**22** Meryl Streep, actress, 1949
**23** Randy Jackson, TV personality, 1956
**24** Mindy Kaling, actress, 1979
**25** Sonia Sotomayor, U.S. Supreme Court justice, 1954
**26** Derek Jeter, baseball player, 1974
**27** Ed Westwick, actor, 1987
**28** John Elway, football player, 1960
**29** Nicole Scherzinger, singer, 1978
**30** Michael Phelps, Olympic champion, 1985

**Sonia Sotomayor**

Frida Kahlo

## JULY
BIRTHSTONE: RUBY

**1** Carl Lewis, Olympic champion, 1961
**2** Ashley Tisdale, actress, 1986
**3** Olivia Munn, actress, 1980
**4** Neil Simon, playwright, 1927
**5** P. T. Barnum, showman/circus founder, 1810
**6** Frida Kahlo, artist, 1907
**7** Satchel Paige, baseball player, 1906
**8** Jaden Smith, actor/rapper, 1998
**9** Tom Hanks, actor, 1956
**10** Sofía Vergara, actress, 1972
**11** E. B. White, author, 1899
**12** Andrew Wyeth, painter, 1917
**13** Ken Jeong, actor, 1969
**14** Jane Lynch, actress, 1960
**15** Rembrandt van Rijn, artist, 1606
**16** Will Ferrell, actor, 1967
**17** Luke Bryan, singer, 1976
**18** Kristen Bell, actress, 1980
**19** Edgar Degas, artist, 1834
**20** Julianne Hough, dancer/singer, 1988
**21** Ernest Hemingway, author, 1899
**22** Selena Gomez, actress/singer 1992
**23** Daniel Radcliffe, actor, 1989
**24** Amelia Earhart, aviator, 1897
**25** Walter Payton, football player, 1954
**26** Stanley Kubrick, director, 1928
**27** Alex Rodriguez, baseball player, 1975
**28** Beatrix Potter, author, 1866
**29** Tim Gunn, TV personality, 1953
**30** Laurence Fishburne, actor, 1961
**31** J. K. Rowling, author, 1965

## AUGUST
BIRTHSTONE: PERIDOT

**1** Yves Saint Laurent, designer, 1936
**2** Sam Worthington, actor, 1976
**3** Tom Brady, football player, 1977
**4** Barack Obama, 44th president, 1961
**5** Neil Armstrong, astronaut, 1930
**6** Andy Warhol, artist, 1928
**7** Charlize Theron, actress, 1975
**8** Matthew Henson, explorer, 1866
**9** Anna Kendrick, actress, 1985
**10** Suzanne Collins, author, 1962
**11** Chris Hemsworth, actor, 1983
**12** Pete Sampras, tennis player, 1971
**13** Alfred Hitchcock, filmmaker, 1899
**14** Mila Kunis, actress, 1983
**15** Jennifer Lawrence, actress, 1990
**16** Steve Carell, actor, 1963
**17** Robert De Niro, actor, 1943
**18** Meriwether Lewis, explorer, 1774
**19** Bill Clinton, 42nd president, 1946
**20** Demi Lovato, actress/singer, 1992
**21** Usain Bolt, Olympic champion, 1986
**22** Kristen Wiig, actress, 1973
**23** Kobe Bryant, basketball player, 1978
**24** Rupert Grint, actor, 1988
**25** Blake Lively, actress, 1987
**26** Chris Pine, actor, 1980
**27** Aaron Paul, actor, 1979
**28** Quvenzhané Wallis, actress, 2003
**29** Lea Michele, actress, 1986
**30** Ted Williams, baseball player, 1918
**31** Tom Coughlin, football coach, 1946

Jimmy Fallon

## SEPTEMBER
BIRTHSTONE: SAPPHIRE

**1** Rachel Zoe, stylist, 1971
**2** Christa McAuliffe, teacher/astronaut, 1948
**3** Shaun White, snowboarder, 1986
**4** Beyoncé Knowles, singer/actress, 1981
**5** Katerina Graham, actress, 1989
**6** Roger Waters, musician, 1943
**7** Buddy Holly, musician, 1936
**8** Pink, singer, 1979
**9** Michelle Williams, actress, 1980
**10** Roger Maris, baseball player, 1934
**11** Paul "Bear" Bryant, football coach, 1913
**12** Jennifer Hudson, singer/actress, 1981
**13** Roald Dahl, author, 1916
**14** Tyler Perry, director, 1969
**15** Prince Harry of Great Britain, 1984
**16** David Copperfield, magician, 1956
**17** Alexander Ovechkin, hockey player, 1985
**18** James Marsden, actor, 1973
**19** Jimmy Fallon, comedian/talk show host, 1974
**20** Brian Joubert, figure skater, 1984
**21** Stephen King, author, 1947
**22** Tom Felton, actor, 1987
**23** Ray Charles, musician, 1930
**24** Jim Henson, Muppet creator, 1936
**25** Will Smith, actor/rapper, 1968
**26** T. S. Eliot, poet, 1888
**27** Gwyneth Paltrow, actress, 1972
**28** Naomi Watts, actress, 1968
**29** Kevin Durant, basketball player, 1988
**30** Elie Wiesel, author, 1928

Jennifer Lawrence

Marie Curie

## OCTOBER
BIRTHSTONE: OPAL

**1** Zach Galifianakis, actor, 1969
**2** Mohandas Gandhi, activist, 1869
**3** Dave Winfield, baseball player, 1951
**4** Anne Rice, author, 1941
**5** Jesse Eisenberg, actor, 1983
**6** Roshon Fegan, actor, 1991
**7** Yo-Yo Ma, cellist, 1955
**8** Matt Damon, actor, 1970
**9** John Lennon, musician, 1940
**10** Maya Lin, sculptor and architect, 1960
**11** Steve Young, football player, 1961
**12** Josh Hutcherson, actor, 1992
**13** Jerry Rice, football player, 1962
**14** Usher, singer, 1978
**15** Friedrich Nietzsche, philosopher, 1844
**16** Eugene O'Neill, playwright, 1888
**17** Eminem, rapper/actor, 1972
**18** Zac Efron, actor, 1987
**19** Ty Pennington, TV personality, 1965
**20** Danny Boyle, director, 1956
**21** Dizzy Gillespie, trumpet player, 1917
**22** Ichiro Suzuki, baseball player, 1973
**23** Ang Lee, director, 1954
**24** Brian Vickers, racecar driver, 1983
**25** Katy Perry, singer, 1984
**26** Keith Urban, musician, 1967
**27** Theodore Roosevelt, 26th president, 1858
**28** Bill Gates, software pioneer, 1955
**29** Gabrielle Union, actress, 1972
**30** Matthew Morrison, actor, 1978
**31** Willow Smith, singer/actress, 2000

Mohandas Gandhi

## NOVEMBER
BIRTHSTONE: TOPAZ

**1** Penn Badgley, actor, 1986
**2** James K. Polk, 11th president, 1795
**3** John Barry, composer, 1933
**4** Matthew McConaughey, actor, 1969
**5** Lamar Odom, basketball player, 1979
**6** Emma Stone, actress, 1988
**7** Marie Curie, scientist/Nobel laureate, 1867
**8** Gordon Ramsay, TV personality, 1966
**9** Carl Sagan, scientist, 1934
**10** Miranda Lambert, musician, 1983
**11** Leonardo DiCaprio, actor, 1974
**12** Ryan Gosling, actor, 1980
**13** Robert Louis Stevenson, author, 1850
**14** Josh Duhamel, actor, 1972
**15** Shailene Woodley, actress, 1991
**16** Maggie Gyllenhaal, actress, 1977
**17** Rachel McAdams, actress, 1978
**18** Alan Shepard, astronaut, 1923
**19** Ryan Howard, baseball player, 1979
**20** Joe Biden, 47th vice president, 1942
**21** Carly Rae Jepsen, singer, 1985
**22** Scarlett Johansson, actress, 1984
**23** Robin Roberts, journalist, 1960
**24** Sarah Hyland, actress, 1990
**25** Joe DiMaggio, baseball player, 1914
**26** Charles Schulz, cartoonist, 1912
**27** Kathryn Bigelow, director, 1951
**28** Jon Stewart, TV host, 1962
**29** Louisa May Alcott, author, 1832
**30** Elisha Cuthbert, actress, 1982

## DECEMBER
BIRTHSTONE: TURQUOISE

**1** Sarah Silverman, actress/comedienne, 1970
**2** Lucy Liu, actress, 1968
**3** Amanda Seyfried, actress, 1985
**4** Jay-Z, rapper, 1969
**5** Walt Disney, cartoonist/filmmaker, 1901
**6** Judd Apatow, filmmaker, 1967
**7** Larry Bird, basketball player/coach, 1956
**8** Nicki Minaj, rapper, 1982
**9** Simon Helberg, actor, 1980
**10** Bobby Flay, chef, 1964
**11** John Kerry, politician/diplomat, 1943
**12** Frank Sinatra, singer/actor, 1915
**13** Taylor Swift, singer, 1989
**14** Vanessa Hudgens, actress/singer, 1988
**15** Michelle Dockery, actress, 1981
**16** Jane Austen, author, 1775
**17** Manny Pacquiao, boxer, 1978
**18** Ashley Benson, actress, 1989
**19** Jake Gyllenhaal, actor, 1980
**20** Jonah Hill, actor, 1983
**21** Samuel L. Jackson, actor, 1948
**22** Giacomo Puccini, composer, 1858
**23** Hanley Ramírez, baseball player, 1983
**24** Stephenie Meyer, author, 1973
**25** Clara Barton, American Red Cross founder, 1821
**26** Carlton Fisk, baseball player, 1947
**27** Louis Pasteur, scientist, 1822
**28** Denzel Washington, actor, 1954
**29** Charles Goodyear, inventor, 1800
**30** LeBron James, basketball player, 1984
**31** Gabrielle Douglas, gymnast, 1995

John Kerry

# What's Your SIGN?

**Astrology** is a study of the positions of celestial bodies—such as the Sun, Moon, planets, and stars—that looks to find connections between these bodies and things that happen on Earth. Most scientists do not believe that there are connections. Still, many people enjoy learning about astrology and using it for entertainment.

**The Zodiac** is very important to people who follow astrology. The zodiac is a belt-shaped section of the sky that has been divided into twelve constellations. A constellation is a cluster of stars that can be seen from Earth. Astrologers believe that every person is influenced by one of these twelve constellations—or twelve signs—depending on his or her birthday. For example, a person born between July 23 and August 22 is a Leo. Leos are said to be confident and generous, but stubborn.

**A Horoscope** is a prediction about a person's future based on his or her astrological sign. Daily or monthly horoscopes can be found in many newspapers and magazines, in print or online, and on other websites.

## Signs of the Zodiac

**Aries**
Mar. 21 - Apr. 19
RAM

**Taurus**
Apr. 20 - May 20
BULL

**Gemini**
May 21 - June 20
TWINS

**Cancer**
June 21 - July 22
CRAB

**Leo**
July 23 - Aug. 22
LION

**Virgo**
Aug. 23 - Sept. 22
MAIDEN

**Libra**
Sept. 23 - Oct. 22
SCALES

**Scorpio**
Oct. 23 - Nov. 21
SCORPION

**Sagittarius**
Nov. 22 - Dec. 21
ARCHER

**Capricorn**
Dec. 22 - Jan. 19
GOAT

**Aquarius**
Jan. 20 - Feb. 18
WATER CARRIER

**Pisces**
Feb. 19 - Mar. 20
FISHES

**Did You KNOW?**

**The *Shēngxiào*, or Chinese zodiac, is a system that relates every birth year to a different animal. For example, people who were born in 2001 (a year of the snake) are said to be smart and proud. Those born in 2002 (a year of the horse) are considered cheerful and charming. And people born in 2003 (a year of the sheep) are said to be calm and capable.**

# Celebrity Crossword Puzzle

Think you know a lot about celebrities? It's time to put that knowledge to the test! Fill in the words that go with each clue. If you're stumped, the answers can all be found in *The World Almanac for Kids*. Look in these chapters: Birthdays, Faces & Places, Movies & TV, and Music & Dance. Good luck!

***Hint***: When the clue is about a person, the answer will be the last name, unless the person goes by only one name.

## ACROSS

2. "Kid President" YouTube star
5. Kids' Choice Awards host in 2013
7. Voice of Smurfette in *The Smurfs*
10. *Glee* actress born in February
11. Author of *The Great Gatsby*
12. Character played by Hugh Jackman
14. Author of *The Perks of Being a Wallflower*
15. Youngest Best Actress Academy Award nominee

## DOWN

1. *The Wonderful Wizard of Oz* author
3. "What Makes You Beautiful" singers
4. Third book of the Hunger Games trilogy
6. *The 20/20 Experience* singer
8. Animated movie featuring Emma Stone and Ryan Reynolds
9. Singer with the best selling album of 2011 and 2012
13. *The Way, Way Back* actress

ANSWERS ON PAGES 334-336.

# BOOKS

→Which children's author is a well-known sports writer? PAGE 45

# 2013 BOOK AWARDS

**Newbery Medal**

For the author of the best children's book

**2013 winner:**
***The One and Only Ivan,***
by Katherine Applegate

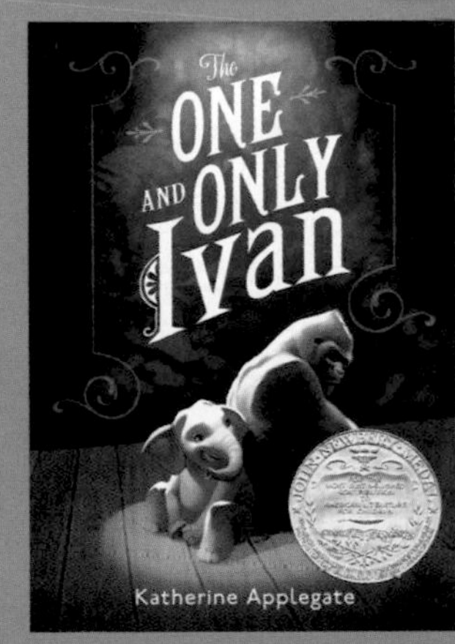


**Caldecott Medal**

For the artist of the best children's picture book

**2013 winner:**
***This Is Not My Hat,***
by Jon Klassen

For a complete list of previous Newbery and Caldecott winners, visit: www.ala.org/alsc/awardsgrants/bookmedia

**Michael L. Printz Award**

For excellence in literature written for young adults

**2013 winner:**
***In Darkness,***
by Nick Lake

**Coretta Scott King Award**

For artists and authors whose works encourage expression of the African-American experience

**2013 winners:**
**Author Award:**
***Hand in Hand: Ten Black Men Who Changed America,***
by Andrea Davis Pinkney

**Illustrator Award:**
***I, Too, Am America,***
illustrated by Bryan Collier

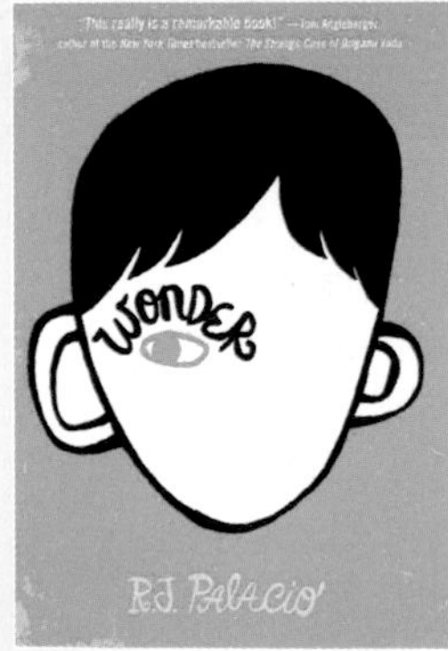


## NEW BOOK SPOTLIGHT

***I won't describe what I look like. Whatever you're thinking, it's probably worse.***

Ten-year-old August Pullman, called Auggie, shares those powerful words at the beginning of ***Wonder***. In R. J. Palacio's heartwarming first novel, Auggie is an ordinary kid—except for the fact that he was born with a severe facial deformity. After being schooled at home for years, Auggie bravely decides to enter fifth grade at Beecher Prep. The story that unfolds centers on the importance of kindness and acceptance.

# Famous Children's Authors

**Suzanne Collins** (1962– ) is the author of The Hunger Games trilogy. She began her career writing for children's television. The Hunger Games series is rooted in her interest in Greek mythology. She got the idea for the books while watching TV. She observed people competing on a reality show on one channel and fighting a war on another channel.

- *The Hunger Games*
- *Catching Fire*
- *Mockingjay*

**Lois Lowry** (1937– ) was born in Hawaii. Her books have looked at many issues, from cancer to the Holocaust. She won Newbery Medals for *Number the Stars* and for *The Giver*, which is the first of a four-book series.

- *Number the Stars*
- *The Giver*
- *Gathering Blue*
- *Messenger*
- *Son*

**Mike Lupica** (1952– ) is one of America's most famous sports writers. He is a newspaper columnist, a TV sports commentator, and the author of many books for adults and kids. His first children's book, *Travel Team*, published in 2004, became a best-seller.

- *Heat*
- *Summer Ball*
- *Travel Team*
- *The Underdogs*

**Stephenie Meyer** (1973– ) is the author of the world-famous Twilight vampire-romance series. Her four novels have sold more than 100 million copies and been translated into 37 languages. In June 2003, a dream sparked the idea for the series. Three months later, she finished writing *Twilight*, her first novel in the saga.

- *Twilight*
- *New Moon*
- *Eclipse*
- *Breaking Dawn*

**Walter Dean Myers** (1937– ) was born Walter Milton Myers in West Virginia. After his mother died when he was only two, his foster parents, Florence and Herbert Dean, raised him in New York City. He changed his middle name to honor them. Growing up, Myers loved basketball and writing. In fourth grade, his first poem was published in the school yearbook.

- *Monster*
- *Lockdown*
- *Scorpions*
- *Somewhere in the Darkness*

**E. B. White** (1899–1985), born Elwyn Brooks White, is the author of the beloved children's classics *Stuart Little*, *The Trumpet of the Swan*, and *Charlotte's Web*. White worked as a reporter, essayist, and magazine writer.

- *Charlotte's Web*
- *The Trumpet of the Swan*

# COOL READS

Calling all bookworms! There are two main types of literature: **fiction** and **nonfiction**. Fiction is a made-up story. Nonfiction, on the other hand, is a true story. Within these two groups are different types of stories called **genres** (ZHAHN-ruhz). Check out these recommended reads from various genres.

## FICTION

### ADVENTURE, FANTASY, and SCIENCE FICTION

**These stories transport you to imaginary worlds filled with unusual characters and magical creatures.**

**TRY THESE**

*The Hunger Games*, by Suzanne Collins; **Storm Runners** series, by Roland Smith; *A Wrinkle in Time*, by Madeleine L'Engle

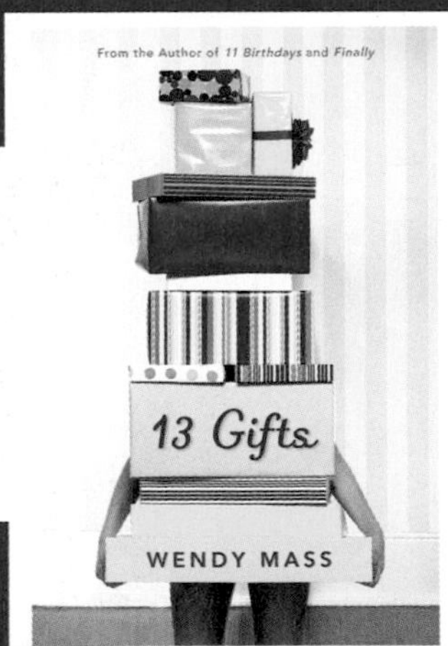


### REALISTIC FICTION

**Do you enjoy reading stories that you can relate to? This genre is about real-life situations that kids and teens deal with every day.**

**TRY THESE**

***13 Gifts***, by Wendy Mass; *Tales of a Fourth Grade Nothing*, by Judy Blume

### MYSTERIES and THRILLERS

**These suspense-filled tales follow a secret that needs to be uncovered or a crime that needs to be solved.**

**TRY THESE**

**The 39 Clues** series, by Rick Riordan; The Mysterious Benedict Society series, by Trenton Lee Stewart

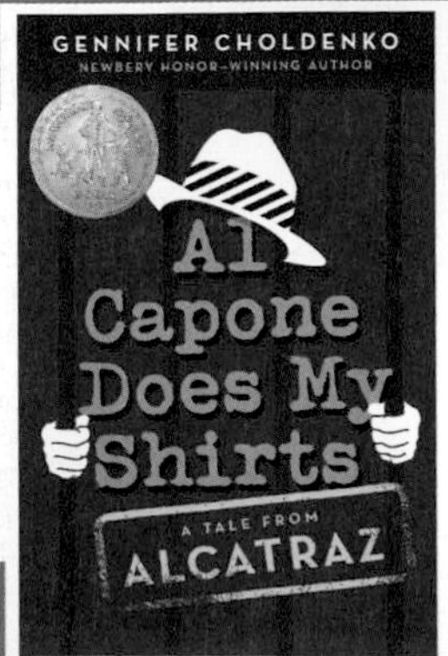


### HISTORICAL FICTION

**Authors of this genre put a new twist on history. They take exciting historical events or periods and place intriguing fictional characters smack in the middle of them.**

**TRY THESE**

***Al Capone Does My Shirts***, by Gennifer Choldenko; *Bud, Not Buddy*, by Christopher Paul Curtis

## GRAPHIC NOVELS, COMICS, AND MANGA

**These types of books convey their stories with drawings and text.**

**TRY THESE** Lunch Lady series, by Jarrett J. Krosoczka; ***Sita's Ramayana***, written by Samhita Arni and illustrated by Moyna Chitrakar

## MYTHS AND LEGENDS

**These made-up stories go way back. Many tell of how things in nature came to be.**

**TRY THESE**
*Amazing Greek Myths of Wonder and Blunders*, by Mike Townsend; *Anansi the Spider: A Tale From the Ashanti*, by Gerald McDermott

# NONFICTION

## MEMOIRS, BIOGRAPHIES, AND AUTOBIOGRAPHIES

**Do you like reading about the details of a real person's life? Then get up-close and personal with this genre!**

**TRY THESE** *Helen's Big World: The Life of Helen Keller*, by Doreen Rappaport; ***Justin Bieber: First Step 2 Forever: My Story***, by Justin Bieber; *Steve Jobs: The Man Who Thought Different*, by Karen Blumenthal

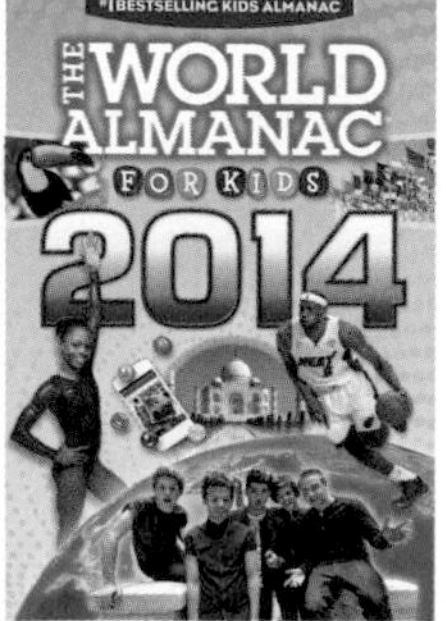


## REFERENCE

**Reference books provide reliable facts and sources of information. Almanacs, atlases, dictionaries, and encyclopedias are examples of reference books.**

**TRY THIS**
*The World Almanac for Kids*

## HISTORY

**Books in this genre can be about an event, an era, a country, or even a war.**

**TRY THESE**
*Abraham Lincoln and Frederick Douglass: The Story Behind an American Friendship*, by Russell Freedman; *Titanic: Voices From the Disaster*, by Deborah Hopkinson

# BOOKS THROUGH TIME

If a Roman emperor wanted to read a book, he had to unroll it from a scroll. Around A.D. 100, the codex was invented. It was made up of a stack of pages stitched together at the side and protected by a cover. Books on paper that we read today look something like a codex.

In the Middle Ages, books were made by monks who copied them by hand onto prepared animal skins called parchment. The monks often decorated the pages with beautiful color illustrations called illuminations. Books were scarce and very expensive, and few people who were not priests or monks could read.

A big change came with the inventions of paper and printing in China. Paper came into Europe through the Muslim world and was common by the 14th century. Johann Gutenberg of Germany perfected printing in the 1450s. Once books could be printed they became more common.

At first, books were still not easy to make. A typesetter had to put each letter into place individually. Once all the letters for the page were in place, they were covered with ink and printed, one page at a time, by hand on a press. By the 19th century, however, steam-powered presses could print out hundreds of pages at a time. Another invention was the linotype machine, which stamped out individual letters and set them up much faster than a typesetter could. Today, many people read books using electronic devices.

## Who Am I?

**I was born in a suburb of Cleveland, Ohio, in 1945. My family, which included my sister and three brothers, was a noisy bunch! We usually went on a car trip each summer. A five-day drive to Idaho when I was twelve would become the basis for my book *Walk Two Moons,* which won the Newbery Medal. Some of my other books for young readers include *Absolutely Normal Chaos, The Wanderer, Love That Dog, Hate That Cat,* and most recently, *The Great Unexpected.* I write some of my stories in verse. My advice for kids who want to be writers? "Read a lot and write a lot. Try different forms when you write: poetry, short stories, and plays. Have fun and experiment."**

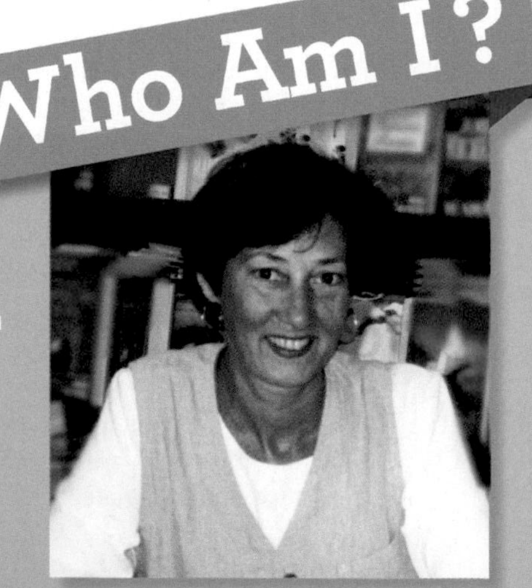

Answer: Sharon Creech

# DIGITAL READS

## E-Books and E-Readers

The age of the electronic book is here! The number of people reading e-books continues to rise. More than one-quarter of Americans age 16 and older were reading e-books in 2013, according to a recent study. Some well-known e-book readers include the Kindle, the Nook, and the Sony Reader. Many people also read e-books on tablet computers.

E-readers allow users to download books, magazines, newspapers, and other material wirelessly from the Internet. They have a number of interactive features. You can control screen brightness, type size, and other aspects of how each page looks. On some devices, you turn a page using a page button. On others, you run your finger across the screen.

Some e-readers have a keyboard, which allows you to add comments to the page as you read. Others have a touch screen keyboard. Some allow website access and some let you download books as audio files.

## Time for Tablets!

Tablets are a line of computers that allow you to read books and also access the Internet, play music, email, watch videos, and download apps with the touch of your finger. Thin and light, a tablet is like a laptop computer, e-reader, and smartphone combined. A Pew Research Center study found that, in 2013, about 31 percent of American adults owned a tablet computer. One of the most popular is Apple's iPad.

# BUILDINGS

→What is a pylon? PAGE 55

## TALLEST BUILDINGS IN THE WORLD

Here are the world's tallest buildings as of early 2013, with the year each was completed. Heights listed don't include antennas or other outside structures.

***Burj Khalifa (Khalifa Tower)***
Dubai, United Arab Emirates (2010)
Height: 163 stories, 2,720 feet

***Makkah Royal Clock Tower Hotel***
Mecca, Saudi Arabia (2012)
Height: 120 stories, 1,972 feet

***Taipei 101***
Taipei, Taiwan (2004)
Height: 101 stories, 1,667 feet

***World Financial Center***
Shanghai, China (2008)
Height: 101 stories, 1,614 feet

***International Commerce Center***
Hong Kong, China (2010)
Height: 108 stories, 1,588 feet

***Petronas Towers 1 & 2***
Kuala Lumpur, Malaysia (1998)
Height: each building is 88 stories, 1,483 feet

## WORLD'S TALLEST WHEN BUILT

**Great Pyramid of Giza, Egypt**
**Built c. 2250 B.C. Height: 480 feet**

**Washington Monument, Washington, D.C.**
**Built 1848–1884, Height: 555 feet**

**Eiffel Tower, Paris, France**
**Built 1887–89. Height: 984 feet**

**Chrysler Building, New York, NY**
**Built 1930. Height: 1,046 feet**

**Empire State Building, New York, NY**
**Built 1931. Height: 1,250 feet**

### One World Trade Center

A major new skyscraper in New York City—One World Trade Center—was scheduled to be completed by late 2013. Built near the site of the World Trade Center towers destroyed in the September 11, 2001, terrorist attacks, One World Trade Center will have 105 stories. If completed as planned, it will be the tallest building in the U.S. (In early 2013, that honor was held by the Willis Tower in Chicago, at 1,450 feet.) One World Trade Center is designed to rise 1,776 feet into the air (a reference to the year the American colonies declared independence). The building will include offices, restaurants, shops, and an observation deck.

**Did You KNOW?**

**The tallest building in Western Europe opened in London on February 1, 2013. Known as the Shard, the new skyscraper is a slender, glass-covered pyramid that stands 1,016 feet tall. The building includes offices, a hotel, luxury apartments, and restaurants. From its observation deck, visitors can see for 40 miles.**

***←The Shard, London***

# A Short History of TALL BUILDINGS

Throughout history, tall buildings have been symbols of power, wealth, and personal importance. Think about how impressed we are by the ancient Pyramids in Egypt, and then imagine how much more impressive they must have seemed to ancient people, who weren't used to seeing such enormous structures. But, in addition to trying to impress other people, the makers of tall buildings had to figure out how to support them and keep them from collapsing from their own weight. One answer was to have a huge, thick base that could support the weight above. The base of the Washington Monument, for example, has walls that are 15 feet thick!

By the 1880s, three **key factors in the evolution of tall buildings** were in place:

**1. A NEED FOR SPACE** Crowded cities had less space for building, and land got expensive. To create more space, buildings had to go up instead of out.

**2. BETTER STEEL PRODUCTION** Mass-producing steel meant more of it was available for construction. Long vertical **columns** and horizontal girders could be joined to form a strong cube-like grid that was lighter than a similar one made of stone or brick. Weight was also directed down the columns to a solid **foundation**, usually underground, instead of to walls.

**3. THE ELEVATOR** Tall buildings need elevators! The first elevator, powered by steam, was installed in a New York store in 1857. Electric elevators came along in 1880.

As buildings got taller, a new problem sprang up—**wind**. Too much movement could damage buildings or make the people inside uncomfortable. Some tall buildings, like New York's Citicorp Center, actually have a counter-weight near the top. A computer controls a 400-ton weight, moving it back and forth to lessen the building's sway.

In places such as California and Japan, **earthquakes** are a big problem, and special techniques are needed to make tall buildings safer from quakes.

***Chrysler Building, New York City*** →

# NOT YOUR AVERAGE BUILDING

When it comes to buildings, the tall ones grab people's attention. But many other buildings are interesting and fun to look at. Here are a few really cool buildings.

## BASKET HOUSE, Newark, Ohio

The Basket House is the headquarters of a company that makes—yes, you guessed it—baskets. Seven stories tall, it was built in 1997 in the style of one of the company's most popular products. The handles alone weigh 150 tons. The building has become a huge tourist attraction and gets about a half a million visitors a year.

## ELEPHANT BUILDING, Bangkok, Thailand

This unusual building (also called the Chang Building) was completed in 1997. It has 32 stories and is 335 feet tall. Inside, there are apartments, shops, and office space. The elephant is Thailand's national animal, so the design honors an important part of the country's heritage. Far from being beautiful, the structure has actually won a competition for the world's ugliest building!

## CROOKED HOUSE, Sopot, Poland

The Crooked House was built in 2004 and is part of a shopping center. Its designers said they were influenced by children's fairytale illustrations by two Polish writers. The style of the building is similar to other buildings around it, but the Crooked House looks as if it has collapsed from exhaustion or perhaps melted in the sun. It is said to be the most-photographed building in the entire country.

## ALEXANDRIA LIBRARY, Alexandria, Egypt

The new library in Alexandria has as its goal to recapture the glory of the Royal Library, which was a major center of learning in the ancient world. The new library opened in 2002 on the site of the old one, destroyed almost 2,000 years ago following the Roman conquest of Egypt. The building's striking granite exterior is intended to make visitors think of the Sun rising over the Mediterranean Sea.

# ARCHITECTURAL MARVELS



## HAGIA SOPHIA

### Istanbul, Turkey; built 532–537

Located on the site of an earlier church, the present Hagia Sophia was built by the Byzantine Emperor Justinian I. Used in the past as a Christian church and then an Islamic mosque, the building is now a museum. It is considered one of the greatest examples of Byzantine architecture in the world. The massive interior is decorated with marble, mosaics, and ancient paintings.

## MAYAN TEMPLES OF TIKAL

### El Petén region, Guatemala; built 700s

The city of Tikal was a center of Mayan culture. Major buildings that survive today include five pyramid-shaped temples. The tallest, Temple IV, rises more than 200 feet. Temple I, on the city's Great Plaza, was built to house the tomb of a king. Constructed of limestone, it has a typical Mayan "comb," or crest, at the top with a carved image of the seated king.

## BOROBUDUR TEMPLE

### Java, Indonesia; built 700s–800s

The stone temple at Borobudur was built as a shrine to Buddha and as a destination for Buddhist pilgrims. The base is in the form of a pyramid. Above it are five square terraces, topped by five circular platforms, all lavishly carved. As pilgrims climbed the different levels, they symbolically went through different levels of the Buddhist religion. Restored in the 19th century, the site is now Indonesia's biggest tourist attraction.

## ALHAMBRA PALACE

### Granada, Spain; built 1300s

The sprawling Alhambra palace was a royal residence. It was built by Muslim leaders from North Africa who ruled much of Spain at that time. Created on the site of a 9th-century fort, the palace complex also contains a bath and a mosque. Its architecture is in the Moorish style. All the rooms open onto interior courtyards surrounded by graceful arcades (covered walkways). The carvings that surround the arches and the lavish fountains and reflecting pools in the courtyards add to the beauty of the complex.

# BRIDGES

There are four main bridge designs: truss, arch, beam, and suspension or cable-stayed.

## TRUSS

The truss bridge uses mainly steel beams, connected in triangles to increase strength and span greater distances.

## ARCH

You can easily recognize an arch bridge, because it has arches holding it up from the bottom. The columns that support the arches are called abutments. Arch bridges were invented by the ancient Greeks.

## BEAM

The beam bridge is the most basic kind. A log across a stream is a simple style of beam bridge. Highway bridges are often beam bridges. The span of a beam bridge, or the length of the bridge without any support under it, needs to be fairly short. Long beam bridges need many supporting poles, called piers.

## SUSPENSION

On suspension bridges, the roadway hangs from smaller cables attached to a pair of huge cables running over two massive towers. The ends of the giant cables are anchored firmly into solid rock or huge concrete blocks at each end of the bridge. The weight of the roadway is transferred through the cables to the anchors. On a cable-stayed bridge, the cables are attached directly from the towers (pylons) to the deck.

## BUILDING QUIZ

Can you unscramble these words to make the names of famous buildings described on pages 50-53?

pleEthan ludiBgin
agHai Shipoa
flEief eworT
heT draSh
barhmAal alecPa
atsBek seuHo

ANSWERS ON PAGES 334-336.

## PARTS OF A SUSPENSION BRIDGE

**Anchorage** Main cables are attached here, adding strength and stability

**Deck** Surface of the bridge

**Main cable** Primary load-bearing cables, secured by anchorages

**Pier** Supports for pylons

**Pylon** Tower supports that hold up cables and decks

**Suspender cable** Vertical cables that hold up the deck

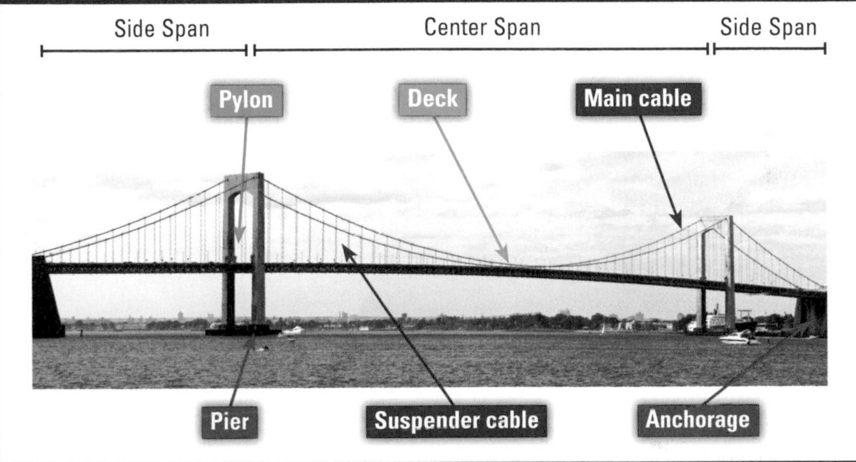


## DAM FACTS

Dams are built to control the flow of rivers. They can provide water for drinking or farming, prevent flooding, and create electricity. The first dams were embankment dams built thousands of years ago out of walls of rocks and dirt to prevent flooding or to make lakes called reservoirs for irrigation. Today, most dams are made of concrete. "Hydroelectric" dams are used to generate electricity by channeling the force of rivers and waterfalls into tunnels in the dam to move enormous machines called turbines.

***Bonneville Dam on the Columbia River***

# CALENDAR

→When is Labor Day? PAGE 61

Holidays and calendars go hand in hand. Using a calendar, you can see what day of the week it is and look for the next special day. Calendars divide time into days, weeks, months, and years.

## MAJOR TYPES OF CALENDARS

→ **GREGORIAN CALENDAR** Most of the world, including the United States, uses the Gregorian calendar. A year consists of 365 and a quarter days, the time it takes for Earth to circle the Sun. The quarter is why we have a leap year every four years. For simplicity, most years have 365 days. In a leap year, an extra day—February 29—is added to make up for the extra quarter days. The next leap year is 2016.

→ **ISLAMIC CALENDAR** The Islamic calendar is used by Muslim people around the world. Twelve lunar months, each beginning with the new Moon, make up the year. The year is 354 days long (355 days in leap years). Al-Hijra/Muharram (Islamic New Year) in Islamic year 1436 starts at Moon crescent on October 24, 2014.

→ **JEWISH CALENDAR** The Jewish calendar has months of 29 and 30 days, and its years are either 12 or 13 months long. It is a lunar-solar calendar, which means its months are lunar, but its years adjust to the movement of Earth around the Sun. It is the official calendar in Israel and is used as a religious calendar by Jewish people worldwide. Rosh Hashanah (New Year) in the year 5775 begins at sundown on September 24, 2014, on the Gregorian calendar.

→ **CHINESE CALENDAR** The Chinese calendar is a lunar-solar calendar that runs on a 60-year cycle. Within the cycle, years are given one of twelve animal designations: Rat, Ox, Tiger, Rabbit, Dragon, Snake, Horse, Sheep, Monkey, Rooster, Dog, and Pig. On January 31, 2014, the Year of the Horse starts.

## THE NAMES OF THE MONTHS

The table shows the names of the months and their meanings.

| Month | Named for |
|---|---|
| JANUARY | Roman god Janus, guardian of gates |
| FEBRUARY | Februalia, a Roman time of sacrifice |
| MARCH | Mars, the Roman god of war (the end of winter meant fighting could begin again) |
| APRIL | Aperire, the Latin word meaning "to open," as in flower buds |
| MAY | Maia, the goddess of plant growth |
| JUNE | Junius, the Latin word for the goddess Juno |
| JULY | Julius Caesar, the Roman ruler |
| AUGUST | Augustus, the first Roman emperor |
| SEPTEMBER | Septem, the Latin word for seven (the Roman year began in March) |
| OCTOBER | Octo, the Latin word for eight |
| NOVEMBER | Novem, the Latin word for nine |
| DECEMBER | Decem, the Latin word for ten |

# HOLIDAY HIGHLIGHTS

**Each month brings new chances to celebrate famous people, historic events, and special occasions. On federal holidays, U.S. government offices are closed as are many schools and businesses. There are also other holidays that might not mean a day off from school, but they are still enthusiastically celebrated. Holidays marked with an asterisk (*) are federal holidays.**

## JANUARY 2014

**January is National Oatmeal Month and National Skating Month. Learn how to ice skate—for free—at events at participating ice rinks nationwide. Grab a bowl of oatmeal beforehand for a nutritious way to stay warm from the inside out.**

### * January 1: New Year's Day

Until the year 1753, New Year's Day was celebrated on March 25 every year. When the Gregorian calendar was adopted in 1582, the date was switched to January 1.

### * January 20: Martin Luther King Jr. Day

Martin Luther King Jr. Day takes place on the third Monday in January. The holiday honors the famous civil rights leader who was born on January 15, 1929.

### JANUARY 31: CHINESE NEW YEAR

The year 4712 begins on January 31 according to China's traditional lunar-solar calendar. The celebration lasts for 15 days, ending with the Lantern Festival.

## FEBRUARY 2014

**February is Black History Month. Learn about the contributions of some important African Americans who changed history.**

### February 2: Groundhog Day

On February 2, thousands of people gather in the small town of Punxsutawney, Pennsylvania, to see if Punxsutawney Phil will see his shadow. According to legend, if the famous groundhog sees his shadow, winter will last six more weeks. If he doesn't, spring will come early.

### FEBRUARY 14: VALENTINE'S DAY

Valentine's Day is mostly a way to celebrate those you care about. People have been exchanging Valentine cards with loved ones since the 1500s.

### * February 17: Presidents' Day

Observed on the third Monday in February, Presidents' Day honors George Washington and Abraham Lincoln. Both presidents were born in February. George Washington was born on February 22, 1732, and Abraham Lincoln was born on February 12, 1809.

# MARCH 2014

**March is Women's History Month. From science to sports, discover some of history's leading ladies. March is also National Nutrition Month. It is a good time to learn how to eat well and stay fit all year long.**

## MARCH 17: ST. PATRICK'S DAY

This day honors the patron saint of Ireland. Festivities include wearing green, attending parades, and eating corned beef and cabbage, a traditional Irish food.

### March 20: First Day of Spring

Today marks the first day of spring in the Northern Hemisphere. Also known as the Vernal Equinox, the first day of spring is observed when the center of the Sun appears directly above Earth's equator.

# APRIL 2014

**April is National Poetry Month. Visit the library for books of poetry (try *Where the Sidewalk Ends*, by Shel Silverstein). Then try writing some of your own.**

### April 1: April Fools' Day

People have been celebrating April Fools' Day with pranks and gags for more than 400 years.

### At sundown, April 14-22: Passover

This Jewish holiday celebrates the freeing of Israelites from slavery in ancient Egypt. The eight-day celebration (seven in Israel) includes a seder meal and other religious rituals.

### April 20: Easter

This Christian holiday celebrates the resurrection of Jesus Christ. Traditions include coloring eggs and filling Easter baskets with candy and gifts.

## APRIL 22: EARTH DAY

First celebrated in the United States in 1970, Earth Day is an occasion for people to take action and care for our environment. Today, more than one billion people around the globe commemorate Earth Day.

# MAY 2014

**May is National Bike Month. Riding your bike is a great way to stay fit and have fun. Be sure to wear a helmet every time you ride, even if you're going just a short distance.**

### May 5: Cinco de Mayo

This holiday commemorates Mexico's defeat of the French army in the Battle of the Puebla on this day in 1862.

### May 11: Mother's Day

Since 1914, Mother's Day has been celebrated on the second Sunday of May. Each year, more than 155 million cards are bought and given to moms across the United States. And that doesn't even include the special homemade cards that moms receive!

### * MAY 26: MEMORIAL DAY

Originally celebrated in honor of members of the military who died during the Civil War, Memorial Day now honors all men and women who have died while serving in the U.S. military. It falls on the last Monday in May.

# JUNE 2014

**June is Great Outdoors Month. Be sure to get outside and get active at special events, from National Boating and Fishing Week to the Great American Backyard Campout, to celebrate the Great Outdoors.**

### June 14: Flag Day

This day remembers the adoption of the first version of the Stars and Stripes by the Continental Congress in 1777. Flag Day is not an official federal holiday, but many communities hold celebrations to honor the American flag.

### June 15: Father's Day

We celebrate fathers on the third Sunday in June.

### June 19: Juneteenth

Juneteenth, also known as Emancipation Day, celebrates a military order on June 19, 1865, that formally completed the freeing of the slaves.

### JUNE 21: FIRST DAY OF SUMMER

The first day of summer in the Northern Hemisphere is observed on the Summer Solstice, when the Sun rises and sets the farthest north on the horizon and daylight hours are longest.

# JULY 2014

**July is Cell Phone Courtesy Month. This month reminds the more than 285 million cell phone users in the United States to be more aware of how cell phone use in public places affects other people.**

### July 1: Canada Day

Canada Day (called Dominion Day until 1982) celebrates the creation of the Dominion of Canada on July 1, 1867. Like the Fourth of July in the United States, Canada Day is celebrated with parades and fireworks.

### * JULY 4: INDEPENDENCE DAY

Commonly known as the Fourth of July, this federal holiday marks the anniversary of the adoption of the Declaration of Independence on July 4, 1776. Americans celebrate with picnics, parades, barbecues, and fireworks.

### July 14: Bastille Day

This holiday commemorates the beginning of the French Revolution by the storming of the Bastille, an event that eventually led to the formation of modern France.

### AT MOON CRESCENT, JULY 27: EID AL-FITR

This Muslim holiday marks the end of Ramadan, the Islamic month of fasting. During Ramadan, observers refrain from eating from dawn to sunset. A special meal is part of Eid al-Fitr festivities to celebrate the end of fasting.

# AUGUST 2014

**August is American Adventures Month. Celebrate vacations in North, South, and Central America by going on one of your own or remembering a fun vacation you've taken in the past.**

### AUGUST 26: WOMEN'S EQUALITY DAY

This day commemorates the adoption, in 1920, of the 19th Amendment to the U.S. Constitution. This amendment granted women the right to vote.

# SEPTEMBER 2014

**September is Library Card Sign-Up Month and Hispanic Heritage Month (September 15-October 15). Take advantage of the library to learn about the 500-year-old roots of Hispanic culture in the Americas.**

### * September 1: Labor Day

A federal holiday that takes place on the first Monday in September, Labor Day celebrates workers with a day off in their honor. Labor Day has its roots in the late 19th-century labor movement, when workers began to organize to demand shorter hours and fairer pay. It was made a federal holiday in 1894.

### September 17: Constitution or Citizenship Day

Constitution Day is celebrated on September 17, the date the U.S. Constitution was signed in 1787.

### SEPTEMBER 22: FIRST DAY OF AUTUMN

Today is the first day of autumn, or fall, in the Northern Hemisphere. Also known as the Autumnal Equinox, the first day of fall occurs when the center of the Sun appears directly above Earth's equator.

### At sundown, September 24-26: Rosh Hashanah

Rosh Hashanah is a two-day holiday that celebrates the beginning of the Jewish new year. The day is marked with prayer and symbolic foods, such as apples dipped in honey.

# OCTOBER 2014

**Smile! October is National Dental Hygiene Month—a time to brush up on keeping your teeth healthy.**

### At sundown, October 3-4: Yom Kippur

Also known as the Day of Atonement, Yom Kippur is the holiest and most solemn day of the year for Jewish people. The holiday is observed with fasting and prayer to atone, or make up, for one's sins.

### At Moon crescent, October 4-5: Eid al-Adha

This Muslim holiday celebrates Abraham's willingness to sacrifice his son Ishmael to Allah prove his faith. The celebration includes a special meal, prayer, and other rituals.

### * October 13: Columbus Day

Celebrated on the second Monday in October, Columbus Day marks Christopher Columbus's landing on an island in the Bahamas, then thought of as the New World, in 1492.

### October 23: Diwali

This Hindu holiday is also known as the Festival of Lights. People decorate their homes with lights, candles, and oil lamps to celebrate.

### OCTOBER 31: HALLOWEEN

Halloween always falls on the last day of October. Popular ways to celebrate include trick-or-treating and going to costume parties.

# NOVEMBER 2014

**November is National American Indian Heritage Month. Learn about Native Americans and their roles in American history.**

### November 4: Election Day

The first Tuesday after the first Monday in November, Election Day is a mandatory holiday in some states.

### * November 11: Veterans Day

On this special day, Americans honor U.S. veterans—men and women who have served in the armed forces.

### * NOVEMBER 27: THANKSGIVING

Every year on the fourth Thursday in November, American families gather together to give thanks and enjoy a big turkey meal.

# DECEMBER 2014

**December is National Drunk and Drugged Driving Prevention Month. Help raise awareness of the danger of impaired driving this month.**

### At sundown, December 16-24: Hanukkah

Also known as the Festival of Lights, this Jewish holiday lasts eight days and commemorates the rededication of the Holy Temple in Jerusalem. Each night, families light a candle in a special holder called a menorah.

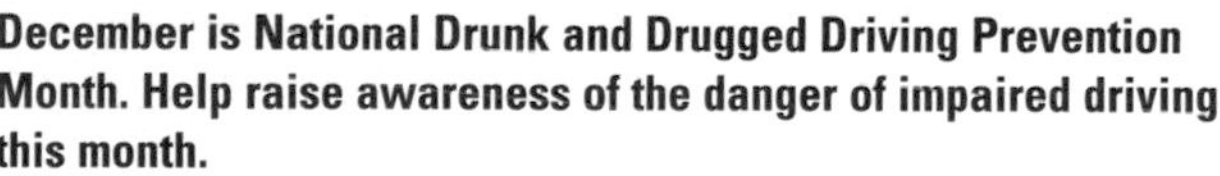

### DECEMBER 21: FIRST DAY OF WINTER

The first day of winter, in the Northern Hemisphere, is observed on the Winter Solstice, when the Sun rises and sets the farthest south on the horizon and daylight hours are shortest.

### * December 25: Christmas

This Christian holiday celebrates the birth of Jesus Christ. People celebrate by decorating trees, exchanging presents, and gathering with family and friends.

### December 26-January 1, 2015: Kwanzaa

This week-long holiday honors African culture. People light candles in holders called kinaras and exchange gifts to celebrate.

### December 31-New Year's Eve

This day isn't technically a holiday, but you'll find a lot of people celebrating the end of one year and the start of the next.

# MORE WAYS TO CELEBRATE

## Here are some other special days you don't want to miss in 2014!

**January 17: Kid Inventors' Day** — Honor young minds on the birthday of Benjamin Franklin, who invented the first swim fins at age 12.

**February 2: Super Bowl XLVIII** — The year's biggest game is the grand finale of the NFL season. The Super Bowl is scheduled to take place at MetLife Stadium in East Rutherford, New Jersey.

**March 2: Read Across America Day** — Celebrate Read Across America Day with a good book and green eggs and ham for breakfast! This nationwide reading celebration takes place each year on Dr. Seuss' birthday.

**April 25: National Arbor Day** — Give a tree a hug today. Arbor Day, observed each year on the last Friday in April, encourages people to plant and care for trees.

**May 3: Kentucky Derby** — Known as "The Most Exciting Two Minutes in Sports," the Kentucky Derby is held each year on the first Saturday in May at Churchill Downs in Louisville, Kentucky.

**June 8: World Oceans Day** — Catch the wave! Help protect the world's oceans, which cover about 70 percent of Earth's surface.

**July 20: National Ice Cream Day** — Let's all scream for ice cream! Also known as "Sundae Sunday," National Ice Cream Day celebrates America's popular dessert.

**August 3: National Watermelon Day** — Cool off from the heat with a slice of summer's favorite fruit.

**September 7: National Grandparents Day** — This day honors grandparents and their special place in our families.

**October 29: National Cat Day** — It's a purr-fect day to celebrate one of America's most popular pets. Our feline friends can be found in one-third of American homes.

**November 7: International Tongue Twister Day** — "Peter Piper picked a peck of pickled peppers." Can you say that three times fast? Celebrate this day by practicing some of your favorite tongue twisters.

**December 4: National Cookie Day** — Bake up a batch of your favorite cookies to celebrate this sweet day!

***O say, can you see...*** **"The Star-Spangled Banner" celebrates its 200th anniversary! Francis Scott Key wrote the U.S. national anthem on September 14, 1814.**

→Who are the only people who don't have unique DNA? PAGE 64

# FIGHTING CRIME WITH SCIENCE

The use of scientific evidence to solve crimes is known as **forensics**. Many different methods can be used to help find out the facts in a case and identify suspects.

**FINGERPRINTS:** In 1880, a court in Japan made the first-ever use of fingerprints to charge a person with a crime. Later advances in technology have made it easier to use fingerprint evidence in solving crimes. Certain chemicals can show up a hidden fingerprint, and modern computer networks allow investigators to quickly compare the fingerprints from a crime scene to the prints of many known individuals on file.

**GUNS:** A bullet that has gone through a gun barrel may pick up markings that can help identify the gun that was used to fire it. The science of analyzing guns, bullets, and their impact on a crime scene is called **ballistics**.

**DNA:** DNA, or genetic, evidence can be very helpful in identifying individuals. Except in identical twins, every person's DNA is unique. Investigators often gather it from sources such as blood, saliva, hairs, and skin.

**CHEMISTRY:** Chemistry is a valuable tool for solving crimes. For example, an investigator may apply a chemical such as luminol at a crime scene to make hidden bloodstains visible. Well-equipped crime labs use the latest techniques to learn the makeup of unknown substances found at a crime scene.

**Did You KNOW?** DNA evidence has been used to re-open many cases considered solved long ago. Despite many safeguards, it may happen that a person gets convicted of a crime by mistake. DNA evidence can show that someone was wrongly found guilty. In 2013, for example, 58-year-old Randolph Arledge was released after some 30 years in prison for a 1981 murder in north Texas. Hairs from the victim's car were saved all this time and finally tested for DNA with the latest techniques. They pointed to a different suspect. A Texas law now allows convicts to seek DNA testing that may show they were wrongly convicted.

Arledge (right) with his son

## ON THE JOB

# Supervisory Federal Air Marshal

**Alfred Burgess** works for the Federal Air Marshal Service, a part of the Department of Homeland Security. He travels on airplanes in order to watch out for and handle any possible threat to the security of passengers. He also supervises other air marshals. He agreed to talk to *The World Almanac for Kids* about his work.

**What do you do in a typical day?** When serving as a Federal Air Marshal, I am the federal law enforcement officer on the airplane. I make sure the plane and everyone on board arrive at their destination safely. I do this by blending in with other passengers and staying alert to what is going on around me. As a supervisor, it's also my job to see that the air marshals who work for me have all they need to train hard and complete each mission successfully.

**What interests and strengths of yours make this job right for you?** I am self-motivated, I like to stay in shape, and I have a thirst for knowledge. Federal air marshals travel all over the world. We also complete 40 hours of special training every three months. We are always trying to learn how to do our jobs better, and we strive to learn from every experience and every encounter.

**What kind of education or training did you need to get in order to do your job?** The Federal Air Marshal Service hires people from different backgrounds with all levels of educational and job-related experience. We strive to be as diverse as the people we are sworn to keep safe. I have a bachelor's degree in fine arts from New York Institute of Technology. On being hired, I received approximately 16 weeks of intense training. The first part of the training focused on the basic skills required of any law enforcement officer, including use of firearms, handcuffing, and defensive measures. The final portion of training included practice in realistic situations, designed to test my knowledge, physical skills, and decision-making ability on board aircraft.

**What do you like best about your job? What is most challenging?** Every day is a new day where I get to meet new people and visit various places within the United States and overseas. Each person I meet reaffirms my commitment to making sure everyone arrives safely, whether you travel for business or for pleasure. Working at 30,000 feet in the sky leaves me no backup or room for error. I enjoy the challenge of training hard and being in a constant state of readiness.

→What is the wind speed in a Category 4 hurricane? PAGE 69

# EARTHQUAKES

There are thousands of earthquakes each year. Most are small, but about 1 in 500 causes damage. Some quakes are incredibly powerful and destructive.

## WHAT CAUSES EARTHQUAKES?

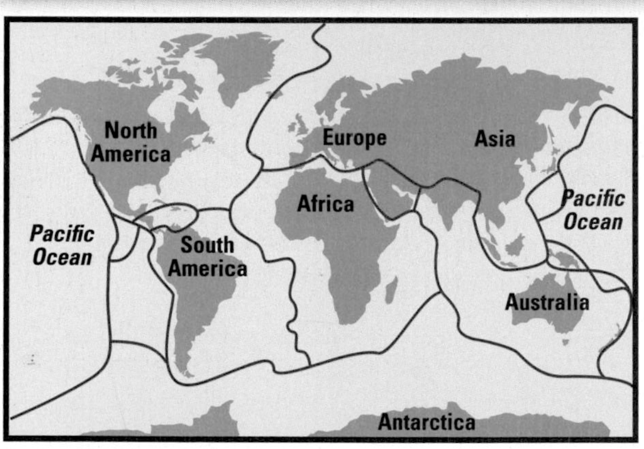


To understand earthquakes, imagine Earth as an egg with a cracked shell. The cracked outer layer (the eggshell) is called the lithosphere, and it is divided into huge pieces called plates (see map). The plates are constantly moving away from, toward, or past one another. Earthquakes result when plates collide or scrape against each other. The cracks in the lithosphere are called faults. Many quakes occur along these fault lines.

## CALIFORNIA'S SAN ANDREAS FAULT

Perhaps the most famous fault in the world, the San Andreas fault runs for about 700 miles north-south through California. Along this fault, which is about 10 miles deep, the North American and Pacific Ocean plates are scraping past each other. In some parts of California, a crack in the ground can be seen where the fault is located. The San Andreas fault is responsible for some of the worst earthquakes in U.S. history, including the 1906 quake in San Francisco that caused more than 3,000 deaths and destroyed large parts of the city.

## MAJOR EARTHQUAKES*

| Year | Location | Magnitude | Deaths (estimated) |
|---|---|---|---|
| **1960** | near Chile | 9.5** | 1,655 |
| **1970** | Northern Peru | 7.9 | 70,000 |
| **1976** | Tangshan, China | 7.5 | 242,769 |
| **1988** | Soviet Armenia | 6.8 | 25,000 |
| **1989** | United States (San Francisco area) | 6.9 | 63 |
| **1990** | Western Iran | 7.4 | 40,000+ |
| **1999** | Western Turkey | 7.6 | 17,000+ |
| **2001** | Western India | 7.6 | 20,085 |
| **2004** | Sumatra, Indonesia | 9.1 | 227,898 |
| **2005** | Pakistan and India | 7.6 | 86,000 |
| **2008** | Sichuan, China | 7.9 | 87,857 |
| **2010** | Haiti | 7.0 | 316,000 |
| **2011** | Northeastern Japan | 9.0 | 20,896 |

*Since 1960. **Strongest earthquake ever recorded.

## WHAT ARE TSUNAMIS?

Tsunami (pronounced ***tsoo-NAH-mee***) comes from two Japanese words: "tsu" (harbor) and "nami" (wave). Tsunamis are huge waves. They are sometimes called tidal waves, but they have nothing to do with the tides. The strongest tsunamis happen when a big part of the sea floor lifts along a fault, pushing up a huge volume of water. Many times this happens after an undersea earthquake.

## MAJOR TSUNAMIS

| Year | Location | What Happened? | Deaths (estimated) |
|---|---|---|---|
| 1755 | Lisbon, Portugal | Three earthquakes struck Portugal's capital, creating a tsunami with waves 100 feet high. | 60,000 |
| **1782** | South China Sea near Taiwan | After a major underwater earthquake, a tsunami sent waves inland more than 60 miles. | 40,000 |
| 1883 | Indonesia | The Krakatau, or Krakatoa, volcano erupted four times, causing a massive tsunami more than 100 feet tall. | 36,000 |
| **1908** | Southern Italy | A major earthquake triggered a devastating tsunami. | 72,000 |
| 2004 | Indian Ocean | After a 9.1-magnitude earthquake hit Indonesia, a tsunami with waves up to 100 feet high struck 14 countries. | 227,898 |
| **2011** | Northeastern Japan | A 9.0-magnitude earthquake touched off a huge tsunami. | 20,896 |

# VOLCANOES

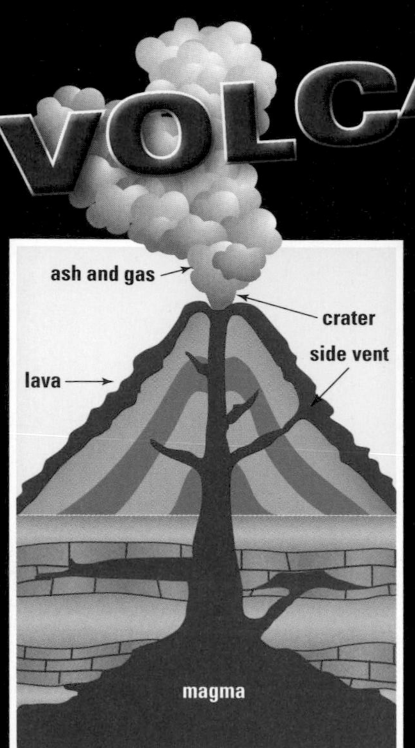


A volcano is a mountain or hill (cone) with an opening on top known as a crater. Hot melted rock (magma), gases, and other material from inside Earth mix together and rise up through cracks and weak spots. When enough pressure builds up, the magma can escape. It erupts through the crater and sometimes through smaller openings called side vents. Magma that comes out of a volcano is called lava. Lava may be hotter than 2,000°F. The cone of a volcano is often made of layers of lava and ash that have erupted, then cooled.

## Some Famous Volcanic Eruptions

| Year | Volcano (place) | Deaths (estimated) |
|---|---|---|
| 79 | Mount Vesuvius (Italy) | 16,000 |
| 1586 | Kelut (Indonesia) | 10,000 |
| 1792 | Mount Unzen (Japan) | 14,500 |
| 1815 | Tambora (Indonesia) | 10,000 |
| 1883 | Krakatau, or Krakatoa (Indonesia) | 36,000 |
| 1902 | Mount Pelée (Martinique) | 28,000 |
| 1980 | Mount St. Helens (U.S.) | 57 |
| 1982 | El Chichón (Mexico) | 1,880 |
| 1985 | Nevado del Ruiz (Colombia) | 23,000 |
| 1986 | Lake Nyos (Cameroon) | 1,700 |
| 1991 | Mount Pinatubo (Philippines) | 800 |

## Where is the RING OF FIRE?

**The hundreds of active volcanoes near the edges of the Pacific Ocean make up what is called the Ring of Fire. They mark the boundary between the plates under the Pacific Ocean and the plates under the surrounding continents. (Earth's plates are explained on page 66, with the help of a map.) The Ring of Fire runs from Alaska, along the west coast of North and South America, to the southern tip of Chile. The ring also runs down the east coast of Asia. Starting in the far north, it passes through Russia, Japan, the Philippines, and New Guinea. It continues down past Australia. Some of the most destructive volcanic eruptions ever recorded have occurred along the Ring of Fire.**

## What happened at POMPEII?

Two thousand years ago, at the time of the Roman Empire, Pompeii was a vacation resort. Located near the Bay of Naples in Italy, it was popular with wealthy Romans. In A.D. 79, nearby Mount Vesuvius, an active volcano, erupted. The eruption sent huge amounts of hot rock, gases, and dense ash over the unsuspecting city. Thousands of people died, and the city was buried under millions of tons of ash. The incredibly well-preserved ruins were rediscovered in 1748, and today millions of people visit Pompeii each year.

# HURRICANES



## Categories

| | |
|---|---|
| 1 | 74-95 mph |
| 2 | 96-110 mph |
| 3 | 111-130 mph |
| 4 | 131-155 mph |
| 5 | over 155 mph |

Hurricanes—called typhoons or cyclones in the Pacific—are Earth's biggest storms. When conditions are right, they form over the ocean from collections of storms and clouds known as tropical disturbances. Strong winds create a wall of clouds and rain that swirl in a circle around a calm center called the eye. If wind speeds reach 39 mph, the storm is named. If wind speeds top 74 mph, the storm is called a **hurricane**. Hurricanes are classified into five categories depending on their wind speeds.

## Hurricane Names

The U.S. began using women's names for hurricanes in 1953 and added men's names in 1979. When all letters (except Q, U, X, Y, and Z) are used in one season, any additional storms are named with Greek letters.

### 2014 Atlantic Hurricane Names

Arthur, Bertha, Cristobal, Dolly, Edouard, Fay, Gonzalo, Hanna, Isaias, Josephine, Kyle, Laura, Marco, Nana, Omar, Paulette, Rene, Sally, Teddy, Vicky, Wilfred

Hurricanes can be hundreds of miles wide. On land, the storm can snap trees and tear buildings apart. Strong winds blowing toward shore can create a rise in the ocean water called a **storm surge**. It can combine with heavy rains to cause flooding and massive damage.

For the Atlantic Ocean, Caribbean Sea, and Gulf of Mexico, hurricane season runs from June 1 to November 30.

## NOTABLE U.S. HURRICANES

| Date | Location | What Happened? | Deaths (estimated) |
|---|---|---|---|
| Sept. 8, 1900 | Galveston, TX | Category 4 storm flooded the island with 15-foot waves. | 8,000+ |
| Sept. 16-17, 1928 | Central/ southern FL | Category 5 storm, the fourth-largest to hit the U.S. mainland, caused 9-foot waves. | 1,836 |
| Sept. 21, 1938 | NY, CT, RI, MA | "The Long Island Express," with storm surges rising 10-25 feet, caused $306 million in damages. | 682 |
| Aug. 25-29, 2005 | LA, MS, AL, GA, FL | Hurricane Katrina, with 175 mph winds and a 25-foot high storm surge, caused about $125 billion in damage. | 1,833+ |
| Oct. 29-30, 2012 | NY, NJ, other eastern states | Sandy, a huge storm measuring 1,000 miles wide, caused at least $50 billion in damage. | 72+ |

**Did You KNOW?**

**Sandy was the second-most-destructive tropical storm ever to hit the United States. It made landfall (came onshore) in southern New Jersey on the evening of October 29, 2012. Besides bringing high winds and heavy rain, it caused a huge storm surge. Walls of water, some more than 9 feet tall, hit coastal areas in New Jersey; New York City; Long Island, NY; and southern New England. Hundreds of thousands of buildings were destroyed or severely damaged.**

*New Jersey shore*

# TORNADOES

## Enhanced Fujita Scale

**WEAK**

EF0: 65-85 mph
EF1: 86-110 mph

**STRONG**

EF2: 111-135 mph
EF3: 136-165 mph

**VIOLENT**

EF4: 166-200 mph
EF5: over 200 mph

Tornadoes, or twisters, are rapidly spinning columns of air. They usually form when winds change direction, speed up, and spin around in or near a thunderstorm.

Tornadoes can happen any time that the weather is right, but they are more common between March and July. They can happen in any state, but strong tornadoes often touch down in the U.S. Midwest and Southeast. A group of states including Texas, Oklahoma, Kansas, Nebraska, Iowa, and South Dakota is sometimes called Tornado Alley because of the large number of twisters that occur in the region.

According to the National Oceanic and Atmospheric Administration (NOAA), about 1,000 tornadoes occur in the U.S. each year.

Tornadoes are measured by how much damage they cause. In February 2007, the U.S. began using the Enhanced Fujita (EF) Scale to measure tornadoes. The EF-Scale provides an estimate of a tornado's wind speed based on the amount of damage. If a tornado doesn't hit anything, it may be hard to classify it.

Wind speeds are difficult to measure directly, because measuring instruments can be destroyed in more violent winds. The highest speed ever recorded—302 mph—was taken in May 1999 in an Oklahoma tornado. A huge EF5 tornado hit the same area, in and around Moore, OK, in May 2013.

## U.S. Tornado Records

(since record keeping began in 1950)

**YEAR:** The 1,817 tornadoes reported in **2004** topped the previous record of 1,424 in 1998.

**MONTH:** In **April 2011**, there were a total of 758 tornadoes, easily passing the old record of 542 set in May 2003.

**SINGLE EVENT:** On **April 25-28, 2011**, an estimated 305 tornadoes touched down in Alabama and a number of other states, mostly in the Southeast, causing more than 300 deaths.

**Did You KNOW?**

**Most tornadoes and the storm clouds that create them are very dark gray. But some tornadoes look red. These red tornadoes are most common in parts of Oklahoma and Kansas that have reddish soil. The swirling winds inside a tornado pick up enough dust to turn the twister red.**

# OTHER MAJOR DISASTERS

*The* Lusitania

## SHIP DISASTERS

| Date | Location | What Happened? | Deaths |
|---|---|---|---|
| April 14, 1912 | near Newfoundland | Luxury liner *Titanic* collided with iceberg. | 1,503 |
| May 7, 1915 | Atlantic Ocean, near Ireland | British steamer *Lusitania* torpedoed and sunk by German submarine. | 1,198 |
| Jan. 30, 1945 | Baltic Sea | Liner *Wilhelm Gustloff* carrying German refugees and soldiers sunk by Soviet sub. Highest death toll for a single ship. | 9,000 |

## AIRCRAFT DISASTERS

| Date | Location | What Happened? | Deaths |
|---|---|---|---|
| May 6, 1937 | Lakehurst, NJ | German zeppelin (blimp) *Hindenburg* caught fire as it prepared to land. | 36 |
| March 27, 1977 | Tenerife, Canary Islands | Two Boeing 747s collide on the runway of Los Rodeos airport. | 583 |
| Sept. 11, 2001 | New York, NY; Arlington, VA; Shanksville, PA | Two hijacked planes crashed into the World Trade Center, one plane hit the Pentagon, and a fourth went down in a PA field. | Nearly 3,000 |

## EXPLOSIONS AND FIRES

| Date | Location | What Happened? | Deaths |
|---|---|---|---|
| March 25, 1911 | New York, NY | Triangle Shirtwaist Factory caught fire, trapping garment workers, mostly women. | 146 |
| Nov. 28, 1942 | Boston, MA | Fire swept through the Cocoanut Grove nightclub; patrons panicked. Deadliest nightclub fire in U.S. history. | 492 |
| Dec. 3, 1984 | Bhopal, India | A pesticide factory explosion spread toxic gas. Worst industrial accident in history. | 15,000 |
| April 17, 2013 | West, TX | A fire and explosion at a fertilizer plant caused hundreds of casualties and destroyed a large part of the town. | 15 |

## FLOODS

| Date | Location | What Happened? | Deaths |
|---|---|---|---|
| 1927 | Mississippi River | From Illinois to Louisiana, the Mississippi River overflowed its banks, flooding 16 million acres of land and leaving 600,000 people homeless. Most destructive river flood in U.S. history. | 246+ |
| Aug. 1931 | China | Vast flooding on the Huang He River. Highest known death toll from a flood. | 3,700,000 |

# ENERGY

→What is biomass? PAGE 73

**Energy** can take many forms. Electricity is a form of energy. The Sun's warmth is energy in the form of heat. The energy we use every day—to heat and light buildings, travel around, run machinery, and power our electronic devices—comes from many sources. Some of these are **renewable** and will not get used up over time. Others are **nonrenewable** and will run out.

## Which Countries **PRODUCE** and **USE** the MOST ENERGY?

China both produces and uses more energy than any other country in the world. The United States is a close second in both categories. The table on the left lists the world's top ten energy producers and the percentage of the world's production that each nation was responsible for in 2010. One of these countries—Saudi Arabia—is the world's largest oil producer. The table on the right lists the world's top energy users and the percentage of the world's energy that each nation consumed that same year.

**TOP ENERGY PRODUCERS**

| Country | Percent |
|---|---|
| China | 18% |
| United States | 15% |
| Russia | 10% |
| Saudi Arabia | 5% |
| Canada | 4% |
| India | 3% |
| Iran | 3% |
| Indonesia | 3% |
| Australia | 3% |
| Brazil | 2% |

**TOP ENERGY USERS**

| Country | Percent |
|---|---|
| China | 20% |
| United States | 19% |
| Russia | 6% |
| India | 4% |
| Japan | 4% |
| Germany | 3% |
| Canada | 3% |
| Brazil | 2% |
| France | 2% |
| South Korea | 2% |

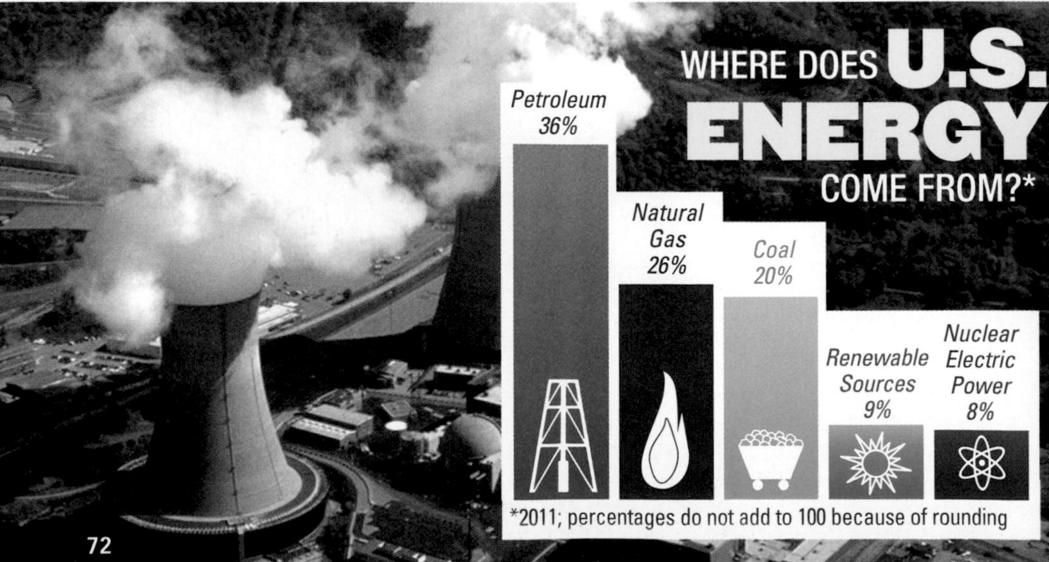

# Sources of ENERGY



## What are NONRENEWABLE sources of energy?

- **Nonrenewable** sources are available in only limited supplies that will eventually run out.
- **Fossil fuels**—especially **coal**, **oil**, and **natural gas**—are the most commonly used nonrenewable sources in the U.S. They are the decayed remains of ancient animals and plants that took millions of years to form.
- **Uranium** is another nonrenewable energy source. U-235, the type of uranium that is split in nuclear power plants to produce energy, is relatively rare.

## What are RENEWABLE sources of energy?

- **Renewable** energy sources, such as wind and water, won't run out.
- We can use the force of moving water, such as rivers and waterfalls, to create **hydropower**.
- The heat from sunlight can be converted into **solar power**.
- Steady winds can be used to spin giant propellers, or wind turbines, generating **wind power**.
- Renewable material made from plants and animals, such as wood and garbage, is called **biomass**. It can be burned to make energy.
- Heat from within Earth, called **geothermal energy**, can be collected at natural hot springs where hot magma boils the surface water.

## How do we POWER homes?

- The most common uses of energy in the home are to control heating and cooling and to provide electricity for lighting and appliances.
- Most electricity is generated at power stations by wheel-shaped engines called turbines. Water, wind, or steam can push turbines. Water is heated into steam by burning biomass or fossil fuels, by splitting uranium atoms during nuclear fission, or by using the heat of sunlight.
- More than two-fifths of America's electricity comes from burning coal.
- Some homes have **solar collectors** that capture the Sun's energy to heat water or **solar panels** → that convert sunlight directly into electricity.
- Many homes use natural gas, delivered through pipes, for heat and hot water.

# RENEWABLE ENERGY ENERGY IN ACTION

**Projects around the world are taking advantage of renewable sources to produce clean energy. Here are a few examples.**

## SOLAR

Plans are under way to build the largest solar energy plant in Africa. A British company is heading the project, taking place in the Central African country of Ghana. The plant will have the capacity to generate 155 megawatts of electricity, making it the fourth-largest solar power producer in the world when it opens in 2015. It is expected to boost Ghana's electricity production by 6 percent, while reducing air pollution. Ghana, which has a fast-growing economy, hopes that by 2020 renewable sources will provide 10 percent of its energy needs, a tenfold increase over 2012.

## GEOTHERMAL

← The world's largest production of geothermal power occurs in an area known as the Geysers, in the Mayacamas Mountains north of San Francisco. Almost 20 power plants at the Geysers draw on fields of steam about 4 miles below Earth's surface, where molten rock causes underground water to boil. The plants have the capacity to produce enough electricity to power about 900,000 homes.

## TIDAL

More reliable than sunshine are the tides, and energy companies are working to harness the energy of the ocean's movements to produce electricity. The world's first plant to generate electricity from changing tides is the Rance Tidal Power Station in Brittany, France. It began operating in 1966, and it is the second-largest such plant in the world today. The plant uses the movement of tides into and out of the mouth of the Rance River to turn turbines that can generate about 240 megawatts of electricity. The plant is nonpolluting, although it has affected populations of some kinds of fish in nearby waters. →

# PRODUCING ELECTRICITY: Pros and Cons

## Wind

**Pros:** Clean; land for wind farms can be used for other purposes like farming; can be built offshore.

**Cons:** Wind farms take up a lot of space; can kill birds if placed in migratory paths; require winds of at least 12 to 14 mph; can be noisy.

## Nuclear Fission

**Pros:** No greenhouse gases; produces a large amount of energy from a small amount of fuel; cannot explode like a nuclear bomb.

**Cons:** Creates dangerous nuclear waste that takes thousands of years to become safe; accidents might contaminate large areas with radiation; expensive.

## Biomass

**Pros:** Reduces trash in landfills; cuts down on release of methane; plants, such as corn for ethanol fuel, a renewable resource.

**Cons:** Burning some trash releases toxins and some greenhouse gases into the air; leaves ash; plants require large farms and specific climate conditions; more extensive use of corn for ethanol could raise food prices.

## Solar

**Pros:** No pollution; little maintenance required.

**Cons:** Solar panels are expensive and take up a lot of space; energy can't be gathered when the Sun isn't shining; manufacturing the solar cells produces waste products.

## Fossil Fuels
**(primarily coal)**

**Pros:** Affordable because equipment is in wide use; needs smaller space to generate power than most other sources.

**Cons:** Limited supply; major contributor to global warming; causes chemical reactions that create acid rain and smog; releases pollutants that cause breathing problems like asthma; can harm land and pollute water.

## Hydroelectric

**Pros:** Does not pollute or heat the water or air; no waste products; runs nonstop; very inexpensive.

**Cons:** Massive dams are expensive and difficult to build; alters the environment around the dam; can affect fish migratory patterns.

# ENERGY in the NEWS

## What Is "FRACKING"?

"Fracking," short for "hydraulic fracturing," is a technique for drilling as much as 4 miles deep into rock formations to get oil or natural gas. Once a hole is drilled, water or chemicals under great pressure are used to create openings called "fractures" in the rock. Oil or gas trapped in the rock seeps into and fills the fractures. This oil or gas can then be extracted.

Fracking has been around since the 1940s, but its use has grown significantly in recent years. The technique is controversial. Supporters say that it can help the U.S. import less oil from foreign countries. Opponents say that the chemicals used in the process can get into water supplies and harm wildlife and people. Some scientists also claim that the natural gas produced through fracking gives off more pollutants than natural gas from other sources.

## What Is BIKE SHARING?

Cities around the world are setting up bike-sharing stands where you can rent a bike for a small fee and then return it to another stand someplace else. These programs are aimed at reducing the use of cars—and therefore reducing pollution—in crowded city centers. Denver, Miami Beach, Minneapolis, New York, and Washington, D.C., are among the U.S. cities with bike programs.

# How Does a NUCLEAR POWER PLANT Work?

**There are different types of nuclear power plants, but they all rely on one basic fact: when the nucleus of an atom of uranium is split, a tremendous amount of energy is produced.**

Atoms contain three different kinds of particles: protons, neutrons, and electrons. Protons and neutrons are found in the atom's nucleus, or core. Electrons orbit around the nucleus. When the nucleus is split, in a process called **nuclear fission**, two new nuclei are created and energy is released. This energy is used to boil water, which turns into steam. This steam turns the blades of a turbine, producing electricity.

Neutrons hit **fuel rods** made of uranium to split the uranium atoms. By having the right number of neutrons hit the right amount of fuel at the right speed, scientists can create a **chain reaction** in which atoms keep splitting at a controlled rate, producing a steady supply of energy. Cool water and devices called **control rods** keep the fuel rods from getting too hot and keep the chain reaction from getting out of control.

# "GREENER" CARS, CLEANER AIR

About 1 billion motor vehicles, most of them passenger cars, fill the world's roads. Nearly all of them burn fossil fuels, mainly gasoline or diesel fuel, putting gases and dust particles into the air. Some of these gases and particles, called **emissions**, are harmful to people's health. They also contribute to **smog** and other types of air pollution. Some, such as carbon dioxide, are called **greenhouse gases** and promote climate change. As interest in reducing auto emissions to protect the environment has grown, new "green" cars with no or reduced emissions have come on the market. More are on the way.

## ALL ELECTRIC!

One way to deal with the emission problem is to replace gasoline or diesel fuel with a different power source for cars—such as electricity. **Electric cars** don't give off any emissions at all. They first appeared at the end of the 19th century but failed to catch on, largely because their batteries had a very limited capacity. Batteries are better today, and electric cars are making a comeback. The Nissan Leaf, for example, can go about 75-100 miles on a single charge, so it's useful for people who don't need to drive long distances.

Batteries are not the only possible source of electricity. Many car companies have been studying **hydrogen fuel cells** as a means of powering cars. These devices use hydrogen as a fuel. They combine it with oxygen in a process that yields electricity and a very nonpolluting by-product: water. Korean automaker Hyundai began producing hydrogen fuel cell cars in 2013.

## HYBRID CARS

Another approach to dealing with automobile emissions in recent years seeks not to eliminate them but to reduce them. Hybrid cars feature both a gasoline (or diesel) engine and an electric motor. The two work together to make the vehicle go, cutting its fossil fuel consumption.

In 2012, about 440,000 hybrid cars were sold in the United States. The Toyota Prius remained one of the most popular models.

## CLEANER-BURNING CARS

Carmakers have also brought out nonelectric, fuel-burning cars that pollute less than those of the past. Some of these vehicles use alternative fuels, such as biofuels or the relatively clean-burning fossil fuel natural gas. Also, many modern gasoline and diesel engines are simply more efficient and run more cleanly. They offer better fuel economy (and thus a lower rate of emissions per mile).

→How do LED bulbs help the environment? PAGE 81

# CLIMATE CHANGE Q&A

Most scientists agree that our planet is currently experiencing a type of climate change known as **global warming**. This is a gradual increase in the average temperature at Earth's surface. Most of the Sun's rays are absorbed by Earth's surface and converted into heat energy. The heat radiates from the surface, and some of it escapes into space. But some is prevented from escaping by **greenhouse gases** in the atmosphere. The most common greenhouse gases are water vapor, carbon dioxide, methane, nitrous oxide, ozone, and fluorinated gases. Most greenhouse gases occur naturally, and a natural **greenhouse effect** helps to make life on Earth possible. But now, greenhouse gases in the atmosphere are increasing. They are trapping more heat and raising global temperatures.

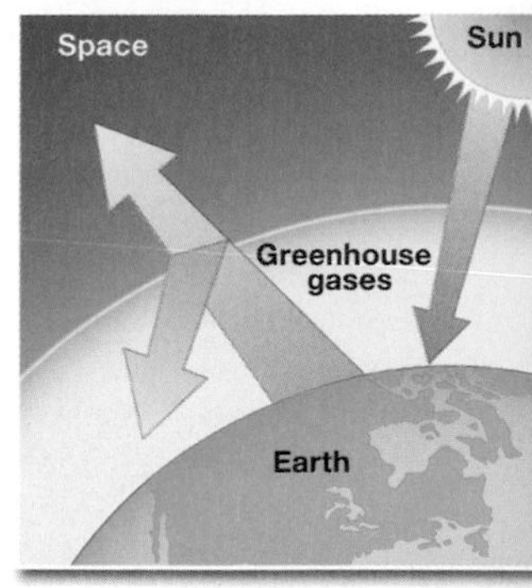


## Why Are Greenhouse Gases Increasing?

Since the mid-1700s, humans have been releasing more and more greenhouse gases into the atmosphere. Mostly these additions have come from burning fossil fuels—such as coal, natural gas, and oil—which produce carbon dioxide. **Deforestation** (cutting down or otherwise destroying forests) adds to the problem, because trees absorb carbon dioxide.

There is more carbon dioxide and methane in the atmosphere today than has been normal for the last 650,000 years, trapping more of the Sun's energy. The decade from 2000 to 2009 was the warmest recorded for the planet since good temperature records began in 1880. For the U.S., not including Hawaii and Alaska, 2012 was the hottest year on record. Almost all scientists believe humans are the main cause of this climate change.

**Sources of Carbon Dioxide in 2010***

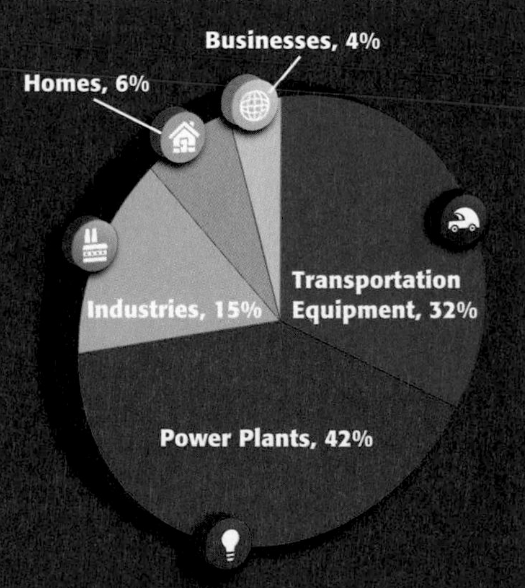


*Carbon dioxide released by burning fossil fuels in the U.S. Percentages do not add to 100% because of rounding.

## How Do We Know About Climate Change?

Worldwide records of climate have been kept since around the mid-1800s. They show global increases in air and ocean temperatures, a rise in sea level, and melting glaciers. Scientists drill thousands of feet into ice caps in Antarctica and Greenland to remove ice core samples. The layers of ice and air pockets trapped in them can be read like a timeline of climate change over the past 800,000 years.

## What Will Happen?

**RISING SEA LEVELS:** Scientists have created computer climate models that identify patterns and make predictions. In the short run, average temperatures may go up or down in a given year. But in the long run, current estimates predict that they will rise. In fact, by the year 2100, Earth's average temperature may increase at least 2°F and oceans will rise 7 inches. The worst-case scenarios suggest that Earth could warm by more than 11°F and sea levels could rise 2 feet or more.

As Earth warms, sea levels rise:

- Water expands slightly as it warms.
- The ice sheets covering Greenland and the Arctic Ocean are melting. Chunks of ice (icebergs) are breaking off ice sheets in Antarctica and Greenland.
- Glaciers are melting in non-polar regions, producing more water.

**MELTING POLAR ICE:** The Arctic region may warm up more than many other places because of the albedo effect, or a surface's power to reflect light. Ice reflects the Sun's rays. With less ice on Earth, more of the Sun's heat will be absorbed by the oceans. Warmer water raises sea levels and melts ice faster.

**CHANGING WATER CYCLE:** Warmer air affects the water cycle (see page 82). More water evaporates, and the atmosphere can hold more water vapor. Places with plenty of water will have more rain and floods. But in places where water is scarce, evaporation will dry out the land even more. Vapor will take more time to condense, meaning less rain and more droughts.

Rising sea levels already threaten some coastal settlements and small Pacific islands.

Many scientists believe that warmer oceans will lead to more intense tropical cyclones (also called hurricanes and typhoons).

As environments change, animals must find new homes or they may become extinct. Warmer global climates will allow disease-carrying creatures such as mosquitoes to spread to new places.

# LIVING GREEN

Protecting the environment is important to humans and every other living thing on Earth. Helping the environment includes keeping air, water, and soil as clean as possible. It also includes preserving Earth's resources for the future, saving the many **biomes** around the world in which different plants and animals live, and reducing the amount of **greenhouse gases** that are being added to the air and are likely changing Earth's climate. Everyone can have an impact, however small, on protecting the environment. Here are some ways people are "living green."

## SHOPPING GREEN

- **Rent or reuse:** Every time something new is made, energy and raw materials are used up to make it. If you or your family needs to use something for a short time, find out whether it can be rented, rather than bought new. You also might find used books, toys, party decorations, and even clothing at garage sales or thrift shops.
- **Think about batteries:** When you buy something that requires batteries, use rechargeable batteries rather than batteries that just go into the trash when they're used up.
- **Check out packaging:** The more packaging there is on a food item, toy, or other purchase, the more trash there will be to throw away. When shopping, look for items that don't have a lot of wasteful packaging.
- **Reuse bags:** Bring your own reusable bags to the supermarket to carry your purchases, rather than getting plastic bags at the store.
- **Be aware of ingredients:** Try to buy only products that don't contain harmful chemicals and that are produced in a way that does the least harm to the environment. You can find shampoos, household cleansers, and clothing that are made without harmful chemicals.

## TRAVELING GREEN

- **Walk or bike:** Try walking or biking to places that aren't too far away, rather than depending on a car. Most cars burn fuel and put pollution into the air.
- **Use trains and buses:** Encourage your family to think about using a train or a bus the next time you go on vacation, rather than driving.
- **Think about carpooling:** Set up carpools for traveling to places that you and your friends go to all the time, rather than having everyone go in separate cars.

## EATING GREEN

- **Think local:** Eat foods that are grown locally so that they don't have to be shipped long distances. Shipping foods by truck or airplane is a major source of air pollution. Is there a greenmarket or a farmer's market near where you live that sells locally produced food?
- **Remember the season:** Eat fresh fruits and other foods that are in season. When you eat a fruit that's not in season, you're eating something that had to be picked and stored and then shipped a long way to your neighborhood store—all of which uses energy and causes pollution.
- **Check out gardening:** Think about planting a small vegetable garden in your yard. If you don't have a yard, maybe there's a community garden in your neighborhood where people are growing their own food. Could you suggest that your school start a small garden?

## THINKING GREEN EVERY DAY

- **Avoid things you use once:** Avoid products that you use just once and then throw away, such as plastic forks, knives, and cups. Try taking your lunch in a container that you can wash and reuse many times, rather than putting it in a paper bag that you'll just throw away.
- **Save water:** Make sure you turn off the faucet tightly to avoid drips that waste water. Don't let the water run when you're not using it—for example, while you brush your teeth. Take showers rather than baths, because they use much less water—and keep your showers short.
- **Use tap water:** Drink tap water rather than bottled water. Making the bottles and shipping the water both use energy. You can fill a glass container with tap water and chill it in the refrigerator so that it will be cold.
- **Use the sponge:** Instead of using paper towels to wipe up spills, use a sponge. Paper towels become trash.
- **Be smart about using appliances:** Don't run a half-full washing machine or dishwasher. Wait until the machine is full, and you can clean twice as much using the same amount of water and energy.
- **Conserve electricity:** To save electricity, turn off the lights when you leave a room. Turn off TVs, computers, and other devices when they're not being used. Encourage your family to buy energy-efficient light bulbs.

**Did You KNOW?**

**There's good news for the environment in a new type of light bulb that is now widely available. These LED bulbs, as they're called, use as little as one-tenth the electricity of the incandescent bulbs that have been used for over a century. What's more, the LED bulbs last 25 times longer. So they require less energy, and they make less trash.**

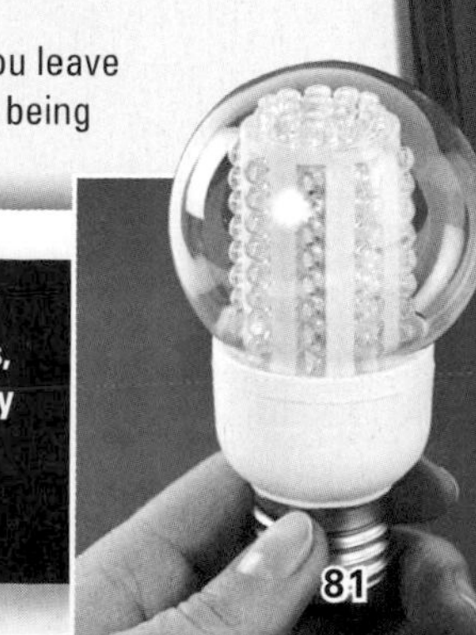

# Water, Water EVERYWHERE

Earth is the water planet. More than two-thirds of its surface is covered with water, and every living thing on it needs water to live. Humans can survive for about a month without eating food, but only for about a week without drinking water. People also use water for cooking and cleaning, to produce power, to irrigate farmland, and for recreation.

About 97% of the world's water is salt water in the oceans and inland seas, which can be drunk only after special treatment. Another 2% of the water is frozen in ice caps and glaciers. Half of the 1% left is too far underground to be reached. That leaves only 0.5% for all the people, plants, and animals on Earth.

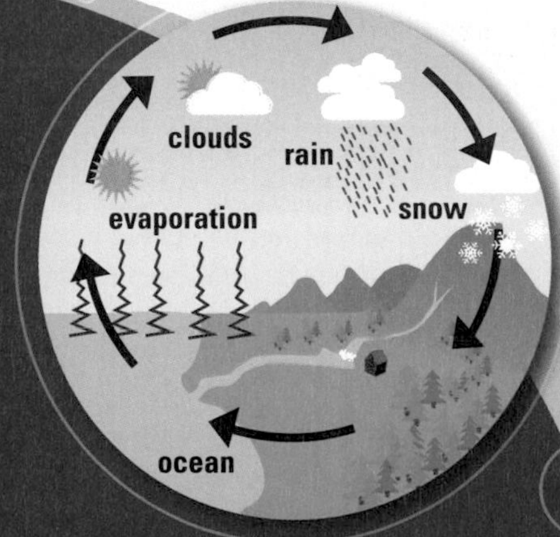


## THE WATER CYCLE

Water is the only thing on Earth that exists naturally in **all three normal physical states**: solid (ice), liquid, and gas (water vapor). The water cycle describes how water changes as it moves through the environment. The cycle has no starting or ending point but is driven by the Sun.

### *HOW DOES WATER GET INTO THE AIR?*

Heat from the Sun causes surface water in oceans, lakes, swamps, and rivers to turn into water vapor. This is called **evaporation**. Plants release water vapor into the air as part of the process called **transpiration**. Animals release a little bit when they breathe and when they perspire.

### *HOW DOES WATER COME OUT OF THE AIR?*

Warm air holds more water vapor than cold air. As the air rises into the atmosphere, it cools and the water vapor **condenses**—changes back into tiny water droplets. These droplets form clouds. As the drops get bigger, gravity pulls them down to Earth as **precipitation** (such as rain, snow, or sleet).

### *WHERE DOES THE WATER GO?*

Depending on where the precipitation lands, it can: **1.** evaporate back into the atmosphere, **2.** run off into streams and rivers, **3.** be absorbed by plants, **4.** soak down into the soil as groundwater, or **5.** fall as snow on a glacier and be trapped as ice for thousands of years.

## WATER WOES

**Pollution:** Polluted water can't be used for drinking, swimming, or watering crops, nor can it provide a good habitat for plants and animals. Major sources of water pollutants are sewage, chemicals from factories, fertilizers and pesticides, and landfills that leak.

**Overuse:** When more water is taken out of lakes and reservoirs (for drinking, washing, watering lawns, and other uses) than is put back in, the water levels begin to drop. This can be devastating. In some cases, lakes become salty or dry up completely.

# WHERE GARBAGE GOES

The disposal of garbage is a serious issue. The problem is that we now produce more garbage than our natural environment can absorb.

## WHAT HAPPENS TO THINGS WE THROW AWAY?

### LANDFILLS

About half of our trash goes to places called landfills. A **landfill** (or dump) is a low area of land that is filled with garbage. Most modern landfills are lined with a layer of plastic or clay to try to keep dangerous liquids from seeping into the soil and underground water supplies (**groundwater**). The number of landfills is one-fourth of what it was in 1988, but they're much larger.

#### *The Problem With LANDFILLS*

Because of the unhealthy materials many of them contain, landfills do not make good neighbors. But where can we dispose of waste?

### INCINERATORS

One way to get rid of trash is to burn it. Trash can be burned in a furnace-like device called an **incinerator** to make electricity.

#### *The Problem With INCINERATORS*

Leftover ash and smoke from burning trash such as rubber tires may contain harmful chemicals, including greenhouse gases. Pollutants can make it hard for some people to breathe. They can harm plants, animals, and people.

### Reduce, Reuse, Recycle

**Reducing garbage helps protect the environment. Reuse products. Recycle products so that materials can be used again rather than become garbage.**

## What Is Made From RECYCLED MATERIALS?

- ***From* RECYCLED PAPER we get newspapers, cereal boxes, wrapping paper, cardboard containers, and insulation.**
- ***From* RECYCLED PLASTIC we get soda bottles, benches, bike racks, cameras, backpacks, carpeting, and clothes.**
- ***From* RECYCLED ALUMINUM we get cans, cars, bicycles, computers, and pots and pans.**
- ***From* RECYCLED GLASS we get glass jars and tiles.**
- ***From* RECYCLED RUBBER we get mousepads, shoe soles, floor tiles, and playground equipment.**

# HOME SWEET BIOME

**A** biome is a large natural area that is home to certain types of plants. The animals, climate, soil, and even the amount of water in the region also help distinguish a biome. There are many kinds of biomes in the world. But the following types cover most of Earth's surface.

## Forests

*Evergreen forest, Europe*

Forests cover about one-third of Earth's land surface. Pines, hemlocks, firs, and spruces grow in the cool **evergreen forests** farthest from the equator. These trees are called evergreens because they keep their leaves year-round. They are also known as **conifers** because they produce cones.

**Temperate forests** tend to have warm, rainy summers and cool, snowy winters. They often are home to **deciduous trees** (trees that lose their leaves in the fall and grow new ones in the spring), such as maple, oak, beech, and poplar. Mixtures of deciduous trees and evergreens also occur, and some temperate forests are primarily coniferous. Areas where temperate forests can be found include the United States, southern Canada, southern Chile, Europe, Asia, eastern Australia, and New Zealand.

Still closer to the equator are the **tropical rain forests**, home to the greatest variety of plants on Earth. Typically, more than 80 inches of rain fall each year. Tropical trees stay green all year. They grow close together, shading the ground. There are several layers of trees. The top, **emergent layer** has trees that can reach 200 feet in height. The **canopy**, which gets lots of sunlight, comes next, followed by the **understory**. The **forest floor**, covered with roots, gets little sunlight. Many plants cannot grow there.

*Amazon Rain Forest Destruction*

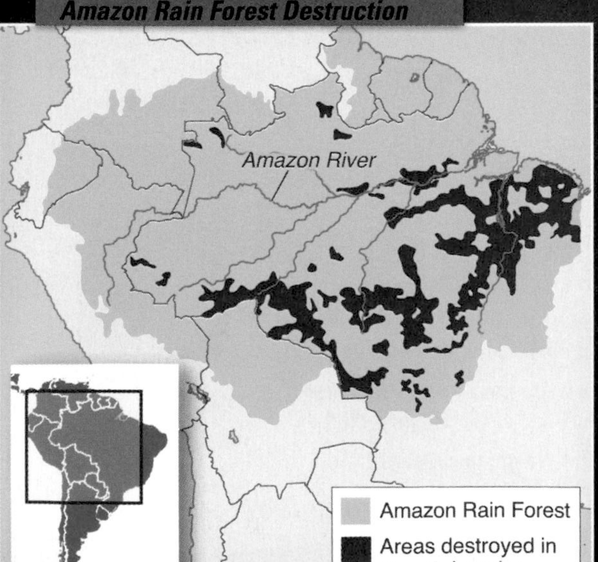


Tropical rain forests are found mainly in Central America, South America, Africa, Southeast Asia, and Australia and nearby islands. They once covered as much as 12% of Earth's land surface or nearly 7 million square miles. Today, because of destruction by humans, fewer than 2.5 million square miles of rain forest remain. The Amazon Rain Forest in South America is the world's largest tropical rain forest, but it is shrinking. Large areas have been cleared for agriculture.

## Tundra

Tundra, the coldest biome, is a treeless plain. In the Arctic tundra—located in the northernmost regions of North America, Europe, and Asia surrounding the Arctic Ocean—the temperature rarely rises above 50°F. Water in the ground freezes the subsoil solid **(permafrost)** so plant and tree roots can't dig down. Most plants are mosses and lichens without roots. In some areas, the top layer of soil thaws for about two months each year. This may allow wildflowers or small shrubs to grow. Alpine tundra is located on top of the world's highest mountains (such as the Himalayas, Alps, Andes, and Rockies). Plants and low shrubs may be found here, and patches of permafrost may occur.

**What Is the Tree Line?** On mountains, there is an altitude above which trees will not grow. This is the **tree line** or **timberline**.

## Deserts

The driest areas of the world are the **deserts**. They receive less than 10 inches of rain in a year. Some desert areas have very few plants. But others contain an amazing number of plants that store water in thick bodies or roots deep underground. Rain can make fields of wildflowers bloom. Shrubby sagebrush and spiny cacti are native to dry regions of North and South America. Prickly pear, barrel, and saguaro cacti can be found in the southwestern United States. Date palms grow in desert oases of the Middle East and North Africa.

*Desert, Nevada*

*Savanna, Tanzania*

## Grasslands

Areas that are too dry to have green forests but not dry enough to be deserts are **grasslands**. The most common plants are grasses. Cooler grasslands are found in the Great Plains of the United States and Canada, in the steppes of Europe and Asia, and in the pampas of Argentina. Drier grasslands called steppes have short grasses and are used for grazing cattle and sheep. In **prairies**, characterized by tall grasses, there is a little more rain. The warmer grasslands, called **savannas**, are found in central and southern Africa, Venezuela, southern Brazil, and Australia. Most savannas have moist summers and cool, dry winters.

## Marine

Covering more than two-thirds of Earth's surface, marine regions are the largest biome. The marine biome includes the **oceans, coastal areas, tidal zones,** and **coral reefs**. Reefs are found most often in relatively shallow warm water, including coastal waters of the Caribbean Sea. Like tropical rain forests, reefs are home to thousands of species of plant and animal life. Australia's Great Barrier Reef is the largest in the world.

*Great Barrier Reef, Australia*

→Which fashion designer was once a figure skater? PAGE 88

# Today's Fashion Trends

Every generation likes to have its own style, so fashion is always changing. Some items may come back into fashion over time, but they are almost always given a fresh spin. Here are some looks that are trending right now.

## MAXI DRESSES

"Maxi dresses" are a popular and comfortable warm-weather trend for women. These dresses usually feature bold colors or patterns and may have fabric cutouts at the back or on the sides. They are often worn with flat sandals.

*Actress Tasie Lawrence →*

## SLIM-FIT JEANS

Slim-fitting jeans remain popular with teens and adults alike. These jeans can be found in a variety of colors and may have zippers at the ankle. Women often pair them with loose-fitting tops and high heels.

*←Actress Taylor Stanley*

## HATS

Men's hats are making a fashion comeback, especially the traditional fedora, which was invented in the 1880s. Many of today's fashion-forward men are matching this classic hat style with modern accessories.

*← Singer Bruno Mars*

**Did You KNOW?**

**Many people today have taken fashion into their own hands. Do-it-yourself (DIY) clothing and accessories are often less expensive and better for the planet than new store-bought items. Using old clothing from their closets or thrift stores, do-it-yourselfers are turning last year's jeans into a pair of shorts with fabric patches, or making a colorful T-shirt into a scarf. Some fashion DIYers are learning how to sew clothes from scratch or make their own jewelry from recycled items—a major money saver!**

# BLASTS from the PAST

**Around the globe and in every period of history, people have chosen their own styles and created new looks. Here are a few examples.**

## ←100s B.C.: Wigs

Wigs were very popular for men and women in Egypt in the second century B.C. The wealthiest members of society shaved their heads to prevent lice and to help keep cool in the extreme heat of the climate. They wore wigs for formal occasions and to protect their bare heads from the sun. The wigs were generally made of human, sheep, or horse hair.

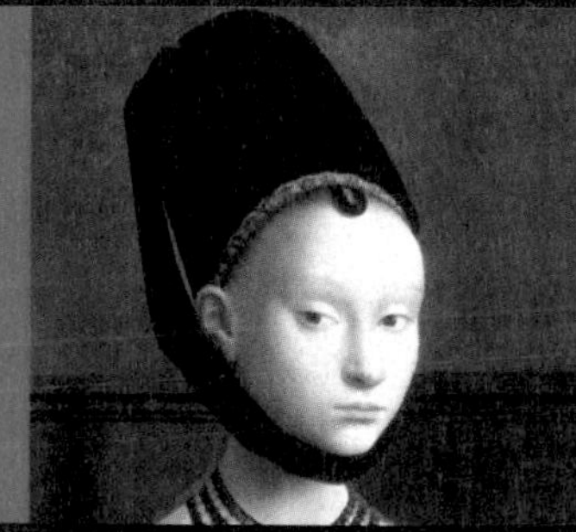

## ←1400s: Hennins

Fashionable women in the 1400s in France wore a tall, cone-shaped headdress known as a hennin. Women often shaved their eyebrows and pulled their hair back tightly to create a more dramatic look. The hennin inspired the hats worn by princesses in many traditional fairy tales.

## ←1800s: Corsets

In the 1800s, women in England went to extreme measures to make their waists look smaller. Corsets, often lined with whalebone or steel, were worn under dresses and tied so tightly that many women suffered from health problems as a result. As women became more aware of these health risks, the corset fell out of fashion and loose-fitting dresses became more popular.

## ←1980s: Miami Style

In the 1980s, men embraced the styles shown in the TV show *Miami Vice.* Stars Don Johnson and Philip Michael Thomas introduced a trend of pastel-colored T-shirts or ties worn with suit jackets. Johnson often paired his look with sockless loafers, which also became a hit.

# Some Famous FASHION DESIGNERS

## VERA WANG

**Vera Wang** was born in 1949 in New York City. She was a competitive figure skater for many years—she began skating when she was six. After graduating from Sarah Lawrence College, she decided to pursue a career in fashion. She accepted a job at *Vogue* magazine and later worked as a designer for Ralph Lauren. When Wang was married in 1989, she had a difficult time finding a wedding dress she loved. The following year, she opened her own bridal boutique. At first, her store carried wedding dresses from other designers, but after a few years, she began selling her own designs. Besides wedding gowns, Wang designs other formal dresses, as well as costumes for some of the world's leading women figure skaters. Her wedding dresses remain extremely popular—many celebrities, including Alicia Keys and Chelsea Clinton, have been married in Vera Wang gowns.

← *Chelsea Clinton (with her father, former President Bill Clinton)*

## RALPH LAUREN

**Ralph Lauren**—originally named Ralph Lifshitz—was born in New York City in 1939. He became interested in fashion while in middle school, after taking a part-time job at a department store. Lauren worked as a designer for a few years before starting his own company and creating his own brand, Polo. He rose to fame with the design of his simple collared shirts with a horse and rider logo. His brands now include Polo Ralph Lauren, Polo Sport, and the Ralph Lauren Collection. One of the world's best-known and most successful designers, he is estimated to be worth about $7 billion.

**Did You KNOW?** Tavi Gevinson was just 11 years old when she created her fashion blog, The Style Rookie, in 2008. Soon, she had tens of thousands of daily readers and was commissioned to write feature articles for leading fashion magazines. In 2011, Gevinson co-founded an online teen magazine called *Rookie*. Within six days of its launch, *Rookie* had more than 1 million page views. Gevinson serves as editor-in-chief of the magazine.

ON THE JOB

# Costume Designer

Fashion and the performing arts have always gone hand in hand. The clothing worn by performers in movies and plays helps tell the story to the audience. Designers create these costumes. **Barry Doss,** a costume designer, agreed to talk to *The World Almanac for Kids* about his work.

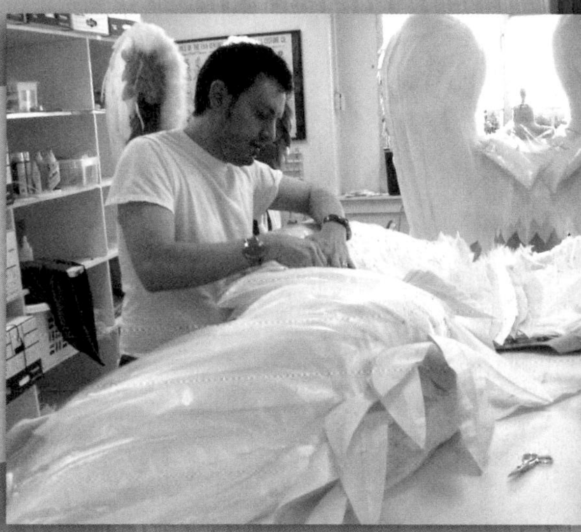

**What do you do in a typical day?** I work with teams of directors, actors, and designers to create characters through the construction of custom-made costumes. I work primarily in Broadway theater, but I do some projects for movies and TV. At the beginning of a project, I often spend a lot of time shopping for fabrics and accessories. Once the garments are ready, then I start fittings. This requires working closely with actors to perfect the fit of the clothing. I also need to make sure the performer can move comfortably in the design, especially if he or she will be dancing.

**What interests and strengths of yours make this job right for you?** I have always had a great love for storytelling and the performing arts, but also for visual arts like painting and crafts. Costume design has allowed me to enjoy all of these elements in one field.

**What kind of education or training did you need to get in order to do your job?** I have a bachelor of arts degree in theater with a focus in costume design, and a minor in fashion design. I also spent a great deal of time in my university's costume shop and worked at summer Shakespeare festivals. This practical experience helped me to develop my knowledge of pattern drafting, cutting and sewing, and garment construction.

**What do you like best about your job? What is most challenging?** Working with fabric and color to create beautiful costumes is always inspiring and fun. I also love being a part of the creative process in the arts and getting to work with so many talented people like actors, singers, and dancers. Sometimes, production schedules can be very tight, and working for long hours can be a challenge. But once the show is up on the stage, the lights are focused, and the audience is applauding . . . it's always worth it!

# GAMES

→In what year was Nintendo's Wii introduced? PAGE 91

In the past few years, the most popular games have been those played on smartphones, other mobile devices, and Facebook. The games—like *Angry Birds, FarmVille, Draw Something*, and *Words With Friends*—tend to be easier to play and less expensive than traditional video games. Still, over the years, individual Nintendo games, developed for traditional platforms, have racked up the most sales.

| Game | Console | U.S. Release | Units Sold* |
|---|---|---|---|
| *Wii Sports* | Wii | 2006 | 81.31 million |
| *Super Mario Bros.* | NES | 1985 | 40.24 million |
| *Mario Kart Wii* | Wii | 2008 | 33.76 million |
| *Wii Sports Resort* | Wii | 2009 | 31.68 million |
| *Pokémon Red / Green / Blue* | Game Boy | 1998 | 31.37 million |

*Through June 10, 2013; sales figures are worldwide. Source: VGChartz

## GAME SPOTLIGHT

*Candy Crush Saga*, developed by King.com, is the most popular game on Facebook, with more than 15 million daily users. Its popularity continued when it also became available to download on iOS and Android devices. Players join Mr. Toffee and Tiffi as they journey through the world of candy, trying to get pieces in rows of three or more.

## WHAT'S NEW

Gamers were excited about new sequels to some popular games in 2013.

**Sly Cooper: Thieves in Time:** The fourth title in the Sly Cooper series, for PlayStation, follows the adventures of the title character, a clever raccoon who is a master thief. Sly and his gang reunite to travel through time to find out who is responsible for stealing pages from the book chronicling the Cooper family history—before the family is destroyed forever.

**Temple Run 2:** The sequel to the popular ***Temple Run***, this "endless running" game is available on iOS and Android. As they try to escape with a stolen golden idol, players move through such obstacles as zip-lines and flames of fire as they outrun a giant ape. →

# GAMING TIMELINE

1972 — The Magnavox Odyssey is the first commercial home video-game console. The system has no sound.

1975 — The home version of Atari's *Pong* debuts. It features two lines (or paddles) that players use to hit a dot back and forth.

1977 — The Atari VCS (later renamed the 2600) is the first popular system to feature cartridges for different games.

1980 — The pie-shaped pellet-eating character Pac-Man chomps its way into arcades.→

1985 — Known as Famicom in Japan, the Nintendo Entertainment System invades the United States.

1989 — Nintendo's first handheld game system, Game Boy, is a huge hit.

1995 — Sony releases its popular PlayStation, which uses CD-Roms instead of cartridges.

2001 — Computer software giant Microsoft gets into the action with the Xbox.

2004 — The Nintendo DS (dual-screen) ushers in a new era of handheld gaming.

2006 — Nintendo Wii changes gaming with the introduction of wand-like controllers.

2009 — The first version of the game *Angry Birds* is released on iOS; it eventually becomes the top-selling paid app of all time.

2010 — The motion-sensing Kinect system for the Xbox 360 console allows users to play games without the need of a controller.

2012 — Sony's PlayStation Vita gives users a full-motion 3-D gaming experience in portable form, with built-in satellite ↑ navigation and access to cellphone networks.

## TEEN GAMER MAKES GOOD

Jordan Casey, a 13-year-old from Waterford, Ireland, believes in starting early. He already has his own game company—Casey Games. Jordan taught himself programming when he was 9 years old and soon began making games. His first successful venture, released for iPhone in February 2012, was *Alien Ball vs Humans*, in which an alien ball tries to save his world. He followed that with *Greenboy Touch* and *Save the Day*. Jordan's latest projects are *Food World*, an online multiplayer game, and *My Little World*, a cross-platform game about a tiny creature who decides to go on an adventure.

# GEOGRAPHY

→What Moroccan explorer reached China in the 1300s? PAGE 95

## SIZING UP PLANET EARTH

The word "geography" comes from the Greek word **geographia**, meaning "writing about Earth." It was first used by the Greek scholar Eratosthenes, who was head of the great library of Alexandria in Egypt. Around 230 B.C., when many people believed the world was flat, he did a remarkable thing. He calculated Earth's circumference. His figure of about 25,000 miles was close to the modern measurement of 24,901 miles!

Actually, Earth is not perfectly round. It's flatter at the poles and bulges out a little at the middle. This bulge around the equator is due to Earth's rotation. Although Earth seems solid to us, it is really slightly plastic, or flexible. As Earth spins, material flows toward its middle, piling up and creating a slight bulge. Earth's diameter is 7,926 miles at the equator, but only 7,900 miles from North Pole to South Pole. The total surface area of Earth is 196,940,000 square miles.

## Geography 1-2-3

| | |
|---|---|
| **Longest Rivers** | **1. Nile (Egypt and Sudan)—4,160 miles**<br>**2. Amazon (Brazil and Peru)—4,000 miles**<br>**3. Chang (China)—3,964 miles (formerly called the Yangtze)** |
| **Tallest Mountains** | **1. Mount Everest (Tibet and Nepal)—29,035 feet**<br>**2. K2 (Kashmir)—28,250 feet**<br>**3. Kanchenjunga (India and Nepal)—28,208 feet** |
| **Biggest Islands** | **1. Greenland (Atlantic Ocean)—840,000 square miles**<br>**2. New Guinea (Pacific Ocean)—306,000 square miles**<br>**3. Borneo (Pacific Ocean)—280,100 square miles** |
| **Biggest Desert Regions** | **1. Sahara Desert (North Africa)—3.5 million square miles**<br>**2. Australian Deserts—1.3 million square miles**<br>**3. Arabian Peninsula—1 million square miles** |
| **Biggest Lakes** | **1. Caspian Sea (Europe and Asia)—143,244 square miles**<br>**2. Superior (U.S. and Canada)—31,700 square miles**<br>**3. Victoria (Kenya, Tanzania, Uganda)—26,828 square miles** |
| **Highest Waterfalls** | **1. Angel Falls (Venezuela)—3,212 feet**<br>**2. Tugela Falls (South Africa)—2,800 feet**<br>**3. Monge Falls (Norway)—2,540 feet** |

# How to Read a MAP

**DIRECTION** Maps usually have a **compass rose** that shows you which way is north. On most maps, like this one, north is straight up. The compass rose on this map is located in the upper left corner.

**DISTANCE** As you can see, the distances on a map are much shorter than the distances in the real world. The **scale** shows you how to estimate the real distance. This map's scale is in the lower left corner.

**PICTURES** Maps usually have little pictures or symbols to represent real things such as roads, towns, airports, or other points of interest. The map **legend** (or **key**) tells what they mean.

**FINDING PLACES** Rather than use latitude and longitude to locate features, many maps use a grid with numbers on one side and letters on another. An index, listing place names in alphabetical order, gives a letter and a number for each. The letter and number tell you in which square to look for a place on the map's grid. For example, Landisville can be found at A1.

**USING THE MAP** People use maps to help them travel from one place to another. What if you lived in East Petersburgh and wanted to go to the Hands-on-House Children's Museum? First, locate the two places on the map. East Petersburgh is C1, and the Hands-on. House Children's Museum is E1. Next, look at the roads that connect them and decide on the best route. One way is to travel east on Route 722, then southeast on Valley Road until you see the Children's Museum.

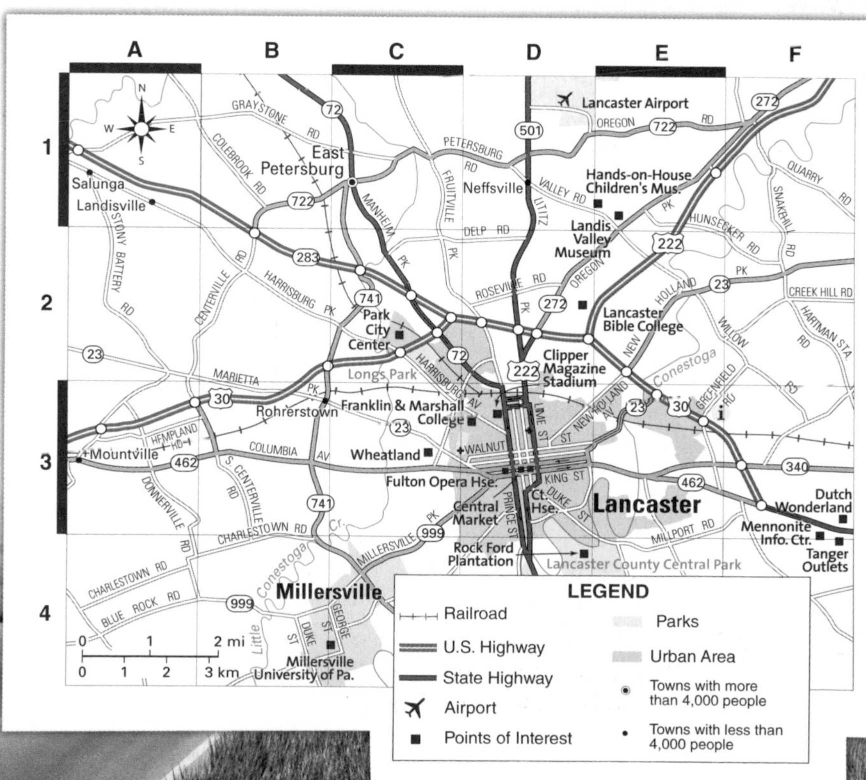

# EARLY EXPLORATION

AROUND 1000 — **Leif Ericson**, from Iceland, explored "Vinland," which may have been the coasts of northeast Canada and New England.

1271–1295 — **Marco Polo** (Italian) traveled through Central Asia, India, China, and Indonesia.

1488 — **Bartolomeu Dias** (Portuguese) explored the Cape of Good Hope in southern Africa.

1492–1504 — **Christopher Columbus** (Italian) sailed four times from Spain to America and started colonies there.

1497–1498 — **Vasco da Gama** (Portuguese) sailed farther than Dias, around the Cape of Good Hope to East Africa and India. →

1513 — **Juan Ponce de León** (Spanish) explored and named Florida.

1513 — **Vasco Núñez de Balboa** (Spanish) explored Panama and reached the Pacific Ocean.

1519–1521 — **Hernán Cortés** (Spanish) explored and conquered Mexico.

1519–1522 — **Ferdinand Magellan** (Portuguese) sailed from Spain around the tip of South America and across the Pacific Ocean to the Philippines, where he died in 1521. His expedition continued around the world, returning to Spain the next year.

1527–1542 — **Alvar Núñez Cabeza de Vaca** (Spanish) explored the southwestern United States, Brazil, and Paraguay.

1532–1535 — **Francisco Pizarro** (Spanish) explored the west coast of South America and conquered Peru.

1534–1536 — **Jacques Cartier** (French) sailed up the St. Lawrence River to the site of present-day Montreal.

1539–1542 — **Hernando de Soto** (Spanish) explored the southeastern United States and the lower Mississippi Valley.

1603–1613 — **Samuel de Champlain** (French) traced the course of the St. Lawrence River and explored the northeastern United States.

1609–1610 — **Henry Hudson** (English), sailing from Holland, explored the Hudson River, Hudson Bay, and Hudson Strait.

1682 — **René-Robert Cavelier, sieur de La Salle** (French), traced the Mississippi River to its mouth in the Gulf of Mexico.

1768–1778 — **James Cook** (English) charted many of the world's major bodies of water and explored Australia, New Zealand, Antarctica, the South Pacific, and Hawaii.

1804–1806 — **Meriwether Lewis and William Clark** (American) traveled from St. Louis along the Missouri and Columbia rivers to the Pacific Ocean and back.

1849–1859 — **David Livingstone** (Scottish) explored southern Africa.

SOME FAMOUS

# EXPLORERS



These explorers, and many others, risked their lives on trips to faraway and often unknown places. Some sought fame. Some sought fortune. Some just sought challenge. All of them increased people's knowledge of the world.

## 1304–1369 IBN BATTUTA

Moroccan explorer who traveled the world for almost 30 years, covering 75,000 miles, and wrote about what he saw. Beginning in 1325, he journeyed through North Africa, the Middle East, Europe, Central Asia, India, and China.

## 1371–1433 ZHENG HE

Chinese explorer who in the early 1400s built a fleet of enormous wooden ships and explored the Indian Ocean and beyond. He sailed into the Persian Gulf, reached East Africa, and brought back ivory, pearls, and spices.

## 1451–1506 CHRISTOPHER COLUMBUS

Italian navigator who sailed for Spain. He had hoped to find a fast route to Asia by going west from Europe. Instead he became the first European (other than the Vikings) to reach America, landing in the Bahamas in October 1492.

## 1480–1521 FERDINAND MAGELLAN

Portuguese explorer who sailed from Spain in 1519, seeking a western route to the Spice Islands of Indonesia. He became the first European to cross the Pacific Ocean but was killed by natives in the Philippines. Because he passed the easternmost point he had reached on an earlier voyage, he is considered the first person to circumnavigate Earth.

## 1779–1813 ZEBULON PIKE

American military officer who explored the Southwest. After the Louisiana Purchase, Pike first led an expedition (1805–1806) to find the source, in Minnesota, of the Mississippi River. In 1806–1807, he explored the southern part of the Louisiana Territory—an area most Americans knew nothing about. Traveling from Missouri through present-day Kansas, Nebraska, and Colorado, he reached the Rocky Mountains. Pikes Peak is named for him. Pike was killed in battle in the War of 1812.

## 1866–1955 MATTHEW HENSON

The first famous African-American explorer. As an assistant to explorer Robert Peary (1856–1920), he traveled on seven expeditions to Greenland and the Arctic region. In April 1909, Peary and Henson became the first to reach, or nearly reach, the North Pole. Recent research suggests they may have fallen short.

## 1951–2012 SALLY RIDE

American astronaut who, in 1983, became the first American woman to go into space. She joined NASA in 1978 and served as a mission specialist on two space shuttle missions. Ride was the first person to operate a robot arm in space. After leaving NASA, Ride taught physics at the University of California and then started her own company to encourage girls to pursue careers in science.

# LOOKING at our WORLD

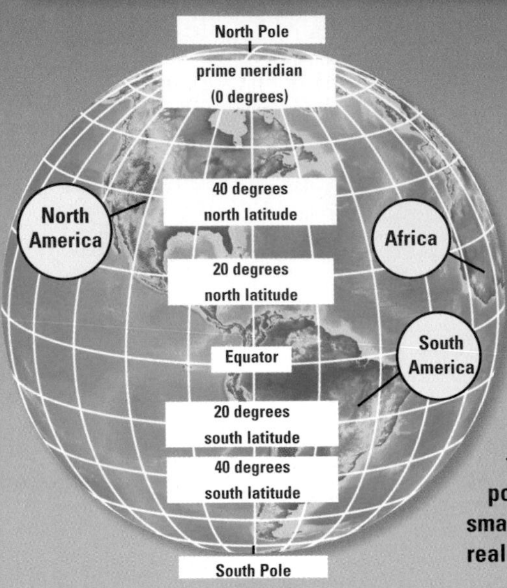


## THINKING GLOBAL

**Shaped like a ball or sphere, a globe is a model of our planet. Like Earth, it's not perfectly round. It is an oblate spheroid (called a "geoid") that bulges a little in the middle.**

**In 1569, Gerardus Mercator found a way to project Earth's curved surface onto a flat map. One problem with a Mercator map (like the one on page 97) is that land closer to the poles appears bigger than it is. Australia looks smaller than Greenland on this type of map, but in reality it's not.**

## LATITUDE AND LONGITUDE

Imaginary lines that run east and west around Earth, parallel to the equator, are called **parallels**. They tell you the **latitude** of a place, or how far it is from the equator. The equator is at 0 degrees latitude. As you go farther north or south, the latitude increases. The North Pole is at 90 degrees **north latitude**. The South Pole is at 90 degrees **south latitude**.

Imaginary lines that run north and south around the globe, from one pole to the other, are called **meridians**. They tell you the degree of **longitude**, or how far east or west a place is from the prime meridian (0 degrees).

## Which Hemispheres Do You Live In?

Draw an imaginary line around the middle of Earth. This is the **equator**. It splits Earth into two halves called **hemispheres**. The part north of the equator, including North America, is the **northern hemisphere**. The part south of the equator is the **southern hemisphere**.

An imaginary line called the **Greenwich meridian** or **prime meridian** divides Earth into east and west. It runs north and south around the globe, passing through the city of Greenwich in England. North and South America are in the **western hemisphere**. Africa, Asia, and most of Europe are in the **eastern hemisphere**.

## THE TROPICS OF CANCER AND CAPRICORN

If you find the equator on a globe or map, you'll often see two dotted lines running parallel to it, one above and one below (see pages 150-151). The top one marks the Tropic of Cancer, an imaginary line marking the latitude (about 23°27′ North) where the sun is directly overhead on June 21 or 22, the beginning of summer in the northern hemisphere.

Below the equator is the Tropic of Capricorn (about 23°27′ South). This line marks the sun's path directly overhead at noon on December 21 or 22, the beginning of summer in the southern hemisphere. The area between these dotted lines is the tropics, where it is consistently hot because the sun's rays shine more directly than they do farther north or south.

# THE SEVEN CONTINENTS AND FIVE OCEANS

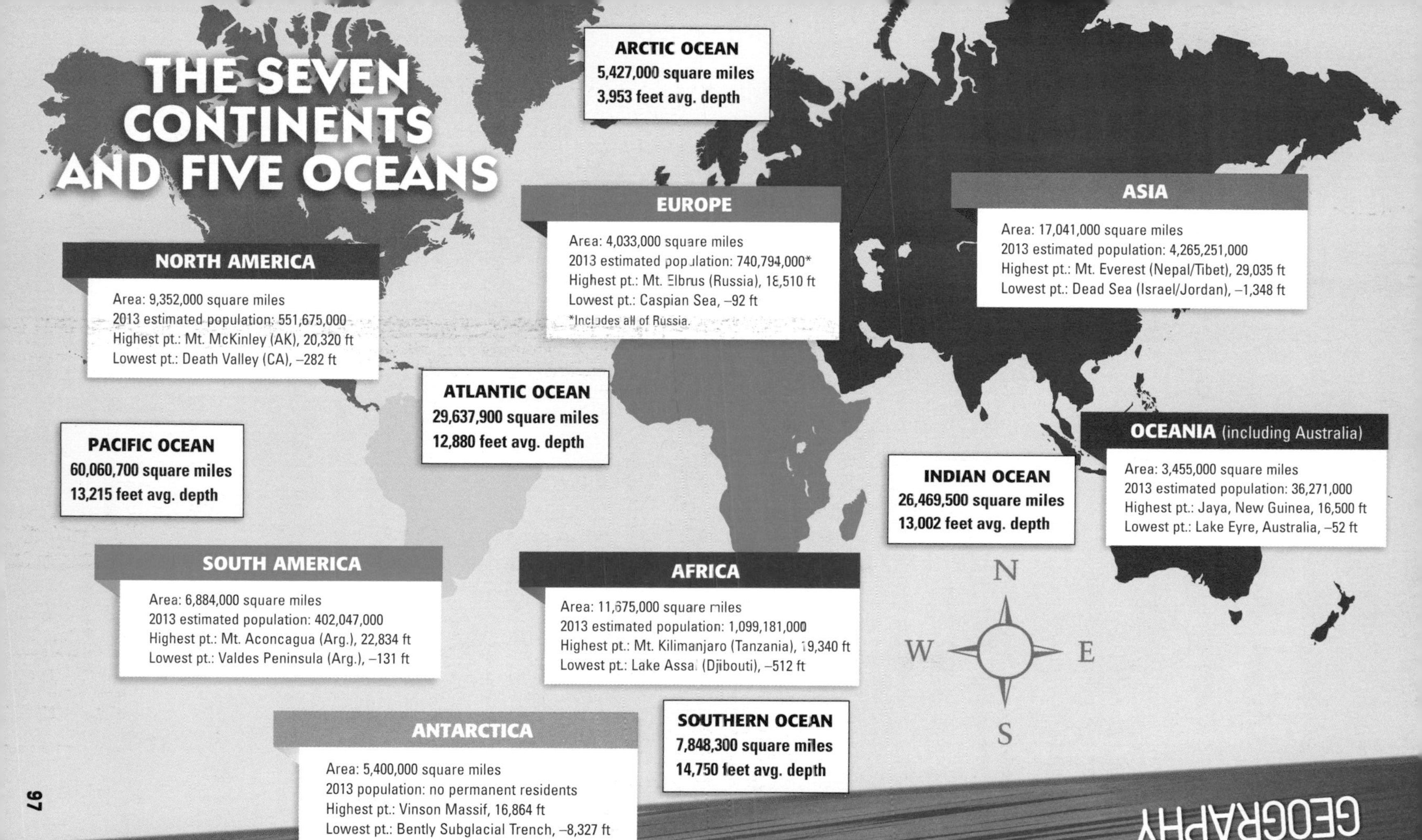

**ARCTIC OCEAN**
**5,427,000 square miles**
**3,953 feet avg. depth**

## NORTH AMERICA

Area: 9,352,000 square miles
2013 estimated population: 551,675,000
Highest pt.: Mt. McKinley (AK), 20,320 ft
Lowest pt.: Death Valley (CA), –282 ft

## EUROPE

Area: 4,033,000 square miles
2013 estimated population: 740,794,000*
Highest pt.: Mt. Elbrus (Russia), 18,510 ft
Lowest pt.: Caspian Sea, –92 ft
*Includes all of Russia.

## ASIA

Area: 17,041,000 square miles
2013 estimated population: 4,265,251,000
Highest pt.: Mt. Everest (Nepal/Tibet), 29,035 ft
Lowest pt.: Dead Sea (Israel/Jordan), –1,348 ft

**ATLANTIC OCEAN**
**29,637,900 square miles**
**12,880 feet avg. depth**

**PACIFIC OCEAN**
**60,060,700 square miles**
**13,215 feet avg. depth**

## OCEANIA (including Australia)

Area: 3,455,000 square miles
2013 estimated population: 36,271,000
Highest pt.: Jaya, New Guinea, 16,500 ft
Lowest pt.: Lake Eyre, Australia, –52 ft

**INDIAN OCEAN**
**26,469,500 square miles**
**13,002 feet avg. depth**

## SOUTH AMERICA

Area: 6,884,000 square miles
2013 estimated population: 402,047,000
Highest pt.: Mt. Aconcagua (Arg.), 22,834 ft
Lowest pt.: Valdes Peninsula (Arg.), –131 ft

## AFRICA

Area: 11,675,000 square miles
2013 estimated population: 1,099,181,000
Highest pt.: Mt. Kilimanjaro (Tanzania), 19,340 ft
Lowest pt.: Lake Assal (Djibouti), –512 ft

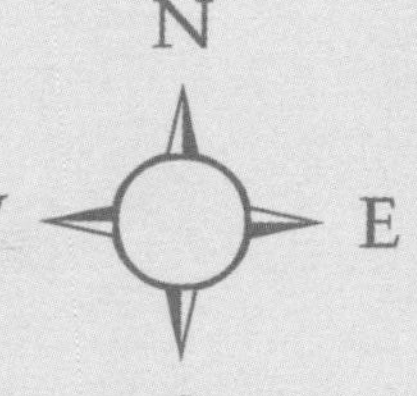


## ANTARCTICA

Area: 5,400,000 square miles
2013 population: no permanent residents
Highest pt.: Vinson Massif, 16,864 ft
Lowest pt.: Bently Subglacial Trench, –8,327 ft

**SOUTHERN OCEAN**
**7,848,300 square miles**
**14,750 feet avg. depth**

# INSIDE PLANET EARTH

**Starting at Earth's surface and going down, you find the crust, the mantle, and then the core.**

The **crust** is Earth's rocky outer shell. It is part of a layer called the **lithosphere**, which extends for about 60 miles and also includes the very top of the mantle.

The dense, heavy inner part of Earth is divided into a thick shell, the **mantle**, surrounding an innermost sphere, the **core**. The mantle extends from the base of the crust to a depth of about 1,800 miles and is mostly solid.

Then there is Earth's core. It has two parts: an inner sphere of scorchingly hot, solid iron almost as large as the Moon and an outer region of molten iron. The inner core is much hotter than the outer core. The intense pressure near the center of Earth squeezes the iron in the inner core into a solid ball nearly as hot as the surface of the Sun. Scientists believe the core formed billions of years ago during the planet's fiery birth. Iron and other heavy elements sank into the planet's hot interior while the planet was still molten. As this metallic soup cooled over millions of years, crystals of iron hardened at the center.

crust

mantle about 1,800 miles

outer core about 1,300 miles

core about 1,500 miles

In 1996, after nearly 30 years of research, it was found that, like Earth itself, the inner core spins on an axis from west to east, but at its own rate, outpacing Earth by about one degree per year.

**There are three types of rock:**

1. **IGNEOUS** rocks form from underground magma (melted rock) that cools and becomes solid. Granite is an igneous rock made from quartz, feldspar, and mica.
2. **SEDIMENTARY** rocks form on low-lying land or the bottom of seas. Layers of small particles harden into rock such as limestone or shale over millions of years.
3. **METAMORPHIC** rocks are igneous or sedimentary rocks that have been changed by chemistry, heat, or pressure (or all three). Marble is a metamorphic rock formed from limestone.

# CONTINENTS in MOTION



Earth's landmasses didn't always look the way they do now. The continents are constantly in motion. It was only in the early 20th century, though, that geologist Alfred Lothar Wegener came up with the theory he called continental drift. Wegener got the idea by looking at matching rock formations and fossils on the west coast of Africa and the east coast of South America. He named the enormous continent that existed more than 250 million years ago Pangaea. The maps below show how the continents have moved since then. Today, Wegener's theory is called plate tectonics, and scientists know that the continents sit on huge sections of Earth's surface called plates (see page 66). These plates move about 2 inches a year.

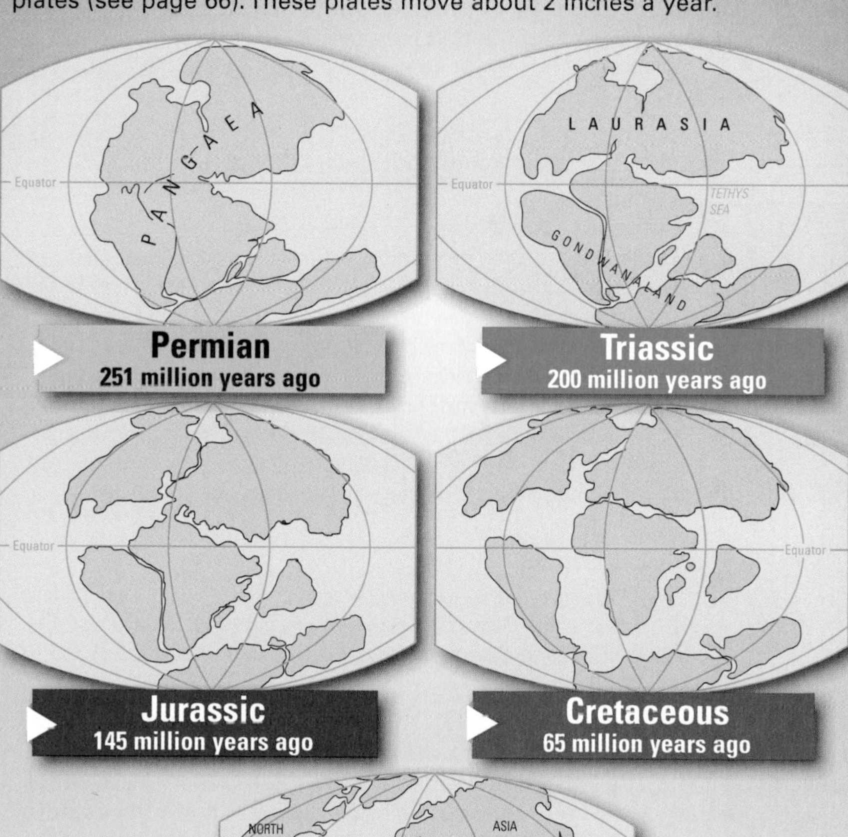


**Permian**
251 million years ago

**Triassic**
200 million years ago

**Jurassic**
145 million years ago

**Cretaceous**
65 million years ago



**Present Day**

→Which body system lets you breathe? PAGE 104

# KIDS' HEALTH ISSUES

## ALLERGIES

Our immune systems protect us from harmful substances. Certain people's immune systems, however, try to fight off even harmless substances. Common **allergens**—the things people are allergic to—include dust mites, pollen, peanuts, shellfish, and pets. If a person inhales, eats, or touches an allergen, he or she might have an allergic reaction.

## ASTHMA

Asthma is a condition that makes breathing difficult. It is caused when the airways narrow and can't carry as much air to the lungs.

## EATING DISORDERS

Millions of teens suffer from eating disorders. People with **anorexia nervosa** have an overwhelming desire to be thin. **Anorexics** may think they are fat even when they are significantly underweight. They skip meals and drastically reduce the amount of food they eat. They lose so much weight that they endanger their health. Other teenagers suffer from **bulimia nervosa**, also known as bulimia. **Bulimics** alternate between bingeing, when they eat huge amounts of food, and purging, when they empty their bodies of everything they've eaten. Unlike anorexics, most bulimics are of normal or above-normal weight.

## OBESITY

Generally, someone who is significantly overweight is considered obese. Nearly one in three kids today is overweight or obese. Being obese can lead to health problems, such as heart disease and diabetes.

## What Are Vaccines?

**Vaccines** help protect people from getting very sick. They are substances that contain dead, weakened, or living organisms. Vaccines build up your body's immunity to diseases caused by those organisms. Most vaccines are given as shots, but some can also be taken orally or through nose sprays. Some common vaccines protect us from the flu, measles, whooping cough, polio, chicken pox, and many other contagious diseases. Some people are concerned about having serious reactions to vaccines. However, doctors say they are safe and one of the best ways to prevent diseases.

# HAVE FUN GETTING FIT

## How To Work Out

→Begin with a five-minute warm-up! Warm-up exercises heat the body up so muscles are ready for more intense activity. Warm-up exercises include jumping jacks, walking, and stretching.

→After warming up, do an activity that you like, such as running or playing basketball with your friends. This increases your heart rate.

→After working out, cool down for 5 to 10 minutes. Cooling down lets your heart rate slow gradually. Walking is an example of a cool-down activity. Afterward, do some stretching. This helps your muscles remove waste, such as lactic acid, made when you exercise. Be sure to drink water during and after exercise.

→Building up strength through your workouts can be very beneficial. This doesn't mean you should lift the heaviest weights possible! It's better to do more lifts using light weights (1/2 lb or 1 lb) than fewer lifts with very heavy weights. Give your body time to recover between strength workouts.

## WHY WORK OUT?

**Exercise is a great way to prevent obesity and improve health. Children should get at least 60 minutes of exercise every day. Be sure to make exercise fun. Do yoga, bike, swim, shoot hoops, or play catch with a friend. The table below shows how many calories you'll burn from different types of activities.**

| ACTIVITY | CALORIES BURNED PER MINUTE |
|---|---|
| Racquetball | 10 |
| Jogging (6 miles per hour) | 8 |
| Martial arts | 8 |
| Basketball | 7 |
| Soccer | 6 |
| Bicycling (10-12 miles per hour) | 5 |
| Raking leaves | 4 |
| Skating or rollerblading (easy pace) | 4 |
| Swimming (25 yards per minute) | 3 |
| Walking (3 miles per hour) | 3 |
| Yoga | 3 |
| Playing catch | 2 |

**Did You KNOW?**

**Sweat helps your body cool down when you're hot from exercise. It comes out of tiny openings in the skin called pores.**

# BALANCE YOUR PLATE!

**Do you want to make sure you're eating a well-balanced diet? Then follow MyPlate! The U.S. government created the MyPlate symbol to show kids and adults how to eat right.**

**The large plate in the symbol is divided into four sections—fruits, vegetables, grains, and protein. The sections are different sizes to represent how much of each food group should be on your plate for a healthful meal. The small circle next to the plate stands for dairy foods, such as milk, cheese, and yogurt.**

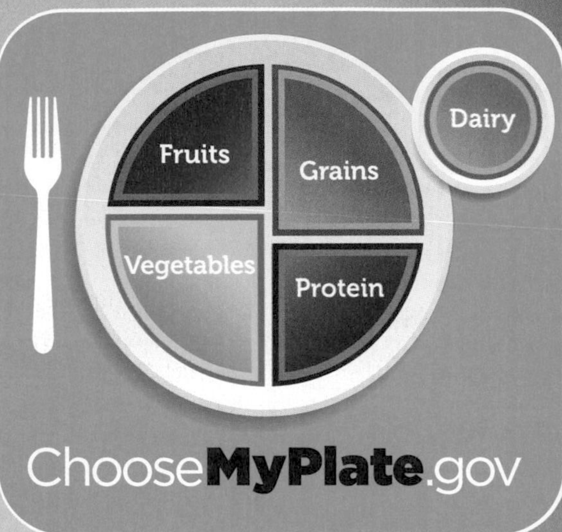


## FOOD FOR THOUGHT

**Check out these tips that go along with the MyPlate symbol to help people make healthful food choices.**

### BALANCING CALORIES

→Enjoy your food, but eat less.

→Avoid oversized portions.

### FOODS TO INCREASE

→Make half your plate fruits and vegetables.

→Drink fat-free or low-fat (1%) milk.

→Make at least half your grains whole grains.

### FOODS TO REDUCE

→Compare sodium (salt) in foods such as soup, bread, and frozen meals—and choose the foods with lower numbers.

→Drink water instead of sugary drinks.

**For more information, visit ChooseMyPlate.gov**

**Did You KNOW?** **Eating an apple a day may really keep the doctor away. Apples help boost your immune system, keep your heart healthy, and even prevent tooth decay.**

# YOUR BODY

## Know What Goes Into It

### HOW TO READ A FOOD LABEL

Every food product approved by the Food and Drug Administration (FDA) has a label that describes its nutrients. For instance, the chips label on this page shows the total calories, fat, cholesterol, sodium, carbohydrate, protein, and vitamin content per serving.

A serving size is always defined (here, it is about 12 chips or 28 grams). This label shows that there are 9 servings per container. Don't be fooled by the calorie count of 140—these are calories per serving and not per container. If you ate the entire bag of chips, you would have eaten 1,260 calories!

**Nutrition Facts**
Serving Size 1 oz. (28g/About 12 chips)
Servings Per Container About 9

| Amount Per Serving | |
|---|---|
| **Calories** 140 | Calories from Fat 60 |
| | **% Daily Value*** |
| **Total Fat** 7g | **11%** |
| Saturated Fat 1g | **5%** |
| Trans Fat 0g | |
| **Cholesterol** 0mg | **0%** |
| **Sodium** 170mg | **7%** |
| **Total Carbohydrate** 18g | **6%** |
| Dietary Fiber 1g | **4%** |
| Sugars less than 1g | |
| **Protein** 2g | |

| | |
|---|---|
| Vitamin A 0% | Vitamin C 0% |
| Calcium 2% | Iron 2% |
| Vitamin E 4% | Thiamin 2% |
| Riboflavin 2% | Vitamin B6 4% |
| Phosphorus 6% | Magnesium 4% |

* Percent Daily Values are based on a 2,000 calorie diet. Your daily values may be higher or lower depending on your calorie needs:

| | Calories: | 2,000 | 2,500 |
|---|---|---|---|
| Total Fat | Less than | 65g | 80g |
| Sat Fat | Less than | 20g | 25g |
| Cholesterol | Less than | 300mg | 300mg |
| Sodium | Less than | 2,400mg | 2,400mg |
| Total Carbohydrate | | 300g | 375g |
| Dietary Fiber | | 25g | 30g |

Calories per gram:
Fat 9 • Carbohydrate 4 • Protein 4

## WHY You Need To Eat:

**Fats** help kids grow and stay healthy. Fats contain nine calories per gram—the highest calorie count of any type of food. So you should limit (but not avoid) fatty foods. Choose unsaturated fats, like the fat in nuts, over saturated fats and trans fats, like the fat in doughnuts.

**Carbohydrates** are a major source of energy for the body. Simple carbohydrates are found in white sugar, fruit, and milk. Complex carbohydrates, also called starches, are found in bread, pasta, and rice.

**Cholesterol** is a soft, fat-like substance produced by your body. It's also present in animal products such as meat, cheese, and eggs but not in plant products. Cholesterol helps with cell membrane and hormone production, but there are two main types. Bad cholesterol, or LDL, gets stuck easily in blood vessels, which can lead to a heart attack or stroke. Good cholesterol, or HDL, helps break down bad cholesterol.

**Proteins** help your body grow and make your immune system stronger. Lean meats and tofu are good options.

**Vitamins and Minerals** are good for all parts of your body. For example, vitamin A, found in carrots, promotes good vision; calcium, found in milk, helps build bones; and vitamin C, found in fruits, helps heal cuts.

**SOME FATTY FOODS**

- Ice cream
- Doughnuts
- Cheeseburgers
- Chocolate candy
- French fries

**SOME LOW-FAT FOODS**

- Strawberries
- Oatmeal
- Plain popcorn
- Carrots
- Bell peppers
- Apples

# BODY Systems

Your body is amazing! Its many parts make up different systems that work together to keep you going.

## CIRCULATORY SYSTEM

In the circulatory system, the **heart** pumps **blood**. Blood travels through tubes, called **arteries**, to all parts of the body. Blood carries oxygen and food that the body needs to stay alive. **Veins** carry blood back to the heart.

## DIGESTIVE SYSTEM

The digestive system moves food through the **esophagus**, **stomach**, and **intestines**. As food passes through, some of it is broken down into tiny particles called **nutrients**. Nutrients enter the bloodstream and are carried to all parts of the body. The digestive system changes whatever food isn't used into waste that is eliminated from the body.

## ENDOCRINE SYSTEM

The endocrine system includes glands. There are two kinds of glands. **Exocrine glands** produce liquids such as sweat and saliva. **Endocrine glands** produce chemicals called **hormones**. Hormones control body functions like growth.

## NERVOUS SYSTEM

The nervous system enables us to think, feel, move, hear, and see. It includes the **brain**, the **spinal cord**, and **nerves** throughout the body. Nerves in the spinal cord carry signals between the brain and the rest of the body.

## RESPIRATORY SYSTEM

The respiratory system allows us to breathe. Air enters the body through the nose and mouth. It goes through the **windpipe**, or **trachea**, to two tubes called **bronchi**, which carry air to the **lungs**. Oxygen from the air is absorbed by tiny blood vessels in the lungs. The blood then carries oxygen to the heart, from where it is sent to the body's cells.

## MUSCULAR SYSTEM

Muscles are made up of elastic fibers. There are three types of muscles. **Skeletal muscles** help the body move. **Smooth muscles** are found in our digestive system, blood vessels, and air passages. **Cardiac muscle** is found only in the heart.

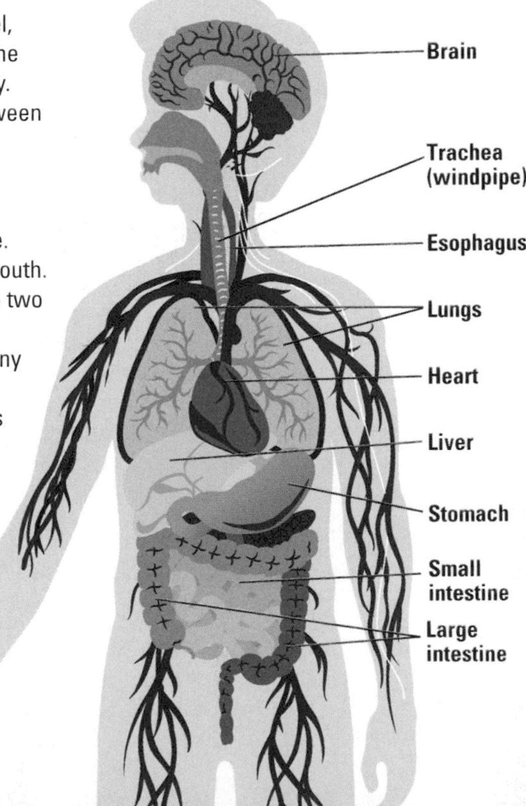

## REPRODUCTIVE SYSTEM

Through the reproductive system, adult human beings are able to create new human beings. Reproduction begins when a man's **sperm** cell fertilizes a woman's **egg** cell.

## URINARY SYSTEM

This system, which includes the **kidneys**, cleans waste from the blood and regulates the amount of water in the body.

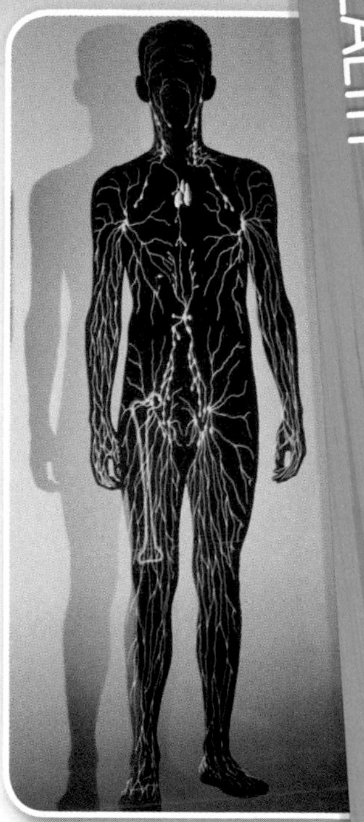

## IMMUNE SYSTEM

The immune system protects your body from diseases by fighting against certain outside substances, or **antigens**. This happens in different ways. For example, white blood cells called **B lymphocytes** learn to fight viruses and bacteria by producing **antibodies** to attack them. Sometimes, as with allergies, the immune system makes a mistake and creates antibodies to fight a substance that's really harmless.

## SKELETAL SYSTEM

The skeletal system is made up of **bones** that hold the body upright. It also gives your body its shape, protects your organs, and works with your muscles to help you move. Babies are born with 350 bones. By adulthood, some of the bones have grown together for a total of 206.

### HOMEWORK TIP

- The largest bone in your body is the thigh bone.
- The smallest bones are in your ear.
- More than half of your body's bones are located in your hands and feet.

For more information and fun facts about the skeletal system, check out **kidshealth.org/kid/htbw/bones.html**

# Brain Power

The typical human brain weighs only about three pounds. But it's like the control center of the body, responsible for making sure everything functions properly. Different parts of the brain do different things.

***Right hemisphere of cerebrum***

- Controls left side of body
- Location of things relative to other things
- Recognizes faces
- Music
- Emotions

***Left hemisphere of cerebrum***

- Controls right side of body
- Ability to understand language and speech
- Ability to reason
- Numbers

**Cerebrum**

**Brain stem**

Regulates vital activities like breathing and heart rate

**Cerebellum**

Controls coordination, balance

# THE Five SENSES

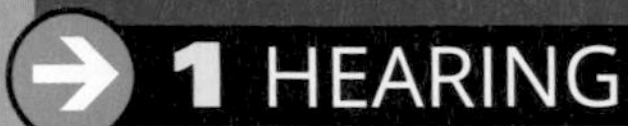

## 1 HEARING

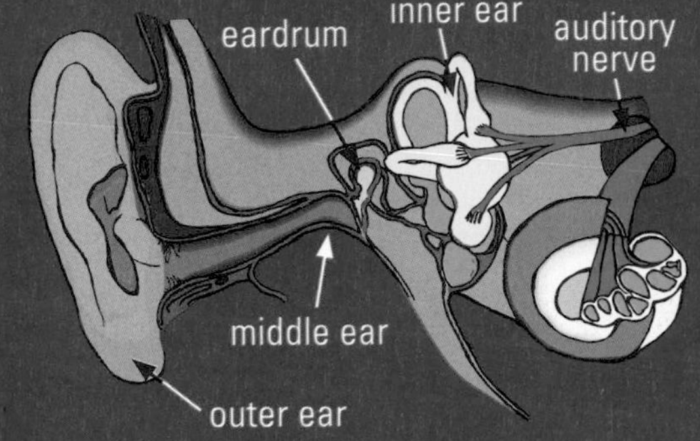


The human ear is divided into three parts—the outer, middle, and inner. The **outer ear** is mainly the flap we can see on the outside. Its shape guides sound waves into the **middle ear**, where the eardrum is located. The **eardrum** vibrates when sound waves hit it. These vibrations are picked up in the **inner ear** by the **auditory nerve**. This nerve sends sound messages to your brain.

## 2 SIGHT

The **lens** of the eye is the first stop for light waves, which tell you the shapes and colors of things around you. The lens focuses light waves onto the **retina**, located on the back wall of the eye. The retina has light-sensitive nerve cells. These cells translate the light waves into patterns of nerve impulses that travel along the **optic nerve** to your brain, where an image is produced.

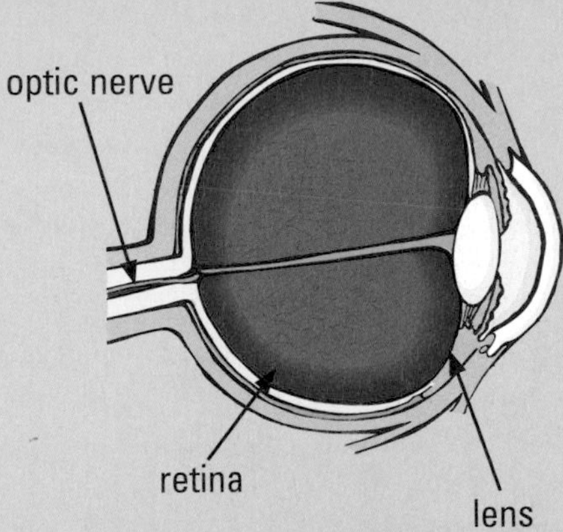


## 3 SMELL

Nerve cells inside the nose called **olfactory receptors** help you smell. Tiny hairs from these receptors trap smells from the air. Nerves then send messages to your brain about what you're smelling.

## 4 TASTE

You have many tiny bumps on your tongue called **taste buds**. They let you experience different tastes, such as sweet, salty, sour, or bitter. Taste buds work with cells inside the nose to give you a food's full flavor.

## 5 TOUCH

Your sense of touch lets you feel temperature, pain, and pressure. Your skin is your body's largest organ. Nerve endings in your skin work with your brain and nervous system so you know what you're touching.

## ON THE JOB

# Pediatrician

**P**ediatricians are doctors who care for babies and kids. **Saidi Clemente** is the Chief of Developmental and Behavioral Pediatrics at Staten Island University Hospital in New York City. She helps children with special needs. She agreed to talk to *The World Almanac for Kids* about her work.

**What do you do in a typical day?**

I work with children who are developing more slowly than usual and have behavior problems. A typical day includes seeing new patients for evaluations. An evaluation may involve giving a child tests to check his or her ability to learn, speak, understand, and behave. It's important for a doctor to know each child's specific needs in order to come up with the best plan to help that child. Some of my patients need to take medication to help them behave and learn better. My day also includes seeing children for follow-up visits, to make sure they are doing well and making as much progress as possible. In addition, I teach pediatricians in training, so that they will be able to identify children with developmental problems and know how to help them.

**What interests and strengths of yours make this job right for you?**

I was driven to this specialty because of my family experiences. My younger brother was a child with special needs. I saw firsthand how the help these children receive can take them very far. I am raising a child with special needs myself. Developmental disabilities is a field very close to my heart, so I put a big effort into evaluating patients thoroughly and making sure the children receive the help they need.

**What kind of education or training did you need to get in order to do your job?**

I did four years of college, four years of medical school, three years of pediatrics, and two years of a fellowship in developmental disabilities. Hard studying!

**What do you like best about your job? What is most challenging?**

The most challenging part about my job is that some of the children have complicated cases, and their behavior is difficult to manage. Many times, the medications these children need require special monitoring, to make sure a child does not have a bad reaction to a drug. The things I like best are seeing children progress and thrive thanks to my treatment or recommendations, and the special bond I develop with my families. I also like knowing that I am helping train pediatricians who will be better able to treat many children with disabilities.

→What is plagiarism? PAGE 109

# HOW to RESEARCH and WRITE A REPORT

**Researching and writing a report can seem overwhelming, but it doesn't have to be. Follow these easy steps to produce an A+ research paper!**

## BRAINSTORM

Before you start, you'll need to choose a topic. Brainstorm ideas for your subject with lists or word webs.

## RESEARCH

Once you decide on a topic, research to learn more. Going online from home or going to the library are great ways to start. Here are some helpful resources.

- **Books and Databases:** Most libraries have an electronic catalog of their nonfiction books (including almanacs like this one!) and reference databases, which companies create for research. Those databases often include encyclopedias with current information. You can read e-books and database articles on a library computer (or find a book on the shelves). Often, you can also search the catalog and access e-books and databases from your home computer, by using the library's website. When using the library catalog, you can search for information by author, title, or subject.
- **Magazines and Newspapers:** Along with recent print issues of magazines and newspapers, many libraries have online electronic archives of past editions of newspapers or magazines. You can also check a magazine or newspaper's website to see if you can search for past articles.
- **Internet:** You can find information on just about everything on the web. Look for topics using search engines such as Google (www.google.com), Yahoo! (www.yahoo.com), and Bing (www.bing.com). Start by typing a few search terms that describe your topic. Try to make them as specific as possible. Once the search engine produces the results, be sure to carefully evaluate and verify the source of the information. Anyone can put stuff on the web—but it might not be true or accurate. Ask yourself: Who is the source? Is it trustworthy? Is the author an expert on the subject matter? If you're doing a report on exploring Mars, for example, the U.S. space agency NASA's site would be a trustworthy, reliable source for this topic.

**The ending of a website can offer clues to the type of site:**

| Type of site | Usually ends in... | Example |
|---|---|---|
| Government site | .gov or .us | www.nasa.gov |
| Nonprofit group | .org | www.redcross.org |
| Educational institution | .edu | www.yale.edu |
| Business | .com | www.amazon.com |

## PREWRITING: NOTES AND OUTLINE

- **Take detailed notes** as you do your research. Keep track of the sources you use for your information—books, articles, and websites—and cite them in a **bibliography** at the end of your paper.
- **Use your information** to organize your thoughts into an **outline**. The outline shows the order in which the information will appear in your paper.
- **When you write your report, use your own words** Be careful not to copy directly from books, articles, or the Internet. That's called **plagiarism**—and it's a form of cheating. If you quote someone, use quotation marks and give the person credit.

## DRAFT

Based on your notes and outline, develop a **draft** (rough copy) to get your ideas down on paper. A draft generally contains three main parts:

- **Introduction:** The paper's opening paragraph(s) explain the topic and focus of the report.
- **Body:** The ideas for your paper are developed here. Use specific facts, examples, and details to support your main ideas. Use separate paragraphs for each new idea, and be sure to include the supporting details. Use words and phases that link one paragraph to the next so your ideas flow smoothly.
- **Conclusion:** Summarize the main points of your paper in a final paragraph.

## REVISE

Reread your rough draft and improve your writing. Ask yourself: Does each sentence make sense? Is the order of information or sequence of events accurate? Do my points support my topic? Have I explained my topic or position clearly? Is there extra information not relevant to the topic that I should cut?

## EDIT

Now is the time to proofread your paper. Check for misspelled words, and correct any grammar, capitalization, or punctuation errors. You might ask an adult or classmate to read your paper. He or she may be able to offer suggestions to help improve it.

## PUBLISH!

You're just about there. Give your paper a final, thorough read. After you make any last-minute changes, it's time to hand in your work. **Congratulations!**

There are many study and learning tips throughout *The World Almanac for Kids*. Look for the "Homework Tip" icon!

# SAY IT RIGHT!

## WRITE ON!

**Check out these tips for writing good sentences:**

√ Does the group of words make sense and express a complete thought?

√ Does the sentence begin with a capital letter and end with the correct punctuation?

√ Are the words in the sentence spelled correctly?

√ Does the sentence have a **subject** and a **predicate**? (The subject names whom or what the sentence is about. The predicate tells about the subject.)

**Example: The family saw seals at the aquarium.**

## COMMON PARTS OF SPEECH

**Nouns** name a person, place, or thing.

**→The doctor is here. (person)**

**→I love the beach. (place)**

**→We sat on the couch. (thing)**

**Verbs** express action or a state of being.

**→The audience clapped. (action)**

**→The girl is sleepy. (state of being)**

**Adjectives** describe nouns or pronouns.

**→The furry cat meowed.**

**→The large apple is in the bowl.**

**Adverbs** usually describe a verb or an adjective. They tell how, when, or where something happens. Or they tell you something specific about a thing or action. They often end in –ly.

**→The furry cat meowed loudly.**

**→The extremely large apple is in the bowl.**

**Pronouns** are words that take the place of nouns. Some pronouns are I, he, she, we, you, they, his, her, me, us, and them.

**→She plays the violin.**

**Prepositions** are words or a group of words that show the relation of a noun or pronoun to other parts of a sentence.

**→The cat hid under the bed.**

**→The teacher stood next to her students.**

## PUNCTUATION

**Periods** are used…

- at the end of a sentence that is a statement or command.

  **→The wolf howled.**
- after abbreviations.

  **→We live on Jefferson St. near the park.**
- after an initial.

  **→Franklin D. Roosevelt**

**Question marks** are used at the end of sentences that ask a question.

**→Did you study for the test?**

**Exclamation points** are used at the end of sentences to express strong feelings.

**→The movie was incredible!**

**Commas** are used…

- to separate items in a series.

  **→The student has pens, pencils, and paper.**
- to separate the name of a city from a state.

  **→He lives in Sacramento, California.**
- between two complete statements in the same sentence.

  **→I visited my aunt, but I had to leave early for baseball practice.**

**YOUR TURN:**

**Can you identify the part of speech for each word in this sentence?**

**Jonah carefully washed his dirty dishes.**

**ANSWERS ON PAGES 334-336.**

## SOME COMMONLY CONFUSED WORDS

### Affect/Effect

**Affect** is a verb that means to change or to influence.

→**The storm may affect our plans.**

**Effect** is a noun that means result or impact.

→**Eating right can have a good effect on your health.**

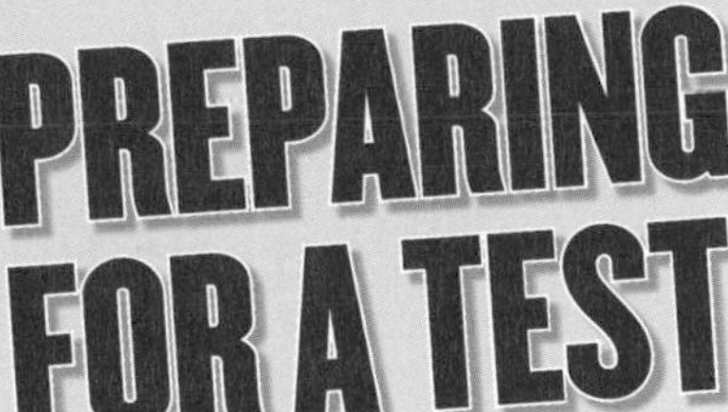

### Its/It's

**Its** shows ownership.

→**The family has its own traditions.**

**It's** is a contraction of it is.

→**It's time to go home.**

### Their/There/They're

**Their** indicates something belongs to certain people or things

→**Their homework is done.**

**There** is a place.

→**Put the dishes over there.**

**They're** is a contraction meaning they are.

→**They're coming to dinner.**

## MORE COMMONLY CONFUSED WORDS

Use a dictionary to learn about the differences:

**accept/except**
**advice/advise**
**capital/capitol**
**desert/dessert**
**hear/here**
**loose/lose**
**passed/past**
**principal/principle**
**than/then**
**to/too/two**
**weak/week**
**your/you're**

# PREPARING FOR A TEST

## GETTING READY

- Take good notes in class and keep up with assignments, so you don't have to learn material at the last minute!
- Make a study schedule and stick to it!
- Start reviewing early if you can—don't wait until the night before the test.
- Go over the headings, summaries, and questions in each chapter of your textbook to review key points. Read your notes and highlight important topics.
- Get a good night's sleep, and eat a nutritious breakfast before the test.

## THE BIG EVENT

- If you are allowed, skim through the entire exam so you know what to expect and how long it may take.
- Read directions carefully.
- Read each question carefully before answering. For a multiple-choice question, check every possible answer before you decide on one.
- Don't spend too much time on any one question. Skip hard questions and go back to them at the end.
- Keep track of time so you can pace yourself. Use any time left at the end to go back and review your answers.

# INVENTIONS

→Who invented potato chips? PAGE 113

## Invention Timeline

| YEAR | INVENTION/INVENTOR (COUNTRY) |
|---|---|
| 105 | **paper** Cai Lun (China) |
| 1440s | **printing press/movable type** Johann Gutenberg (Germany) |
| 1608 | **telescope** Hans Lippershey (Netherlands) |
| 1714 | **mercury thermometer** Gabriel D. Fahrenheit (Germany) |
| 1752 | **lightning rod** Benjamin Franklin (U.S.) |
| 1783 | **parachute** Sebastien Lenormand (France) |
| 1800 | **electric battery** Alessandro Volta (Italy) |
| 1804 | **steam locomotive** Richard Trevithick (England) |
| 1837 | **telegraph** Samuel F. B. Morse (U.S.), Charles Wheatstone (England), & William F. Cooke (England) |
| 1870s | **telephone*** Antonio Meucci (Italy), Alexander G. Bell (U.S.) |
| 1879 | **practical lightbulb** Thomas A. Edison (U.S.) |
| 1886 | **automobile (gasoline)** Karl Benz (Germany) → |
| 1892 | **moving picture viewer** Thomas A. Edison & William K. Dickson (U.S.) |
| 1894 | **cereal flakes** Will Keith Kellogg (U.S.) |
| 1897 | **diesel engine** Rudolf Diesel (Germany) |
| 1923 | **television**** Vladimir K. Zworykin (U.S.) |
| 1926 | **liquid-fuel rocket engine** Robert H. Goddard (U.S.) |
| 1928 | **penicillin** Alexander Fleming (Scotland) |
| 1930 | **packaged quick-frozen food** Clarence Birdseye (U.S.) → |
| 1939 | **jet airplane** Hans von Ohain (Germany) |
| 1942 | **electronic computer** John V. Atanasoff & Clifford Berry (U.S.) |
| 1955 | **TV wireless remote control** Eugene Polley (U.S.) |
| 1957 | **digital image** Russell Kirsch (U.S.) |
| 1973 | **personal computer** André Thi Truong (France) |
| 1975 | **digital camera** Steven Sasson (U.S.) |
| 1989 | **World Wide Web** Tim Berners-Lee (England) |
| 2007 | **iPhone** Apple (U.S.) |
| 2012 | **Google Glass wearable computer** Google (U.S.) → |

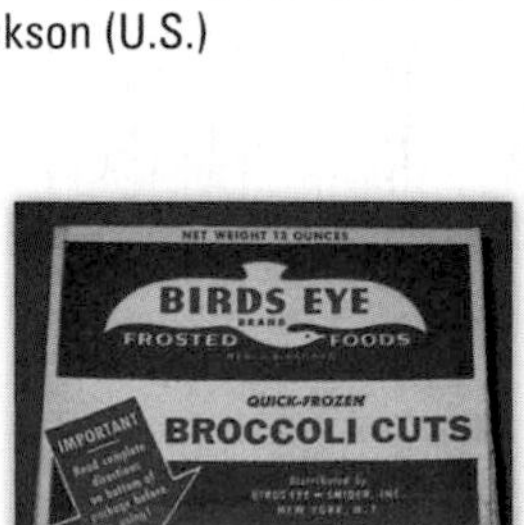

*Meucci developed a type of telephone (early 1870s); Bell received a patent for a telephone in 1876.
**Others who helped invent the television in the 1920s were Philo T. Farnsworth and John Baird.

# They've Come a Long Way

**Many inventions that changed our lives have also changed a great deal themselves over the years. Here are just a couple of examples.**

## Submarines

Dutchman Cornelis Drebbel invented the first submarine in about 1620. The oar-powered wooden boat was covered in greased leather. Tubes, supported by floats, supplied air to the occupants. The boat traveled about 12 feet below the water surface.

Various American inventors, including steamboat pioneer Robert Fulton, developed other hand-powered submarines. In 1898, John P. Holland built a craft powered underwater by an electric motor and on the surface by a gas engine. The *Holland* was the first U.S. Navy submarine.

By World War I, diesel-electric submarines were used by the major navies. The German *Unterseeboot* ("undersea boat"), or U-boat, was fitted with deck guns and torpedo tubes and required a crew of 44 sailors. In 1954, the U.S. launched the world's first nuclear-powered submarine, the *Nautilus*. Today, nuclear reactors power high-speed submarines.

Submarines also have nonmilitary uses. In 2012, filmmaker and explorer James Cameron designed the 12-ton *Deepsea Challenger* to go to the → deepest known point on Earth. Equipped with digital 3-D cameras, the sub traveled 7 miles below the surface of the Pacific Ocean. It is now a research craft at the Woods Hole Oceanographic Institution in Massachusetts.

## Radios

The first radio transmission across the Atlantic Ocean took place on December 12, 1901. Electric waves traveled almost 2,000 miles from Cornwall, England, to Newfoundland, Canada. There Italian inventor Guglielmo Marconi picked them up on a few coils, condensers, and a radio signal detector called a coherer. This new technology changed the way the world communicated.

Various inventions improved on Marconi's crude radio. The simple, inexpensive crystal radio required earphones and a thin antenna called a "cat's whisker" to pick up radio signals. In the mid-1920s, amplifying receivers used the new technology of vacuum tubes. By the late-1920s, receivers with loudspeakers and plugged-in power allowed families to listen to their favorite broadcasts together. The large radios of the 1930s and 1940s were handsome pieces of furniture. In the 1950s, the invention of the transistor resulted in smaller portable radios, powered by batteries.

Today, signals from satellites allow people to listen, for a fee, to hundreds of sports, news, and entertainment channels anywhere on the planet 24 hours a day. It's called satellite radio.

**Did You KNOW?**

**Potato chips were invented in 1853 after a customer at a restaurant in Saratoga Springs, New York, complained that his French fries were too thick. The insulted cook, named George Crum, quickly thought of a plan to get even. He sliced the potatoes very thin, soaked them in ice water, and fried them to a crisp. After salting the preparation heavily, Crum returned the plate to the customer. To everyone's surprise, the crunchy potatoes were an instant hit.**

# LANGUAGE

→What does *Ni hao!* mean? PAGE 115

## TOP LANGUAGES

**What is the "top language" spoken in the world? More people speak some form (dialect) of Chinese than any other language. Spanish ranks as the second most common native, or first, language. The table below and this world map show the languages with at least 100 million native speakers.***

*2013 estimates

| LANGUAGE | KEY PLACES WHERE SPOKEN | NATIVE SPEAKERS |
|---|---|---|
| Chinese | China, Taiwan | 1.197 million |
| Spanish | Latin America, Spain | 406 million |
| English | U.S., Canada, Britain, Australia | 335 million |
| Hindi | India | 260 million |
| Arabic | Middle East, North Africa | 223 million |
| Portuguese | Portugal, Brazil | 202 million |
| Bengali | Bangladesh, India | 193 million |
| Russian | Russia | 162 million |
| Japanese | Japan | 122 million |

## Which LANGUAGES Are SPOKEN in the UNITED STATES?

Most Americans speak English at home. But since the beginning of American history, immigrants have come to the U.S. from all over the world. Many have brought other languages with them.

The table below lists the most frequently spoken languages in the U.S. in 2011, according to estimates from the Census Bureau.

| | LANGUAGE USED AT HOME | SPEAKERS 5 YEARS AND OLDER |
|---|---|---|
| 1 | Speak only English | 230,947,071 |
| 2 | Spanish or Spanish Creole | 37,579,787 |
| 3 | Chinese | 2,882,497 |
| 4 | Tagalog | 1,594,413 |
| 5 | Vietnamese | 1,419,539 |
| 6 | French (including Patois, Cajun) | 1,301,443 |
| 7 | Korean | 1,141,277 |
| 8 | German | 1,083,637 |
| 9 | Arabic | 951,699 |
| 10 | Russian | 905,843 |

| | LANGUAGE USED AT HOME | SPEAKERS 5 YEARS AND OLDER |
|---|---|---|
| 11 | African languages | 884,660 |
| 12 | Other Asian languages | 855,303 |
| 13 | Other Indic languages | 815,345 |
| 14 | French Creole | 753,990 |
| 15 | Italian | 723,632 |
| 16 | Portuguese or Portuguese Creole | 673,566 |
| 17 | Hindi | 648,983 |
| 18 | Polish | 607,531 |
| 19 | Other Indo-European languages | 449,600 |
| 20 | Japanese | 436,110 |

# LANGUAGE EXPRESS

Hallo! (German)
Hello! (English)
Salam! (Arabic)

Surprise your friends and family with words from other languages.

| English | Arabic* | Chinese | French | German |
|---|---|---|---|---|
| January | yanāyir | yi-yue | janvier | Januar |
| February | fibrāyir | er-yue | février | Februar |
| March | māris | san-yue | mars | Marz |
| April | abrīl *or* ibrīl | si-yue | avril | April |
| May | māyū | wu-yue | mai | Mai |
| June | yūnyū *or* yūnya | liu-yue | juin | Juni |
| July | yūlyū *or* yūlia | qi-yue | juillet | Juli |
| August | aġustus | ba-yue | août | August |
| September | sibtambir | jiu-yue | septembre | September |
| October | uktūbar | shi-yue | octobre | Oktober |
| November | nūfambir | shi-yi-yue | novembre | November |
| December | dīsambir | shi-er-yue | décembre | Dezember |
| blue | asrag | lan | bleu | blau |
| red | ahmar | hong | rouge | rot |
| green | akhdar | lu | vert | grün |
| yellow | asfar | huang | jaune | gelb |
| black | aswad | hei | noir | schwarz |
| white | abyad | bai | blanc | weiss |
| Happy birthday! | Eid meelad sa'eed! | Sheng-ri kuai le! | Joyeux anniversaire! | Glückwunsch zum Geburtstag! |
| Hello! | Salam! | Ni hao! | Bonjour! | Hallo! |
| Good-bye! | Ma salamah! | Zai-jian! | Au revoir! | Auf Wiedersehen! |
| fish | samakah | yu | poisson | Fisch |
| bird | altair | niao | oiseau | Vogel |
| horse | hisan | ma | cheval | Pferd |
| one | wahed | yi | un | eins |
| two | ithnaan | er | deux | zwei |
| three | thalatha | san | trois | drei |
| four | arba'a | si | quatre | vier |
| five | khamsa | wu | cinq | fünf |

*The line over a vowel indicates a long sound.

## LANGUAGE Q&As

How many languages are spoken on Earth? *More than 7,000.*

What country has the highest number of spoken languages? *Papua New Guinea, with 836.*

How many languages of the world have fewer than 10 remaining speakers? *135.*

# ¡Say It in Español!

After English, Spanish is the most commonly spoken language in the U.S. More than 37 million people speak Spanish at home. That's about 12 percent of all people in the U.S.

## Pronouncing Spanish Words

In Spanish, the vowels only make one type of sound. The sound each vowel makes in Spanish is the same sound it makes in the English words at right.

| | |
|---|---|
| A | water |
| E | bet |
| I | feet |
| O | slow |
| U | tube |

Also, if you see the letters *j, g,* or *x* followed by a vowel, pronounce them like the English *h.* So, *frijoles* (beans) sounds like free-HOLE-lehs. *México* sounds like MAY-hee-co. The *h* in Spanish is always silent. So *hermano* (brother) sounds like er-MAN-o.

**Try pronouncing the Spanish on this page.**

## *Basic* Spanish Phrases

| | |
|---|---|
| Hello | Hola |
| Good-bye | Adiós |
| How are you? | ¿Cómo estás? |
| Please | Por favor |
| Thank you | Gracias |
| What is your name? | ¿Cómo te llamas? |

## Find the False Friends

**Some Spanish and English words that look or sound the same have similar meanings. But some of these words can have very different meanings. They are called false friends. Can you spot which of these Spanish words have false friends? Check the answers to see if you're right!**

**basamento**
**blanco**
**compromiso**
**doctor**
**éxito**
**motel**
**similar**

Answers: There are four false friends: *basamento* means "base of a column," not "basement"; *blanco* means "white," not "blank"; *compromiso* means "commitment," not a "compromise"; and *éxito* means "success," not an "exit." The other three words mean the same thing in Spanish and English: *doctor, motel,* and *similar.*

## FOOD

**Ask your parent to make you *pollo* for dinner.**

# Your Bedroom
## Es Su Dormitorio

**Do you know what a *silla* is? See if you can say and remember these items from a bedroom (*dormitorio*) in Spanish.**

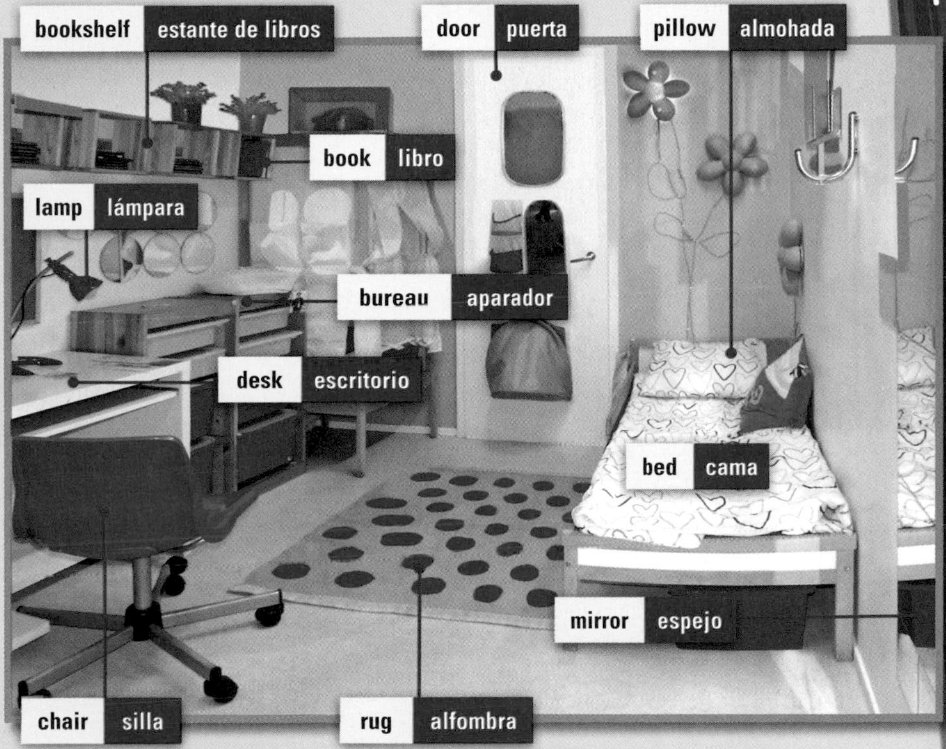

|  |  |
|---|---|
| bookshelf | estante de libros |
| door | puerta |
| pillow | almohada |
| book | libro |
| lamp | lámpara |
| bureau | aparador |
| desk | escritorio |
| bed | cama |
| mirror | espejo |
| chair | silla |
| rug | alfombra |

## Numbers

| | | | | | | | | | |
|---|---|---|---|---|---|---|---|---|---|
| 1 | uno | 3 | tres | 5 | cinco | 7 | siete | 9 | nueve |
| 2 | dos | 4 | cuatro | 6 | seis | 8 | ocho | 10 | diez |

## Joke en Español

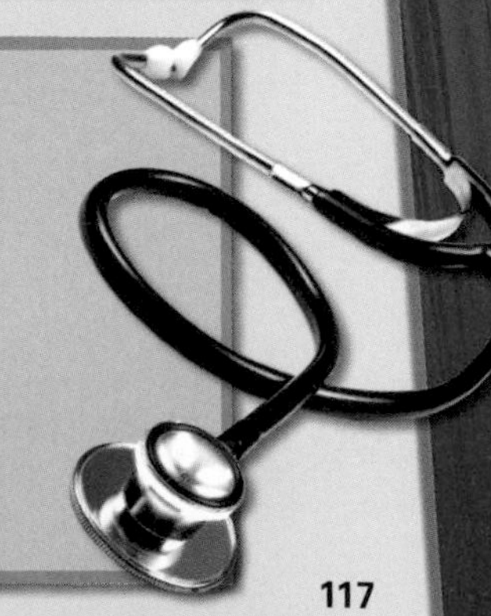

**PATIENT:** *Doctor, doctor, no puedo recordar nada.* (Doctor, doctor, I can't remember anything.)

**DOCTOR:** *Vaya, y desde cuando tiene usted este problema?* (Wow, and how long have you had this problem?)

**PATIENT:** *¿Qué problema?* (What problem?)

# The English Language

## New Words

**English is always changing as new words are born and old ones die out. Many new words come from the latest technology, from weather events, or from slang.**

**brain cramp:** temporary mental confusion that results in a mistake

**dumbphone:** a basic mobile phone without the advanced functions of a smartphone

**floordrobe:** a storage solution that involves dropping clothes on the floor instead of hanging them in the closet

**Frankenstorm:** a massive storm resulting from multiple weather systems →

**minimoon:** a short trip taken by a newly married couple in anticipation of a longer honeymoon later

**user experience:** the overall appeal of using a website or computer application

## FACTS ABOUT ENGLISH

- According to the *Oxford English Dictionary*, the English language contains between 250,000 and 750,000 words. (Some people count different meanings of the same word as separate words and include unusual technical terms.)
- The most common vowel in English is the letter *e*. The most common consonant is *t*. The least common letters are *q*, *j*, *z*, and *x*.
- The most common nouns in English are *time*, *person*, and *year*.

## IN OTHER WORDS: SIMILES

*Similes are comparisons of two things that use "as" or "like." Here are some to wrap your brain around.*

**fresh as a daisy = "alert and ready to go."** A well-rested, energetic person is often compared to a daisy, which opens its petals in the morning.

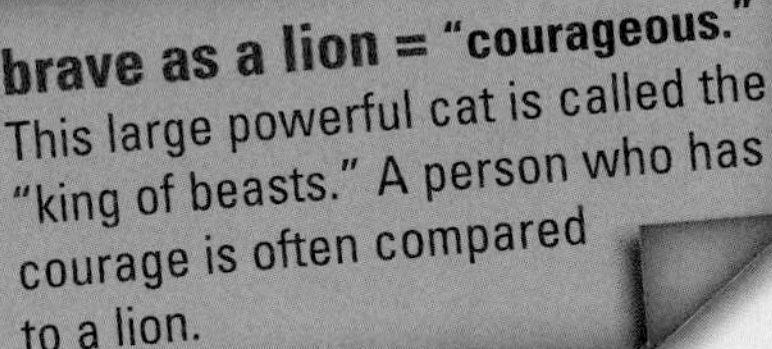

**brave as a lion = "courageous."** This large powerful cat is called the "king of beasts." A person who has courage is often compared to a lion.

**cold as ice = "very cold, freezing."** If your friend has been outside during winter without wearing gloves, you might describe her hands as being cold as ice.

LANGUAGE

# Getting to the ROOT

Many English words and parts of words can be traced back to Latin or Greek. If you know the meaning of parts of a word, you can probably guess what it means. A **root** (also called a stem) is the part of the word that gives its basic meaning but can't be used by itself. Roots need other word parts to complete them: either a **prefix** at the beginning, or a **suffix** at the end, or sometimes both. The following tables give some examples of Latin and Greek roots, prefixes, and suffixes.

## Latin

| root | basic meaning | example |
|---|---|---|
| -alt- | high | *altitude* |
| -dict- | to say | *dictate* |
| -port- | to carry | *transport* |
| -scrib-/ -script- | to write | *prescription* |
| -vert- | turn | *invert* |

| prefix | basic meaning | example |
|---|---|---|
| de- | away, off | *defrost* |
| in-/im- | not | *invisible* |
| non- | not | *nontoxic* |
| pre- | before | *prehistoric* |
| re- | again, back | *rewrite* |
| trans- | across, through | *transatlantic* |

| suffix | basic meaning | example |
|---|---|---|
| -ation | (makes verbs into nouns) | *invitation* |
| -fy/-ify | make or cause to become | *horrify* |
| -ly | like, to the extent of | *highly* |
| -ment | (makes verbs inton nouns) | *government* |
| -ty/-ity | state of | *purity* |

## Greek

| root | basic meaning | example |
|---|---|---|
| -anthrop- | human | *anthropology* |
| -bio- | life | *biology* |
| -dem- | people | *democracy* |
| -phon- | sound | *telephone* |
| -psych- | soul | *psychology* |

| prefix | basic meaning | example |
|---|---|---|
| anti-/ant- | against | *antisocial* |
| auto- | self | *autopilot* |
| biblio-/ bibl- | book | *bibliography* |
| micro- | small | *microscope* |
| tele- | far off | *television* |

| suffix | basic meaning | example |
|---|---|---|
| -graph | write, draw, describe, record | *photograph* |
| -ism | act, state, theory of | *realism* |
| -ist | one who believes in, practices | *capitalist* |
| -logue/ -log | speech, to speak | *dialogue* |
| -scope | see | *telescope* |

# MILITARY

→What was duct tape first used for by the U.S. military? PAGE 123

## MAJOR WARS IN U.S. HISTORY

**Since the colonists fought the British for American independence more than 200 years ago, U.S. troops have been involved in a number of conflicts, both at home and abroad.**

### AMERICAN REVOLUTION

***Why?*** The British king sought to control American trade and tax the 13 colonies without their consent. The colonies wanted independence from Great Britain.

***Who?*** British vs. Americans with French support

***When?*** 1775–1783

***Result?*** The 13 colonies gained their independence.

**When George Washington took command of the Continental Army in 1775, many of his soldiers did not have guns. To fool the British, they carved fake weapons out of wood.**

### WAR OF 1812

***Why?*** Britain interfered with American commerce and forced American sailors to join the British navy.

***Who?*** Britain vs. United States

***When?*** 1812–1814

***Result?*** There was no clear winner. The U.S. unsuccessfully invaded Canada. The British burned Washington, D.C., but were defeated in other battles.

### MEXICAN-AMERICAN WAR

***Why?*** The U.S. annexed Texas and wanted control of California, a Mexican province.

***Who?*** Mexico vs. United States

***When?*** 1846–1848

***Result?*** Mexico gave up its claim to Texas and ceded to the U.S. California and all or part of six other Western states.

### CIVIL WAR

***Why?*** Eleven Southern states (the Confederacy) seceded from the U.S. (the Union). The U.S. fought to keep them.

***Who?*** Confederacy vs. Union

***When?*** 1861–1865

***Result?*** The Confederacy was defeated. The United States remained a unified country. Slavery was abolished.

Did You KNOW?

**Former schoolteacher Clara Barton risked her life to nurse thousands of soldiers during the Civil War. She later helped start the American Red Cross.**

## SPANISH-AMERICAN WAR

***Why?*** The Americans supported Cuban independence from Spain.

***Who?*** United States vs. Spain

***When?*** 1898

***Result?*** Spain lost the Philippines, Guam, and Puerto Rico to the U.S. Cuba became independent.

**Did You KNOW?** **Future president Theodore Roosevelt became a national hero when he led a cavalry unit called the Rough Riders that fought in Cuba during the Spanish-American War.**

## WORLD WAR I

***Why?*** Colonial and military competition between European powers.

***Who?*** Allies (including the U.S., Britain, France, Russia, Italy, and Japan) vs. Central Powers (including Germany, Austria-Hungary, and Turkey)

***When?*** 1914–1918 (U.S. entered in 1917)

***Result?*** The Allies defeated the Central Powers. An estimated 8 million soldiers and close to 10 million civilians died.

**Did You KNOW?** **Tanks were developed and used for the first time in World War I. Attacking forces used them to break through well-defended enemy trenches.**

## WORLD WAR II

↑ ***U.S. troops land in France on D-Day***

***Why?*** The Axis sought world domination.

***Who?*** Axis (including Germany, Italy, and Japan) vs. Allies (including the U.S., Britain, France, and the Soviet Union). The U.S. did not enter the war until Japan attacked Pearl Harbor in 1941.

***When?*** 1939–1945 (U.S. dropped atomic bombs on Hiroshima and Nagasaki in August 1945.)

***Result?*** The Allies defeated the Axis. The Holocaust (the Nazi effort to wipe out the Jews) was stopped. The U.S. helped rebuild Western Europe and Japan. The Soviet Union set up Communist governments in Eastern Europe.

## KOREAN WAR

***Why?*** North Korea invaded South Korea. In many ways, the conflict was part of the Cold War between the Communist and non-Communist nations.

***Who?*** North Korea with support from China and the Soviet Union vs. South Korea backed by the United States and its allies

***When?*** 1950–1953

***Result?*** The war ended in a stalemate. Korea remains divided.

**Did You KNOW?** **More than 5.7 million American troops served in the Korean War. Almost 140,000 of them were killed or wounded.**

## VIETNAM WAR

***Why?*** Communists (Viet Cong) backed by North Vietnam attempted to overthrow South Vietnam's government.

***Who?*** North Vietnam and the Viet Cong with support from the Soviet Union and China vs. South Vietnam with support from the U.S. and its allies

***When?*** 1959–1975

***Result?*** The U.S. withdrew its troops in 1973. In 1975, South Vietnam surrendered. Vietnam became a unified Communist country.

## AFGHANISTAN WAR

***Why?*** The U.S. demanded that the Taliban regime in Afghanistan turn over Osama bin Laden, the man who planned the 9/11 terrorist attacks in 2001.

***Who?*** Taliban vs. Afghan forces, supported by the U.S. and its allies

***When?*** 2001–

***Result?*** The Taliban was driven from power but later regained control over large parts of the country. In 2009 and 2010, the U.S. increased its troop strength but later began reducing forces, with the goal of bringing at least most troops home by 2014.

↑ ***President Obama with Afghanistan's President Hamid Karzai***

## PERSIAN GULF WAR

***Why?*** Iraq invaded and annexed Kuwait. It refused to withdraw despite United Nations demands.

***Who?*** Iraq vs. U.S.-led coalition

***When?*** 1991

***Result?*** The coalition drove out Iraqi forces from Kuwait.

## IRAQ WAR

***Why?*** The U.S. accused Iraq of hiding weapons of mass destruction (WMDs) and supporting terrorists.

***Who?*** Iraq vs. United States, Great Britain, and their allies

***When?*** 2003–2011

***Result?*** Saddam Hussein's government was toppled. Hussein was tried and executed. No WMDs were found. The U.S. withdrew its last combat support troops in 2011. ↓

## Top 10 Nations With Largest Armed Forces*

| Rank | Country | Troops | Rank | Country | Troops |
|---|---|---|---|---|---|
| 1. | China | 2,285,000 | 6. | South Korea | 655,000 |
| 2. | United States | 1,569,000 | 7. | Pakistan | 642,000 |
| 3. | India | 1,325,000 | 8. | Iran | 523,000 |
| 4. | North Korea | 1,190,000 | 9. | Turkey | 511,000 |
| 5. | Russia | 956,000 | 10. | Vietnam | 482,000 |

*Troops on active duty in 2012. Source: *The Military Balance*/International Institute for Strategic Studies.

# The Military: Mother of Inventions

When you think about the military, you probably think of tanks, fighter planes, and submarines. But all kinds of inventions that have become part of everyday life were first developed for use by the armed forces. Here are a few of those inventions.

**DUCT TAPE** Duct tape was developed during World War II to keep water out of cases that held ammunition. It was nicknamed "duck tape," probably because it was waterproof. The U.S. military quickly figured out that the tape was practical for many things, including fixing jeeps and tanks. By the 1950s, the tape was available in hardware stores around the country. It was often used to connect ducts and tubes in heating and air conditioning systems, and the name evolved into duct tape.

**GLOBAL POSITIONING SYSTEM (GPS)**

GPS was originally used by the armed forces to track military vehicles. The system went into operation in 1993, soon after the U.S. Air Force completed placing 24 Navstar satellites in orbit over different parts of the globe. If a vehicle had a receiver picking up signals from Navstar, its exact location could be determined. The system was opened to civilian use in 1996, and today, receivers in cars, smartphones, computers, and other devices help people get directions, find nearby places of interest, and find their way when they get lost.

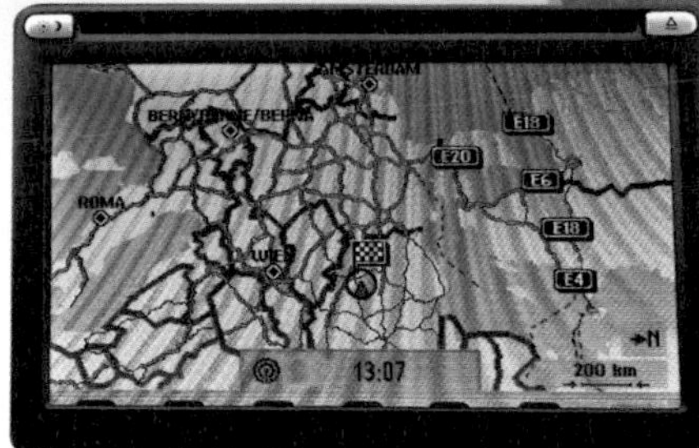


**THE INTERNET** An early version of the Internet—a system of connected computer networks—was developed for the U.S. military in the 1960s and 1970s. Called ARPAnet, it was used for military communications and transmission of information.

**PENICILLIN** Although penicillin had been discovered in the 1920s, research on the drug was spurred by World War II. Doctors were eager to find a medication to prevent and treat infections in wounded soldiers. By the end of the war, penicillin had saved countless lives, and soon after, it was being used by doctors worldwide.

**Did You KNOW?** In 2013, the U.S. military ended its ban on women serving in ground combat roles. Under the new policy, to be phased in over three years, women in the military can now serve in combat roles in infantry, artillery, and other types of ground fighting units.

# MONEY

→How many Mexican pesos can you get for one dollar? PAGE 125

## WORLD'S TEN RICHEST PEOPLE*

| Name | Age | Country | Industry | Worth |
|---|---|---|---|---|
| **Carlos Slim Helú†** | 73 | Mexico | Communications | $73.0 billion |
| Bill Gates | 57 | United States | Software (Microsoft) | 67.0 billion |
| Amancio Ortega | 76 | Spain | Fashion | 57.0 billion |
| Warren Buffett | 82 | United States | Investments | 53.5 billion |
| Lawrence Ellison | 68 | United States | Data Management (Oracle) | 43.0 billion |
| Charles Koch | 77 | United States | Diversified | 34.0 billion |
| David Koch | 72 | United States | Diversified | 34.0 billion |
| Li Ka-shing | 84 | Hong Kong | Diversified | 31.0 billion |
| **Liliane Bettencourt†** | 90 | France | Beauty Products (L'Oreal) | 30.0 billion |
| Bernard Arnault† | 64 | France | Luxury goods (LMVH) | 29.0 billion |

*As of March 2013 (Source: www.forbes.com). †Includes other family members.

## WORLD'S YOUNGEST BILLIONAIRES*

| Name | Age | Country | Industry | Worth |
|---|---|---|---|---|
| **Dustin Moskovitz** | 28 | United States | Technology (Facebook, Asana) | $3.8 billion |
| Mark Zuckerberg | 28 | United States | Technology (Facebook) | 13.3 billion |
| Prince Albert von Thurn und Taxis | 29 | Germany | Diversified investments | 1.5 billion |
| Scott Duncan | 30 | United States | Inherited energy company | 5.1 billion |
| Eduardo Saverin | 31 | United States | Technology (Facebook) | 2.2 billion |
| Yang Huiyan | 31 | China | Property development | 5.7 billion |
| Fahd Hariri | 32 | Lebanon | Technology, real estate | 1.4 billion |
| Marie Besnier Beauvalot | 32 | France | Inherited dairy company | 1.5 billion |
| **Sean Parker** | 33 | United States | Technology (Facebook) | 2.0 billion |
| Ayman Hariri | 34 | Lebanon | Technology, real estate | 1.4 billion |

*As of March 2013 (Source: www.forbes.com).

# MONEY AROUND the WORLD

Most countries have their own currency. Sometimes two countries call their currency by the same name, but the money usually has different designs and may have different values. Most currency is decorated with cultural symbols and pictures of important people in the country's history.

An exchange rate is the price of a country's currency in terms of another. For example, one U.S. dollar could buy 6.21 yuan in China in early 2013. These rates are based on a country's economy, the value of products it makes, and inflation, the increase in how much things cost. When people want to buy goods from someone in another country, they need to exchange their money for, or buy, some of the other country's currency.

## the EURO

Because many European nations wanted to make it easier for companies in different countries to do business with one another, they formed an organization to eliminate barriers to trade. This organization, now called the European Union (EU), decided, among other things, to create one currency that could be used by many countries.

The euro, whose symbol is €, became the official currency of 12 EU members on January 1, 2002. As of mid-2013, the euro was used by 17 EU countries (see page 138). It was also used in six other countries.

## HOW MUCH IS THE DOLLAR WORTH?

**In April 2013, here is about how much one dollar could buy of some other currencies.**

| Amount | Currency | Amount | Currency | Amount | Currency |
|---|---|---|---|---|---|
| 0.66 | British pounds | 0.77 | euros | 12.45 | Mexican pesos |
| 1.02 | Canadian dollars | 54.38 | Indian rupees | 31.01 | Russian rubles |
| 6.21 | Chinese yuan | 94.91 | Japanese yen | 1.82 | Turkish lira |

## FAST FACTS ABOUT MONEY

**Money has been in use in one form or another for thousands of years. Here are a few examples:**

- **In China about 3,000 years ago, people used cowrie shells as money. (Cowries are a type of sea snail.)**
- **By 2,000 years ago, the Chinese were making metal coins in the shape of cowrie shells—the world's first coins.**
- **The Lydian Empire (in what is now Turkey) made the first gold coins around 1,700 years ago.**
- **China was the first country to use paper money, starting about A.D. 800.**
- **Some American Indian groups traded animal skins, including buck (male deer) skins—leading to the slang term "buck" for dollar!**

# What's New in COINS

The U.S. Mint is making one-dollar coins that show the faces of the presidents. The coins are being released in the order in which the presidents served in office. The Mint plans to issue four presidential $1 coins per year through 2016.

The new coins to be introduced in 2014 honor Warren Harding, Calvin Coolidge, Herbert Hoover, and Franklin D. Roosevelt. On the back of all the coins is an image of the Statue of Liberty.

The U.S. Mint is also releasing five new America the Beautiful quarters each year, honoring National Park Service sites and other national sites. The five quarters released in 2013 featured White Mountain National Forest, Perry's Victory and International Peace Memorial, Great Basin National Park, Fort McHenry National Monument, and Mount Rushmore National Memorial. →

**For more information on all these coins, visit the U.S. Mint's website at www.usmint.gov**

# OUTSMARTING THE COUNTERFEITERS

In recent years, the U.S. government has increased its efforts to keep counterfeiters from making fake paper money that can pass for the real thing. Because today's laser printers and scanners have made it easier to make realistic copies of actual bills, the government has had to come up with new ways to stop counterfeiters. Among the techniques used by the government in new bills made in recent years are watermarks that don't show up on scanned or copied bills, embedded fibers, and special inks that change color depending on the way light hits the money. The newer bills have fine lines in the background and detailed scrolls running around the edges that copiers and scanners generally can't pick up. They also have enlarged portraits that include difficult-to-copy details.

An even harder-to-counterfeit $100 bill was scheduled to go into circulation in late 2013. This bill has a blue stripe running from top to bottom in the middle of the front. Inside this blue stripe, depending on how you tilt the bill, you'll see either small images of the Liberty Bell or the number 100. On the right side of the bill, there's an image of an inkwell inside of which is another picture of the Liberty Bell that changes color if you tilt the bill.

# What's on the $1 Bill?

**Everybody knows that George Washington is on the front of the U.S. one-dollar bill, but did you ever wonder what all that other stuff is?**

**Plate position**
Shows where on the 32-note plate this bill was printed.

**Treasury Department seal**
The scales represent justice. The stripe across the middle has 13 stars for the 13 colonies. The key represents authority.

**Plate serial number**
Shows which printing plate was used for the face of the bill.

**Serial number**
Each bill has its own.

**Federal Reserve District number**
Shows which district issued the bill.

**Treasurer of the U.S. signature**

**Series indicator**
(year note's design was first used)

**Secretary of the Treasury signature**

**Federal Reserve District seal**

The name of the Federal Reserve Bank that issued the bill is printed in the seal. The letter tells you which of the 12 Federal Reserve Districts the bill is from:

A: Boston
B: New York
C: Philadelphia
D: Cleveland
E: Richmond
F: Atlanta
G: Chicago
H: St. Louis
I: Minneapolis
J: Kansas City
K: Dallas
L: San Francisco

**Did You KNOW?** The back of the $1 bill shows the front and back of the Great Seal of the United States (see page 255).

# TIPS ON BUDGETS AND SAVING UP

**Many kids get an allowance or earn money by doing chores or working a part-time job. Here are some tips for budgeting your money wisely and even having some left over to save for the future.**

1. Figure out how much money you take in each week.
2. About how much do you spend each week? Do you pay for your own movies? Music downloads?
3. Compare the two numbers. If you have money left over each week, good for you! Try putting it into a bank savings account. Then, when you want to buy something for yourself, buy a gift, or help your favorite charity, you'll have a way to pay for it.
4. If you're coming up short, look for ways to make a bit of money. Can you take on extra chores at home? Walk a neighbor's dog?
5. And think about ways to spend less. Look for what's on sale when you're shopping. Or maybe you can put off buying something if you don't really need it.

**For more about budgeting and saving, go to www.themint.org/kids**

# MOVIES & TV

→How many films will be made from the Hunger Games books? PAGE 130

## MOVIE & TV FACTS

**RECORD BREAKERS** When the 2013 Academy Award nominees were announced, history was made. The category of Best Actress included both the oldest and youngest actresses who had ever been nominated for the award. Quvenzhané Wallis, nominated for her role in *Beasts of the Southern Wild*, was just 9 years old. Emmanuelle Riva was nominated at age 85 for her role in *Amour*.

***SECRET* NEWS** *The Secret Life of the American Teenager* made headlines in March 2013 when the show aired an episode told almost entirely in American Sign Language (ASL). All of the show's sounds were muted, except for background music.

*Quvenzhané Wallis*

### ALL-TIME TOP ANIMATED MOVIES*

| Rank | Title (Year released) | Gross (in millions) |
|---|---|---|
| 1 | *Shrek 2* (2004) | $436.7 |
| 2 | *Toy Story 3* (2010) | 415.0 |
| 3 | *Finding Nemo* (2003) | 339.7 |
| 4 | *Shrek the Third* (2007) | 322.7 |
| 5 | *The Lion King* (1994) | 312.9 |
| 6 | *Up* (2009) | 293.0 |
| 7 | *Shrek* (2001) | 267.7 |
| 8 | *The Incredibles* (2004) | 261.4 |
| 9 | *Monsters, Inc.* (2001) | 255.9 |
| 10 | *Despicable Me* (2010) | 251.5 |

### ALL-TIME TOP MOVIES*

| Rank | Title (Year released) | Gross (in millions) |
|---|---|---|
| 1 | *Avatar* (2009) | $760.5 |
| 2 | *The Avengers* (2012) | 623.4 |
| 3 | *Titanic* (1997) | 600.8 |
| 4 | *The Dark Knight* (2008) | 533.3 |
| 5 | *Star Wars* (1977) | 461.0 |
| 6 | *The Dark Knight Rises* (2012) | 448.1 |
| 7 | *Shrek 2* (2004) | 436.7 |
| 8 | *E.T. the Extra-Terrestrial* (1982) | 435.0 |
| 9 | *Star Wars: Episode I—The Phantom Menace* (1999) | 431.1 |
| 10 | *Pirates of the Caribbean: Dead Man's Chest* (2006) | 423.3 |

Source: © 2013 by Rentrak Corporation. Rankings are for movies rated G, PG, or PG-13.
*Through June 14, 2013, based on box office sales in the U.S. and Canada.

# Viral Video STARS

**Many of today's stars, including Justin Bieber, first became famous through online videos. Anyone can upload videos to sites such as YouTube and Vimeo. Here are some examples of success stories.**

**Robby Novak** became a YouTube sensation → in 2013. His "Kid President" videos, which include inspirational tips and jokes, have been seen by tens of millions of viewers. In April 2013, Kid President was invited to Washington, D.C., where he took a tour of the White House and met President Barack Obama.

The character of Miranda Sings was created by actress **Colleen Ballinger**. Ballinger has been posting funny videos of her character (often singing badly) since 2008. Her videos have become so popular that she now performs her act in a live touring show. Ballinger's YouTube videos have been viewed more than 39 million times.

**Did You KNOW?** **TV series produced for viewing on the web are becoming more common. In April 2013, Amazon released 14 different pilots (first episodes) and asked viewers to decide which shows should be made into full streaming-only series. Netflix announced a plan to partner with DreamWorks Animation and release streaming-only animated programs for kids in Fall 2013.**

# COMING TO THEATERS

## IN THE SECOND HALF OF 2013

- Logan Lerman returns as Percy in *Percy Jackson: Sea of Monsters.* (August)
- Lily Collins stars in *The Mortal Instruments: City of Bones,* based on the first book in the bestselling series. (August)
- Dane Cook and Julia Louis-Dreyfus provide voices for the animated film *Planes.* (August)
- Jennifer Lawrence returns for *The Hunger Games: Catching Fire.* (November)
- Peter Jackson directs *The Hobbit: The Desolation of Smaug.* (December)

## ...AND IN 2014

- Chris Pratt and Will Arnett star in *The Lego Movie,* which hits theaters in March.
- Miss Piggy and Kermit are back in *The Muppets . . . Again,* due in March.
- **Chris Evans suits up for *Captain America: The Winter Soldier,* coming in April. →**
- *The Hunger Games: Mockingjay—Part 1* opens in November.

# BOOKS to FILM

**MOVIE:** ***The Perks of Being a Wallflower*** **(2012)**
**BOOK:** ***The Perks of Being a Wallflower*** **(1999)**
**BY STEPHEN CHBOSKY**

*The Perks of Being a Wallflower* is a novel written by Stephen Chbosky. The book tells the story of Charlie, who is shy and quiet, and the two close friends he makes in his freshman year of high school. The movie version, released in 2012, starred Logan Lerman as Charlie. His friends, Sam and Patrick, were played by Emma Watson and Ezra Miller. Chbosky directed the movie and wrote its screenplay.

**MOVIE:** ***Oz: The Great and Powerful*** **(2013)**
**BOOK:** ***The Wonderful Wizard of Oz*** **(1900)**
**BY L. FRANK BAUM**

L. Frank Baum is the author of 14 books in a series about the Land of Oz. Several movies have been made about his characters, including the beloved 1939 film *The Wizard of Oz*. The most recent movie, *Oz: The Great and Powerful*, was called a "prequel" to the first book in Baum's series. The movie's writers imagined what might have happened to the characters before the story in the book took place.

**MOVIE:** ***The Hunger Games: Catching Fire*** **(2013)**
**BOOK:** ***Catching Fire*** **(2009)**
**BY SUZANNE COLLINS**

Suzanne Collins is the author of three books, known as the Hunger Games trilogy, about Katniss Everdeen, a girl who must fight in a violent competition between kids. Each of the books has been or will be made into a movie. As with the Twilight books, the last title in the series will be made into two movies. Josh Hutcherson, Jennifer Lawrence, and Liam Hemsworth star in the films.

**THE HUNGER GAMES TRILOGY**

1 ***The Hunger Games*** **(book: 2008; movie: 2012)**
2 ***Catching Fire*** **(book: 2009; movie: 2013)**
3 ***Mockingjay*** **(book: 2010; movies:** ***Part 1*****, 2014, and** ***Part 2*****, 2015)**

# TOP TV Shows in 2012-2013

## FOR AGES 6-11

| NETWORK | CABLE |
|---|---|
| 1. *American Idol* | 1. *Dog With a Blog* |
| 2. *NBC Sunday Night Football* | 2. *Jessie* |
| 3. *The Voice* | 3. *Big Time Rush* |
| 4. *The Big Bang Theory* | 4. *Austin & Ally* |
| 5. *Fox NFL Sunday* | 5. *Gravity Falls* |

## FOR AGES 12-17

| NETWORK | CABLE |
|---|---|
| 1. *NBC Sunday Night Football* | 1. *NFL on ESPN* |
| 2. *Family Guy* | 2. *Victorious* |
| 3. *American Idol* | 3. *Big Time Rush* |
| 4. *The Voice* | 4. *Family Guy* |
| 5. *Glee* | 5. *Drake and Josh* |

Source: © 2013, Nielsen. Top 5 programs with 10 telecasts or more, excluding motion pictures, September 9, 2012, through April 19, 2013.

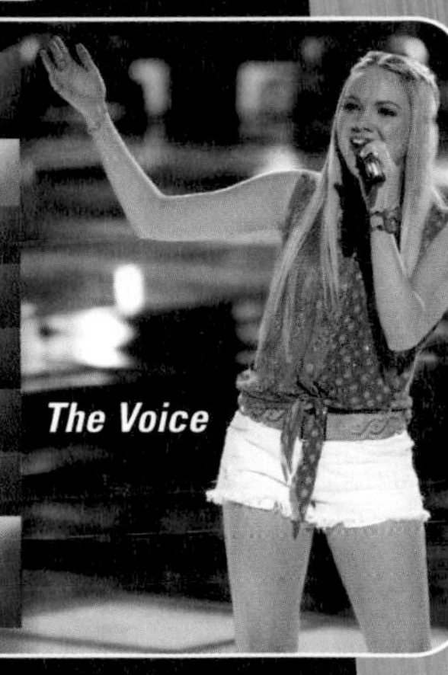
*The Voice*

## MOVIES & TV WORD SEARCH

Find the name of each movie or TV show listed. The names may appear running up, down, forward, backward, or diagonally.

**NAMES TO FIND:**

- Gravity Falls
- The Avengers
- Drake and Josh
- The Voice
- Mockingjay
- Avatar
- Finding Nemo
- Big Time Rush

| | | | | | | | | | | | | | | |
|---|---|---|---|---|---|---|---|---|---|---|---|---|---|---|
| G | T | H | E | V | O | I | C | E | P | F | J | D | Y | H |
| D | R | R | A | F | N | K | G | G | D | P | Z | R | A | S |
| J | O | A | I | V | Z | Q | N | D | W | M | T | A | J | Q |
| E | V | H | V | K | A | Y | R | N | D | H | P | K | G | J |
| R | H | J | S | I | H | T | E | C | E | I | S | E | N | J |
| H | R | F | R | U | T | M | A | A | C | Z | I | A | I | S |
| E | S | N | C | B | R | Y | V | R | F | W | Y | N | K | L |
| S | Q | X | T | G | Y | E | F | S | Q | E | P | D | C | P |
| P | H | M | S | C | N | R | M | A | F | C | M | J | O | I |
| X | F | T | T | G | F | Y | B | I | L | T | S | O | M | H |
| T | Q | L | E | Y | M | R | U | O | T | L | U | S | Q | O |
| Q | S | R | S | F | N | T | P | N | R | G | S | H | D | C |
| L | S | O | M | E | N | G | N | I | D | N | I | F | E | E |
| L | B | N | B | N | Z | N | T | S | B | S | E | B | M | X |
| W | S | Y | H | Q | Z | U | G | R | O | I | T | U | M | B |

ANSWERS ON PAGES 334-336.

→What is "K-pop"? PAGE 134

## TOP ALBUMS OF 2012

1. *21* ........ Adele →
2. *Christmas* ........ Michael Bublé
3. *Take Care* ........ Drake
4. *Red* ........ Taylor Swift
5. *Up All Night* ........ One Direction
6. *Tailgates and Tanlines* ........ Luke Bryan
7. *Babel* ........ Mumford & Sons
8. *Talk That Talk* ........ Rihanna
9. *Tuskegee* ........ Lionel Richie
10. *El Camino* ........ The Black Keys

Source: *Billboard 200*/The Nielsen Company

## THE GRAMMY AWARDS

The Grammy Awards—for best recorded music and recording artists—have been held every year since 1959. Winners are chosen by the National Academy of Recording Arts and Sciences, a group made up of people involved in the music industry. Winners at the 2013 Grammy Awards ceremony, hosted by LL Cool J, ↓ included the following.

| Award | Winner |
|---|---|
| Record of the Year | "Somebody That I Used to Know," Gotye featuring Kimbra |
| Album of the Year | *Babel*, Mumford & Sons |
| Song of the Year | "We Are Young," fun. featuring Janelle Monáe |
| Best New Artist | fun. |
| Best Pop Vocal Album | *Stronger*, Kelly Clarkson |
| Best Traditional Pop Vocal Album | *Kisses on the Bottom*, Paul McCartney |
| Best Rock Album | *El Camino*, The Black Keys |
| Best Rap Album | *Take Care*, Drake |
| Best Country Album | *Uncaged*, Zac Brown Band |

# WHO'S HOT NOW?

## KATY PERRY

**BORN:** October 25, 1984, in Santa Barbara, California

**ALBUMS:** *One of the Boys* (2008), *Teenage Dream* (2010)

Singer-songwriter Katy Perry fell in love with music at church—both of her parents are pastors. She pursued a career in gospel music, but had little success. After three record deals fell through, she struck gold with her album *One of the Boys*. The album produced several hit singles and was a huge success. Her second album, *Teenage Dream*, was another huge hit. Perry has crossed over into movie success, providing the voice of Smurfette in 2011's *The Smurfs* and releasing *Katy Perry: Part of Me* in 2012. She is also well-known for her colorful, energetic concert tours. Perry planned to release her third studio album in the second half of 2013.

## ONE DIRECTION

**ALBUMS:** *Up All Night* (2011); *Take Me Home* (2012)

The five members of the band One Direction are Harry Styles, Zayn Malik, Louis Tomlinson, Liam Payne, and Niall Horan. All are from England except for Horan, who is from Ireland. The band got its start on the British TV show *The X Factor*. In 2010, each boy auditioned separately for the show. The judges suggested that they form a group. The band finished in third place, and its first single, "What Makes You Beautiful," was a hit. When One Direction's first album, *Up All Night*, was released in the U.S., the group became the first British band in history to enter the charts at the top spot with a debut album.

**Did You KNOW?**

**Adele's *21* was best-selling album of the year twice in a row—in 2011 and 2012. It was the first time this had happened since Michael Jackson's *Thriller* was the best selling album of 1983 and 1984.**

# Reality TV Competitions

Many popular reality shows highlight singing and dancing competitions. These shows usually feature celebrity judges or mentors who offer tips to the contestants—the winners are chosen through a combination of judge input and votes from viewers. Many celebrities, from Jennifer Hudson to One Direction, were discovered through reality TV competitions. Here are a few examples of these shows.

***American Idol*** has been popular since the program's first season, which aired in 2002. The show's judges select a group of semifinalists, who sing each week on the program. Viewers decide who advances or goes home. In 2013, the winner was **Candice Glover.** →

***The X Factor*** was created by former *American Idol* judge Simon Cowell, and it originally aired in Britain. Contestants are divided into four categories—Boys, Girls, Over 30s, and Groups—with judges assigned to act as mentors for each category. The winner of the second U.S. season was **Tate Stevens**.

***Dancing With the Stars*** pairs celebrities with professional dancers. Each pair dances live on the show every week. The dancers receive scores and advice from the judges. Viewers also cast their votes. The winners of the show's 16th season were **Kellie Pickler** and her partner **Derek Hough**. →

***The Voice*** starts each season with "blind auditions." Celebrity judges listen from chairs turned so that the judges can't see who is singing. If a judge wants to mentor the contestant, he or she hits a button that turns the chair around. Team members compete against each other for the judges before advancing to performances decided by public votes. In 2013, the winner was **Danielle Bradbery**, mentored by **Blake Shelton**.

**Did You KNOW?**

**"K-pop," which stands for Korean pop, is a type of popular music that originated in South Korea and is now enjoyed worldwide. One of the best-known examples of K-pop is "Gangnam Style," a song by Psy that went viral in late 2012. By mid-2013, the song had more than 1.5 billion hits on YouTube.**

# Musical INSTRUMENTS

There are many kinds of musical instruments. Instruments in an orchestra are divided into four groups, or sections: string, woodwind, brass, and percussion.

**PERCUSSION** instruments make sounds when they are struck. They include **drums**, cymbals, triangles, gongs, bells, and xylophones. Keyboard instruments, like the piano, are sometimes included in percussion instruments.

**WOODWINDS** are cylindrical and hollow inside. They make sounds when air is blown into them. The clarinet, **flute**, oboe, bassoon, and piccolo are woodwinds.

**STRING** instruments make sounds when the strings are either stroked with a bow or plucked with the fingers. The **violin**, viola, cello, bass, and harp are used in an orchestra. The guitar, banjo, and mandolin are other stringed instruments.

**BRASSES** are hollow inside. They make sounds when air is blown into a mouthpiece. The trumpet, French horn, trombone, and **tuba** are brasses.

# Dancing Around THE World

**All over the world, different cultures enjoy dance in celebrations and performances, or just for recreation and to stay healthy—dancing can be great exercise. Here are two types of dance that trace their roots back to particular cultures.**

**SALSA dancing is performed in many different cultures, but it is especially popular in in Cuba and Puerto Rico. Salsa dancing is typically performed by couples and goes with a special type of music, also called salsa. The dances usually involve quick steps combined with hip movements.**

**← BOLLYWOOD dancing originated in India and is often shown in movies. ("Bollywood" is a combination of the words Bombay and Hollywood.) This type of dancing combines traditional Indian dances with modern moves taken from jazz and hip hop.**

# MYTHOLOGY

→Who was the first woman created by the Greek gods? PAGE 137

## A FAMILY OF GODS

Poseidon/Neptune

**The Ancient Greeks believed that a big family of gods and goddesses watched over them from Mount Olympus. Farmers planting crops, sailors crossing the sea, and poets writing verses thought that these powerful beings could help or harm them. Stories about the gods and goddesses are called myths.**

After the Romans conquered Greece, in 146 B.C., they adopted Greek myths but gave Roman names to the main gods and goddesses. Except for Earth, the planets in our solar system are named after Roman or Greek gods.

### Greek & Roman Gods

Some of the most important Greek and Roman gods are listed here. Those with an * are children of Zeus (Jupiter).

| Greek Name | Roman Name | Description |
|---|---|---|
| Aphrodite | Venus | Goddess of beauty and of love |
| *Apollo | Apollo | God of prophecy, music, and medicine |
| *Ares | Mars | God of war; protector of the city |
| *Artemis | Diana | Goddess of the Moon and of the hunt |
| *Athena | Minerva | Goddess of wisdom and of war |
| Cronus | Saturn | Father of Zeus (Jupiter), Poseidon (Neptune), Hades (Pluto), Hera (Juno), and Demeter (Ceres) |
| Demeter | Ceres | Goddess of crops and harvest, sister of Zeus (Jupiter) |
| *Dionysus | Bacchus | God of wine, dancing, and theater |
| Hades | Pluto | Ruler of the Underworld, brother of Zeus (Jupiter) |
| Hephaestus | Vulcan | God of fire |
| Hera | Juno | Queen of the gods, wife of Zeus (Jupiter), goddess of marriage |
| *Hermes | Mercury | Messenger god, had winged helmet and sandals |
| Poseidon | Neptune | God of the sea and of earthquakes, brother of Zeus (Jupiter) |
| Zeus | Jupiter | Sky god (grandson of Uranus), ruler of gods and mortals |

**In Greek mythology, Medusa was one of the Gorgons, monsters who had the face of an ugly woman and long, writhing snakes for hair. Anyone who looked directly at Medusa would immediately be turned to stone.**

# MAKING SENSE OF THE WORLD

Re

Myths were once thought to be true. Most ancient peoples explained many things in nature by referring to gods and heroes with superhuman qualities. To the Greeks, a rough sea meant that **POSEIDON** was angry. Lightning was **THOR'S** hammer in Norse mythology. Egyptians worshipped the sun god **RE,** who sailed across the sky in a ship each day. In Japan, **AMATERASU** was the Shinto sun goddess who gave light to the land. Her brother **SUSANOO** was the storm god who ruled the sea.

There are even stories of gods or heroes who chose brain over brawn to get what they wanted. **COYOTE** was wild and cunning, a true trickster for many American Indian tribes throughout the West. He was never simply good or bad. **ANANSI** was a spider in the stories of the Akan tribes of West Africa. The tiny spider used his wits to capture the hornet, python, and leopard.

Myths have remained popular long after people knew they weren't true because the stories hold important life lessons and morals for cultures around the world. Myths have also inspired countless stories and works of art.

# GREEK & ROMAN HEROES

**Besides stories about the gods, Greek and Roman mythology has many stories about other heroes with amazing qualities.**

**ODYSSEUS**, the king of Ithaca, was a hero of the Trojan War in the epic poem the *Iliad.* It was his idea to build a huge wooden horse, hide Greek soldiers inside, and smuggle them into the city of Troy to capture it. The long poem the *Odyssey* is the story of his long and magical trip home after the war.

**PANDORA** was the first woman created by the Greek gods. Zeus ordered Hephaestus to create a beautiful woman out of earth. All the gods on Olympus gave her gifts. Hera's gift was curiosity. When Pandora was finished, she received a box that she was never to open. But, because of her curiosity, Pandora could not resist. She opened the box and released all the evil spirits into the world.

**JASON** and the Argonauts set out on a quest to find the golden fleece so that Jason could reclaim his rightful throne. Among the Argonauts were Herakles and Orpheus. After many adventures and with the help of Medea, Jason slew the Minotaur and claimed the fleece. He later betrayed Medea and eventually died when a beam from his ship, the Argo, fell off and hit him on the head.

**HERCULES**, or Herakles, was said to have superhuman strength. The most famous of his deeds were his 12 labors. They included killing the **Hydra**, a many-headed monster, and capturing the three-headed dog **Cerberus**, who guarded the gates of the Underworld. Hercules was so great a hero that the gods granted him immortality. When his body lay on his funeral pyre, Athena came and carried him off to Mount Olympus.

*Jason with the Golden Fleece*

# NATIONS

→What nation's capital has 137 different museums? PAGE 159

## KINDS OF GOVERNMENT

**As of 2013, there were 196 independent nations, with various kinds of governments.**

**Totalitarianism** In **totalitarian** countries, the rulers have strong power, and the people have little freedom. Elections are controlled, so that people do not have a real choice. North Korea is an example of a totalitarian country.

**Monarchy** A **monarchy** is a country headed by a king or queen (or occasionally by a ruler with a different title), who usually has inherited the title from a parent or other relative. There still are some monarchies in the world today. The United Kingdom (Great Britain) is one.

**Democracy** The word **democracy** comes from the Greek words demos ("people") and kratos ("rule"). In modern democracies, people govern themselves through the leaders they choose in elections. The United States and many other countries are democracies. Some monarchies, like the United Kingdom, are also democracies because the main decisions are actually made by elected leaders.

## THE EUROPEAN UNION (EU)

**The EU is a group of nations with a total population of over 500 million people. The organization was expected to have 28 members by July 2013, when Croatia was scheduled to join. Each nation is still independent, but the EU is like a super-government.**

- The European Union has many policies all member nations must follow.
- The EU has its own flag and anthem.
- Leaders from the EU countries meet regularly to help set common policies.
- The Council of the European Union (with one representative from each nation) and the European Parliament (with 736 elected members) help make laws.
- A Court of Justice interprets laws and resolves disputes between members.
- Citizens can move freely from one EU country to another, to live and work.
- Goods can be traded freely between member countries.

As of early 2013, 17 of the member nations had a common currency, known as the euro.

### Members of the EU*

| | | |
|---|---|---|
| Austria** | Germany** | Netherlands** |
| Belgium** | Greece** | Poland |
| Bulgaria | Hungary | Portugal** |
| Cyprus** | Ireland** | Romania |
| Czech Republic | Italy** | Slovakia** |
| Denmark | Latvia | Slovenia** |
| Estonia** | Lithuania | Spain** |
| Finland** | Luxembourg** | Sweden |
| France** | Malta** | United Kingdom |

*As of early 2013.
**These countries used the euro as of early 2013.

# THE UNITED NATIONS (UN)

The UN emblem shows the world surrounded by olive branches of peace.

The **United Nations** was founded in 1945, after World War II, to help promote peace and cooperation among nations. By 2013, there were 193 member nations. Kosovo, Taiwan, and Vatican City were not members. The UN has its headquarters in New York City.

## HOW THE UN IS ORGANIZED

- **GENERAL ASSEMBLY** **What It Does:** Discusses world problems, admits new members, appoints the secretary-general, decides the UN budget. **Members:** All UN members; each country has one vote.
- **SECURITY COUNCIL** **What It Does:** Handles questions of peace and security. **Members:** Five permanent members (China, France, the United Kingdom, Russia, and the United States) and ten members elected by the General Assembly to two-year terms. If any permanent member votes against a proposal, it is blocked.
- **ECONOMIC AND SOCIAL COUNCIL** **What It Does:** Deals with issues related to economic development, population, education, health, and human rights. **Members:** 54 member countries elected to three-year terms.
- **INTERNATIONAL COURT OF JUSTICE (WORLD COURT)** located in The Hague, Netherlands. **What It Does:** UN court for disputes between countries. **Members:** 15 judges, each from a different country, elected to nine-year terms.
- **SECRETARIAT** **What It Does:** Carries out the UN's day-to-day operations. **Members:** UN staff, headed by the secretary-general.

For more information, go to **www.un.org**

## Food for the Hungry

About 870 million people in the world do not have enough to eat. The Food and Agriculture Organization (FAO), a special agency of the UN, was founded in 1945 to help farmers grow crops efficiently. World Food Day is celebrated every year in October, to draw attention to the problem of hunger and the role of the FAO. This agency works year after year to try to make food as cheap and plentiful as possible in the developing world, and give struggling farmers a better chance to escape poverty. For example, through the FAO, farmers in Ghana recently learned to plant cassava plants (which bees love) next to their chili peppers (which bees won't eat). The bees came and spread pollen among the chili plants, which greatly increased their yield.

# MAPS SHOWING NATIONS OF THE WORLD



Maps showing the continents and nations of the world appear on pages 140-151. Flags of the nations appear on pages 152-177. A map of the United States appears on pages 288-289.

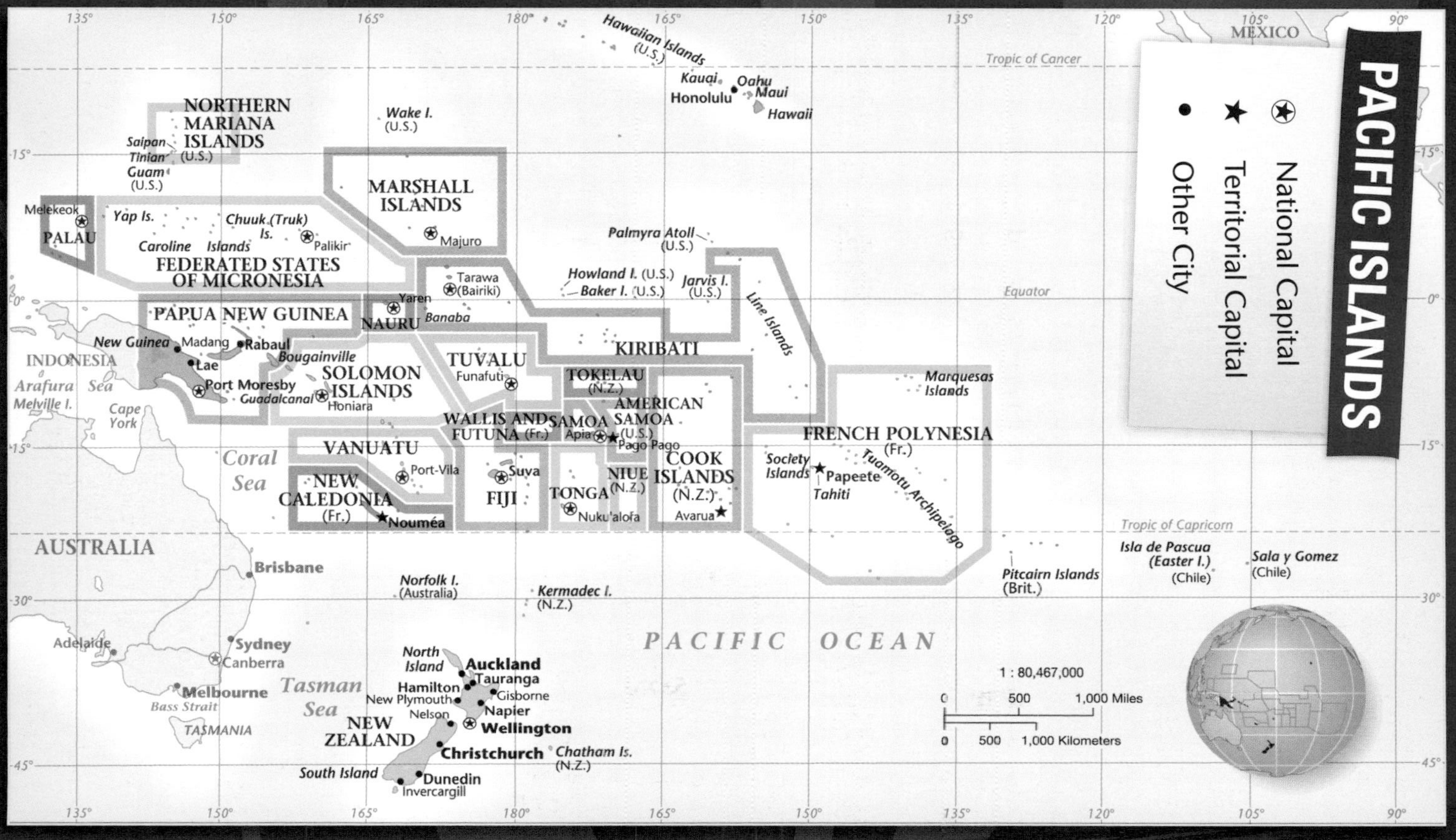
PACIFIC ISLANDS
National Capital
Territorial Capital
Other City
MEXICO
Tropic of Cancer
Equator
Tropic of Capricorn
Hawaiian Islands (U.S.)
Kauai
Oahu
Maui
Hawaii
Honolulu
Palmyra Atoll (U.S.)
Jarvis I. (U.S.)
Howland I. (U.S.)
Baker I. (U.S.)
Line Islands
Marquesas Islands
FRENCH POLYNESIA (Fr.)
Tuamotu Archipelago
Society Islands
Papeete
Tahiti
Pitcairn Islands (Brit.)
Isla de Pascua (Easter I.) (Chile)
Sala y Gomez (Chile)
KIRIBATI
TOKELAU (N.Z.)
AMERICAN SAMOA (U.S.)
Pago Pago
SAMOA
Apia
COOK ISLANDS (N.Z.)
Avarua
NIUE (N.Z.)
TONGA
Nuku'alofa
WALLIS AND FUTUNA (Fr.)
TUVALU
Funafuti
FIJI
Suva
Kermadec I. (N.Z.)
Chatham Is. (N.Z.)
MARSHALL ISLANDS
Majuro
Wake I. (U.S.)
Tarawa (Bairiki)
Banaba
NAURU
Yaren
SOLOMON ISLANDS
Honiara
Guadalcanal
Bougainville
VANUATU
Port-Vila
NEW CALEDONIA (Fr.)
Nouméa
Norfolk I. (Australia)
NORTHERN MARIANA ISLANDS (U.S.)
Saipan
Tinian
Guam (U.S.)
Yap Is.
Chuuk (Truk) Is.
Palikir
Caroline Islands
FEDERATED STATES OF MICRONESIA
PALAU
Melekeok
PAPUA NEW GUINEA
Rabaul
Madang
Lae
Port Moresby
New Guinea
INDONESIA
Arafura Sea
Melville I.
Cape York
Coral Sea
AUSTRALIA
Brisbane
Sydney
Canberra
Melbourne
Adelaide
Bass Strait
TASMANIA
Tasman Sea
NEW ZEALAND
North Island
South Island
Auckland
Hamilton
Tauranga
Gisborne
Napier
New Plymouth
Nelson
Wellington
Christchurch
Dunedin
Invercargill
PACIFIC OCEAN
1 : 80,467,000
0 500 1,000 Miles
0 500 1,000 Kilometers

RUSSIA
SWEDEN
Svalbard (Nor.)
NORWAY
North Pole
Cape Morris Jessup
Nord
Greenland Sea
Arctic Ocean
UNITED KINGDOM
Alert
Knud Rasmussen Land
Arctic Circle
Point Hope
Point Barrow
Bering Strait
GREENLAND (KALAALLIT NUNAAT) (Den.)
ICELAND
Bering Sea
Kotzebue
Barrow
Nome
Oaanaaq (Thule)
Queen Elizabeth Islands
Ellesmere I.
Grise Fiord
Baffin Bay
BROOKS RANGE
Beaufort Sea
ALASKA
Denmark Strait
Bethel
Banks I.
Resolute
Tasiilaq
Mt. McKinley 6,194 m. (20,320 ft.)
Yukon
Sachs Harbour
Arctic Bay
Pond Inlet
Fort Yukon
Fairbanks
Inuvik
Fort McPherson
Holman
Davis Strait
ALASKA RANGE
Victoria I.
Cambridge Bay
Baffin Island
Nuuk
Cape Farewell
Kenai
Anchorage
Seward
Valdez
Great Bear L.
Mackenzie
Dawson
Kodiak
Mayo
Kugluktuk
Pangnirtung
YUKON
Mt. Logan 5,959 m (19,551 ft)
Déline
Carmacks
Repulse Bay
NORTHWEST TERRITORIES
Iqaluit
Gulf of Alaska
Yakutat
Whitehorse
NUNAVUT
Southampton I.
Watson Lake
Ft. Simpson
Yellowknife
Hudson Strait
Labrador Sea
Skagway
Great Slave L.
Juneau
Sitka
Ungava Peninsula
Hebron
COAST MOUNTAINS
BRITISH COLUMBIA
Hay River
Fort Smith
CANADA
Povungnituk
Uranium City
Athabasca
Ketchikan
Hudson Bay
ALBERTA
NEWFOUNDLAND AND LABRADOR
Prince Rupert
Queen Charlotte Is.
Peace
Peace River
SASK.
Churchill
MANITOBA
Schefferville
St. Anthony
Happy Valley-Goose Bay
Belcher Is.
Kitimat
Prince George
Ft. McMurray
La Loche
York Factory
Island of Newfoundland
Labrador City
Thompson
Athabasca
Edmonton
La Ronge
QUEBEC
St. John's
Williams Lake
Jasper
Saskatchewan
Flin Flon
James Bay
Vancouver I.
Anticosti I.
Corner Brook
Prince Albert
Sept-Iles
ROCKY
GREAT
L. Winnipeg
CANADIAN
SHIELD
Mooseonee
St. Pierre & Miquelon (Fr.)
Fraser
Vancouver
Columbia
Calgary
Saskatoon
Chibougamau
RANGE
P.E.I.
Victoria
Regina
ONTARIO
Chicoutimi
NEW BRUNS.
Sydney
Seattle
Brandon
Winnipeg
St. Lawrence
WASH.
Spokane
Thunder
Saint John

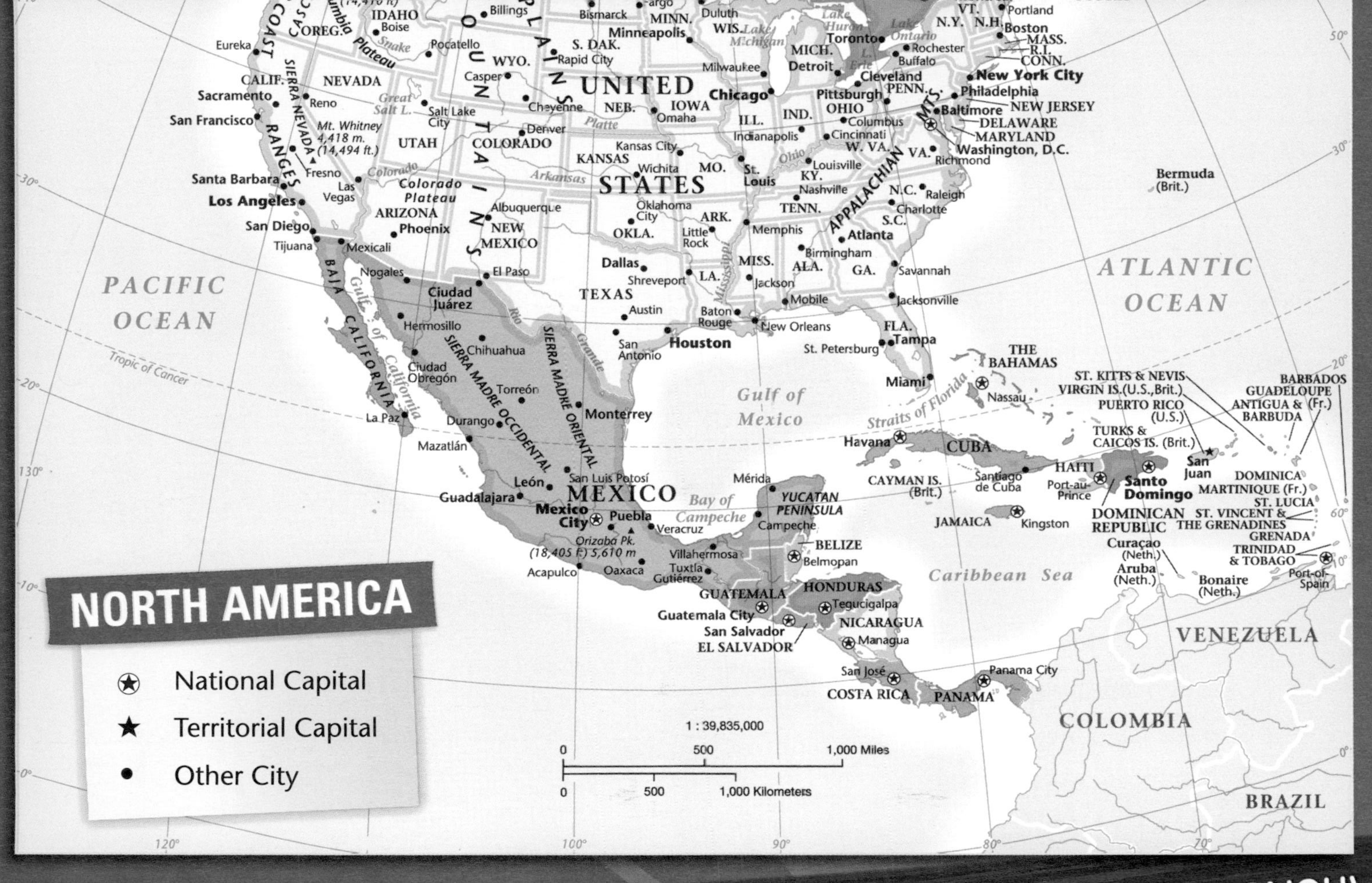
NORTH AMERICA
National Capital
Territorial Capital
Other City
1 : 39,835,000
0
500
1,000 Miles
0
500
1,000 Kilometers
PACIFIC OCEAN
ATLANTIC OCEAN
Gulf of Mexico
Caribbean Sea
Bay of Campeche
Gulf of California
Straits of Florida
Tropic of Cancer
UNITED STATES
MEXICO
CALIF.
NEVADA
IDAHO
OREG.
WYO.
UTAH
COLORADO
ARIZONA
NEW MEXICO
TEXAS
OKLA.
KANSAS
NEB.
S. DAK.
MINN.
IOWA
MO.
ARK.
LA.
MISS.
ALA.
GA.
FLA.
S.C.
N.C.
TENN.
KY.
ILL.
IND.
OHIO
MICH.
WIS.
W. VA.
VA.
PENN.
N.Y.
VT.
N.H.
MASS.
R.I.
CONN.
NEW JERSEY
DELAWARE
MARYLAND
COAST RANGES
SIERRA NEVADA
Snake Plateau
Great Salt L.
Colorado Plateau
Mt. Whitney 4,418 m. (14,494 ft.)
Platte
Arkansas
Ohio
Mississippi
Rio Grande
APPALACHIAN MTS.
Lake Michigan
Lake Huron
Lake Erie
Lake Ontario
Eureka
Sacramento
San Francisco
Reno
Fresno
Santa Barbara
Los Angeles
San Diego
Tijuana
Las Vegas
Mexicali
Boise
Pocatello
Billings
Casper
Rapid City
Bismarck
Salt Lake City
Cheyenne
Denver
Phoenix
Albuquerque
El Paso
Minneapolis
Duluth
Omaha
Kansas City
Wichita
Oklahoma City
Dallas
Shreveport
Austin
San Antonio
Houston
Little Rock
Baton Rouge
New Orleans
Jackson
Memphis
Mobile
Birmingham
Nashville
Atlanta
St. Louis
Milwaukee
Chicago
Indianapolis
Louisville
Cincinnati
Columbus
Detroit
Cleveland
Pittsburgh
Toronto
Buffalo
Rochester
Portland
Boston
New York City
Philadelphia
Baltimore
Washington, D.C.
Richmond
Raleigh
Charlotte
Savannah
Jacksonville
Tampa
St. Petersburg
Miami
Bermuda (Brit.)
BAJA CALIFORNIA
SIERRA MADRE OCCIDENTAL
SIERRA MADRE ORIENTAL
Nogales
Ciudad Juárez
Hermosillo
Chihuahua
Ciudad Obregón
Torreón
La Paz
Durango
Mazatlán
Monterrey
San Luis Potosí
León
Guadalajara
Mexico City
Puebla
Veracruz
Orizaba Pk. (18,405 ft.) 5,610 m
Acapulco
Oaxaca
Villahermosa
Tuxtla Gutiérrez
Mérida
YUCATAN PENINSULA
Campeche
BELIZE
Belmopan
GUATEMALA
Guatemala City
San Salvador
EL SALVADOR
HONDURAS
Tegucigalpa
NICARAGUA
Managua
San José
COSTA RICA
PANAMA
Panama City
THE BAHAMAS
Nassau
CUBA
Havana
Santiago de Cuba
CAYMAN IS. (Brit.)
JAMAICA
Kingston
HAITI
Port-au-Prince
Santo Domingo
DOMINICAN REPUBLIC
TURKS & CAICOS IS. (Brit.)
PUERTO RICO (U.S.)
San Juan
VIRGIN IS.(U.S.,Brit.)
ST. KITTS & NEVIS
BARBADOS
GUADELOUPE (Fr.)
ANTIGUA & BARBUDA
DOMINICA
MARTINIQUE (Fr.)
ST. LUCIA
ST. VINCENT & THE GRENADINES
GRENADA
TRINIDAD & TOBAGO
Port-of-Spain
Curaçao (Neth.)
Aruba (Neth.)
Bonaire (Neth.)
VENEZUELA
COLOMBIA
BRAZIL

SOUTH AMERICA
National Capital
Territorial Capital
Other City
CARIBBEAN SEA
PACIFIC OCEAN
Equator
TRINIDAD AND TOBAGO
PANAMA
COLOMBIA
VENEZUELA
GUYANA
SURINAME
FRENCH GUIANA (Fr.)
ECUADOR
PERU
BOLIVIA
BRAZIL
PARAGUAY
ANDES MTS.
LLANOS
GUIANA HIGHLANDS
AMAZON BASIN
SELVAS
MATO GROSSO PLATEAU
BRAZILIAN HIGHLANDS
ALTIPLANO
CHACO
DESERT
Panama City
Santa Marta
Barranquilla
Cartagena
Sincelejo
Montería
Medellín
Barrancabermeja
Bucaramanga
Cúcuta
Valledupar
Maracaibo
Cabimas
Coro
Valencia
Barquisimeto
Maracay
Caracas
Cumaná
Maturín
El Tigre
Ciudad Guayana
Ciudad Bolívar
San Fernando de Apure
Puerto Ayacucho
Valera
Mérida
L. Maracaibo
San Cristóbal
Tunja
Bogotá
Villavicencio
Neiva
Manizales
Pereira
Armenia
Ibagué
Palmira
Cali
Buenaventura
Popayán
Pasto
Esmeraldas
Quito
Ambato
Chimborazo 6,310 m. (20,702 ft.)
Cuenca
Portoviejo
Guayaquil
Machala
Tumbes
Talara
Sullana
Piura
Chiclayo
Cajamarca
Trujillo
Chimbote
Yurimaguas
Iquitos
Mt. Huascarán 6,768 m. (22,205 ft.)
Huánuco
Cerro de Pasco
Pucallpa
Huancayo
Callao
Lima
Ica
Ayacucho
Cusco
Puerto Maldonado
Juliaca
Puno
Arequipa
Tacna
Arica
Iquique
Calama
L. Titicaca
L. Poopó
La Paz
Oruro
Cochabamba
Sucre
Potosí
Tarija
Santa Cruz
Trinidad
Riberalta
Cobija
Guajará-Mirim
Porto Velho
Rio Branco
Cruzeiro do Sul
Benjamin Constant
Manaus
Boa Vista
Georgetown
New Amsterdam
Paramaribo
Kourou
Cayenne
Macapá
Santarém
Marajó I.
Belém
São Luís
Parnaíba
Teresina
Fortaleza
Natal
João Pessoa
Recife
Campina Grande
Maceió
Aracaju
Juàzeiro do Norte
Salvador
Feira de Santana
Ilhéus
Itabuna
Vitória da Conquista
Montes Claros
Governador Valadares
Vitória
Belo Horizonte
Juiz de Fora
Imperatriz
Gurupi
Brasília
Anápolis
Goiânia
Uberlândia
Ribeirão Prêto
São José do Rio Prêto
Cuiabá
Corumbá
Campo Grande
Magdalena R.
Orinoco R.
Negro R.
Amazon R.
Putumayo R.
Ucayali R.
Marañón R.
Juruá R.
Purus R.
Madeira R.
Mamoré R.
Beni R.
Guaporé R.
Tapajós R.
Xingu R.
Araguaia R.
Tocantins R.
Parnaíba R.
São Francisco R.
Paraguay R.

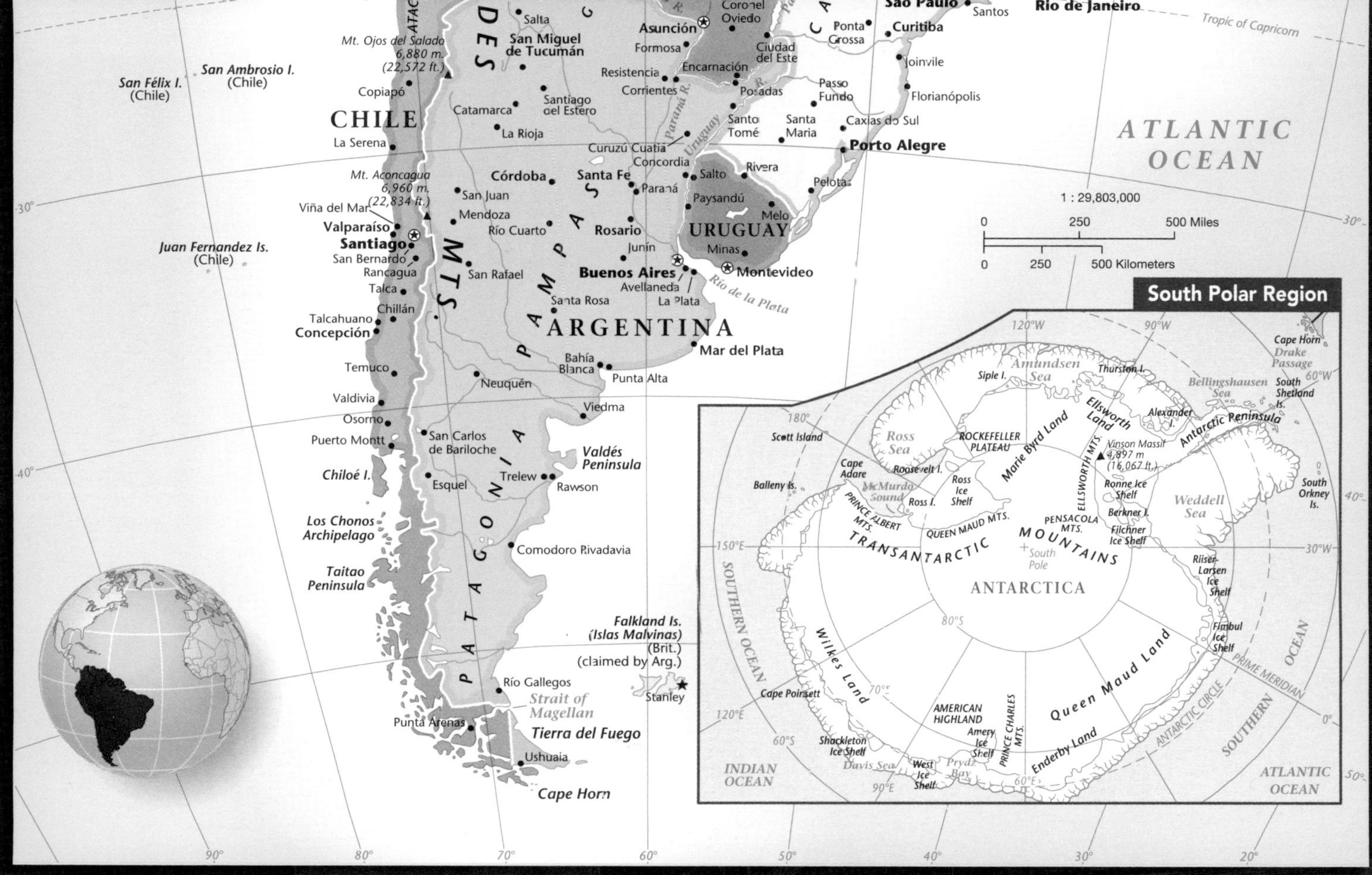
CHILE
ARGENTINA
URUGUAY
ATLANTIC OCEAN
ANDES MTS.
PAMPAS
PATAGONIA
Tropic of Capricorn
Mt. Ojos del Salado 6,880 m. (22,572 ft.)
Mt. Aconcagua 6,960 m. (22,834 ft.)
San Félix I. (Chile)
San Ambrosio I. (Chile)
Juan Fernandez Is. (Chile)
Copiapó
La Serena
Viña del Mar
Valparaíso
Santiago
San Bernardo
Rancagua
Talca
Chillán
Talcahuano
Concepción
Temuco
Valdivia
Osorno
Puerto Montt
Chiloé I.
Los Chonos Archipelago
Taitao Peninsula
Salta
San Miguel de Tucumán
Catamarca
Santiago del Estero
La Rioja
Córdoba
San Juan
Mendoza
Río Cuarto
San Rafael
Santa Fe
Paraná
Rosario
Junín
Buenos Aires
Avellaneda
La Plata
Santa Rosa
Mar del Plata
Bahía Blanca
Punta Alta
Neuquén
Viedma
San Carlos de Bariloche
Esquel
Trelew
Rawson
Valdés Peninsula
Comodoro Rivadavia
Río Gallegos
Strait of Magellan
Punta Arenas
Tierra del Fuego
Ushuaia
Cape Horn
Falkland Is. (Islas Malvinas) (Brit.) (claimed by Arg.)
Stanley
Asunción
Coronel Oviedo
Formosa
Resistencia
Corrientes
Encarnación
Ciudad del Este
Posadas
Paraná R.
Uruguay R.
Santo Tomé
Curuzú Cuatiá
Concordia
Salto
Paysandú
Rivera
Melo
Minas
Montevideo
Río de la Plata
Santa Maria
Passo Fundo
Caxias do Sul
Porto Alegre
Pelotas
Ponta Grossa
Curitiba
Joinvile
Florianópolis
São Paulo
Santos
Rio de Janeiro
1 : 29,803,000
0 250 500 Miles
0 250 500 Kilometers
30°
40°
50°
60°
70°
80°
90°
20°
South Polar Region
ANTARCTICA
TRANSANTARCTIC MOUNTAINS
South Pole
Cape Horn
Drake Passage
South Shetland Is.
South Orkney Is.
Antarctic Peninsula
Bellingshausen Sea
Alexander I.
Thurston I.
Amundsen Sea
Siple I.
Ellsworth Land
Vinson Massif 4,897 m (16,067 ft.)
ELLSWORTH MTS.
Marie Byrd Land
ROCKEFELLER PLATEAU
Ross Sea
Ross Ice Shelf
Roosevelt I.
Ross I.
McMurdo Sound
Cape Adare
Scott Island
Balleny Is.
PRINCE ALBERT MTS.
QUEEN MAUD MTS.
PENSACOLA MTS.
Ronne Ice Shelf
Berkner I.
Filchner Ice Shelf
Weddell Sea
Riiser-Larsen Ice Shelf
Fimbul Ice Shelf
Queen Maud Land
Enderby Land
PRINCE CHARLES MTS.
AMERICAN HIGHLAND
Amery Ice Shelf
Prydz Bay
West Ice Shelf
Davis Sea
Shackleton Ice Shelf
Cape Poinsett
Wilkes Land
SOUTHERN OCEAN
INDIAN OCEAN
ATLANTIC OCEAN
ANTARCTIC CIRCLE
PRIME MERIDIAN
120°W
90°W
60°W
30°W
0°
180°
150°E
120°E
90°E
60°E
80°S
70°S
60°S

EUROPE
National Capital
Other City
1 : 22,667,000
0
250
500 Miles
0
250
500 Kilometers
Arctic Circle
Reykjavík
Akureyri
ICELAND
Tromsø
Kiruna
Bodø
Norwegian Sea
Faroe Is. (Den.)
Shetland Is. (Brit.)
Orkney Is.
Hebrides
Trondheim
Sundsvall
NORWAY
SWEDEN
Bergen
Oslo
Stavanger
Uppsala
Stockholm
Linköping
Gotland
Öland
Skagerrak
Kattegat
Göteborg
Aberdeen
Glasgow
Edinburgh
Belfast
UNITED KINGDOM (GREAT BRITAIN)
Newcastle
Dublin
IRELAND
Irish Sea
Liverpool
Leeds
Cork
Manchester
Sheffield
North Sea
Jutland
Århus
Copenhagen
Helsingborg
Malmö
DENMARK
Odense
Baltic
Birmingham
Cardiff
Bristol
NETHERLANDS
Amsterdam
The Hague
Rotterdam
London
Portsmouth
Land's End
Antwerp
Hamburg
Bremen
Elbe
Hannover
Gdańsk
Szczecin
Vistula
Berlin
Poznań
ATLANTIC OCEAN
English Channel
Channel Is. (Brit.)
Brussels
Lille
BELGIUM
Liège
Essen
Cologne
Bonn
GERMANY
Leipzig
Dresden
Oder
Łódź
Wrocław
Le Havre
Brest
Rouen
LUXEMBOURG
Luxembourg
Frankfurt
Prague
Katowice
Paris
Mannheim
CZECH REP.
Brno
Ostrava
Nantes
Loire
Strasbourg
Rhine
Stuttgart
Danube
SLOVAKIA
Bay of Biscay
FRANCE
Dijon
Munich
Linz
Vienna
Bratislava
Bern
Zürich
LIECHTENSTEIN
AUSTRIA
Budapest
Cape Finisterre
Geneva
SWITZERLAND
Graz
HUNGARY
Gijón
Bordeaux
Lyon
ALPS
Mt. Blanc 4807 m (15,771 ft)
Milan
SLOVENIA
Ljubljana
Pécs
Vigo
Bilbao
Turin
Verona
Zagreb
Porto
Ebro
Toulouse
Rhône
Genoa
Venice
Bologna
DINARIC
Valladolid
PYRENEES
Marseille
Nice
Po
APENNINES
CROATIA
BOSNIA & HERZEGOVINA
SAN MARINO
Florence
MONACO
Sarajevo
PORTUGAL
IBERIAN
Pico de Aneto 3404 m (11,168 ft)
Zaragoza
Toulon
Ligurian Sea
Adriatic
ALPS
Lisbon
Madrid
ANDORRA
Split
MONTENEGRO
Tagus
Barcelona
Corsica (Fr.)
Elba
Dubrovnik
Badajoz
PENINSULA
Podgorica
Valencia
Balearic Sea
VATICAN CITY
Rome
Sea
SPAIN
Majorca
ITALY
Córdoba
Palma
Minorca
Bari
Cape St. Vincent
Sevilla
Alicante
Balearic Is. (Sp.)
Sardinia (It.)
Naples
Salerno
Cádiz
Granada
Málaga
Tyrrhenian Sea
Cagliari
Corfu
Strait of Gibraltar
GIBRALTAR (Brit.)
Mediterranean
Ionian Sea
Palermo
Rabat
Algiers
Catania
Mt. Etna 3323 m (10,902 ft)
Casablanca
Tunis
Sicily
MOUNTAINS
MOROCCO
ATLAS
ALGERIA
TUNISIA
Valletta
MALTA
Sea

North Cape
Barents Sea
Nar'yan-Mar
Pechora
Murmansk
KOLA PENINSULA
Apatity
Arctic Circle
White Sea
Ukhta
URAL MOUNTAINS
Ob
Irtysh
Arkhangel'sk
RUSSIA
Serov
Oulu
Belomorsk
Syktyvkar
Divina
Bereznki
Petropavl
FINLAND
Kotlas
Yekaterinburg
Lake Onega
Perm'
Petrozavodsk
Kirov
Chelyabinsk
PLAIN
Tampere
Lahti
Lake Ladoga
Izhevsk
Kama
Qostanay
Helsinki
Vologda
Ufa
St. Petersburg
Gulf of Finland
Cherepovets
Naberezhnyye Chelny
Magnitogorsk
Tallinn
Kazan
ESTONIA
Velikiy Novgorod
Yaroslavl'
Nizhniy Novgorod
Tartu
Ivanovo
Pskov
EUROPEAN
Ul'yanovsk
Tol'yatti
Orenburg
Orsk
LATVIA
Tver'
Saransk
Samara
Moscow
Daugavpils
Ryazan'
Penza
Aktobe
Vitsyebsk
Smolensk
Tula
Oral
Vilnius
Tambov
Volga
Mahilyow
Lipetsk
Saratov
Ural
KAZAKHSTAN
Minsk
Hrodna
Bryansk
Voronezh
Aral Sea
BELARUS
Homyel'
Kursk
Brest
Atyraū
Volgograd
Kharkiv
Kyiv
UZBEKISTAN
Luhans'k
UKRAINE
Dnieper
Donets'k
Astrakhan'
L'viv
Don
Dniester
Dnipropetrovs'k
Zaporizhzhia
Rostov na Donu
Aktaū
Chernivtsi
MOLDOVA
Kryvyy Rih
Mariupol'
Caspian Sea
MTS.
Mykolaiv
Sea of Azov
Stavropol'
Chişinău
Makhachkala
Iaşi
Groznyy
ROMANIA
Odesa
CRIMEA
Krasnodar
Mt. Elbrus 5642 m (18,510 ft)
TURKMENISTAN
CAUCASUS
Simferopol'
Sevastopol'
GEORGIA
Türkmenbashy
Ploieşti
Bucharest
Constanţa
Tbilisi
Baku
Black Sea
AZERBAIJAN
Danube
ARMENIA
Varna
BULGARIA
Yerevan
Sofia
Burgas
Trabzon
Plovdiv
Skopje
Tabriz
Tehran
İstanbul
Thessaloniki
Ankara
TURKEY
IRAN
Larisa
Aegean Sea
İzmir
Athens
Adana
Tigris
Cyclades
Baghdad
SYRIA
Rhodes
Euphrates
Sea of Crete
Nicosia
IRAQ
LEBANON
Crete
Iraklion
CYPRUS
Beirut
Damascus
Persian Gulf

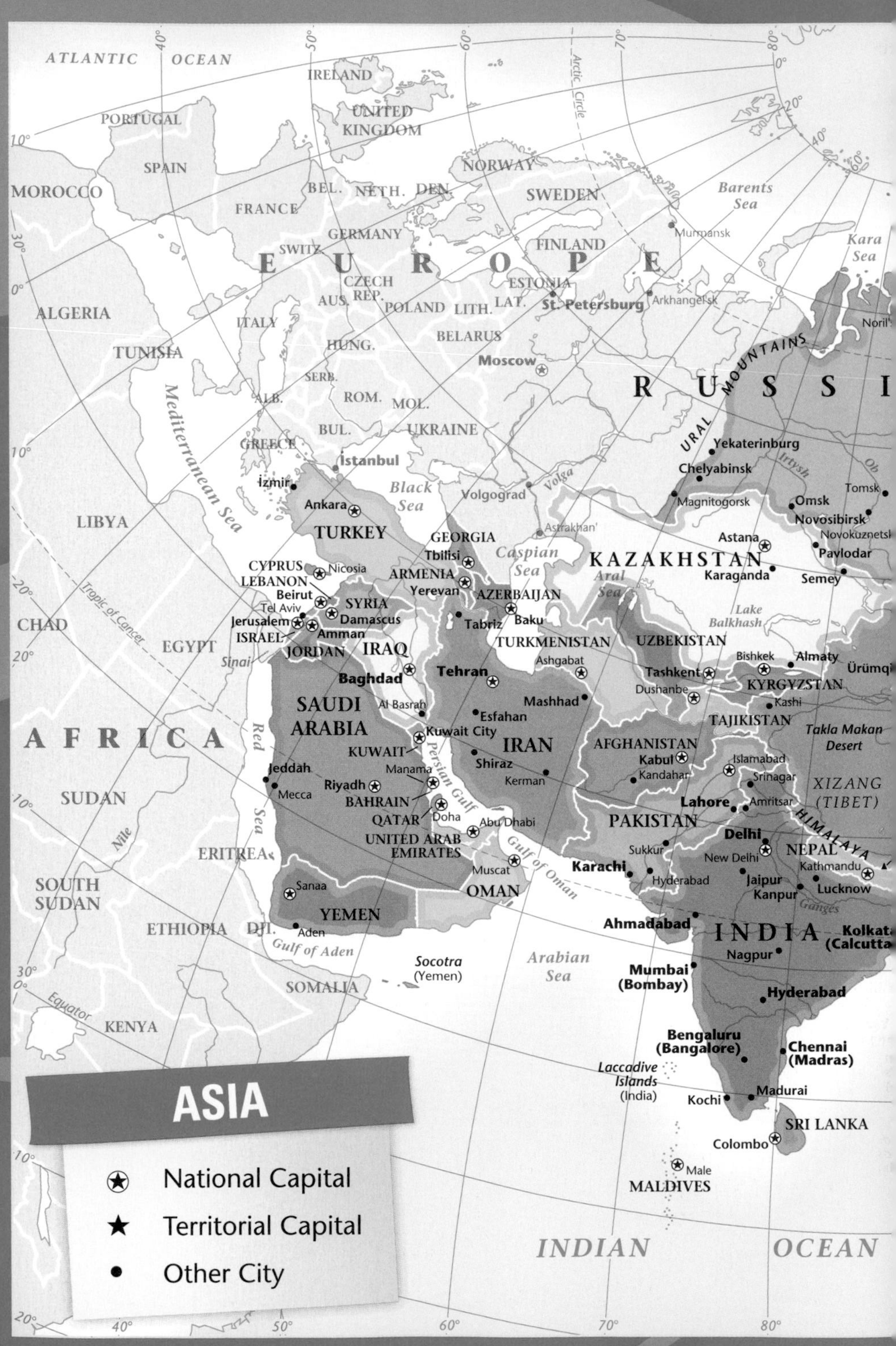
ASIA
National Capital
Territorial Capital
Other City
ATLANTIC OCEAN
IRELAND
UNITED KINGDOM
PORTUGAL
SPAIN
MOROCCO
FRANCE
BEL.
NETH.
DEN.
NORWAY
SWEDEN
Barents Sea
Kara Sea
Murmansk
GERMANY
SWITZ.
FINLAND
E U R O P E
CZECH REP.
AUS.
ESTONIA
ALGERIA
POLAND
LITH.
LAT.
St. Petersburg
Arkhangelsk
ITALY
BELARUS
Noril'sk
TUNISIA
HUNG.
Moscow
URAL MOUNTAINS
SERB.
R U S S I
ALB.
ROM.
MOL.
BUL.
UKRAINE
Mediterranean Sea
GREECE
İstanbul
Yekaterinburg
Chelyabinsk
Irtysh
Ob
İzmir
Black Sea
Volgograd
Volga
Tomsk
Ankara
Magnitogorsk
Omsk
Novosibirsk
LIBYA
TURKEY
Astrakhan'
Novokuznetsk
GEORGIA
Astana
Pavlodar
CYPRUS
Nicosia
Tbilisi
Caspian Sea
KAZAKHSTAN
Aral Sea
Karaganda
Semey
LEBANON
ARMENIA
Yerevan
Beirut
SYRIA
AZERBAIJAN
Tel Aviv
Damascus
Baku
Lake Balkhash
CHAD
Jerusalem
Amman
Tabriz
ISRAEL
EGYPT
TURKMENISTAN
UZBEKISTAN
JORDAN
IRAQ
Ashgabat
Bishkek
Almaty
Ürümqi
Sinai
Tashkent
Baghdad
Tehran
KYRGYZSTAN
Dushanbe
SAUDI ARABIA
Mashhad
Kashi
Al Basrah
Esfahan
TAJIKISTAN
Takla Makan Desert
A F R I C A
Red Sea
Kuwait City
IRAN
AFGHANISTAN
KUWAIT
Shiraz
Kabul
Islamabad
Jeddah
Manama
Kerman
Kandahar
Srinagar
XIZANG (TIBET)
Mecca
Riyadh
Persian Gulf
SUDAN
BAHRAIN
Lahore
Amritsar
QATAR
Doha
PAKISTAN
HIMALAYA
Abu Dhabi
Nile
UNITED ARAB EMIRATES
Delhi
ERITREA
Sukkur
New Delhi
NEPAL
Gulf of Oman
Muscat
Karachi
Kathmandu
SOUTH SUDAN
Sanaa
Hyderabad
Jaipur
Lucknow
OMAN
Kanpur
Ganges
ETHIOPIA
DJI.
YEMEN
Ahmadabad
Aden
I N D I A
Kolkata (Calcutta)
Gulf of Aden
Socotra (Yemen)
Arabian Sea
Nagpur
SOMALIA
Mumbai (Bombay)
Hyderabad
Equator
KENYA
Bengaluru (Bangalore)
Chennai (Madras)
Laccadive Islands (India)
Madurai
Kochi
SRI LANKA
Colombo
Male
MALDIVES
INDIAN OCEAN
Tropic of Cancer
Arctic Circle
40°
50°
60°
70°
80°
10°
20°
30°
0°

Chukchi Sea
Bering Sea
East Siberian Sea
ALASKA
Anadyr
Laptev Sea
KAMCHATKA PENINSULA
Magadan
Petropavlovsk-Kamchatskiy
Sea of Okhotsk
Yakutsk
Sakhalin
Kuril Islands (Russia)
SIBERIA
Komsomolsk na Amure
Khabarovsk
Bratsk
Blagoveshchensk
Lake Baikal
Chita
Sapporo
Irkutsk
Ulan-Ude
Harbin
JAPAN
Vladivostok
Sea of Japan (East Sea)
Sendai
Ulaanbaatar
Changchun
Tokyo
Shenyang
Yokohama
MONGOLIA
N. KOREA
Pyongyang
Kyoto
Kobe
Osaka
GOBI DESERT
Beijing
Seoul
Dalian
Hohhot
Tianjin
Sejong City
S. KOREA
Hiroshima
PACIFIC OCEAN
Jinan
Qingdao
Nagasaki
Taiyuan
Yellow Sea
Zhengzhou
Lanzhou
Shanghai
CHINA
Xi'an
Nanjing
East China Sea
Wuhan
Ryukyu Islands
Okinawa (Japan)
Chengdu
Wenzhou
Chongqing
Changsha
Fuzhou
Lhasa
Xiamen
Taipei
TAIWAN
Guangzhou
Hong Kong
Philippine Sea
Kunming
Nanning
Macao
Hanoi
Gulf of Tonkin
LUZON
Mandalay
LAOS
Nay Pyi Taw
Vientiane
Mekong
MYANMAR (BURMA)
Manila
PHILIPPINES
Da Nang
THAILAND
South China Sea
Yangon (Rangoon)
VIETNAM
Cebu
MINDANAO
CAMBODIA
Bangkok
Sulu Sea
Davao
Phnom Penh
Ho Chi Minh City
Andaman Sea
Gulf of Thailand
Kota Kinabalu
Bandar Seri Begawan
Celebes Sea
NEW GUINEA
BRUNEI
Manado
Kuala Lumpur
MALAYSIA
Medan
Putrajaya
Kuching
BORNEO
SINGAPORE
Singapore
INDONESIA
Banda Sea
Arafura Sea
SUMATRA
Banjarmasin
Makassar
Timor Sea
Padang
Palembang
Java Sea
Dili
TIMOR-LESTE
Jakarta
Surabaya
Kupang
Bandung
JAVA
AUSTRALIA
1 : 51,914,000
0
500
1,000 Miles
0
500
1,000 Kilometers

ATLANTIC OCEAN
AZORES (Port.)
MADEIRA (Port.)
CANARY IS. (Sp.)
Las Palmas
WESTERN SAHARA (occ. by Morocco)
Laayoune
Nouadhibou
MOROCCO
Marrakech
Safi
Casablanca
Rabat
Tangier
Fez
ATLAS MOUNTAINS
PORTUGAL
Lisbon
SPAIN
Madrid
FRANCE
Paris
SWITZ.
GERMANY
CZECH REP.
AUSTRIA
SLOVE.
CRO.
ITALY
Rome
BOS. & HER.
MONT.
SERB.
KOS.
MAC.
ALBANIA
GREECE
Athens
SLOVAKIA
HUNGARY
ROMANIA
Bucharest
BULGARIA
MOLDOVA
UKRAINE
RUSSIA
KAZAKHSTAN
Aral Sea
UZBEKISTAN
TURKMENISTAN
Caspian Sea
AZERBAIJAN
GEORGIA
ARMENIA
Black Sea
İstanbul
Ankara
TURKEY
CYPRUS
LEBANON
ISRAEL
SYRIA
Damascus
Jerusalem
JORDAN
IRAQ
Baghdad
IRAN
Tehran
KUWAIT
Persian Gulf
BAHRAIN
QATAR
Tropic of Cancer
SAUDI ARABIA
Riyadh
OMAN
YEMEN
Sanaa
Gulf of Aden
DJIBOUTI
Djibouti
Berbera
Hargeysa
SOMALIA
ALGERIA
Oran
Algiers
Constantine
Annaba
Oujda
Béchar
Ghardaia
I-n-Salah
Tamanrasset
AHAGGAR MTS.
TUNISIA
Bizerte
Tunis
Sfax
MALTA
Mediterranean Sea
Gulf of Sidra
Tripoli
Misratah
Benghazi
al-Bayda
Tobruk
LIBYA
al-Jawf
LIBYAN DESERT
EGYPT
Alexandria
Port Said
Cairo
Suez Canal
Siwa
Luxor
Aswan
L. Nasser
NUBIAN DESERT
Red Sea
Port Sudan
Atbara
Nile
SUDAN
Omdurman
Khartoum
Kassala
Wad Medani
Blue Nile
El Obeid
El Fasher
ERITREA
Asmara
Assab
Gonder
L. Tana
ETHIOPIAN HIGHLANDS
Addis Ababa
Jima
Harer
GREAT RIFT VALLEY
ETHIOPIA
Kelafo
L. Turkana
SOUTH SUDAN
Malakal
Juba
Wau
White Nile
CHAD
TIBESTI
Faya-Largeau
Abéché
N'Djamena
L. Chad
Sarh
CENTRAL AFRICAN REPUBLIC
Bangui
Bouar
Ubangi
NIGER
AIR
Agadez
Zinder
Niamey
SAHARA
SAHEL
MALI
Timbuktu
Niger
Ségou
Bamako
MAURITANIA
Nouakchott
Senegal
SENEGAL
Dakar
Kaolack
THE GAMBIA
Banjul
GUINEA-BISSAU
Bissau
GUINEA
Labe
Kankan
Kayes
Conakry
SIERRA LEONE
Freetown
LIBERIA
Monrovia
CÔTE D'IVOIRE
Bouake
Yamoussoukro
Abidjan
BURKINA FASO
Ouagadougou
Bobo-Dioulasso
GHANA
Kumasi
Accra
Sekondi-Takoradi
TOGO
Lomé
BENIN
Cotonou
Porto-Novo
NIGERIA
Sokoto
Zaria
Kano
Maiduguri
Abuja
Ogbomosho
Ibadan
Lagos
Enugu
Onitsha
Port Harcourt
Benue
CAMEROON
Garoua
Maroua
Yaoundé
Douala
Malabo

AFRICA
National Capital
Other City
1 : 39,580,000
0
500
1,000 Miles
0
500
1,000 Kilometers
ATLANTIC OCEAN
INDIAN OCEAN
ASCENSION (Brit.)
ST. HELENA (Brit.)
SAO TOME AND PRINCIPE
São Tomé
Libreville
GABON
Port-Gentil
Franceville
REP. OF THE CONGO
Brazzaville
Pointe-Noire
Cabinda (Ang.)
Kinshasa
Mbandaka
DEMOCRATIC REPUBLIC OF THE CONGO
Kisangani
Kikwit
Tshikapa
Kananga
Mbuji-Mayi
Matadi
KATANGA
PLATEAU
Kolwezi
Likasi
Lubumbashi
Kasai
Congo
RWANDA
Kigali
Bukavu
Bujumbura
BURUNDI
GREAT RIFT VALLEY
Kampala
Kisumu
KENYA
Nakuru
Nairobi
Kilimanjaro
5895 m (19,340 ft)
Mwanza
SERENGETI PLAIN
Arusha
Mombasa
Kismaayo
L. Victoria
L. Tanganyika
L. Mweru
L. Nyasa
L. Kariba
Tabora
Dodoma
Tanga
Zanzibar
TANZANIA
Dar es Salaam
Mbeya
Mtwara
COMOROS
Moroni
Antsiranana
Luanda
Malanje
ANGOLA
Lobito
Benguela
Huambo
Namibe
Menongue
Cuene
MALAWI
Lilongwe
Kitwe
Ndola
Chipata
ZAMBIA
Kabwe
Lusaka
Zambezi
Blantyre
Livingstone
Nacala-Porto
Nampula
MOZAMBIQUE
Mozambique Channel
MADAGASCAR
Toamasina
Antananarivo
Fianarantsoa
Toliara
Quelimane
Harare
Mutare
ZIMBABWE
Bulawayo
Beira
Grootfontein
NAMIBIA
NAMIB DESERT
Walvis Bay
Windhoek
Francistown
BOTSWANA
KALAHARI DESERT
Gaborone
Limpopo
Inhambane
Tropic of Capricorn
Equator
Pretoria
Maputo
Johannesburg
Mbabane
SWAZILAND
Klerksdorp
Newcastle
Kimberley
LESOTHO
Pietermaritzburg
Bloemfontein
Maseru
Durban
Lüderitz
Orange
SOUTH AFRICA
Cape Town
Cape of Good Hope
Cape Agulhas
East London
Port Elizabeth
0°
10°
20°
30°
40°
50°
60°

# FACTS ABOUT NATIONS

**Here are basic facts about the world's independent nations. The color of the heading for each country tells you what continent it belongs in. The population is an estimate for 2013. The area includes both land and inland water. The language entry gives official languages and other common languages.**

## Afghanistan

**Capital:** Kabul

**Population:** 31,108,077

**Area:** 250,001 sq mi (647,500 sq km)

**Language:** Afghan Persian (Dari), Pashtu

**Did You Know?** Afghanistan has both high mountains and desert valleys. Summer temperatures in some areas may hit 120°F. Winter temperatures in the mountains can fall to –15°F.

## Albania

**Capital:** Tirana

**Population:** 3,011,405

**Area:** 11,100 sq mi (28,748 sq km)

**Language:** Albanian, Greek

**Did You Know?** In Albania, when you agree to something out loud and seal the agreement with a handshake or a hug, it is considered more binding than any written contract.

## Algeria

**Capital:** Algiers (El Djazair)

**Population:** 38,087,812

**Area:** 919,595 sq mi (2,381,740 sq km)

**Language:** Arabic, French, Berber dialects

**Did You Know?** Turkey ruled Algeria for more than 300 years, until France took control in 1830. But the Algerian people revolted against French rule and won independence in the early 1960s.

## Andorra

**Capital:** Andorra la Vella

**Population:** 85,293

**Area:** 181 sq mi (468 sq km)

**Language:** Catalan, French, Castilian

**Did You Know?** Tiny Andorra lies in the mountains between France and Spain. Visitors from around the world go there to enjoy outdoor activities.

## Angola

**Capital:** Luanda

**Population:** 18,565,269

**Area:** 481,354 sq mi (1,246,700 sq km)

**Language:** Portuguese, African languages

**Did You Know?** Luanda was first settled by Portuguese colonists back in 1576. Every year on January 25, people celebrate its founding with traditional food, music, and dancing.

## Antigua and Barbuda

**Capital:** St. John's

**Population:** 90,156

**Area:** 171 sq mi (443 sq km)

**Language:** English

**Did You Know?** Snorkelers in the waters off Antigua may brush up against a wide range of marine life, from colorful reef fish to moray eels, sea turtles, barracudas, and the occasional nurse shark.

**COLOR KEY**

- Africa
- Asia
- Australia
- Europe
- North America
- Pacific Islands
- South America

ENGLISH HARBOUR, ANTIGUA

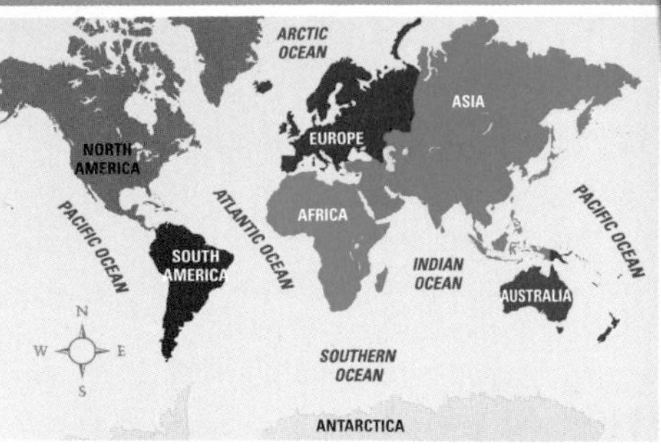


## Argentina

**Capital:** Buenos Aires

**Population:** 42,610,981

**Area:** 1,068,302 sq mi (2,766,890 sq km)

**Language:** Spanish, English, Italian, German, French

**Did You Know?** Mount Aconcagua, in western Argentina, is 22,831 feet high, making it the tallest mountain in the western hemisphere. Every year, thousands of people brave the cold, wind, and altitude to climb to the summit.

## Armenia

**Capital:** Yerevan

**Population:** 2,974,184

**Area:** 11,484 sq mi (29,743 sq km)

**Language:** Armenian, Russian

**Did You Know?** On September 21, 1991, Armenians voted overwhelmingly to drop out of what was then the Soviet Union. This day is now known in Armenia as Independence Day. It is celebrated each year with parades and other festive events.

## Australia

**Capital:** Canberra

**Population:** 22,262,501

**Area:** 2,967,909 sq mi (7,686,850 sq km)

**Language:** English, Aboriginal languages

**Did You Know?** Uluru, or Ayers Rock, in central Australia, is the biggest monolith, or single rock, in the world. It is over 2 miles long and about 1.5 miles wide.

ULURU (AYERS ROCK), AUSTRALIA

## Austria

**Capital:** Vienna

**Population:** 8,221,646

**Area:** 32,382 sq mi (83,870 sq km)

**Language:** German, Slovene, Croatian, Hungarian

**Did You Know?** Austria is one of the few countries where people can vote when they reach the age of 16.

## Azerbaijan

**Capital:** Baku

**Population:** 9,590,159

**Area:** 33,436 sq mi (86,600 sq km)

**Language:** Azeri, Russian, Armenian

**Did You Know?** Former world chess champion Garry Kasparov was born and raised in the city of Baku, where he first learned to play the game.

## The Bahamas

**Capital:** Nassau

**Population:** 319,031

**Area:** 5,382 sq mi (13,940 sq km)

**Language:** English, Creole

**Did You Know?** There are about 700 islands in the Bahamas, but only 30 of these have people living on them.

## Bahrain

**Capital:** Manama

**Population:** 1,281,332

**Area:** 257 sq mi (665 sq km)

**Language:** Arabic, English, Farsi, Urdu

**Did You Know?** Most of the people in this small island kingdom in the Persian Gulf are Shiite Muslims. However, Sunni Muslims have most of the power in the government.

## Bangladesh

**Capital:** Dhaka
**Population:** 163,654,860
**Area:** 55,599 sq mi (144,000 sq km)
**Language:** Bangla, English
**Did You Know?** Look out below! The heaviest hailstone ever measured fell in south-central Bangladesh on April 14, 1986. It weighed 2.25 pounds.

## Barbados

**Capital:** Bridgetown
**Population:** 288,725
**Area:** 166 sq mi (431 sq km)
**Language:** English
**Did You Know?** The so-called green monkeys of Barbados arrived on the islands about 350 years ago from West Africa. Their fur looks greenish in certain light.

GREEN MONKEYS OF BARBADOS

## Belarus

**Capital:** Minsk
**Population:** 9,625,888
**Area:** 80,155 sq mi (207,600 sq km)
**Language:** Belarusian, Russian
**Did You Know?** The Pripyat, or Pripet, Marshes, in Belarus and Ukraine, is a vast wetlands region. Elk, lynx, wolves, foxes, and beavers live there, along with many kinds of birds.

## Belgium

**Capital:** Brussels
**Population:** 10,444,268
**Area:** 11,787 sq mi (30,528 sq km)
**Language:** Dutch, French, German
**Did You Know?** *Speculoos,* a cookie made with mild spices and brown sugar, is a popular treat in Belgium. It was originally baked for children to eat on St. Nicholas Day, December 6. Today, people of all ages enjoy it year-round.

## Belize

**Capital:** Belmopan
**Population:** 334,297
**Area:** 8,867 sq mi (22,966 sq km)
**Language:** English, Spanish, Mayan, Garifuna, Creole
**Did You Know?** Belize—a neighbor of Mexico and Guatemala—was a British colony before it became independent in 1981.

## Benin

**Capital:** Porto-Novo (constit.); Cotonou (admin.)
**Population:** 9,877,292
**Area:** 43,483 sq mi (112,620 sq km)
**Language:** French, Fon, Yoruba
**Did You Know?** The people of Benin have their own version of French fries: fried yams. They even celebrate a yam festival every year, in mid-August.

## Bhutan

**Capital:** Thimphu
**Population:** 725,296
**Area:** 18,147 sq mi (47,000 sq km)
**Language:** Dzongkha, Tibetan dialects
**Did You Know?** More than 90 percent of the working people in Bhutan are involved in farming.

## Bolivia

**Capital:** La Paz (admin.); Sucre (legislative/judicial)
**Population:** 10,461,053
**Area:** 424,164 sq mi (1,098,580 sq km)
**Language:** Spanish, Quechua, Aymara
**Did You Know?** It is a polite custom in Bolivia to stand close to the person you are talking to.

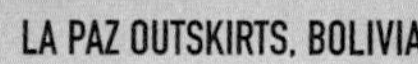

LA PAZ OUTSKIRTS, BOLIVIA

## Bosnia and Herzegovina

**Capital:** Sarajevo

**Population:** 3,875,723

**Area:** 19,772 sq mi (51,209 sq km)

**Language:** Bosnian, Croatian, Serbian

**Did You Know?** Breads and roasted meats are common Bosnian foods. For dessert you might eat *Tufahijia,* or apples stuffed with walnuts and topped with whipped cream.

## Botswana

**Capital:** Gaborone

**Population:** 2,127,825

**Area:** 231,804 sq mi (600,370 sq km)

**Language:** Setswana, English

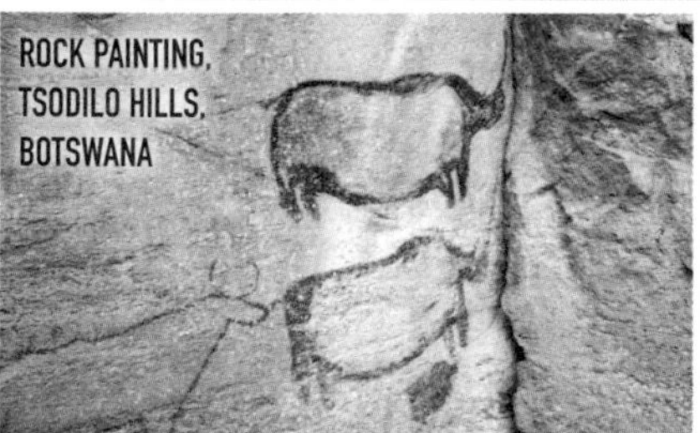

ROCK PAINTING, TSODILO HILLS, BOTSWANA

**Did You Know?** The Tsodilo Hills is a rock formation in Botswana where people have lived for over 100,000 years. More than 4,500 rock paintings survive from ancient times.

## Brazil

**Capital:** Brasília

**Population:** 201,009,622

**Area:** 3,286,488 sq mi (8,511,965 sq km)

**Language:** Portuguese, Spanish, English, French

**Did You Know?** About 180 million people in the world speak Portuguese. Most of them live in Brazil.

## Brunei

**Capital:** Bandar Seri Begawan

**Population:** 415,717

**Area:** 2,228 sq mi (5,770 sq km)

**Language:** Malay, English, Chinese

**Did You Know?** Brunei is ruled by a sultan who is one of the richest people in the world.

## Bulgaria

**Capital:** Sofia

**Population:** 6,981,642

**Area:** 42,823 sq mi (110,910 sq km)

**Language:** Bulgarian, Turkish

**Did You Know?** Plovdiv, Bulgaria's second-largest city, is very old. People were living at the site as early as 6,000 years ago.

## Burkina Faso

**Capital:** Ouagadougou

**Population:** 17,812,961

**Area:** 105,869 sq mi (274,200 sq km)

**Language:** French, indigenous languages

**Did You Know?** Visitors to Burkina Faso can ride camels into the desert, explore needle-like rock formations, and hike to lakes where hippos float in the water or crocodiles bask on the shore.

## Burundi

**Capital:** Bujumbura

**Population:** 10,888,321

**Area:** 10,745 sq mi (27,830 sq km)

**Language:** Kirundi, French, Swahili

**Did You Know?** The Master Drummers of Burundi sing, dance, and drum to exciting rhythms, following a tradition passed down through many generations. In the past, they performed in special ceremonies for the king. Today, they entertain audiences of ordinary people in Burundi and around the world.

## Cambodia

**Capital:** Phnom Penh

**Population:** 15,205,539

**Area:** 69,900 sq mi (181,040 sq km)

**Language:** Khmer, French, English

**Did You Know?** The powerful Khmer Empire that flourished from the 9th to the 13th centuries included large parts of present-day Laos, Thailand, and Vietnam, as well as Cambodia.

### COLOR KEY

- Africa
- Asia
- Australia
- Europe
- North America
- Pacific Islands
- South America

## Cameroon

**Capital:** Yaoundé

**Population:** 20,549,221

**Area:** 183,568 sq mi (475,440 sq km)

**Language:** English, French, African languages

**Did You Know?** The most popular sport in Cameroon is soccer. Teams from Cameroon have won the Africa Cup of Nations soccer championship four times.

## Canada

**Capital:** Ottawa

**Population:** 34,568,211

**Area:** 3,855,103 sq mi (9,984,670 sq km)

**Language:** English, French

**Did You Know?** Canada has more lakes than any other country in the world. Great Slave Lake, in Canada's Northwest Territories, is more than 2,000 feet deep, making it the deepest lake in North America.

## Cape Verde

**Capital:** Praia

**Population:** 531,046

**Area:** 1,557 sq mi (4,033 sq km)

**Language:** Portuguese, Crioulo

**Did You Know?** Cidade Velha ("old city"), located in the Cape Verde islands off the coast of West Africa, was first settled by the Portuguese in 1462. Pirates looted the settlement in the early 1700s. It is now in ruins.

## Central African Republic

**Capital:** Bangui

**Population:** 5,166,510

**Area:** 240,535 sq mi (622,984 sq km)

**Language:** French, Sangho

**Did You Know?** It's common in this country to shake hands with the other members of your family after you get up in the morning.

## Chad

**Capital:** N'Djamena

**Population:** 11,193,452

**Area:** 495,755 sq mi (1,284,000 sq km)

**Language:** French, Arabic, Sara

**Did You Know?** Experts estimate that, because of illegal hunting, the number of wild elephants in Chad has dropped from about 4,000 in 2006 to under 2,500 today.

## Chile

**Capital:** Santiago

**Population:** 17,216,945

**Area:** 292,260 sq mi (756,950 sq km)

**Language:** Spanish

**Did You Know?** Nicknamed the "shoestring republic," Chile is more than 2,500 miles long but an average of only about 110 miles wide.

## China

**Capital:** Beijing

**Population:** 1,349,585,838

**Area:** 3,705,407 sq mi (9,596,960 sq km)

**Language:** Mandarin, and many dialects

**Did You Know?** The Forbidden City, in the heart of Beijing, was the home of Chinese emperors for centuries. Most ordinary people were forbidden to enter its walls. It is now visited by thousands of tourists every day.

FORBIDDEN CITY, BEIJING, CHINA

## Colombia

**Capital:** Bogotá

**Population:** 45,745,783

**Area:** 439,736 sq mi (1,138,910 sq km)

**Language:** Spanish

**Did You Know?** Colombia is the only country in South America that touches both the Caribbean Sea and the Pacific Ocean.

**COLOR KEY**

- Africa
- Asia
- Australia
- Europe
- North America
- Pacific Islands
- South America

## Comoros

**Capital:** Moroni

**Population:** 752,288

**Area:** 838 sq mi (2,170 sq km)

**Language:** Arabic, French, Shikomoro

**Did You Know?** On Grande Comore, the largest of the islands in the Comoros, land is traditionally owned and inherited by women, and people take their mothers' last names.

## Congo, Democratic Republic of the

**Capital:** Kinshasa

**Population:** 75,507,308

**Area:** 905,568 sq mi (2,345,410 sq km)

**Language:** French, Lingala, Kingwana, Kikongo, Tshiluba

**Did You Know?** This country in the heart of Africa was ruled by Belgium for about 80 years, until it won independence in 1960.

## Congo, Republic of the

**Capital:** Brazzaville

**Population:** 4,492,689

**Area:** 132,047 sq mi (342,000 sq km)

**Language:** French, Lingala, Monokutuba, Kikongo

**Did You Know?** The Republic of the Congo lies on the equator and contains both tropical rain forests and grasslands. Wild animals include gorillas, giraffes, cheetahs, crocodiles, and many kinds of snakes.

## Costa Rica

**Capital:** San José

**Population:** 4,695,942

**Area:** 19,730 sq mi (51,100 sq km)

**Language:** Spanish, English

**Did You Know?** *Fútbol*, or soccer, is by far the most popular sport in Costa Rica. Even small towns usually have their own team.

RAIN FOREST, COSTA RICA

## Côte d'Ivoire (Ivory Coast)

**Capital:** Yamoussoukro

**Population:** 22,400,835

**Area:** 124,503 sq mi (322,460 sq km)

**Language:** French, Dioula

**Did You Know?** *Mafé*, or meat in a peanut sauce, is a common food in Côte d'Ivoire. It is often served with grated cassava, a root vegetable.

## Croatia

**Capital:** Zagreb

**Population:** 4,475,611

**Area:** 21,831 sq mi (56,542 sq km)

**Language:** Croatian, Serbian

**Did You Know?** The *kolo* is a popular dance in Croatia. It is performed in a circle, with music from violins and a mandolin.

ZAGREB, CROATIA

## Cuba

**Capital:** Havana

**Population:** 11,061,886

**Area:** 42,803 sq mi (110,860 sq km)

**Language:** Spanish

**Did You Know?** There are thousands of species of plants and animals in Cuba that live nowhere else on Earth.

## Cyprus

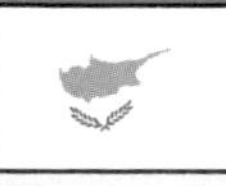

**Capital:** Nicosia

**Population:** 1,155,403

**Area:** 3,571 sq mi (9,250 sq km)

**Language:** Greek, Turkish, English

**Did You Know?** The island of Cyprus is divided into two parts, one mostly Greek, the other almost entirely Turkish.

## Czech Republic

**Capital:** Prague

**Population:** 10,162,921

**Area:** 30,450 sq mi (78,866 sq km)

**Language:** Czech, Slovak

**Did You Know?** The Prague Castle, now used by the Czech Republic's president, dates back to the ninth century.

## Denmark

**Capital:** Copenhagen

**Population:** 5,556,452

**Area:** 16,639 sq mi (43,094 sq km)

**Language:** Danish, Faroese

**Did You Know?** Tivoli Gardens, which opened in Copenhagen in 1853, is one of the world's oldest and best-known amusement parks. The rides are in a beautiful park that is lit up at night.

TIVOLI GARDENS, COPENHAGEN, DENMARK

## Djibouti

**Capital:** Djibouti

**Population:** 792,198

**Area:** 8,880 sq mi (23,000 sq km)

**Language:** French, Arabic, Somali, Afar

**Did You Know?** Common foods in Djibouti include chicken, lentils, flat bread, and baked fish with a spicy sauce.

## Dominica

**Capital:** Roseau

**Population:** 73,286

**Area:** 291 sq mi (754 sq km)

**Language:** English, French patois

**Did You Know?** The Sisserou parrot, seen on Dominica's flag, is the national bird. This parrot lives only in Dominica.

## Dominican Republic

**Capital:** Santo Domingo

**Population:** 10,219,630

**Area:** 18,815 sq mi (48,730 sq km)

**Language:** Spanish

**Did You Know?** More than 500 athletes who have played major league baseball over the years were born in the Dominican Republic.

## Ecuador

**Capital:** Quito

**Population:** 15,439,429

**Area:** 109,483 sq mi (283,560 sq km)

**Language:** Spanish, Quechua

**Did You Know?** The tortoises in Ecuador's Galapagos Islands can weigh more than 500 pounds and live for 150 years or more.

## Egypt

**Capital:** Cairo

**Population:** 85,294,388

**Area:** 386,662 sq mi (1,001,450 sq km)

**Language:** Arabic, English, French

**Did You Know?** The death of the "boy king" Tutankhamun in 1323 B.C., at the age of about 19, is a mystery. Some scholars think he was murdered by a rival. Another theory is that he was attacked by a hippopotamus. Others believe he may have died of malaria after being weakened by a broken leg.

## El Salvador

**Capital:** San Salvador

**Population:** 6,108,590

**Area:** 8,124 sq mi (21,040 sq km)

**Language:** Spanish, Nahua

**Did You Know?** El Salvador, the smallest country in Central America, is known as the "Land of Volcanoes" because it has so many of them. The massive San Salvador volcano lies on the edge of the nation's capital city.

**COLOR KEY**

- Africa
- Asia
- Australia
- Europe
- North America
- Pacific Islands
- South America

## Equatorial Guinea

**Capital:** Malabo

**Population:** 704,001

**Area:** 10,831 sq mi (28,051 sq km)

**Language:** Spanish, French, Fang, Bubi

**Did You Know?** Because Equatorial Guinea lies close to the equator, temperatures do not change much from month to month. But there are dry and rainy seasons. Rainy seasons can be long: lasting from February to June and from September to December.

## Eritrea

**Capital:** Asmara

**Population:** 6,233,682

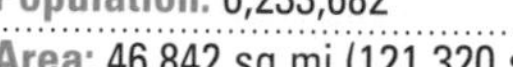

**Area:** 46,842 sq mi (121,320 sq km)

**Language:** Afar, Arabic, Tigre, Kunama, Tigrinya

**Did You Know?** Spicy stews are a popular food in Eritrea. At meals, it is a sign of politeness to take some of your own food and feed it to the person next to you.

## Estonia

**Capital:** Tallinn

**Population:** 1,266,375

**Area:** 17,462 sq mi (45,226 sq km)

**Language:** Estonian, Russian

**Did You Know?** In 1991, Estonia became independent, and it joined the European Union in 2004. In 2011, Estonia became the 17th nation of the EU to adopt the euro as its currency.

## Ethiopia

**Capital:** Addis Ababa

**Population:** 93,877,025

**Area:** 435,186 sq mi (1,127,127 sq km)

**Language:** Amharic, Tigrinya, Oromigna, Guaragigna, Somali, Arabic

**Did You Know?** In rural areas of Ethiopia, when a couple gets married, neighbors often build them a house of their own.

## Fiji

**Capital:** Suva

**Population:** 896,758

**Area:** 7,054 sq mi (18,270 sq km)

**Language:** English, Fijian, Hindustani

**Did You Know?** This country is made up of more than 300 islands in the South Pacific Ocean. Some of them are very tiny, and most of them have no people living there.

## Finland

**Capital:** Helsinki

**Population:** 5,266,114

**Area:** 130,559 sq mi (338,145 sq km)

**Language:** Finnish, Swedish

**Did You Know?** Pesäpallo has been called the national sport of Finland. It's something like baseball, but pitches are thrown straight up, and the batter hits the ball when it drops down.

## France

**Capital:** Paris

**Population:** 65,951,611

**Area:** 248,429 sq mi (643,427 sq km)

**Language:** French

**Did You Know?** The city of Paris has 137 museums. One of them is the Sewer Museum, and tourists can walk through part of the city's sewer system.

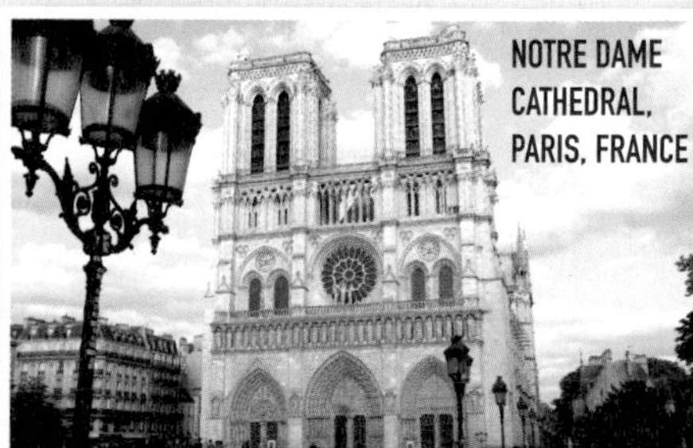

NOTRE DAME CATHEDRAL, PARIS, FRANCE

## Gabon

**Capital:** Libreville

**Population:** 1,640,286

**Area:** 103,347 sq mi (267,667 sq km)

**Language:** French, Fang, Myene, Nzebi

**Did You Know?** Offshore oil deposits were first discovered in the 1970s. Today, Gabon depends on oil for 50 percent of its national income.

## The Gambia

**Capital:** Banjul

**Population:** 1,883,051

**Area:** 4,363 sq mi (11,300 sq km)

**Language:** English, Mandinka, Wolof

**Did You Know?** The River Gambia splits The Gambia in two as it flows west to the Atlantic Ocean.

## Georgia

**Capital:** T'bilisi

**Population:** 4,555,911

**Area:** 26,911 sq mi (69,700 sq km)

**Language:** Georgian, Russian, Armenian, Azeri, Abkhaz

**Did You Know?** Forests in the mountains of Georgia provide a habitat for deer, boar, lynxes, and wolves. In all, Georgia has more than 100 kinds of mammals.

## Germany

**Capital:** Berlin

**Population:** 81,147,265

**Area:** 137,847 sq mi (357,021 sq km)

**Language:** German

**Did You Know?** Fortune-telling on New Year's Eve is an old tradition in Germany. In a one game, called *Bleigiessen*, molten lead is poured into a bowl of cold water to see what shape it takes. A heart or ring shape, for example, is said to mean marriage in the coming year.

## Ghana

**Capital:** Accra

**Population:** 25,199,609

**Area:** 92,456 sq mi (239,460 sq km)

**Language:** English, Akan, Moshi-Dagomba, Ewe, Ga

**Did You Know?** Many European colonies in sub-Saharan Africa became independent countries in the second half of the 20th century. Ghana—in 1957—was the first one.

### COLOR KEY

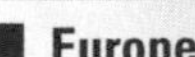

- Africa
- Asia
- Australia
- Europe
- North America
- Pacific Islands
- South America

## Greece

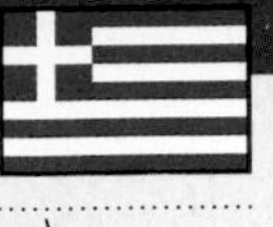

**Capital:** Athens

**Population:** 10,772,967

**Area:** 50,942 sq mi (131,940 sq km)

**Language:** Greek, English, French

**Did You Know?** In the ancient city-state of Athens, almost every adult male citizen could attend meetings of the Assembly and vote on laws. Women and slaves did not get the same privilege.

PARTHENON, ATHENS, GREECE

## Grenada

**Capital:** Saint George's

**Population:** 109,590

**Area:** 133 sq mi (344 sq km)

**Language:** English, French patois

**Did You Know?** Spring in Grenada is often sunny, dry, and windy. There are kite flying competitions all across the country.

## Guatemala

**Capital:** Guatemala City

**Population:** 14,373,472

**Area:** 42,043 sq mi (108,890 sq km)

**Language:** Spanish, Amerindian languages

**Did You Know?** "Worry dolls" from Guatemala are made out of small pieces of wood or wire, with cloth wrapped around them. It's said that if you tell your troubles to the doll, you can get a good night's sleep while the doll does the worrying for you.

## Guinea

**Capital:** Conakry

**Population:** 11,176,026

**Area:** 94,926 sq mi (245,857 sq km)

**Language:** French, Susu, Pulaar, Malinke

**Did You Know?** Snakes, crocodiles, parrots, leopards, monkeys, wild boar, elephants, and hippopotamuses live in Guinea's forests and grasslands.

## Guinea-Bissau

**Capital:** Bissau
**Population:** 1,660,870
**Area:** 13,946 sq mi (36,120 sq km)
**Language:** Portuguese, Crioulo, African languages
**Did You Know?** Guinea-Bissau has six main rivers. Some ocean-going ships can reach the larger riverside towns, while tugs and barges can get to most small towns.

## Guyana

**Capital:** Georgetown
**Population:** 739,903
**Area:** 83,000 sq mi (214,970 sq km)
**Language:** English, Amerindian dialects, Creole, Hindi
**Did You Know?** Guyana, a former British colony, is the only English-speaking country in South America.

## Haiti

**Capital:** Port-au-Prince
**Population:** 9,893,934
**Area:** 10,714 sq mi (27,750 sq km)
**Language:** French, Creole
**Did You Know?** Carnival, held before the religious season of Lent, is the biggest festival of the year in Haiti. Parades feature colorful floats and people dressed in costumes.

## Honduras

**Capital:** Tegucigalpa
**Population:** 8,448,465
**Area:** 43,278 sq mi (112,090 sq km)
**Language:** Spanish, Amerindian dialects
**Did You Know?** Popular foods in Honduras include tacos, tortillas, and tamales, along with conch soup and fried plantains. These are often served with rice and beans.

## Hungary

**Capital:** Budapest
**Population:** 9,939,470
**Area:** 35,919 sq mi (93,030 sq km)
**Language:** Hungarian (Magyar)
**Did You Know?** In the course of Hungary's history, large parts of the country have been part of the Roman Empire, the Mongol Empire, and Turkey's Ottoman Empire.

## Iceland

**Capital:** Reykjavik
**Population:** 315,281
**Area:** 39,769 sq mi (103,000 sq km)
**Language:** Icelandic, English
**Did You Know?** Glaciers, lakes, and a lava desert cover about three-fourths of Iceland's surface area.

## India

**Capital:** New Delhi
**Population:** 1,220,800,539
**Area:** 1,269,346 sq mi (3,287,590 sq km)
**Language:** Hindi, English, Bengali, Urdu
**Did You Know?** There are about 65,000 different species of animals living in India. It is the only country in the world that has both lions and tigers.

## Indonesia

**Capital:** Jakarta
**Population:** 251,160,124
**Area:** 741,100 sq mi (1,919,440 sq km)
**Language:** Bahasa Indonesian, English, Dutch, Javanese
**Did You Know?** Badminton is a very popular sport in Indonesia. The national men's team has won the Thomas Cup world championship 13 times, more than any other country.

ULUN DANU TEMPLE, BALI, INDONESIA

## Iran

**Capital:** Tehran
**Population:** 79,853,900
**Area:** 636,296 sq mi (1,648,000 sq km)
**Language:** Farsi (Persian), Turkic, Kurdish
**Did You Know?** The Persians settled in Iran around 1500 B.C. and made it the center of a vast empire in the 6th century B.C. But the empire fell to Alexander the Great.

## Iraq

**Capital:** Baghdad
**Population:** 31,858,481
**Area:** 168,754 sq mi (437,072 sq km)
**Language:** Arabic, Kurdish
**Did You Know?** Summers in Iraq are very hot and dry. Temperatures in the south sometimes go above 110°F or even 120°F in the daytime, but then drop sharply at night.

## Ireland

**Capital:** Dublin
**Population:** 4,775,982
**Area:** 27,135 sq mi (70,280 sq km)
**Language:** English, Irish
**Did You Know?** Every year, hundreds of thousands of people visit Blarney Castle in County Cork, to kiss the so-called Blarney stone there. According to legend, they get the "gift of gab" in return.

## Israel

**Capital:** Jerusalem
**Population:** 7,707,042
**Area:** 8,019 sq mi (20,770 sq km)
**Language:** Hebrew, Arabic, English
**Did You Know?** When Romans destroyed the Second Temple in Jerusalem, in A.D. 70, an outer wall of the Temple Mount was left standing. This Western Wall, sometimes called the Wailing Wall, is sacred to Jews around the world. It is common for visitors to slip written prayers into the cracks.

## Italy

**Capital:** Rome
**Population:** 61,482,297
**Area:** 116,306 sq mi (301,230 sq km)
**Language:** Italian, German, French, Slovenian
**Did You Know?** In 1173, workers began building a bell tower next to the cathedral in Pisa. It soon started to lean sideways in the soft soil. Today, despite some fixing up, the world-famous Leaning Tower of Pisa still leans—and is a major tourist attraction, visited by 1 million people a year.

LEANING TOWER OF PISA, ITALY

## Jamaica

**Capital:** Kingston
**Population:** 2,909,714
**Area:** 4,244 sq mi (10,991 sq km)
**Language:** English, Jamaican Creole
**Did You Know?** The Jamaican giant swallowtail butterfly is the biggest butterfly in the Americas. It has a wingspan of about 6 inches.

## Japan

**Capital:** Tokyo
**Population:** 127,253,075
**Area:** 145,883 sq mi (377,835 sq km)
**Language:** Japanese
**Did You Know?** Noodles are a favorite food in Japan. And it is fine to slurp loudly as you eat them. People take it as a sign that you are enjoying your meal.

## Jordan

**Capital:** Amman
**Population:** 6,482,081
**Area:** 35,637 sq mi (92,300 sq km)
**Language:** Arabic, English
**Did You Know?** When offered a meal in Jordan, it is considered polite to refuse three times before accepting.

**COLOR KEY**

- Africa
- Asia
- Australia
- Europe
- North America
- Pacific Islands
- South America

## Kazakhstan

**Capital:** Astana

**Population:** 17,736,896

**Area:** 1,049,155 sq mi (2,717,300 sq km)

**Language:** Kazakh, Russian

**Did You Know?** Kazakhstan, the world's biggest landlocked country in area, is located mostly in Central Asia. Like Russia, and unlike the other former Soviet republics, Kazakhstan has large oil reserves—totaling about 30 billion barrels.

## Kenya

**Capital:** Nairobi

**Population:** 44,037,656

**Area:** 224,962 sq mi (582,650 sq km)

**Language:** Kiswahili, English

**Did You Know?** There are only about 2,000 lions left in Kenya. Some farmers kill lions to prevent attacks on livestock.

## Kiribati

**Capital:** Tarawa

**Population:** 103,248

**Area:** 313 sq mi (811 sq km)

**Language:** English, I-Kiribati

**Did You Know?** Tarawa is one of many tiny Pacific islands that are part of Kiribati. It was the site of a fierce battle between Japanese forces and U.S. Marines during World War II.

## Korea, North

**Capital:** Pyongyang

**Population:** 24,720,407

**Area:** 46,541 sq mi (120,540 sq km)

**Language:** Korean

**Did You Know?** The Tower of the Juche Idea, in Pyongyang, was built in 1982 to honor North Korea's ruler at the time, Kim Il Sung, known as the "Great Leader." The tower was made of 25,550 granite blocks, one for each day of his life (excepting February 29ths) up to his 70th birthday that year.

## Korea, South

**Capital:** Seoul; Sejong City (admin.)

**Population:** 48,955,203

**Area:** 38,023 sq mi (98,480 sq km)

**Language:** Korean

**Did You Know?** It is considered polite for young Koreans to avoid looking an older person in the eye.

SEOUL, SOUTH KOREA

## Kosovo

**Capital:** Pristina

**Population:** 1,847,708

**Area:** 4,203 sq mi (10,887 sq km)

**Language:** Albanian, Serbian, Bosnian, Turkish, Roma

**Did You Know?** "Kos" is the Serbian word for "blackbird," and the country's name comes from a place called "field of blackbirds." There, in 1389, the Serbs were defeated in battle by the Ottoman Turks.

## Kuwait

**Capital:** Kuwait City

**Population:** 2,695,316

**Area:** 6,880 sq mi (17,820 sq km)

**Language:** Arabic, English

**Did You Know?** Because of the money that Kuwait earns from oil, the country's citizens get free medical care and pay no taxes.

## Kyrgyzstan

**Capital:** Bishkek

**Population:** 5,548,042

**Area:** 76,641 sq mi (198,500 sq km)

**Language:** Kyrgyz, Russian

**Did You Know?** The Sun in the center of Kyrgyzstan's flag has 40 rays, one for each of the 40 tribes that, it is said, united to form the Kyrgyz nation.

## Laos

**Capital:** Vientiane
**Population:** 6,695,166
**Area:** 91,429 sq mi (236,800 sq km)
**Language:** Lao, French, English
**Did You Know?** Xiang Miang is one of the most popular figures in Laotian folktales. There are many stories about how this trickster cleverly outwits the king and other powerful people.

## Latvia

**Capital:** Riga
**Population:** 2,178,443
**Area:** 24,938 sq mi (64,589 sq km)
**Language:** Latvian, Russian, Lithuanian
**Did You Know?** The president's official home is a castle built in the early 1300s.

## Lebanon

**Capital:** Beirut
**Population:** 4,131,583
**Area:** 4,015 sq mi (10,400 sq km)
**Language:** Arabic, French, English, Armenian
**Did You Know?** Beirut's history goes back about 5,000 years. It was founded as early as 3000 B.C., before Jerusalem, Athens, Damascus, or any other capital city in the world.

## Lesotho

**Capital:** Maseru
**Population:** 1,936,151
**Area:** 11,720 sq mi (30,355 sq km)
**Language:** English, Sesotho, Zulu, Xhosa
**Did You Know?** The high, rugged mountains of Lesotho attract many tourists from South Africa and other countries. Hiking and bird watching are very popular. Visitors often ride ponies to get to remote areas.

MALETSUNYANE FALLS, LESOTHO

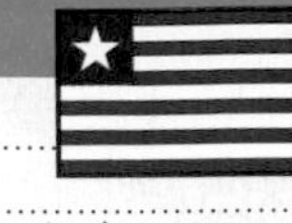

## Liberia

**Capital:** Monrovia
**Population:** 3,989,703
**Area:** 43,000 sq mi (111,370 sq km)
**Language:** English, ethnic languages
**Did You Know?** When visiting people in Liberia, guests normally take their shoes off before entering a house.

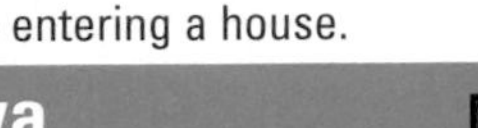

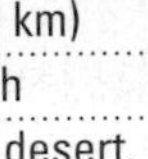

## Libya

**Capital:** Tripoli
**Population:** 6,002,347
**Area:** 679,362 sq mi (1,759,540 sq km)
**Language:** Arabic, Italian, English
**Did You Know?** Most of Libya is desert. Only about 1 percent of the land is naturally suitable for farming.

## Liechtenstein

**Capital:** Vaduz
**Population:** 37,009
**Area:** 62 sq mi (160 sq km)
**Language:** German, Alemannic dialect
**Did You Know?** Nearly half of all the workers in tiny Liechtenstein commute there each day from their homes in Austria, Switzerland, or Germany.

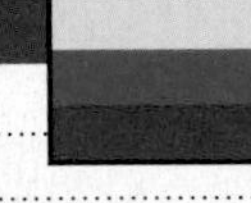

## Lithuania

**Capital:** Vilnius
**Population:** 3,515,858
**Area:** 25,213 sq mi (65,300 sq km)
**Language:** Lithuanian, Russian, Polish
**Did You Know?** Lithuania and France rely on nuclear power for their energy needs more than any other countries in the world.

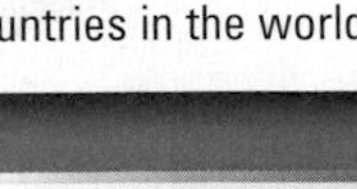

**COLOR KEY**

- Africa
- Asia
- Australia
- Europe
- North America
- Pacific Islands
- South America

## Luxembourg

**Capital:** Luxembourg
**Population:** 514,682
**Area:** 998 sq mi (2,586 sq km)
**Language:** French, German, Luxembourgish
**Did You Know?** Luxembourg's history as a nation dates back to the year 963, when a count built his castle on top of Roman ruins there.

OLD QUARTER, LUXEMBOURG

## Macedonia

**Capital:** Skopje
**Population:** 2,087,171
**Area:** 9,781 sq mi (25,333 sq km)
**Language:** Macedonian, Albanian, Turkish
**Did You Know?** Skopje was rebuilt after an earthquake in 1963 destroyed more than half of the city.

## Madagascar

**Capital:** Antananarivo
**Population:** 22,599,098
**Area:** 226,657 sq mi (587,040 sq km)
**Language:** Malagasy, French, English
**Did You Know?** Lemurs are monkey-like animals with big eyes and, usually, long bushy tails. They can be found only in Madagascar and nearby islands.

## Malawi

**Capital:** Lilongwe
**Population:** 16,777,547
**Area:** 45,745 sq mi (118,480 sq km)
**Language:** English, Chichewa
**Did You Know?** Lake Nyasa, also called Lake Malawi, lies along the eastern border of Malawi. One of the world's biggest and deepest lakes, it is a popular vacation spot and has more kinds of fish than any other lake in the world.

## Malaysia

**Capital:** Kuala Lumpur; Putrajaya (admin.)
**Population:** 29,628,392
**Area:** 127,317 sq mi (329,750 sq km)
**Language:** Malay, English, Chinese, Tamil
**Did You Know?** Singapore was part of the original country of Malaysia that was created in 1963. But two years later, Singapore became a separate nation.

## Maldives

**Capital:** Male
**Population:** 393,988
**Area:** 116 sq mi (300 sq km)
**Language:** Maldivian Divehi, English
**Did You Know?** An island nation that is officially part of Asia, Maldives is that continent's smallest country in area.

## Mali

**Capital:** Bamako
**Population:** 15,968,882
**Area:** 478,767 sq mi (1,240,000 sq km)
**Language:** French, Bambara
**Did You Know?** Salif Keita is a world-renowned singer from Mali. He is a descendant of the 13th-century warrior king who founded the Malian empire.

## Malta

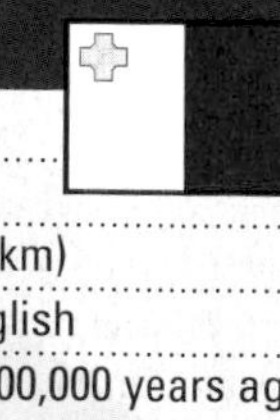

**Capital:** Valletta
**Population:** 411,277
**Area:** 122 sq mi (316 sq km)
**Language:** Maltese, English
**Did You Know?** Some 200,000 years ago, Malta was connected to Sicily by a land bridge. Elephants, hippos, and other big animals lived on the island. Their remains have been found washed into a cave.

MAKUZI BAY, LAKE MALAWI

## Marshall Islands

**Capital:** Majuro

**Population:** 69,747

**Area:** 70 sq mi (181 sq km)

**Language:** English, Marshallese

**Did You Know?** Hiking, swimming, snorkeling, and fly fishing are among popular activities on these islands in the Pacific Ocean.

## Mauritania

**Capital:** Nouakchott

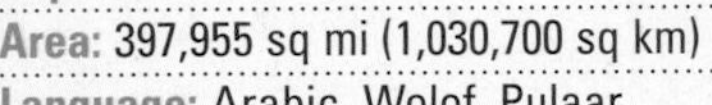

**Population:** 3,437,610

**Area:** 397,955 sq mi (1,030,700 sq km)

**Language:** Arabic, Wolof, Pulaar

**Did You Know?** Ben Amera, one of the biggest monoliths (large single rocks) in the world, lies in the desert sands of Mauritania.

## Mauritius

**Capital:** Port Louis

**Population:** 1,322,238

**Area:** 788 sq mi (2,040 sq km)

**Language:** Creole, Bhojpuri, French, English

**Did You Know?** The island of Mauritius is the longtime home of dodo birds. For many centuries, these birds had no enemies. They lost their fear of danger and their ability to fly. When humans came in large numbers in the 1600s, the birds were easily hunted and soon became extinct.

## Mexico

**Capital:** Mexico City

**Population:** 116,220,947

**Area:** 761,606 sq mi (1,972,550 sq km)

**Language:** Spanish, Mayan languages

**Did You Know?** When the Spanish arrived in Mexico in 1519, the Aztec Empire controlled a huge area that included most of present-day Mexico and large parts of Central America.

AZTEC PYRAMID, MEXICO

## Micronesia

**Capital:** Palikir

**Population:** 106,104

**Area:** 271 sq mi (702 sq km)

**Language:** English, Trukese, Pohnpeian, Yapese

**Did You Know?** Micronesia is made up of 607 separate islands in the Pacific Ocean, spread over a path about 2,000 miles long.

## Moldova

**Capital:** Chisinau

**Population:** 3,619,925

**Area:** 13,067 sq mi (33,843 sq km)

**Language:** Moldovan, Russian

**Did You Know?** Romania is Moldova's next-door neighbor. The Moldavian language is almost the same as Romanian, and about four-fifths of the people in Moldova belong to the Romanian ethnic group.

## Monaco

**Capital:** Monaco

**Population:** 30,500

**Area:** 0.76 sq mi (1.96 sq km)

**Language:** French, English, Italian, Monegasque

**Did You Know?** Monaco is the world's second-smallest country in area (after Vatican City). It is only about three times as big as the Mall in Washington, D.C.

## Mongolia

**Capital:** Ulaanbaatar

**Population:** 3,226,516

**Area:** 603,909 sq mi (1,564,116 sq km)

**Language:** Khalkha Mongolian

**Did You Know?** The Gobi desert covers about 500,000 square miles in China and southern Mongolia. Much of the surface is bare rock, and in winter there can be snow and temperatures as low as –40°F.

### COLOR KEY

- Africa
- Asia
- Australia
- Europe
- North America
- Pacific Islands
- South America

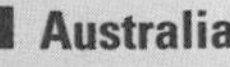

## Montenegro

**Capital:** Podgorica

**Population:** 653,474

**Area:** 5,415 sq mi (14,026 sq km)

**Language:** Serbian, Bosnian, Albanian, Croatian

**Did You Know?** *Montenegro* means "black mountain." The country gets the name from its dark mountain forests.

## Morocco

**Capital:** Rabat

**Population:** 32,649,130

**Area:** 172,414 sq mi (446,550 sq km)

**Language:** Arabic, Berber dialects, French

MOSQUE, CASABLANCA, MOROCCO

**Did You Know?** Parts of Morocco have a tropical climate, but it can get very cold in some areas. On February 11, 1935, the temperature in a mountainous region fell to −11°F, a record low for any place in Africa.

## Mozambique

**Capital:** Maputo

**Population:** 24,096,669

**Area:** 309,496 sq mi (801,590 sq km)

**Language:** Portuguese, Bantu languages

**Did You Know?** For hundreds of years, Mozambique was a colony of Portugal. The first Portuguese settlement was set up in 1505, as a stopping place for Portuguese ships sailing around Africa to reach Asia.

## Myanmar (Burma)

**Capital:** Nay Pyi Taw

**Population:** 55,167,330

**Area:** 261,970 sq mi (678,500 sq km)

**Language:** Burmese

**Did You Know?** In 1989, the military rulers of this country changed its name from Burma to Myanmar. The UN and most countries use the new name, but some nations, including the United States, do not.

## Namibia

**Capital:** Windhoek

**Population:** 2,182,852

**Area:** 318,696 sq mi (825,418 sq km)

**Language:** Afrikaans, English, German

**Did You Know?** The largest naturally occurring piece of iron on Earth is a meteorite that fell in Namibia.

## Nauru

**Capital:** Yaren district

**Population:** 9,434

**Area:** 8 sq mi (21 sq km)

**Language:** Nauruan, English

**Did You Know?** In the 1920s, a flu epidemic left Nauru with only about 1,000 people. The birth of a girl on October 26, 1932, brought the number to 1,500, a milestone. Nauru celebrates that day each year.

## Nepal

**Capital:** Kathmandu

**Population:** 30,430,267

**Area:** 56,827 sq mi (147,181 sq km)

**Language:** Nepali, Maithali, Bhojpuri, English

**Did You Know?** More than 3,000 people have climbed to the top of Mount Everest, on the Nepal-China border. Over 200 have died in the attempt.

## Netherlands

**Capital:** Amsterdam; The Hague (admin.)

**Population:** 16,805,037

**Area:** 16,033 sq mi (41,526 sq km)

**Language:** Dutch, Frisian

**Did You Know?** In the 1600s, the Netherlands was a major world power with colonies in the East Indies, West Indies, Africa, South America, and the present-day United States.

## New Zealand

**Capital:** Wellington
**Population:** 4,365,113
**Area:** 103,738 sq mi (268,680 sq km)
**Language:** English, Maori
**Did You Know?** More than 2 million foreign tourists visit New Zealand every year. Many go there to explore the countryside, which is the backdrop for the popular Lord of the Rings and Hobbit movies.

PORT LEVY, NEW ZEALAND

## Nicaragua

**Capital:** Managua
**Population:** 5,788,531
**Area:** 49,998 sq mi (129,494 sq km)
**Language:** Spanish, Miskito, indigenous languages
**Did You Know?** Uncle Rabbit, or Tio Conejo, is a popular figure from Nicaraguan folktales. He is known for playing tricks on Uncle Tiger (Tio Tigre) and other animal neighbors.

## Niger

**Capital:** Niamey
**Population:** 16,899,327
**Area:** 489,192 sq mi (1,267,000 sq km)
**Language:** French, Hausa, Djerma
**Did You Know?** Horse racing and camel racing are popular sports in Niger, along with wrestling and soccer.

### COLOR KEY

- Africa
- Asia
- Australia
- Europe
- North America
- Pacific Islands
- South America

## Nigeria

**Capital:** Abuja
**Population:** 174,507,539
**Area:** 356,669 sq mi (923,768 sq km)
**Language:** English, Hausa, Yoruba, Ibo
**Did You Know?** Aso Rock, a huge rock formation well over 1,000 feet high, towers over the city of Abuja. There are a number of caves inside the rock.

## Norway

**Capital:** Oslo
**Population:** 4,722,701
**Area:** 125,021 sq mi (323,802 sq km)
**Language:** Norwegian, Sami
**Did You Know?** In Norway's far north, some members of the Sami ethnic group still herd reindeer as their ancestors did. But many Sami today also use cell phones and live in homes that have TV and Internet access.

## Oman

**Capital:** Muscat
**Population:** 3,154,134
**Area:** 82,031 sq mi (212,460 sq km)
**Language:** Arabic, English, Indian dialects
**Did You Know?** The Sultan Qaboos Grand Mosque in Muscat can hold 20,000 worshippers. It has a hand-woven prayer rug that's about 230 feet long and 200 feet wide. It took 600 women to weave the rug, over a period of four years.

## Pakistan

**Capital:** Islamabad
**Population:** 193,238,868
**Area:** 310,403 sq mi (803,940 sq km)
**Language:** Urdu, English, Punjabi, Sindhi
**Did You Know?** Every year Pakistanis throng to Lahore to welcome spring in the annual kite festival. Often dressed in yellow, people fly kites big and small. They compete with one another, and it is considered OK to cut the string of a rival's kite.

## Palau

**Capital:** Melekeok

**Population:** 21,108

**Area:** 177 sq mi (458 sq km)

**Language:** English, Palauan, Sonsoral, Tobi, Angaur

**Did You Know?** Palau has coral reefs, sea caves, shipwrecks, and a wide variety of sea creatures—including giant clams that may weigh as much as 500 pounds.

## Panama

**Capital:** Panama City

**Population:** 3,559,408

**Area:** 30,193 sq mi (78,200 sq km)

**Language:** Spanish, English

**Did You Know?** El Camino Real was a road across Panama used by Spanish conquerers in the 1500s to bring gold from the Pacific to the Atlantic coast, where it was loaded onto ships to be brought to Spain.

## Papua New Guinea

**Capital:** Port Moresby

**Population:** 6,431,902

**Area:** 178,704 sq mi (462,840 sq km)

**Language:** English, Motu, Melanesian pidgin

**Did You Know?** A popular dish in Papua New Guinea is *unu bona boroma,* made of boiled, sliced breadfruit. The fruit tastes a lot like bread and is served in a sauce made of fried bacon, onions, and chicken broth.

## Paraguay

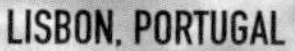

**Capital:** Asunción

**Population:** 6,623,252

**Area:** 157,047 sq mi (406,750 sq km)

**Language:** Spanish, Guarani

**Did You Know?** Myths of the Guarani people describe a wolf-like creature, called the *luison,* with red, glowing eyes and sharp teeth. The *luison* was said to show up at night when the moon is full and to appear in human form during the day.

## Peru

**Capital:** Lima

**Population:** 29,849,303

**Area:** 496,226 sq mi (1,285,220 sq km)

**Language:** Spanish, Quechua, Aymara

**Did You Know?** Potatoes were first grown about 8,000 years ago, in the Andes Mountains of Peru and Bolivia.

## Philippines

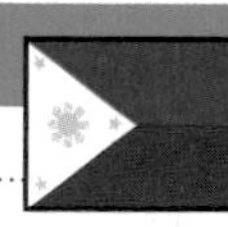

**Capital:** Manila

**Population:** 105,720,644

**Area:** 115,831 sq mi (300,000 sq km)

**Language:** Filipino, English

**Did You Know?** The martial art of *arnis*, also called *escrima* or *kali*, has a long history in the Philippines. In 2009, it was named the national sport.

## Poland

**Capital:** Warsaw

**Population:** 38,383,809

**Area:** 120,726 sq mi (312,679 sq km)

**Language:** Polish, Ukrainian, German

**Did You Know?** Famous people born in Poland include composer Frederic Chopin, Nobel Prize-winning scientist Marie Curie, and Pope John Paul II.

## Portugal

**Capital:** Lisbon

**Population:** 10,799,270

**Area:** 35,672 sq mi (92,391 sq km)

**Language:** Portuguese

**Did You Know?** The city of Guimarães in northern Portugal has a medieval castle dating back to the 12th century.

LISBON, PORTUGAL

## Qatar

**Capital:** Doha
**Population:** 2,042,444
**Area:** 4,416 sq mi (11,437 sq km)
**Language:** Arabic, English
**Did You Know?** The population of this oil-rich nation on the Arabian Peninsula is growing at a rate of about 5 percent a year. This is one of the fastest growth rates of any country in the world.

## Romania

**Capital:** Bucharest
**Population:** 21,790,479
**Area:** 91,699 sq mi (237,500 sq km)
**Language:** Romanian, Hungarian, German
**Did You Know?** At the Pharmaceutical Museum in the city of Cluj-Napoca, you can enter a centuries-old drugstore, learn about medieval medicine and alchemy, and view old scales, prescriptions, and glass cases of mummy dust.

## Russia

**Capital:** Moscow
**Population:** 142,500,482
**Area:** 6,592,772 sq mi (17,075,200 sq km)
**Language:** Russian, many minority languages
**Did You Know?** Peter the Great, who became Russia's ruler in the late 1600s, developed science and industry, built a modern navy, and made his country into a world power. He ruled with an iron hand. In 1696, he had his oldest son executed for treason.

HERMITAGE MUSEUM, ST. PETERSBURG, RUSSIA

## Rwanda

**Capital:** Kigali
**Population:** 12,012,589
**Area:** 10,169 sq mi (26,338 sq km)
**Language:** French, English, Kinyarwanda, Kiswahili
**Did You Know?** Nyungwe National Park in Rwanda is Africa's biggest protected mountain rain forest. It is home to large numbers of monkeys and chimpanzees and to more than 300 species of birds.

## Saint Kitts and Nevis

**Capital:** Basseterre
**Population:** 51,134
**Area:** 101 sq mi (261 sq km)
**Language:** English
**Did You Know?** The island of St. Kitts was named in honor of St. Christopher, patron saint of Christopher Columbus. "Kitt" is actually a nickname for "Christopher." Columbus sighted the island in November 1493, becoming the first European to do so.

COAST OF SAINT LUCIA

## Saint Lucia

**Capital:** Castries
**Population:** 162,781
**Area:** 238 sq mi (616 sq km)
**Language:** English, French patois
**Did You Know?** This tropical island has several kinds of snakes, including the boa constrictor and the poisonous St. Lucia lancehead.

## Saint Vincent and the Grenadines

**Capital:** Kingstown
**Population:** 103,220
**Area:** 150 sq mi (389 sq km)
**Language:** English, French patois
**Did You Know?** The popular Pirates of the Caribbean movies, starring Johnny Depp, were filmed mostly at Wallilabou Bay on the island of St. Vincent.

## Samoa (formerly Western Samoa)

**Capital:** Apia
**Population:** 195,476
**Area:** 1,137 sq mi (2,944 sq km)
**Language:** English, Samoan
**Did You Know?** Robert Louis Stevenson, the Scottish author who wrote *Treasure Island* and other famous classics, lived on an island in Samoa during his last years. He is buried there, on a mountain overlooking the sea.

## San Marino

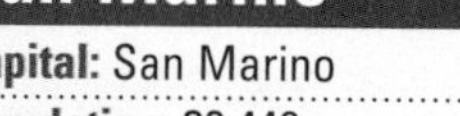

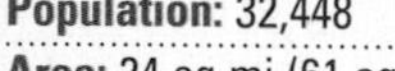

**Capital:** San Marino
**Population:** 32,448
**Area:** 24 sq mi (61 sq km)
**Language:** Italian
**Did You Know?** San Marino claims to be the oldest country in Europe, dating back to the fourth century.

## São Tomé and Príncipe

**Capital:** São Tomé
**Population:** 186,817
**Area:** 386 sq mi (1,001 sq km)
**Language:** Portuguese, Creole
**Did You Know?** The Angolares are a small ethnic group in São Tomé. The first Angolares may have been escaped slaves.

## Saudi Arabia

**Capital:** Riyadh
**Population:** 26,939,583
**Area:** 830,000 sq mi (2,149,960 sq km)
**Language:** Arabic
**Did You Know?** Camel racing is a popular sport in Saudi Arabia. More than 2,000 camels and their riders compete in the annual King's Camel Race, held in Riyadh in February.

## Senegal

**Capital:** Dakar
**Population:** 13,300,410
**Area:** 75,749 sq mi (196,190 sq km)
**Language:** French, Wolof, Pulaar
**Did You Know?** Visiting family and friends is very popular in Senegal, and it is not considered impolite to just drop by without warning. When you do stop in, you are nearly always invited to stay for a meal or for tea.

## Serbia

**Capital:** Belgrade
**Population:** 7,243,007
**Area:** 29,913 sq mi (77,474 sq km)
**Language:** Serbian, Albanian, Romanian
**Did You Know?** In Serbian weddings, it is common for the groom's brother to walk down the aisle with the bride. Towels are a traditional wedding present in Serbia. Many Serbians consider them a symbol of closeness.

BELGRADE, SERBIA

### COLOR KEY

- Africa
- Asia
- Australia
- Europe
- North America
- Pacific Islands
- South America

## Seychelles

**Capital:** Victoria
**Population:** 90,846
**Area:** 176 sq mi (455 sq km)
**Language:** Creole, English, French
**Did You Know?** There are thousands of giant tortoises on Aldabra Island in the Seychelles. They can weigh more than 500 pounds and live for over 100 years.

GIANT TORTOISE, SEYCHELLES

## Sierra Leone

**Capital:** Freetown
**Population:** 5,612,685
**Area:** 27,699 sq mi (71,740 sq km)
**Language:** English, Mende, Temne, Krio
**Did You Know?** The lakes and rivers of Sierra Leone are home to crocodiles and hippos.

## Singapore

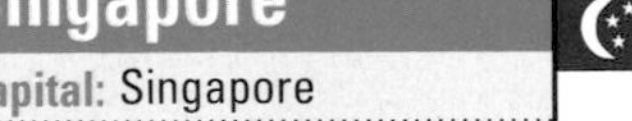

**Capital:** Singapore
**Population:** 5,460,302
**Area:** 269 sq mi (697 sq km)
**Language:** Chinese, Malay, Tamil, English
**Did You Know?** In Singapore you can be given a big fine for spitting in public, carrying chewing gum, or bringing a toy weapon or toy money into the country.

## Slovakia

**Capital:** Bratislava
**Population:** 5,488,339

**Area:** 18,859 sq mi (48,845 sq km)
**Language:** Slovak, Hungarian
**Did You Know?** The artist Andy Warhol, the astronaut Eugene Cernan, and the actress Angelina Jolie all had ancestors who came from this part of central Europe.

## Slovenia

**Capital:** Ljubljana
**Population:** 1,992,690
**Area:** 7,827 sq mi (20,273 sq km)
**Language:** Slovenian, Serbo-Croatian
**Did You Know?** The forests of Slovenia are home to Europe's largest population of brown bears. Less common animals, such as the scarab beetle, moor tortoise, and dormouse, also live in the woods and countryside.

## Solomon Islands

**Capital:** Honiara
**Population:** 597,248
**Area:** 10,985 sq mi (28,450 sq km)
**Language:** English, Melanesian pidgin
**Did You Know?** These islands got their name from a Spanish explorer who found gold in 1568 at the mouth of a river. He thought the site could be one of the places where King Solomon got the gold for his temple in Jerusalem.

## Somalia

**Capital:** Mogadishu
**Population:** 10,251,568
**Area:** 246,201 sq mi (637,657 sq km)
**Language:** Somali, Arabic, Italian, English
**Did You Know?** Former British and Italian colonies combined to form the independent nation of Somalia in 1960.

BRATISLAVA CASTLE, SLOVAKIA

## South Africa

**Capital:** Pretoria (admin.); Cape Town (legis.); Bloemfontein (judicial)

**Population:** 48,601,096

**Area:** 471,011 sq mi (1,219,912 sq km)

**Language:** Afrikaans, English, Ndebele, Sotho, Zulu, Xhosa

**Did You Know?** In the Sterkfontein Caves of South Africa, scientists found the skeleton of a human-like creature more than 3 million years old. Visitors can tour these limestone caves, and there is also an archaeological museum.

## South Sudan

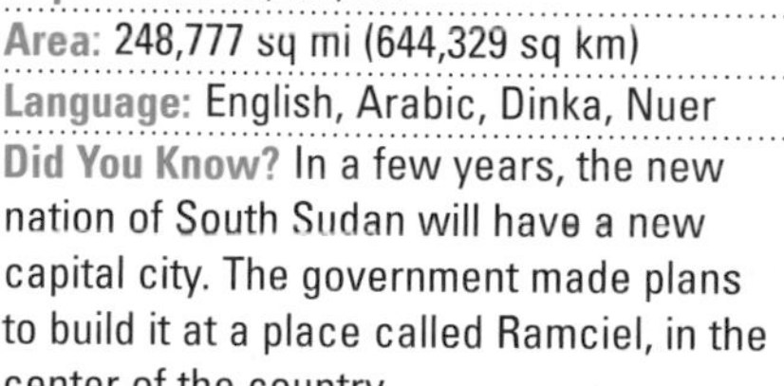

**Capital:** Juba

**Population:** 10,090,104

**Area:** 248,777 sq mi (644,329 sq km)

**Language:** English, Arabic, Dinka, Nuer

**Did You Know?** In a few years, the new nation of South Sudan will have a new capital city. The government made plans to build it at a place called Ramciel, in the center of the country.

## Spain

**Capital:** Madrid

**Population:** 47,370,542

**Area:** 194,897 sq mi (504,782 sq km)

**Language:** Castilian Spanish, Catalan, Galician

**Did You Know?** The Basque language is spoken by hundreds of thousands of Basque people in France and northern Spain. It is the oldest language still spoken in Europe and is not related to other European languages.

**COLOR KEY**

- Africa
- Asia
- Australia
- Europe
- North America
- Pacific Islands
- South America

## Sri Lanka

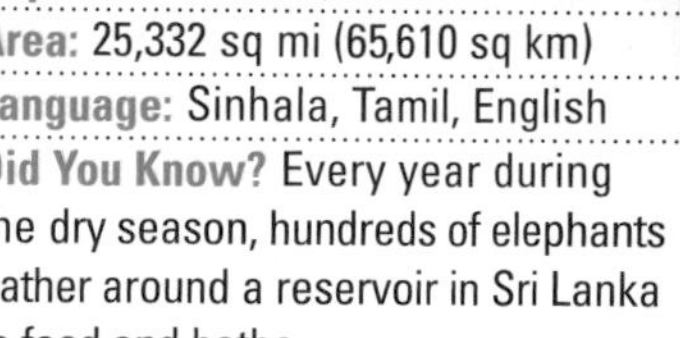

**Capital:** Colombo

**Population:** 21,675,648

**Area:** 25,332 sq mi (65,610 sq km)

**Language:** Sinhala, Tamil, English

**Did You Know?** Every year during the dry season, hundreds of elephants gather around a reservoir in Sri Lanka to feed and bathe.

ELEPHANT GATHERING, SRI LANKA

## Sudan

**Capital:** Khartoum

**Population:** 34,847,910

**Area:** 718,723 sq mi (1,861,484 sq km)

**Language:** Arabic, English, Nubian, Ta Bedawie

**Did You Know?** Khartoum is located where the White Nile and the Blue Nile rivers meet to form the main Nile River.

## Suriname

**Capital:** Paramaribo

**Population:** 566,846

**Area:** 63,039 sq mi (163,270 sq km)

**Language:** Dutch, English, Sranang Tongo

**Did You Know?** Suriname is the smallest country in South America.

## Swaziland

**Capital:** Mbabane

**Population:** 1,403,362

**Area:** 6,704 sq mi (17,363 sq km)

**Language:** English, siSwati

**Did You Know?** Only one out of five people in Swaziland lives in a city.

## Sweden

**Capital:** Stockholm

**Population:** 9,119,423

**Area:** 173,732 sq mi (449,964 sq km)

**Language:** Swedish, Sami, Finnish

**Did You Know?** In Sweden's far north, the Sun doesn't rise in January or set in June.

THE MATTERHORN, SWITZERLAND

## Switzerland

**Capital:** Bern
**Population:** 7,996,026
**Area:** 15,942 sq mi (41,290 sq km)
**Language:** German, French, Italian, Romansch
**Did You Know?** The Gotthard Base tunnel will be the world's longest railway tunnel when it opens for operation in a few years. It extends for 35 miles through the Alps.

## Syria

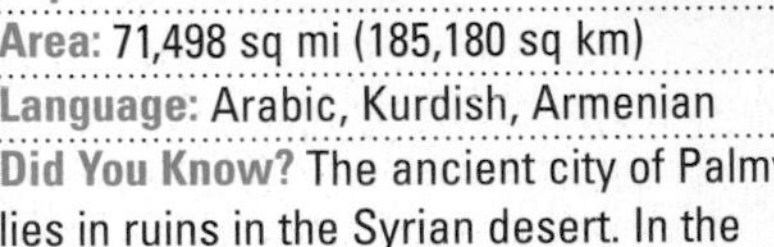

**Capital:** Damascus
**Population:** 22,457,336
**Area:** 71,498 sq mi (185,180 sq km)
**Language:** Arabic, Kurdish, Armenian
**Did You Know?** The ancient city of Palmyra lies in ruins in the Syrian desert. In the third century A.D., it was ruled by a warrior queen named Zenobia. She conquered Egypt but was eventually defeated by the Romans, who led her off to Rome in chains.

## Taiwan

**Capital:** Taipei
**Population:** 23,299,716
**Area:** 13,892 sq mi (35,980 sq km)
**Language:** Mandarin Chinese, Taiwanese
**Did You Know?** Beef noodle soup is a traditional dish from mainland China that is very popular in Taiwan. It is often made with very hot red chili peppers.

## Tajikistan

**Capital:** Dushanbe
**Population:** 7,910,041
**Area:** 55,251 sq mi (143,100 sq km)
**Language:** Tajik, Russian
**Did You Know?** Tajikistan is a landlocked country in Central Asia. Mountains cover more than 90 percent of the land, and the glaciers there are the biggest in Asia.

## Tanzania

**Capital:** Dar es Salaam; Dodoma (legislative)
**Population:** 48,261,942
**Area:** 364,900 sq mi (945,087 sq km)
**Language:** Kiswahili (Swahili), English, Arabic
**Did You Know?** Mount Kilimanjaro, the tallest mountain in Africa, stands by itself in Tanzania. There are no other mountains around it.

## Thailand

**Capital:** Bangkok
**Population:** 67,448,120
**Area:** 198,457 sq mi (514,000 sq km)
**Language:** Thai, English
**Did You Know?** The king of Thailand is said to be the richest royal person in the world, worth about $30 billion.

BANGKOK, THAILAND

## Timor-Leste (East Timor)

**Capital:** Dili
**Population:** 1,172,390
**Area:** 5,743 sq mi (14,874 sq km)
**Language:** Tetum, Portuguese, Indonesian, English
**Did You Know?** Timor-Leste spends a bigger share of its government budget on education than any other country in the world.

## Togo

**Capital:** Lomé
**Population:** 7,154,237
**Area:** 21,925 sq mi (56,785 sq km)
**Language:** French, Ewe, Mina, Kabye, Dagomba
**Did You Know?** Foods popular in Togo include fried yams, grilled chicken with chili sauce, and snails.

## Tonga

**Capital:** Nuku'alofa
**Population:** 105,322
**Area:** 289 sq mi (748 sq km)
**Language:** Tongan, English
**Did You Know?** Children in Tonga enjoy playing *lanita*, a simplified form of cricket, and various traditional games that involve tossing sticks. Friendliness is a big part of Tonga's culture, and many of these games stress cooperation rather than competition.

## Trinidad and Tobago

**Capital:** Port-of-Spain
**Population:** 1,225,225
**Area:** 1,980 sq mi (5,128 sq km)
**Language:** English, Hindi, French, Spanish
**Did You Know?** Many people from India came to Trinidad in the 1800s to work on sugar cane plantations. Today, about 40 percent of Trinidad's population is of Indian descent.

## Tunisia

**Capital:** Tunis
**Population:** 10,835,873
**Area:** 63,170 sq mi (163,610 sq km)
**Language:** Arabic, French
**Did You Know?** "Tatooine" is the name of a fictional planet in the Star Wars movies. In fact, many of the scenes in those films were shot in Tataouine, a desert region and city in southern Tunisia.

**COLOR KEY**

- Africa
- Asia
- Australia
- Europe
- North America
- Pacific Islands
- South America

## Turkey

**Capital:** Ankara
**Population:** 80,694,485
**Area:** 301,384 sq mi (780,580 sq km)
**Language:** Turkish, Kurdish, Arabic
**Did You Know?** The Bosporus Bridge, in Istanbul, spans two continents, linking Asia with Europe. About 3 percent of Turkey is in Europe, and the rest is in Asia.

BOSPORUS BRIDGE, ISTANBUL, TURKEY

## Turkmenistan

**Capital:** Ashgabat
**Population:** 5,113,040
**Area:** 188,456 sq mi (488,100 sq km)
**Language:** Turkmen, Russian, Uzbek
**Did You Know?** Much of the city of Ashgabat was turned into rubble when an earthquake struck the region in October 1948. Some 110,000 people lost their lives.

## Tuvalu

**Capital:** Funafuti
**Population:** 10,698
**Area:** 10 sq mi (26 sq km)
**Language:** Tuvaluan, English
**Did You Know?** Some scientists predict that because of global warming and rising sea levels these nine small islands could disappear within the next 50 years.

## Uganda

**Capital:** Kampala

**Population:** 34,875,809

**Area:** 91,136 sq mi (236,040 sq km)

**Language:** English, Ganda, Swahili

**Did You Know?** Seven out of ten people in Uganda are under the age of 25 (compared to one out of three in the United States).

## Ukraine

**Capital:** Kiev (Kyiv)

**Population:** 44,573,205

**Area:** 233,090 sq mi (603,700 sq km)

**Language:** Ukrainian, Russian

**Did You Know?** One of the most popular heroes in Ukrainian legend is Kyrylo Kozhumiaka, a mythical figure who saved the city of Kiev from a dragon and rescued a princess from certain death.

## United Arab Emirates

**Capital:** Abu Dhabi

**Population:** 5,473,971

**Area:** 32,278 sq mi (83,600 sq km)

**Language:** Arabic, Persian, English, Hindi, Urdu

**Did You Know?** The world's biggest indoor theme park is located in Abu Dhabi, United Arab Emirates. The park's Formula Rossa roller coaster, which starts indoors and travels outside, is the world's fastest roller coaster. It reaches a top speed of 149 miles an hour.

FORMULA ROSSA ROLLER COASTER, ABU DHABI, UNITED ARAB EMIRATES

BUCKINGHAM PALACE, LONDON, UNITED KINGDO

## United Kingdom (Great Britain)

**Capital:** London

**Population:** 63,395,574

**Area:** 94,526 sq mi (244,820 sq km)

**Language:** English, Welsh, Scottish Gaelic

**Did You Know?** In 2012, researchers found a skeleton beneath a parking lot in central England, where an old church once stood. Tests proved the skeleton was the remains of the 15th-century British king Richard III, who was said to be one of the worst villains in history.

## United States

**Capital:** Washington, D.C.

**Population:** 316,668,567

**Area:** 3,795,951 sq mi (9,831,513 sq km)

**Language:** English, Spanish

**Did You Know?** The Statue of Liberty, which welcomes ships entering New York Harbor, was a gift to the United States from France. It took nine years to build and was shipped to New York in 1885, in 214 crates. The statue weighs 225 tons and stands about 111 feet from head to toe.

## Uruguay

**Capital:** Montevideo

**Population:** 3,324,460

**Area:** 68,039 sq mi (176,220 sq km)

**Language:** Spanish, Portunol

**Did You Know?** Despite its relatively small population, Uruguay has had big success in soccer. Uruguay won the first-ever men's World Cup in 1930 and has won the Copa America soccer championship a record 15 times.

## Uzbekistan

**Capital:** Tashkent

**Population:** 28,661,637

**Area:** 172,742 sq mi (447,400 sq km)

**Language:** Uzbek, Russian, Tajik

**Did You Know?** Uzbekistan and Liechtenstein are the only two countries that are "doubly landlocked." They are surrounded entirely by other countries that also have no seacoast.

## Vanuatu

**Capital:** Port-Vila

**Population:** 261,565

**Area:** 4,710 sq mi (12,200 sq km)

**Language:** French, English, Bislama, local languages

**Did You Know?** Pigs have lived on the islands of Vanuatu for over 3,000 years. Owning, or giving away, pigs is a sign of wealth and prestige. Even today, pigs are often traded in place of cash.

## Vatican City

**Population:** 836

**Area:** 0.17 sq mi (0.44 sq km)

**Language:** Italian, Latin, French

**Did You Know?** Vatican City is the headquarters of the Roman Catholic Church. Besides many priests and nuns, people who work there include members of the Swiss Guards. This tiny army has served the popes since the 1500s.

## Venezuela

**Capital:** Caracas

**Population:** 28,459,085

**Area:** 352,144 sq mi (912,050 sq km)

**Language:** Spanish, indigenous dialects

**Did You Know?** Some Venezuelans consider handkerchiefs to be unlucky and could be insulted to receive one as a gift.

## Vietnam

**Capital:** Hanoi

**Population:** 92,447,857

**Area:** 127,244 sq mi (329,560 sq km)

**Language:** Vietnamese, English, French, Chinese

**Did You Know?** The ancient city of Hué, in central Vietnam, served as the nation's capital for more than 100 years, beginning in the early 1800s.

## Yemen

**Capital:** Sana'a

**Population:** 25,408,288

**Area:** 203,850 sq mi (527,970 sq km)

**Language:** Arabic

**Did You Know?** In some parts of Yemen, it rains only once every five or ten years.

## Zambia

**Capital:** Lusaka

**Population:** 14,222,233

**Area:** 290,586 sq mi (752,614 sq km)

**Language:** English, indigenous languages

VICTORIA FALLS, ZAMBIA

**Did You Know?** Victoria Falls, on Zambia's border with Zimbabwe, are also known by the name Mosi-oa-Tunya, which means "the smoke that thunders."

## Zimbabwe

**Capital:** Harare

**Population:** 13,182,908

**Area:** 150,804 sq mi (390,580 sq km)

**Language:** English, Shona, Sindebele

**Did You Know?** Among the Ndebele people of Zimbabwe, married women often wear copper and brass rings, or *idzila,* around their neck, arms, and legs, to show a bond with their husband.

### COLOR KEY

- Africa
- Asia
- Australia
- Europe
- North America
- Pacific Islands
- South America

# NUMBERS

→What does the word "percent" mean? PAGE 180

# ON...AND ON...AND ON...

The set of numbers includes all different types of numbers—positive and negative numbers, fractions and decimals, and even irrational numbers that cannot be expressed as fractions.

There is no highest or lowest number, since you could take any number and add 1 to it or subtract 1 from it. Both positive and negative numbers go on to infinity.

∞

The symbol for infinity looks like an eight lying on its side.

## PRIME TIME

All positive numbers higher than 1 are either prime numbers or composite numbers.

A **prime number** can be divided only by itself and the number 1. So, the set of prime numbers includes 2, 3, 5, 7, 11, 13, 17, and so on. Prime numbers go on into infinity.

All other positive numbers (other than 1) are known as **composite numbers**, because they have at least two factors (numbers they can be divided by evenly) other than 1. For example, 6 is a composite number. It has three factors other than 1: 2, 3, and 6.

## INTEGERS

Integers are whole numbers, both positive and negative. Zero is an integer. So is –1. But fractions, decimals, and percentages are not integers.

## THE PREFIX TELLS THE NUMBER

The table below shows prefixes that stand for various numbers from 1 to 1 billion. Knowing what each prefix means can help you figure out the meanings of words it is part of. For example, a **pent**agon has **five** sides, and an **octo**pus has eight tentacles.

| Number | Prefix(es) | Word(s) |
|---|---|---|
| 1 | uni-, mono- | unicorn, monorail |
| 2 | bi- | binoculars |
| 3 | tri- | triangle |
| 4 | quadr-, tetr- | quadrangle, tetrahedron |
| 5 | pent-, quint- | pentagon, quintuplet |
| 6 | hex-, sext- | hexagon, sextuplet |
| 7 | hept-, sept- | heptathlon, septuplet |

| Number | Prefix(es) | Word(s) |
|---|---|---|
| 8 | oct- | octopus |
| 9 | non- | nonagon |
| 10 | dec- | decade |
| 100 | cent- | century |
| 1,000 | kilo- | kilometer |
| million | mega- | megabyte |
| billion | giga- | gigabyte |

## ZERO

Do you know the Roman numeral for 0? Probably not, because there isn't one!

The Babylonians in Asia, Hindus in India, and Mayans in the Americas were among the first peoples to use the idea of zero as a "placeholder." In the number system that we use today, "10" means 1 "ten" and 0 "ones." The 0 in 10 is a placeholder in the ones column.

Zero has some interesting properties. If you take any number and multiply it by 0, it equals 0. Any number added to 0 equals the original number.

# ROMAN NUMERALS

**The numerals we use today are called Arabic, or Hindu Arabic, numerals, after the ancient peoples who first used them. The ancient Romans had a different system, based on letters, as shown in the table to the left.**

## Numerals

| Arabic | Roman | Arabic | Roman |
|---|---|---|---|
| 1 | I | 16 | XVI |
| 2 | II | 17 | XVII |
| 3 | III | 18 | XVIII |
| 4 | IV | 19 | XIX |
| 5 | V | 20 | XX |
| 6 | VI | 30 | XXX |
| 7 | VII | 40 | XL |
| 8 | VIII | 50 | L |
| 9 | IX | 60 | LX |
| 10 | X | 70 | LXX |
| 11 | XI | 80 | LXXX |
| 12 | XII | 90 | XC |
| 13 | XIII | 100 | C |
| 14 | XIV | 500 | D |
| 15 | XV | 1,000 | M |

If one Roman numeral is followed by one with a greater value, the first is subtracted from the second. For example, IX means 10 – 1 = 9. Think of it as "one less than ten." On the other hand, if a Roman numeral is followed by one or more others that are equal or of lesser value, add them together. Thus, LXI means 50 + 10 + 1 = 61.

A Roman numeral can be repeated only three times to express a number. For example, XXX equals 30. You would have to write XL (50 minus 10) to show the number 40.

Roman numerals are still sometimes used today, such as on clock faces and in the names for Super Bowls.

**In Super Bowl XLVII, played in 2013, the Baltimore Ravens defeated the San Francisco 49ers, 34-31. Which Super Bowl was that, in Arabic numerals? Can you put the year and score in Roman numerals?**

**ANSWERS ON PAGES 334-336.**

## HOMEWORK TIP

Many websites can help you sharpen your math skills—and have fun in the process. Here are a few that are recommended by the American Library Association.

**AAAMath**
aaamath.com

**Gymnasium for the Brain**
gymnasiumforbrain.com

**Hooda Math →**
hoodamath.com

**Johnnie's Math Page**
jmathpage.com

**Math Playground**
MathPlayground.com

**For more suggestions, see:**
gws.ala.org/category/mathematics-computers

# FRACTIONS, PERCENTS, & DECIMALS

## FRACTIONS

A fraction is part of a whole. It helps to think of a fraction as a slice of a circle, with the circle being the whole (represented by the number 1). Check out the common fractions at right.

**1/2**

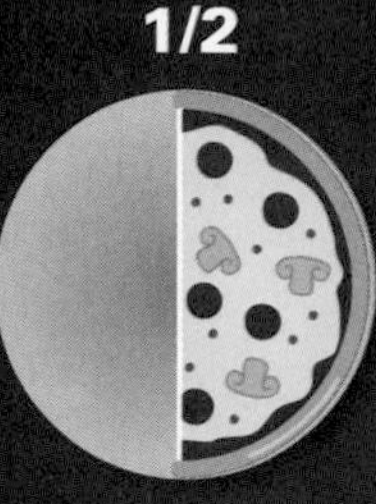

***1/2 is missing***

**2/3**

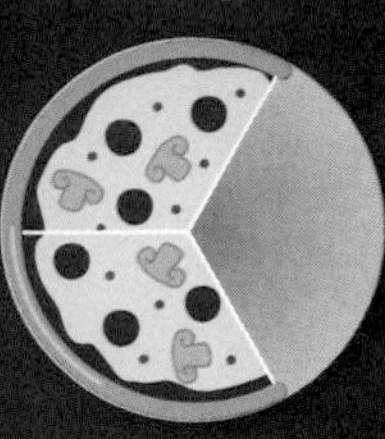

***1/3 is missing***

**7/8**

***1/8 is missing***

To reduce a fraction to its lowest terms, divide both the numerator (top number) and the denominator (bottom number) by the largest number by which both can be divided evenly. For example, to reduce 8/16 to its lowest terms, divide the numerator and denominator by 8. You end up with 1/2.

## PERCENTS

Percents also represent part of a whole. The word *percent* means "per hundred." So, a percent is like a fraction with a denominator of 100. You see percents every day. If you scored 80 percent on a test at school, you received 80 points out of a possible 100. Changing percents to fractions is not hard. Here are two examples:

80% = 80/100; reduced to its lowest terms, 80/100 becomes 4/5
23% = 23/100, which cannot be reduced

## DECIMALS

Decimals are also part of a whole. They are represented with numerals placed to the right of a decimal point. Each position—or place—in a decimal has its own name.

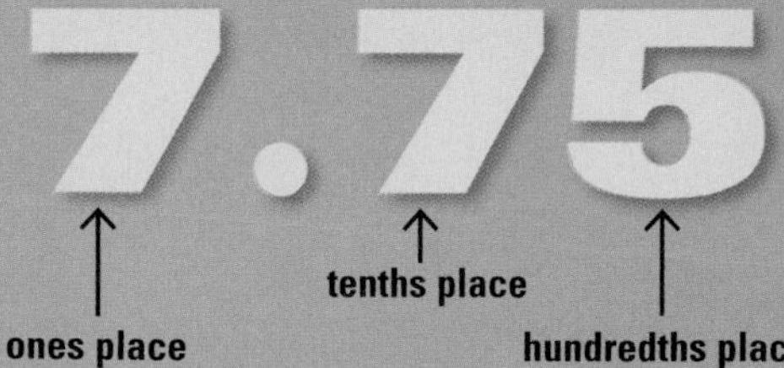

To convert a decimal to a fraction or a percent, you have to pay attention to the placement after the decimal point. For example, 0.2 means 2 tenths, or 2/10, which can be reduced to 1/5. And think of 0.25 as 25 hundredths, or 25/100, which can be reduced to 1/4. To convert a decimal to a percent, just move the decimal point to the right of the hundredths place: 0.25 = 25% and 0.025 = 2.5%

**Can you change these decimals to fractions that are reduced to lowest terms?**
**0.3 0.75 0.6**

**ANSWERS ON PAGES 334-336.**

# BRAIN TEASERS!



## Number Facts

First, figure out the right number to answer each question. Then, add or subtract your answers, as shown, and see if you can get the correct result at the end of it all!

The Roman Empire came to an end in the year CDLXXVI. What year was that in Arabic numerals?

− How many sides does a heptagon have?

+ Rhode Island has an area of about 1,545 square miles, while Alaska is some 665,384 square miles in area. How many Rhode Islands would fit into Alaska? (Just ignore anything after the decimal point.)

− What is the smallest prime number?

+ According to some estimates there were about 1 billion people in the world by 1804 and 2 billion by 1927. How many years did it take for the world population to go from 1 billion to 2 billion?

− Justin Bieber was born on March 1, 1994. So how many years old will he be after his birthday in March 2014?

− How many meters are there in a kilometer?

= What did you end up with?

## Secret Message

Here is a message written in secret code. Luckily, you have already figured out out the code. A is 25, B is 24, C is 23, and so on all the way down to Y, which is 1, and Z, which is 0. Now, decode the message to learn a famous ancient saying.

6 18 21 3 25 1 5 10 17 7 6 18 21 3 25 1
22 11 3 12

## Missing Numbers

Can you figure out what the missing numbers should be in these four groups?

| A | | | | B | | | C | | | D | | |
|---|---|---|---|---|---|---|---|---|---|---|---|---|
| ?? | 4 | 9 | 16 | 2 | 3 | 5 | 45 | 9 | 72 | 19 | 9 | 33 |
| 25 | ?? | 49 | 64 | 7 | ?? | 13 | 69 | 15 | 78 | 90 | ?? | 80 |
| 81 | 100 | ?? | 144 | ?? | 19 | 23 | 20 | ?? | 11 | 14 | 4 | 22 |

## A Little Logic

1. You are picking out socks from your drawer to wear to school, but it's too dark to see the colors, and the socks are all mixed up. There are 12 red socks in there, all exactly the same, and 11 blue socks, also all the same (1 sock got lost in the laundry). How many socks do you have to take out to be sure of getting one matching pair?

2. What if there are 12 red socks, 11 blue socks, and 10 green socks in the drawer. Then, how many would you need to take up to be sure you got a pair?

ANSWERS ON PAGES 334-336

# POPULATION

→ What is the world's biggest "mega-city"? PAGE 183

## *Where Do People Live?*

In 2013, there were more than 7 billion people in the world. Six out of every ten lived in Asia. China, the world's second-biggest country in land area, ranked first in population, with India close behind. Russia, by far the largest country in area, ranked only ninth in population. The United States is the world's third-biggest country, in both land area and population.

## COUNTRY POPULATIONS, 2013

### LARGEST COUNTRIES

### SMALLEST COUNTRIES

| | COUNTRY | POPULATION |
|---|---|---|
| 1. | Vatican City | 836 |
| 2. | Nauru | 9,434 |
| 3. | Tuvalu | 10,698 |
| 4. | Palau | 21,108 |
| 5. | Monaco | 30,500 |

*Excluding Taiwan, pop. 23,299,716, Hong Kong, pop. 7,182,724, and Macao, pop. 583,003

Note: These and most other statistics in this chapter come from the U.S. Census Bureau.

## The *Growing* World Population

Partly because of better living conditions, the world population began increasing rapidly in the 1700s and has grown even faster since then.

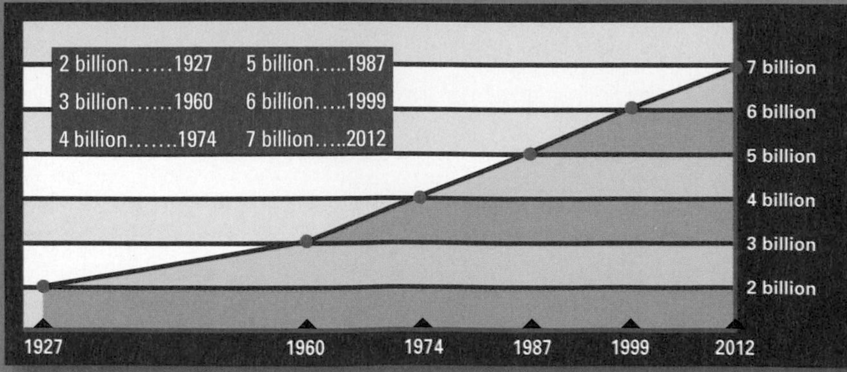

# TRENDS AROUND the WORLD

If current trends continue, the world's population is expected to reach 8 billion around 2023 and 9 billion well before 2050. The population is growing fastest in the developing countries of Africa. In Europe, the population is falling.

| | Population (in millions) | | |
|---|---|---|---|
| **Continent** | **2013** | **2050** | **Change** |
| **Africa** | 1,099 | 2,232 | +104% |
| **Asia** | 4,265 | 5,130 | +20% |
| **Europe**[1] | 741 | 702 | –5% |
| **North America**[2] | 552 | 718 | +30% |
| **South America** | 402 | 490 | +22% |
| **Oceania**[3] | 36 | 49 | +36% |

1. Includes all of Russia. 2. Includes Mexico, Central America, and the Caribbean. 3. Includes Australia.

Eight of the ten fastest-growing nations in the world are developing countries in Africa. Women in the African nations of Niger, Mali, Somalia, Uganda, and Burkina Faso all have an average of six or more children in their lifetime. →

Women in the United States have an average of only two children—basically enough to keep the population level. The U.S. population is growing at about 1 percent a year, but that is mostly because of immigration.

Of the ten countries that are losing population the fastest, seven are in Europe. The population of Moldova, in Eastern Europe, is falling the fastest, by more than 1 percent a year. This is partly because families tend to be small and partly because more people leave the country than come in as immigrants.

# The World's BIGGEST MEGA-CITIES

Many people live in and around cities, in a large area sometimes called a "mega-city." The area may include more than one city when the cities are close together. These are the biggest mega-cities according to United Nations estimates for 2010.

*Mumbai, India*

| | CITY, COUNTRY | POPULATION |
|---|---|---|
| **1.** | Tokyo, Japan | 36,669,000 |
| **2.** | Delhi, India | 22,157,000 |
| **3.** | São Paulo, Brazil | 20,262,000 |
| **4.** | Mumbai, India | 20,041,000 |
| **5.** | Mexico City, Mexico | 19,460,000 |
| **6.** | New York/Newark, U.S. | 19,425,000 |

# The Growing U.S. Population

**The number of Americans has grown from under 4 million in 1790 to over 300 million today. By 2050, it is expected to pass 420 million.**

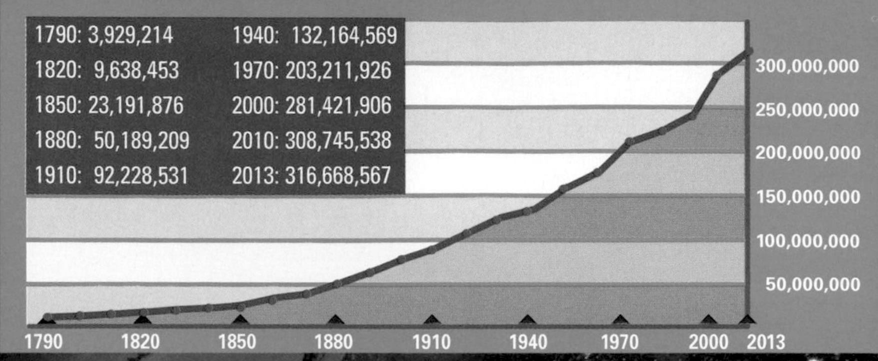


## The U.S. Population by Race, 2011

White people make up by far the largest racial group in the United States today, while African Americans are by far the largest racial minority.

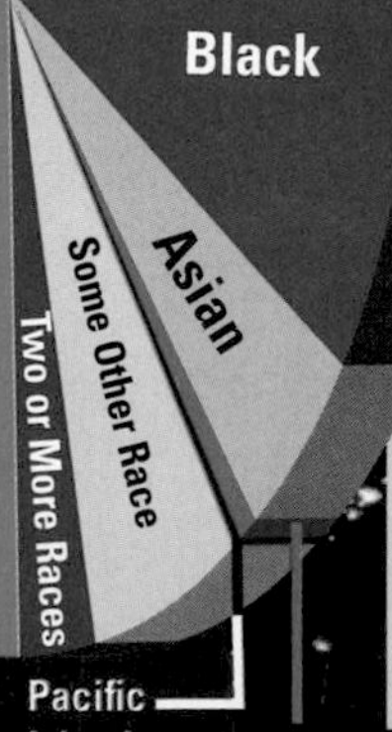


| Race | Number | Percent of Population |
|---|---|---|
| White | 230,879,179 | 74.1% |
| Black | 39,244,071 | 12.6% |
| Asian | 15,027,719 | 4.8% |
| American Indian* | 2,522,316 | 0.8% |
| Pacific Islander | 494,453 | 0.2% |
| Some Other Race | 14,703,533 | 4.7% |
| Two or More Races | 8,720,648 | 2.8% |

*Also includes Alaska Natives

Note: Hispanic Americans, or Latinos, are not listed separately here, since they may be of any race. In 2011, they made up an estimated 16.7 percent of the population.

**Did You KNOW?**

**A majority of people in the United States today (about 63 percent) are both white and non-Hispanic. But as time goes on, this "majority" is expected to become a minority. The Census Bureau recently estimated that in 2011, for the first time, more than half of all children under the age of one were non-white, Hispanic, or both.**

## Population of the United States, 2012

As of July, based on Census Bureau estimates

| STATE AND RANK | POPULATION | STATE AND RANK | POPULATION |
|---|---|---|---|
| 1. California (CA) | 38,041,430 | 27. Oregon (OR) | 3,899,353 |
| 2. Texas (TX) | 26,059,203 | 28. Oklahoma (OK) | 3,814,820 |
| 3. New York (NY) | 19,570,261 | 29. Connecticut (CT) | 3,590,347 |
| 4. Florida (FL) | 19,317,568 | 30. Iowa (IA) | 3,074,186 |
| 5. Illinois (IL) | 12,875,255 | 31. Mississippi (MS) | 2,984,926 |
| 6. Pennsylvania (PA) | 12,763,536 | 32. Arkansas (AR) | 2,949,131 |
| 7. Ohio (OH) | 11,544,225 | 33. Kansas (KS) | 2,885,905 |
| 8. Georgia (GA) | 9,919,945 | 34. Utah (UT) | 2,855,287 |
| 9. Michigan (MI) | 9,883,360 | 35. Nevada (NV) | 2,758,931 |
| 10. North Carolina (NC) | 9,752,073 | 36. New Mexico (NM) | 2,085,538 |
| 11. New Jersey (NJ) | 8,864,590 | 37. Nebraska (NE) | 1,855,525 |
| 12. Virginia (VA) | 8,185,867 | 38. West Virginia (WV) | 1,855,413 |
| 13. Washington (WA) | 6,897,012 | 39. Idaho (ID) | 1,595,728 |
| 14. Massachusetts (MA) | 6,646,144 | 40. Hawaii (HI) | 1,392,313 |
| 15. Arizona (AZ) | 6,553,255 | 41. Maine (ME) | 1,329,192 |
| 16. Indiana (IN) | 6,537,334 | 42. New Hampshire (NH) | 1,320,718 |
| 17. Tennessee (TN) | 6,456,243 | 43. Rhode Island (RI) | 1,050,292 |
| 18. Missouri (MO) | 6,021,988 | 44. Montana (MT) | 1,005,141 |
| 19. Maryland (MD) | 5,884,563 | 45. Delaware (DE) | 917,092 |
| 20. Wisconsin (WI) | 5,726,398 | 46. South Dakota (SD) | 833,354 |
| 21. Minnesota (MN) | 5,379,139 | 47. Alaska (AK) | 731,449 |
| 22. Colorado (CO) | 5,187,582 | 48. North Dakota (ND) | 699,628 |
| 23. Alabama (AL) | 4,822,023 | 49. Vermont (VT) | 626,011 |
| 24. South Carolina (SC) | 4,723,723 | 50. Wyoming (WY) | 576,412 |
| 25. Louisiana (LA) | 4,601,893 | District of Columbia (DC) | 632,323 |
| 26. Kentucky (KY) | 4,380,415 | Puerto Rico (PR) | 3,667,084 |

## LARGEST CITIES in the United States

**Cities grow and shrink in population. Below is a list of the largest U.S. cities, with their population in 2011. Their 1950 populations are shown for comparison. Populations are for people living within the city limits only.**

| RANK & CITY | 2011 | 1950 |
|---|---|---|
| 1. New York, NY | 8,224,910 | 7,891,957 |
| 2. Los Angeles, CA | 3,819,702 | 1,970,358 |
| 3. Chicago, IL | 2,707,120 | 3,620,962 |
| 4. Houston, TX | 2,145,146 | 596,163 |
| 5. Philadelphia, PA | 1,536,471 | 2,071,605 |
| 6. Phoenix, AZ | 1,469,471 | 106,818 |
| 7. San Antonio, TX | 1,359,758 | 408,442 |
| 8. San Diego, CA | 1,326,179 | 434,462 |
| 9. Dallas, TX | 1,223,229 | 334,387 |
| 10. San Jose, CA | 967,487 | 95,280 |

# Americans From Near and Far

About 40 million people in the United States today, or one in eight Americans, were born in some other country. They came to the U.S. in search of a better life. Most recent immigrants are from Latin America (53 percent of the foreign-born today) or Asia (29 percent). About 12 percent were born in Europe.

Not all foreign-born people in the U.S. are legal immigrants. The U.S. government estimates that there are some 11 million unauthorized immigrants living in the country. Many of these people arrived from other nations without permission. Others had permission to visit, work, or attend school in the U.S. for a time, but stayed on afterward.

## Where Do Immigrants Come From?

A total of 757,434 immigrants were naturalized—that is, were sworn in as American citizens—in the 12-month period ending September 30, 2012. About one in ten of these new citizens originally came from Mexico. The table below shows the 14 countries where the largest numbers of new Americans came from.

| COUNTRY | Number | Percent of total |
|---|---|---|
| Mexico | 102,181 | 13.5% |
| Philippines | 44,958 | 5.9% |
| India | 42,928 | 5.7% |
| Dominican Republic | 33,351 | 4.4% |
| China* | 31,868 | 4.2% |
| Cuba | 31,244 | 4.1% |
| Colombia | 23,972 | 3.2% |
| Vietnam | 23,490 | 3.1% |
| Haiti | 18,114 | 2.5% |
| El Salvador | 16,685 | 2.2% |
| Jamaica | 15,531 | 2.1% |
| South Korea | 13,790 | 1.8% |
| Peru | 11,814 | 1.6% |
| Pakistan | 11,150 | 1.5% |

*Excludes Taiwan, Hong Kong, and Macau.

## Where Do Immigrants Settle?

In the 12 months ending September 30, 2012, 1,031,631 people from foreign countries became "legal permanent residents" of the U.S. One out of five, including many from Vietnam, Mexico, and the Philippines, settled in California. Many immigrants born in the Dominican Republic settled in New York. Florida was the destination for most Haitian and Cuban immigrants.

California, 196,622

New York, 149,505

Florida, 103,047

Texas, 95,567

New Jersey, 50,790

Illinois, 38,373

Massachusetts, 31,392

**The states shown here were home to two out of three immigrants who became legal permanent residents of the U.S. in 2012.**

**Did You KNOW?** **Fifty years ago, immigration to the U.S. was at a low point. Only about one in 20 Americans was foreign-born, and three out of four foreign-born Americans came from Europe. The largest numbers were from Italy and Germany.**

# Fast-Growing POPULATIONS



## Hispanic Americans by Background

| Origin | Percent of All Hispanics |
|---|---|
| Mexico | 64.6% |
| Puerto Rico | 9.4% |
| El Salvador | 3.8% |
| Cuba | 3.6% |
| Dominican Rep. | 3.0% |
| Guatemala | 2.3% |
| Colombia | 1.9% |
| Honduras | 1.3% |
| Ecuador | 1.3% |
| Peru | 1.1% |
| All Other or Unknown | 7.7% |

## HISPANIC AMERICANS

More than 50 million Americans trace their heritage back to a Spanish-speaking country or territory, making Hispanic Americans the biggest minority group in the United States. Between 2000 and 2011, the Hispanic-American population grew by 47 percent. By 2050, if current trends continue, three out of every ten Americans will be Hispanic.

There are about 14 million Hispanic Americans living in California, more than in any other state. Some 10 million people of Hispanic origin live in Texas. New Mexico has the highest proportion of Hispanic residents (47 percent in 2011).

## ASIAN AMERICANS

More than 15 million Americans are Asian, not counting those of two or more races. Between 2000 and 2011 alone, the Asian American population grew by 46 percent—faster than any other racial group. In comparison, the number of whites who are not Hispanic grew by only 1.3 percent. About 6 million Asians live in California, more than in any other state.

*Hmong Market Place, St. Paul, MN*

## Asian Americans by Background

| Origin | Percent of All Asians |
|---|---|
| China* | 22.4% |
| India | 19.1% |
| Philippines | 17.3% |
| Vietnam | 10.9% |
| South Korea | 9.8% |
| Japan | 5.2% |
| Pakistan | 2.4% |
| Cambodia | 1.7% |
| Hmong** | 1.7% |
| Laos | 1.4% |
| All Other or Unknown | 8.1% |

*Not including Taiwan.

**The Hmong are an ethnic group from China and Southeast Asia.

# PRIZES & CONTESTS

→Who won the Academy Award for Best Actress in 2013? PAGE 189

## NOBEL PRIZES

**The Nobel Prizes are named after Alfred B. Nobel (1833–1896), a Swedish scientist who invented dynamite and who left money for most of the prizes. They are given every year for promoting peace, as well as for achievements in physics, chemistry, physiology or medicine, literature, and economics.**

### SELECTED WINNERS OF THE NOBEL PEACE PRIZE

| YEAR | NAME | POSITION AND ACTIONS |
|---|---|---|
| 2012 | European Union (EU) | Organization of European countries, for promoting peace, democracy, and human rights in Europe |
| 2009 | Barack Obama | U.S. president, for his efforts in international diplomacy |
| 2007 | Al Gore Jr. | Former U.S. vice president, and the International Panel on Climate Change, for their efforts in educating the world about global warming |
| 2004 | Wangari Maathai | Kenyan environmentalist and social reformer |
| 2002 | Jimmy Carter | Former U.S. president and peace negotiator |
| 1993 | Nelson Mandela, F. W. de Klerk | Leader of South African blacks; president of South Africa |
| 1991 | Aung San Suu Kyi | Activist for democracy in Myanmar (Burma) |
| 1989 | Dalai Lama | Tibetan Buddhist leader, forced into exile in 1959 |
| 1986 | Elie Wiesel | Holocaust survivor and author |
| 1979 | Mother Teresa | Leader of the order of the Missionaries of Charity, who cared for the sick and dying in India → |
| 1964 | Martin Luther King Jr. | Civil rights leader who used only peaceful means to achieve change |
| 1954 | Albert Schweitzer | Missionary, surgeon |
| 1919 | Woodrow Wilson | U.S. president who played a key role in founding the League of Nations |
| 1906 | Theodore Roosevelt | U.S. president who helped negotiate a peace treaty between Japan and Russia |

**Did You KNOW?** Albert Schweitzer, the 1954 Nobel Peace Prize winner, was a church pastor who became a medical doctor because he wanted to help people in Africa receive medical care. He founded a hospital in Gabon in 1913. In addition to his medical work, he was an anti-war activist. Schweitzer used his Nobel Prize winnings to further fund his humanitarian work. He died in his hospital in 1965, at the age of 90. The Albert Schweitzer Hospital is still in operation today, treating nearly 30,000 patients every year.

# 2013 KIDS' CHOICE AWARDS

**The 2013 Kids' Choice Awards** were held March 23, 2013, and hosted by Josh Duhamel. More than 350 million votes were cast by kids to choose the winners. For more information, go to: **www.nick.com**

| Award | Winner |
|---|---|
| Music Group | One Direction |
| Movie | *The Hunger Games* |
| Book | The Hunger Games series |
| Video Game | *Just Dance 4* |
| Favorite App | Temple Run |
| Reality TV Show | *Wipeout* |
| TV Show | *Victorious* |
| Cartoon | *SpongeBob SquarePants* |
| TV Actor | Ross Lynch |
| TV Actress | Selena Gomez |
| Favorite Villain | Simon Cowell (*The X Factor*) |
| Movie Actor | Johnny Depp |
| Movie Actress | Kristen Stewart |
| Animated Movie | *Wreck-It Ralph* |
| Voice from an Animated Movie | Adam Sandler (*Hotel Transylvania*) |
| Male Singer | Justin Bieber |
| Female Singer | Katy Perry |
| Favorite Song | "What Makes You Beautiful" (One Direction) |
| Male Athlete | LeBron James |
| Female Athlete | Danica Patrick → |

# THE ACADEMY AWARDS

The Academy Awards—sometimes called the Oscars—have been held every year since 1929. Winners are chosen by the Academy of Motion Picture Arts and Sciences, a group made up of actors and other people involved in the film industry. Winners at the 2013 Academy Awards ceremony, honoring 2012 movies, included:

| Award | Winner |
|---|---|
| Best Picture | *Argo* |
| Actress in a Leading Role | Jennifer Lawrence (*Silver Linings Playbook*) |
| Actor in a Leading Role | Daniel Day-Lewis (*Lincoln*) |
| Actress in a Supporting Role | Anne Hathaway (*Les Misérables*) |
| Actor in a Supporting Role | Christoph Waltz (*Django Unchained*) |
| Animated Feature Film | *Brave* → |
| Original Song | "Skyfall" (*Skyfall*) |
| Visual Effects | *Life of Pi* |

# BEE INVOLVED

If you have a knack for spelling or an interest in world geography, then these two national contests may be for you.

## NATIONAL SPELLING BEE

The National Spelling Bee was started in Louisville, Kentucky, by the *Courier-Journal* newspaper in 1925. Today, winners of local spelling bees may qualify for the Scripps National Spelling Bee, held in Washington, D.C., in late May or early June. In 2013, the National Spelling Bee was updated to include vocabulary knowledge. In addition to spelling their words, students had to be able to pick the correct definition from a multiple choice list.

**Arvind Mahankali**, 13 years old, from Bayside Hills, New York, → won the 86th annual Scripps National Spelling Bee on May 30, 2013. He won the bee by correctly spelling the word "knaidel," which means a small mass of leavened dough. The word has Yiddish origins. After Mahankali's win, some Yiddish experts argued that the word should actually be spelled differently. The bee's organizers said there was no controversy, however, because the word was spelled as it is written in the official dictionary used by the competition.

**For more information, visit: www.spellingbee.com**

## NATIONAL GEOGRAPHIC BEE

The National Geographic Bee draws 4 million contestants from nearly 12,000 schools in all parts of the United States. To enter, students must be in grades 4-8. School-level bees are followed by state-level bees and then the nationals, which have been moderated by *Jeopardy!* host Alex Trebek. Trebek announced that the 2013 bee would be his last. After a quarter-century as moderator, Trebek said he wanted to spend more time visiting the places he had been asking questions about.

**Sathwik Karnik,** 12 years old, from Norfolk, Massachusetts, won the 25th National Geographic Bee on May 22, 2013. He won by correctly answering this final question: "Because Earth bulges at the Equator, the point that is farthest from Earth's center is the summit of a peak in Ecuador. Name this peak." (The answer: Chimborazo.) Karnik won a $25,000 college scholarship, a trip to the Galápagos Islands, and a lifetime membership in the National Geographic Society.

**For more information, visit: www.nationalgeographic.com/geobee**

**Did You KNOW?**

**Several national science or math contests for students take place every year. One of these contests is the DuPont Challenge. The 2013 winner in the senior division of this science essay contest was Hugo Yen, a student at Troy High School in Fullerton, CA. The title of his essay? *Flavonoids: The Avengers of Rice Bacterial Blight.***

# ODD CONTESTS

It just seems to be part of human nature to find out who is the best at something, no matter what it is! There are state, national, and international competitions in a wide variety of events. Most of them are commonplace ones such as foot races or trivia contests. But then there are others that are more unusual. Here are a few contests that are not very ordinary.

## DUCT TAPE PROM OUTFITS

Couples entering the Duck® Brand Duct Tape Stuck At Prom Contest must attend a high school prom wearing complete outfits and accessories made from duct tape. The winning couple is chosen based on originality, workmanship, quantity of Duck Tape used, use of colors, and creative use of accessories. The first place couple each receives a $5,000 scholarship, and a $5,000 cash prize is awarded to the school that hosted the prom.

For more information, visit: www.stuckatprom.com

Cole Sudduth and Lara Ford

## CREATIVE SANDWICH

Have a great idea for a sandwich? The Jif® peanut butter company awards a $25,000 college scholarship to a student who comes up with a new sandwich recipe using any Jif products. The 2013 winner of the contest was 9-year-old Jacob Crawford from Morganton, North Carolina, for his Magnificent Mole Chicken Torta.

For more information, visit: www jif.com

## ROTTEN SNEAKERS

The National Odor-Eaters® Rotten Sneaker Contest is held annually in Montpelier, Vermont. In 2013, the panel of judges included NASA "Master Sniffer" George Aldrich, a chemical specialist for space missions. Each year, the winner's sneakers are added to the Odor-Eaters "Hall of Fumes." The 2013 winner, Casey Adams, was awarded $2,500, the Golden Sneaker Award trophy, a supply of Odor-Eaters products, and a trip to see the play *Wicked* on Broadway in New York City.

For more information, visit: www.odor-eaters.com

# RELIGION

→Where does the pope live? PAGE 195

How did the universe begin? Why are we here on Earth? What happens to us after we die? For many people, religion provides answers to questions like these. Believing in a God or gods, or in a higher power, is one way people make sense of the world around them. Religion can also help guide people's lives.

Different religions have different beliefs. For example, Christians, Jews, and Muslims are monotheists, meaning they believe in only one God. Hindus are polytheists, meaning they believe in many gods. On this page and the next are some facts about the world's major religions.

## Christianity

**WHO STARTED CHRISTIANITY?** Christianity is based on the teachings of Jesus Christ. He was born in Bethlehem between 8 B.C. and 4 B.C. and died about A.D. 29.

**WHAT WRITINGS ARE THERE?** The **Bible**, consisting of the Old Testament and New Testament, is the main spiritual text in Christianity.

**WHAT DO CHRISTIANS BELIEVE?** There is only one God. God sent his Son, Jesus Christ, to Earth. Jesus died to save humankind but later rose from the dead.

**HOW MANY ARE THERE?** Christianity is the world's biggest religion. In 2011, there were about 2.3 billion Christians worldwide

**WHAT KINDS ARE THERE?** About 1.2 billion Christians are **Roman Catholics**, who follow the Pope's leadership. **Orthodox Christians** accept similar teachings but follow different leadership. **Protestants** disagree with many Catholic teachings. They believe in the Bible's authority.

## Buddhism

**WHO STARTED BUDDHISM?** Siddhartha Gautama (the Buddha), around 525 B.C.

**WHAT WRITINGS ARE THERE?** The Tripitaka, or "Three Baskets," contains three collections of teachings, rules, and commentaries. There are also other texts, many of which are called sutras.

**WHAT DO BUDDHISTS BELIEVE?** Buddha taught that life is filled with suffering. Through meditation and deeds, one can end the cycle of endless birth and rebirth and achieve a state of perfect peace known as nirvana.

**HOW MANY ARE THERE?** In 2011, there were about 468 million Buddhists in the world, 98% of them in Asia.

**WHAT KINDS ARE THERE?** There are two main kinds. Theravada ("Way of the Elders") Buddhism, the older kind, is more common in countries such as Sri Lanka, Myanmar, and Thailand. Mahayana ("Great Vehicle") Buddhism is more common in China, Korea, Japan, and Tibet.

# Hinduism

**WHO STARTED HINDUISM?** The beliefs of Aryans, who migrated to India around 1500 B.C., intermixed with the beliefs of the people who already lived there.

**WHAT WRITINGS ARE THERE?** The **Vedas** ("Knowledge") collect the most important writings, including the ancient hymns in the **Samhita** and the teachings in the **Upanishads.** Also important are the stories the **Bhagavad-Gita** and the **Ramayana**.

**WHAT DO HINDUS BELIEVE?** There is one divine principle, known as **brahman**; the various gods are only aspects of it. Life is an aspect of, yet separate from the divine. To escape a meaningless cycle of birth and rebirth (**samsara**), one must improve one's **karma** (the purity or impurity of one's past deeds).

**HOW MANY ARE THERE?** In 2011, there were about 960 million Hindus, mainly in India and in places that people from India have immigrated to.

**WHAT KINDS ARE THERE?** Most Hindus are primarily devoted to a single deity, the most common being the gods **Vishnu** and **Shiva** and the goddess **Shakti**.

# Islam

**WHO STARTED ISLAM?** Muhammad, the Prophet, about A.D. 622.

**WHAT WRITINGS ARE THERE?** The **Koran** (*al-Qur'an* in Arabic) is regarded as the word of God. The **Sunna**, or example of the Prophet, is recorded in the **Hadith**.

**WHAT DO MUSLIMS BELIEVE?** People who practice Islam are known as Muslims. There is only one God. God revealed the Koran to Muhammad so he could teach humankind truth and justice. Those who "submit" (literal meaning of "Islam") to God will attain salvation.

**HOW MANY ARE THERE?** In 2011, there were about 1.6 billion Muslims, mostly in parts of Africa and Asia.

**WHAT KINDS ARE THERE?** There are two major groups: the Sunnis, who make up about 84% of the world's Muslims, and the Shiites, who broke away in a dispute over leadership after Muhammad died in 632.

# Judaism

**WHO STARTED JUDAISM?** Abraham is thought to be the founder of Judaism, one of the first monotheistic religions. He probably lived between 2000 B.C. and 1500 B.C.

**WHAT WRITINGS ARE THERE?** The most important is the **Torah** ("Law"), the five books of Moses. The **Nevi'im** ("Prophets") and **Ketuvim** ("Writings") are also part of the Hebrew Bible.

**WHAT DO JEWS BELIEVE?** There is one God who created the universe. One should be faithful to God and observe God's laws.

**HOW MANY ARE THERE?** In 2011, there were almost 15 million Jews around the world. Many live in Israel or the United States.

**WHAT KINDS ARE THERE?** In the U.S. there are three main forms: **Orthodox**, **Conservative**, and **Reform**. Orthodox Jews are the most traditional, following strict laws about dress and diet. Reform Jews are the least traditional. Conservative Jews are somewhere in-between.

# Major Holy Days

## FOR CHRISTIANS, JEWS, MUSLIMS, BUDDHISTS, AND HINDUS

## CHRISTIAN HOLY DAYS

| DAY | 2014 | 2015 | 2016 |
|---|---|---|---|
| Ash Wednesday | March 5 | February 18 | February 10 |
| Good Friday | April 18 | April 3 | March 25 |
| Easter Sunday | April 20 | April 5 | March 27 |
| Easter for Orthodox Churches | April 20 | April 12 | May 1 |
| Christmas* | December 25 | December 25 | December 25 |

***Russian and some other Orthodox churches celebrate Christmas in January.**

## JEWISH HOLY DAYS

**The Jewish holy days begin at sundown the night before the first full day of the observance. The dates of first full days are listed below.**

| DAY | 2014–2015 (5775) | 2015–2016 (5776) | 2016–2017 (5777) |
|---|---|---|---|
| Rosh Hashanah (New Year) | September 25, 2014 | September 14, 2015 | October 3, 2016 |
| Yom Kippur (Day of Atonement) | October 4, 2014 | September 23, 2015 | October 12, 2016 |
| Hanukkah (Festival of Lights) | December 17, 2014 | December 7, 2015 | December 25, 2016 |
| Passover | April 4, 2015 | April 23, 2016 | April 11, 2017 |

## ISLAMIC (MUSLIM) HOLY DAYS

**The Islamic holy days begin at sundown the night before the first full day of the observance. The dates of first full days are listed below.**

| DAY | 2013–2014 (1435) | 2014–2015 (1436) | 2015–2016 (1437) |
|---|---|---|---|
| Muharram 1 (New Year) | November 4, 2013 | October 25, 2014 | October 2, 2015 |
| Mawlid (Birthday of Muhammad) | January 13, 2014 | January 3, 2015 | December 12, 2015 |
| Ramadan (Month of Fasting) | June 28, 2014 | June 18, 2015 | June 7, 2016 |
| Eid al-Fitr (End of Ramadan) | July 28, 2014 | July 17, 2015 | July 7, 2016 |
| Eid al-Adha | October 4, 2014 | September 23, 2015 | September 13, 2016 |

## BUDDHIST HOLY DAYS

**Not all Buddhists use the same calendar to determine holidays and festivals. A few well-known Buddhist observances and the months in which they may fall are listed below.**

**NIRVANA DAY, February:** Marks the death of Siddhartha Gautama (the Buddha).

←**VESAK OR VISAKAH PUJA (BUDDHA DAY), April/May:** Celebrates the birth, enlightenment, and death of the Buddha.

**ASALHA PUJA (DHARMA DAY), July:** Commemorates the Buddha's first teaching.

**MAGHA PUJA OR SANGHA DAY, February:** Commemorates the day when 1,250 of Buddha's followers (**sangha**) visited him without his calling them.

**VASSA (RAINS RETREAT), July-October:** A three-month period during Asia's rainy season when monks travel little and spend more time on meditation and study.

## HINDU HOLY DAYS

**Different Hindu groups use different calendars. A few of the many Hindu festivals and the months in which they may fall are listed below.**

**MAHA SHIVARATRI, February/March:** Festival dedicated to Shiva, creator and destroyer.

←**HOLI, February/March:** Festival of spring

**RAMANAVAMI, March/April:** Celebrates the birth of Rama, the seventh incarnation of Vishnu.

**DIWALI, October/November:** Festival of Lights

## A NEW ROMAN CATHOLIC LEADER

On March 13, 2013, cardinals of the Roman Catholic Church elected Cardinal Jorge Mario Bergoglio, archbishop of Buenos Aires, Argentina, to serve as pope. The new pope, who chose to be called Francis, is the first pope to come from Latin America. He is also the first to choose the name Francis. The pope lives in Vatican City, an independent state within Rome, Italy. He is the spiritual leader of the world's Roman Catholics and sets the church's religious policies. He also heads a huge organization that administers church institutions, such as schools, hospitals, and charities. It is the pope who appoints new cardinals (the highest church officials except for the pope), names new saints, and in general represents the church throughout the world. The election of a new pope became necessary when Pope Benedict XVI decided, in February 2013, to resign because of his health.

# SCIENCE

→What are the two main kinds of cells? PAGE 202

## THE WORLD OF SCIENCE

The Latin root of the word "science" is *scire*, meaning "to know." When people use the word *science,* they usually mean a kind of knowledge that can be discovered and backed up by observation or experiments.

There are four main branches of scientific study: Physical Science, Life Science (Biology), Earth Science, and Social Science. Each branch has more specific areas. For example, biology includes zoology (the study of animals), which includes entomology (the study of insects).

Scientists must often draw from more than one discipline. Biochemists, for example, deal with the chemistry that happens inside living things. Paleontologists study fossil remains of ancient plants and animals. Astrophysicists study matter and energy in outer space. And all scientists use mathematics.

### PHYSICAL SCIENCE

**ASTRONOMY:** stars, planets, outer space

**CHEMISTRY:** properties and behavior of substances

**PHYSICS:** matter and energy

### EARTH SCIENCE

**GEOGRAPHY:** Earth's surface and its relationship to humans

**GEOLOGY:** Earth's structure

**HYDROLOGY:** water

**METEOROLOGY:** Earth's atmosphere and weather

**MINERALOGY:** minerals

**OCEANOGRAPHY:** the sea, including currents and tides

**PETROLOGY:** rocks

**SEISMOLOGY:** earthquakes

**VOLCANOLOGY:** volcanoes

### LIFE SCIENCE (BIOLOGY)

**ANATOMY:** structure of the human body

**BOTANY:** plants

**ECOLOGY:** living things in relation to their environment

**GENETICS:** heredity

**PATHOLOGY:** diseases and their effects on the human body

**PHYSIOLOGY:** the body's biological processes

**ZOOLOGY:** animals

### SOCIAL SCIENCE

**ANTHROPOLOGY:** human cultures and physical characteristics

**ECONOMICS:** production and distribution of goods and services

**POLITICAL SCIENCE:** governments

**PSYCHOLOGY:** mental processes and behavior

**SOCIOLOGY:** human society and community life

# HOW SCIENTISTS MAKE DISCOVERIES: THE SCIENTIFIC METHOD

**The scientific method was developed over many centuries. You can think of it as having five steps:**

→ ❶ **Ask a question.**

→ ❷ **Gather information through observation.**

→ ❸ **Based on that information, make an educated guess (hypothesis) about the answer to your question.**

→ ❹ **Design an experiment to test that hypothesis.**

→ ❺ **Evaluate the results.**

If the experiment shows that your hypothesis is wrong, make up a new hypothesis. If the experiment supports your hypothesis, then your hypothesis may be correct! However, it is usually necessary to test a hypothesis with many different experiments before it can be accepted as a scientific law—something that is generally accepted as true.

You can apply the **scientific method** to problems in everyday life. For example, suppose you plant some seeds and they fail to sprout. You would probably **ask** yourself, "Why didn't they sprout?"—and that would be step one of the scientific method. The next step would be to make **observations**; for example, you might take note of how deep the seeds were planted, how often they were watered, and what kind of soil was used. Then, you would make an **educated guess** about what went wrong—for example, you might hypothesize that the seeds didn't sprout because you didn't water them enough. After that, you would **test** your hypothesis—perhaps by trying to grow the seeds again, under the exact same conditions as before, except that this time you would water them more frequently than before.

Finally, you would wait and **evaluate** the results of your experiment. If the seeds sprouted, then you could conclude that your hypothesis may be correct. If they didn't sprout, you'd continue to use the method to find a scientific answer to your original question.

## Darwin's *Origin of Species*

**In his 1859 book *On the Origin of Species,* Charles Darwin sets out his theory of evolution, which he arrived at by using the scientific method. On a five-year voyage to South America, Darwin had studied many different living things. He observed that individuals in a population group were all different, and that many of the differences they showed were inherited from previous generations. His hypothesis was that evolution takes place because of what he called "natural selection." After studying the evidence he had collected and doing experiments, Darwin concluded that life did evolve according to natural selection. In other words, some individuals inherit characteristics that give them a better chance to survive in their environment. These individuals are likely to have more offspring than others in their group. Over time, this leads to a population shift in favor of individuals with certain characteristics.**

# WHAT IS EVERYTHING MADE OF?

Everything we see and use is made of basic ingredients called elements. There are more than 100 elements. They are found in nature or made by scientists.

**Elements in Earth's Crust** (percent by weight)

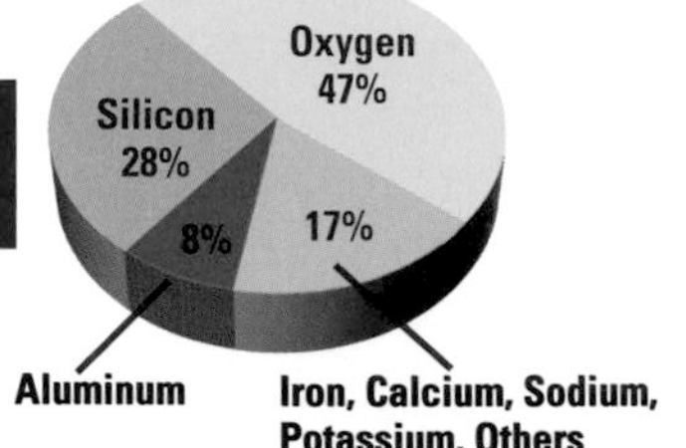


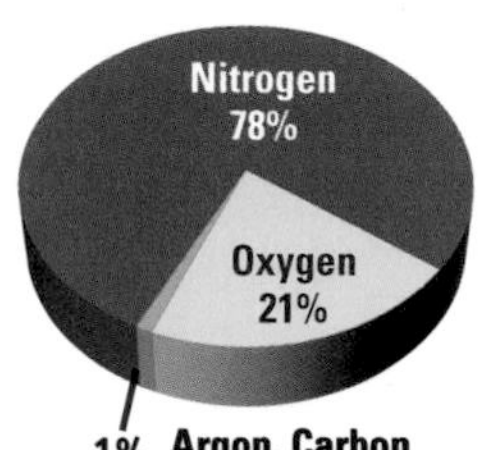


**Elements in the Atmosphere** (percent by volume)

# HOW ARE ELEMENTS NAMED?

Elements are named after places, scientists, figures in mythology, or properties of the element. But no element gets a name until the International Union of Pure and Applied Chemistry (IUPAC) accepts it. In 2011, the IUPAC officially accepted two new elements: No. 114 and No. 116. In 2012, the IUPAC officially approved the name flerovium (honoring the Flerov Laboratory of Nuclear Reactions), and the symbol Fl, for No. 114. The IUPAC also approved the name livermorium (honoring the Lawrence Livermore National Laboratory), and the symbol Lv, for No. 116.

| NAME | SYMBOL | WHAT IT IS | WHEN FOUND | NAMED FOR |
|---|---|---|---|---|
| Bromine | Br | nonmetallic liquid | 1826 | the Greek word *bromos*, which means stench; it smells bad |
| Helium | He | gas | 1868 | the Greek word *helios*, which means Sun; it was discovered during a solar eclipse |
| Hydrogen | H | non-metal | 1766 | the Greek words *hydro* and *genes*, which mean water and forming |
| Iridium | Ir | transitional metal | 1804 | the Latin word *iridis*, which means rainbow |
| Nickel | Ni | transitional metal | 1774 | the German word *kupfernickel*, meaning devil's copper |
| Thorium | Th | radioactive metal | 1828 | Thor, the Scandinavian god of war |

**Did You KNOW?**

**Antiperspirants are chemicals that reduce sweating. They contain a number of ingredients, including aluminum chlorohydrate or aluminum chloride. Antiperspirants block sweat glands located in the armpits. When you apply an antiperspirant, aluminum ions are taken into the cells that line the sweat glands. Water also enters the cells, causing them to swell so that they block sweat from getting out. Eventually, the water in the cells passes back out, the swelling goes down, and you have to reapply your antiperspirant.**

# COMPOUNDS



**Carbon, hydrogen, nitrogen, and oxygen are the most common chemical elements in the human body. Many other elements may be found in small amounts. These include calcium, iron, phosphorus, potassium, and sodium.**

**When elements join together, they form compounds. Water is a compound made up of hydrogen and oxygen. Salt is a compound made up of sodium and chlorine. The element silicon is found in many useful compounds. They are used to make glass, bricks, concrete, transistors, microchips, and other things.**

| COMMON NAME | CONTAINS THE COMPOUND | CONTAINS THE ELEMENTS |
|---|---|---|
| Baking Soda | sodium bicarbonate | sodium, hydrogen, carbon, oxygen |
| Chalk | calcium carbonate | calcium, carbon, oxygen |
| Fool's Gold | iron disulfide | iron, sulfur |
| Lye | sodium hydroxide | sodium, oxygen, hydrogen |
| Marble | calcium carbonate | calcium, carbon, oxygen |
| Sugar | sucrose | carbon, hydrogen, oxygen |
| Toothpaste | sodium fluoride | sodium, fluorine |

## CHEMICAL SYMBOLS

When scientists write the names of elements, they often use a symbol instead of spelling out the full name. The symbol for each element is one or two letters. Scientists write O for oxygen and He for helium. The symbols usually come from the English name for the element (C for carbon). The symbols for some of the elements come from the element's Latin name. For example, the symbol for gold is Au, which is short for *aurum*, the Latin word for gold.

## HOW DO FIREFLIES GLOW?

Fireflies—which are actually beetles, not flies—glow in a process called bioluminescence. The cells in firefly tails contain a chemical called luciferin. The cells also produce an enzyme called luciferase. Luciferin combines with oxygen to form oxyluciferin, with luciferase speeding up the reaction. When oxyluciferin is formed, light is produced. Luckily, very little heat is produced. If the tails got hot when they glowed, fireflies would probably not survive.

## What Is SOUND?

Sound is a form of energy that is made up of waves traveling through matter. When you "hear" a sound, it is actually your ear detecting the vibrations of molecules as the sound wave passes through. To understand sound, you first have to understand waves. Take a bowl full of water and drop a penny into the middle of it. You'll see little circular waves move away from the area where the penny hit, spread out toward the bowl's edges, and bounce back. Sound moves in the same way. The waves must travel through a gas, a liquid, or a solid. In the vacuum of space, there is no sound because there are no molecules to vibrate. When you talk, your vocal cords vibrate to produce sound waves.

## What Is LIGHT?

Light is a little tricky. It is a form of energy known as electromagnetic radiation that is emitted from a source. It travels as waves in straight lines and spreads out over a larger area the farther it goes. Scientists also think it goes along as particles known as photons. Light is produced in many ways. They generally involve changes in the energy levels of electrons inside atoms.

Regular white light is made up of all the colors of the spectrum from red to violet. Each color has its own frequency and wavelength. When you see a color on something, such as a red apple, that means that the apple absorbed all other colors of the spectrum and reflected the red light. Things that are white reflect almost all the light that hits them. Things that are black, on the other hand, absorb all the light that hits them.

## LIGHT VS. SOUND

Sound travels fast but light travels a whole lot faster. You've probably noticed that when you see lightning, you don't hear thunder until several seconds later. That's because the light reaches you before the sound. The speed of sound in air varies depending mainly on temperature (sound also travels faster through liquids and many solids). A jet traveling at about 761 miles per hour is considered to be flying at the "speed of sound." But this is nothing compared to light. In a vacuum, such as in space, it goes 186,000 miles per second! Scientists don't think anything in the universe can travel faster.

# All About Simple Machines

**Simple machines are devices that make our lives easier. They increase the magnitude or change the direction of a force. Using simple machines makes it easier to do many kinds of work.**

## Inclined Plane

**Examples: escalators, staircases, slides**

When trying to get a refrigerator onto the back of a truck, a worker will use a ramp, or inclined plane. Instead of lifting something heavy a short distance, we can more easily push it over a longer distance, but to the same height.

## Screw

**Examples: drills, corkscrews**

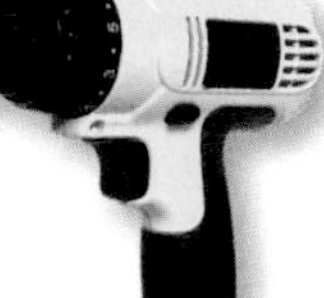

A screw is an inclined plane wrapped around a cylinder. In the case of a wood screw, as it is turned it travels deeper into the piece of wood.

## Lever

**Examples: shovel, seesaw, bottle opener, "claw" part of a hammer used for prying out nails**

Any kind of arm, bar, or plank that can pivot on something (known as a fulcrum) is a lever.

## Wedge

**Examples: axes, knives**

A wedge is two inclined planes fastened onto each other to make a point. Wedges are used to pull things apart and even cut.

## Wheel and Axle

**Examples: cars, bicycles, wagons**

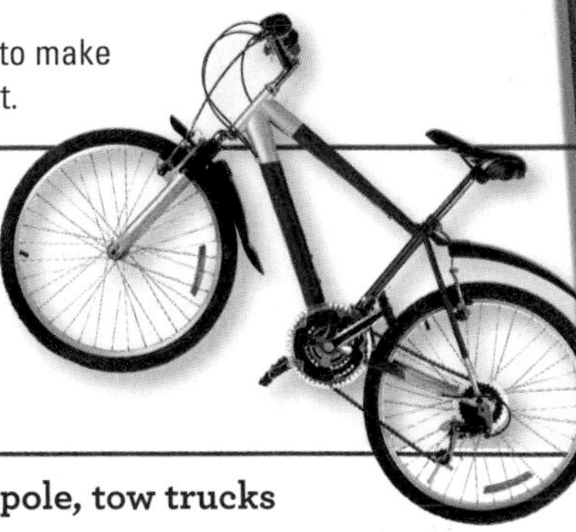

This is another kind of lever, but instead of going up and down, it goes around. The wheel is the lever, and the axle on which it turns is the fulcrum.

## Pulley

**Examples: a block and tackle, a flag pole, tow trucks**

A pulley is similar to a wheel and axle, except that there's no axle. It can be used to change both the direction and level of force needed to move an object.

# FORCES and ACCELERATION

In physics, **acceleration** is a change in an object's speed or direction. To scientists, a car accelerates when it speeds up—and when it slows down or makes a turn. **Force** is whatever causes an object to accelerate, since an object cannot begin to move on its own. Force can be thought of as a push or pull. When you kick a soccer ball lying still on the ground, your foot applies a force that pushes the ball and makes it start moving (accelerate).

# BIOLOGICAL **SCIENCE**

## WHAT ARE **LIVING THINGS** MADE OF?

Cells are sometimes called the "building blocks" of living things. There are trillions of cells in the human body.

There are two main kinds of cells: **eukaryotic** and **prokaryotic.** All the cells in your body—along with the cells of other animals, plants, and fungi—are eukaryotic. These contain several different structures called **organelles.** Each kind of organelle has its own function. The **nucleus,** for example, contains most of the cell's DNA, while the **mitochondria** provide energy for the cell.

Plant and animal cells differ in a few ways. Animal cells rely on mitochondria for energy, but plant cells also have an organelle called a **chloroplast.** This contains chlorophyll, a green chemical plants use to get oxygen and energy from sunlight and water, a process called **photosynthesis.** Plant cells also have a rigid cell wall made largely of **cellulose.**

**Prokaryotes** are living things, or organisms, with prokaryotic instead of eukaryotic cells. Most prokaryotes are single-celled. They don't have the variety of organelles that eukaryotic cells do.

Cell wall
Chloroplast
Nucleus
Mitochondrion

Plant Cell

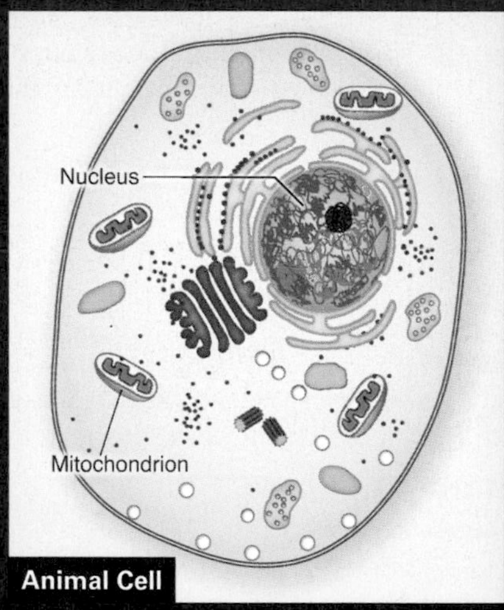


Animal Cell

## WHAT IS **DNA?**

Every cell has **DNA**, a molecule that holds all the information about the organism containing the cell. Lengths of connected bits of a DNA molecule, called **genes**, are tiny pieces of code. They determine what each organism is like. Almost all the DNA and genes come packaged in thread-like structures called **chromosomes**.

Genes are passed on from parents to children. Many things—the color of our eyes or hair, whether we're tall or short, our chances of getting certain diseases—depend on our genes.

## WHAT IS THE **HUMAN GENOME?**

A **genome** is all the DNA in an organism, including its genes. The human genome contains 20,000 to 25,000 genes. Human genes can produce more than one kind of protein. Proteins perform most life functions and make up a large part of cellular structures.

# TINY CREATURES

**Microbes** Anton van Leeuwenhoek (pronounced Lay-wen-ook) made the first practical microscope in 1674. When he looked through it, he saw tiny bacteria, plant cells, and fungi, among other things. Leeuwenhoek called the creatures "wee beasties." We call them **microorganisms** ("micro" means *little*), or microbes. Before the microscope, people had no idea that there were millions of tiny living things crawling all over them.

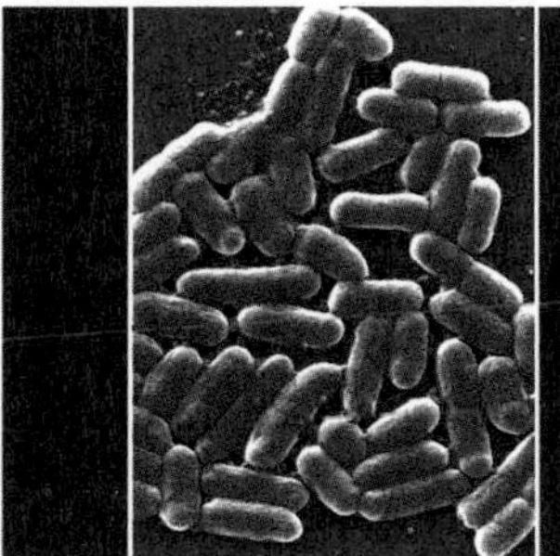

**Bacteria** Bacteria are tiny single-celled microorganisms—bigger than viruses but smaller than, say, human red blood cells. As prokaryotes, they have no organized nucleus. Bacteria are found just about everywhere—in our bodies, in soil, in water, and in plants. They are extremely important because of their chemical effects. In fact, they take part in just about every biological activity on the planet. For example, some bacteria put nutrients into the soil. Others help plants get nutrients from the soil. Some bacteria cause diseases that affect humans or other living things.

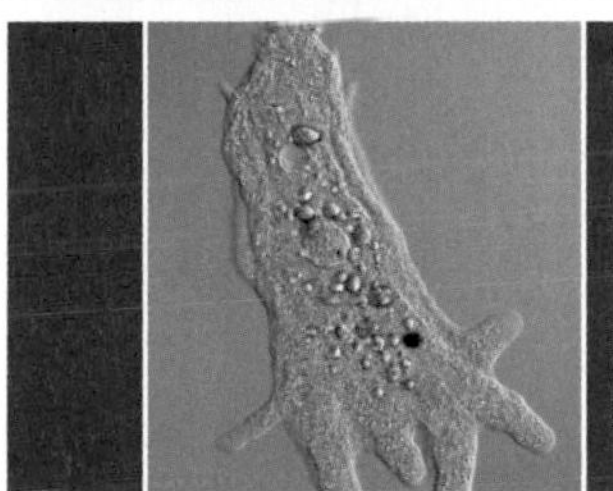

**Amoebas** Amoebas (uh-ME-buhz) are eukaryotic jelly-like blobs of protoplasm that ooze through their microscopic world. They eat by engulfing their food and slowly digesting it. To move around, the cell extends a part of its goo to create something called a **pseudopod** (SOO-doh-pod), which means "false foot." The amoeba uses this to pull the rest of its "body" along. Amoebas normally live in water or on moist surfaces.

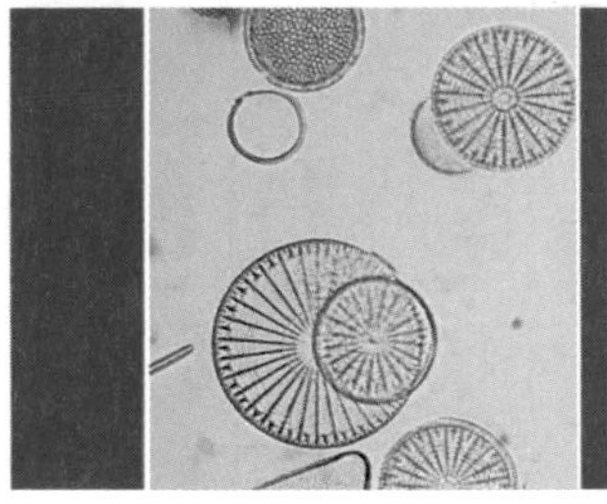

**Diatoms** Diatoms are one-celled algae that make glass shells to protect themselves. When they die, their shells collect at the bottom of the ocean in great numbers and form something called **diatomaceous earth**. It's gritty like sandpaper. Among other things, diatomaceous earth is used as a pesticide—when sprayed in the air, it gets caught in the lungs of insects and slowly suffocates them.

## VIRUSES

**Tiny in size and lacking cells, viruses consist of genetic material—either DNA or the similar RNA—and a protein coat. They don't grow or seem to react to the environment. They don't do anything—unless they are located inside a living thing, in which case they can reproduce, by borrowing the living thing's genetic machinery. In recent years super-sized viruses, dubbed the mimivirus and mamavirus, have been discovered in amoebas. They are as big as small bacteria.**

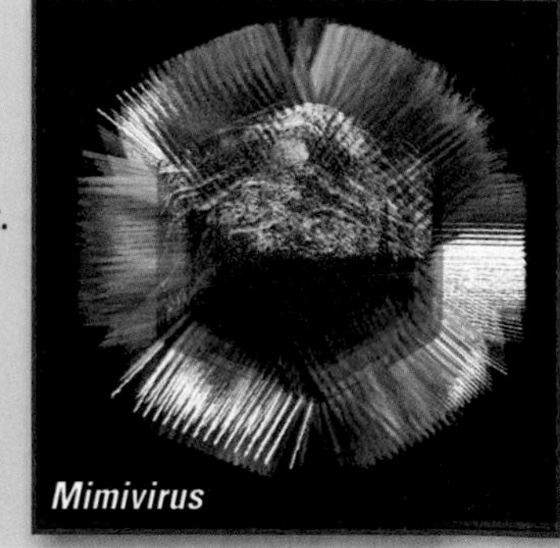

*Mimivirus*

# SOME FAMOUS **SCIENTISTS**

## 1473–1543 NICOLAUS COPERNICUS

Polish scientist known as the founder of modern astronomy. He came up with the theory that Earth and other planets revolve around the Sun. But most thinkers continued to believe that Earth was the center of the universe.

## 1571–1630 JOHANNES KEPLER

German astronomer who developed three laws of planetary motion. He was the first to propose a force (later named gravity) that governs planets' orbits around the Sun.

## 1578–1657 WILLIAM HARVEY

British physician who used the scientific method to prove that blood circulates through the body, pumped by the heart. To reach his conclusions, he dissected many types of animals and conducted thorough experiments. Until then, scientists had thought that the heart only warmed the blood, which was being constantly created and then used up.

## 1867–1934 MARIE CURIE

Polish-born French physicist who discovered the radioactive elements polonium and radium with her husband, Pierre, and later carried out important research on radium. Marie and Pierre Curie shared the Nobel Prize for Physics in 1903, and Marie by herself won the Nobel Prize for Chemistry in 1911. She was the first person to receive two Nobel prizes. She was also the first woman to become a professor at the University of Paris.

## 1879–1955 ALBERT EINSTEIN

German-American physicist who developed a number of revolutionary theories about the relationships between time, space, matter, and energy. Probably the most famous and influential scientist of the 20th century, he won a Nobel Prize in 1921.

## 1881–1955 ALEXANDER FLEMING

Scottish bacteriologist who discovered the life-saving antibiotic penicillin. The development came about as a lucky accident. He failed to clean up some laboratory culture dishes and found that the mold that grew there, which he named penicillin, had microbe-killing power. He shared a Nobel Prize in 1945.

## 1906–1972 MARIA GOEPPERT MAYER

German-born physicist who developed the shell model of the atomic nucleus, to explain the arrangement of protons and neutrons. In 1963, she became only the second woman to be honored with the Nobel Prize for Physics.

## 1928– JAMES D. WATSON

American geneticist who, with British scientist Francis Crick, discovered the molecular structure of DNA. They showed that the molecule was in the shape of a double helix, an arrangement that made it possible for DNA to replicate. In 1962, he shared a Nobel Prize for the discovery. He also was the first director of the Human Genome Project, the effort to map all the parts of the human genome. His 1968 memoir, *The Double Helix*, was a best-seller.

# ON THE JOB
# Biologist

**B**iologists are scientists who study life and living things. **Richard King** is a professor of biology at Northern Illinois University. His special interests are conservation and herpetology—the study of reptiles and amphibians. He agreed to talk to *The World Almanac for Kids* about his work.

**What do you do in a typical day?**

In my job, I have two kinds of days—office days and field-work days. On field-work days, my students and I travel to one of our study locations to find snakes. When we find a snake, we identify what kind it is, measure and weigh it, and mark it before letting it go. That way, if we see the snake again, we know who it is. Office days are spent analyzing the data we collect. I also write reports, teach classes, and help students with their projects.

**What interests and strengths of yours make this job right for you?**

I have always been interested in wildlife and the outdoors, so biology was a natural job area for me. I also enjoy teaching and working with students. I have learned to manage multiple projects at the same time—something that teachers and researchers have to do daily.

**What kind of education or training did you need to get in order to do your job?**

I have an undergraduate degree in zoology and a Ph.D. emphasizing ecology (the study of living things and their environment) and evolution. I also have on-the-job training in conservation biology and statistics.

**What do you like best about your job? What is most challenging?**

Each day is a little different, and I get to do the sorts of things I enjoy: spending time outdoors, training students, and discovering new things about the animals I study. My job has given me the opportunity to travel to nature preserves and natural areas throughout the Midwest. Challenges include managing my time and explaining to people how the work I do can further our understanding of biology and help protect biological diversity.

# SPACE

→Which dwarf planet is not a plutoid? PAGE 209

# THE SOLAR SYSTEM

## The Sun in Our Solar System

Did you know that the Sun is a star, like the other stars you see at night? It is a typical, medium-size star, though it is the largest object in the solar system. But because the Sun is much closer to our planet than any other star, we can study it in great detail. The diameter of the Sun is 865,000 miles, which is more than 100 times Earth's diameter. The gravity of the Sun at its surface is nearly 28 times the gravity of Earth.

> **How hot is the Sun?** The surface temperature of the Sun is close to 10,000° F, and it is believed that the Sun's inner core may reach temperatures around 28 million degrees! The Sun provides enough light and heat energy to support life on our planet.

**HOMEWORK TIP→** Here's a useful way to remember the names of planets in order of their distance from the Sun. Think of this sentence:

My Very Excellent Mother Just Sent Us Nachos.

**M** = Mercury, **V** = Venus, **E** = Earth, **M** = Mars, **J** = Jupiter, **S** = Saturn, **U** = Uranus, **N** = Neptune

# The Planets in Orbit

The planets in the solar system move around the Sun in oval-shaped paths called **orbits**. One complete trip around the Sun is called a **revolution**. Earth takes one year, or 365¼ days, to make one revolution. Planets farther away from the Sun take longer. Most planets have one or more moons. A moon orbits a planet in much the same way that the planets orbit the Sun. Each planet also spins, or rotates, on its axis. An axis is an imaginary line running through the center of a planet. The time it takes Earth to rotate on its axis equals one day.

## TOP PLANETS

- **Largest planet:** Jupiter (88,846 miles diameter)
- **Smallest planet:** Mercury (3,032 miles diameter)
- **Shortest orbit:** Mercury (88 days)
- **Longest orbit:** Neptune (164.8 years)
- **Tallest mountain:** Mars (Olympus Mons, 16.8 miles high)
- **Hottest planet:** Venus (867° F)
- **Coldest planet:** Neptune (–330° F)
- **Shortest day:** Jupiter (9 hours, 55 minutes, 33 seconds)
- **Longest day:** Mercury (175.94 days)
- **No moons:** Mercury, Venus
- **Most moons:** Jupiter (66 known satellites)

# Solar and Lunar Eclipses

During a solar eclipse, the Moon casts a shadow on part of Earth. A total solar eclipse is when the Sun is completely blocked out. When this happens, the halo of gas around the Sun, called the **corona**, can be seen.

The next total solar eclipse is predicted to take place on November 3, 2013. It will be seen in Africa and the Atlantic Ocean. After this, another total solar eclipse will not take place until March 20, 2015. Then, there will be a total solar eclipse on March 9, 2016.

Sometimes Earth casts a shadow on the Moon. During a total lunar eclipse, the Moon remains visible, but it looks dark.

The next total lunar eclipses will occur in 2014, when two are predicted, on April 15 and October 8.

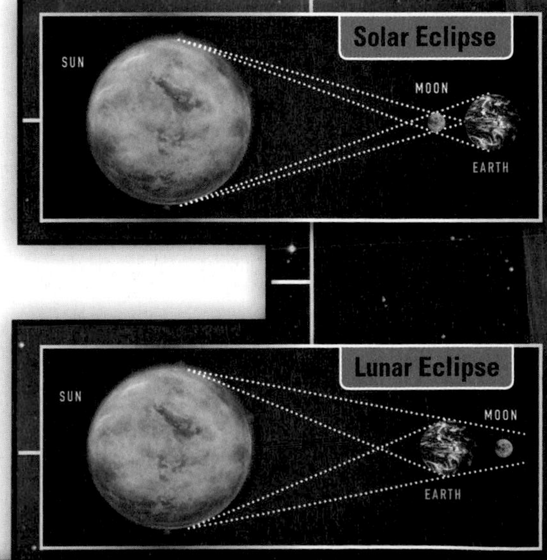

# THE PLANETS

## 1 MERCURY

**Average distance from the Sun:** 36 million miles

**Diameter:** 3,032 miles

**Average temp.:** 333°F

**Surface:** silicate rock

**Time to revolve around the Sun:** 88 days

**Day (synodic—midday to midday):** 175.94 days

**Number of moons:** 0

**Did You KNOW?** Mercury has the most extreme differences in temperature in the solar system.

## 2 VENUS

**Average distance from the Sun:** 67 million miles

**Diameter:** 7,521 miles

**Average temp.:** 867°F

**Surface:** silicate rock

**Time to revolve around the Sun:** 224.7 days

**Day (synodic):** 116.75 days

**Number of moons:** 0

**Did You KNOW?** The "transit of Venus," when the planet passes between Earth and the Sun, is very rare. It occurs in pairs eight years apart every 100 years.

## 3 EARTH

**Average distance from the Sun:** 93 million miles

**Diameter:** 7,926 miles

**Average temp.:** 59°F

**Surface:** water, basalt, and granite rock

**Time to revolve around the Sun:** 365¼ days

**Day (synodic):** 24 h.

**Number of moons:** 1

**Did You KNOW?** A 2011 earthquake in Japan made Earth rotate faster, shortening the day by 1.8 millionths of a second.

## 4 MARS

**Average distance from the Sun:** 142 million miles

**Diameter:** 4,222 miles

**Average temp.:** –81°F

**Surface:** iron-rich basaltic rock

**Time to revolve around the Sun:** 687 days

**Day (synodic):** 24 h., 39 min., 35 s.

**Number of moons:** 2

**Did You KNOW?** NASA's Mars Reconnaissance Orbiter went into orbit around the Red Planet in 2006. Since then, it has sent more data to Earth than all other interplanetary spacecraft put together.

## 5 JUPITER

**Average distance from the Sun:** 484 million miles

**Diameter:** 88,846 miles

**Average temp.:** –162°F

**Surface:** liquid hydrogen

**Time to revolve around the Sun:** 11.9 years

**Day (synodic):** 9 h., 55 min., 33 s.

**Number of moons:** 66

**Did You KNOW?** Jupiter's Great Red Spot is a hurricane-like storm that is three times the diameter of Earth.

## 6 SATURN

**Average distance from the Sun:** 887 million miles

**Diameter: 74,898 miles**

**Average temp.:** –218°F

**Surface:** liquid hydrogen

**Time to revolve around the Sun:** 29.5 years

**Day (synodic):** 10 h., 34 min., 13 s.

**Number of moons:** 62

**Did You KNOW?** Saturn is the only planet in the solar system that is less dense than water. It could float!

## 7 URANUS

**Average distance from the Sun:** 1.8 billion miles

**Diameter:** 31,763 miles

**Average temp.:** –323°F

**Surface:** liquid hydrogen and helium

**Time to revolve around the Sun:** 84 years

**Day (synodic):** 17 h., 14 min., 23 s.

**Number of moons:** 27

**Uranus has at least 13 narrow, dark rings, some of which are surrounded by belts of fine dust.**

## 8 NEPTUNE

**Average distance from the Sun:** 2.8 billion miles

**Diameter:** 30,775 miles

**Average temp.:** –330°F

**Surface:** liquid hydrogen and helium

**Time to revolve around the Sun:** 164.8 years

**Day (synodic):** 16 h., 6 min., 36 s.

**Number of moons:** 13

Did You KNOW?

**Neptune, Jupiter, Saturn, and Uranus are called gas giants because they consist largely of gas.**

# DWARF PLANETS AND PLUTOIDS

In 2006, the International Astronomical Union (IAU) officially changed the definition of "planet." It decided that a planet must "clear the neighborhood" around its orbit. In other words, a planet has to have strong enough gravity that nearby bodies either merge with it or orbit around it. As a result, Pluto lost planet status and was put in a new category called **dwarf planet**.

A dwarf planet orbits the Sun, and its gravity must be strong enough to give it a rounded shape. The first officially classified dwarf planets were Pluto, Ceres, Eris, Haumea, and Makemake. Dwarf planets with orbits beyond Neptune's are called **plutoids.** Pluto, Eris, Haumea, and Makemake are plutoids. Ceres orbits the Sun between Mars and Jupiter.

### →CERES

**Average distance from the Sun:** 257 million miles

**Diameter:** 592 miles

**Number of moons:** 0

### →PLUTO

**Average distance from the Sun:** 3.67 billion miles

**Diameter:** 1,430 miles

**Number of moons:** 5

### →HAUMEA

**Average distance from the Sun:** 4 billion miles

**Diameter:** roughly 900 miles

**Number of moons:** 2

### →MAKEMAKE

**Average distance from the Sun:** 4.2 billion miles

**Diameter:** 930 miles

**Number of moons:** 0

### →ERIS

**Average distance from the Sun:** 6.3 billion miles

**Diameter:** 1,600 miles

**Number of moons:** 1

d You NOW?

**So far, no evidence of life has been found elsewhere in the solar system. But that doesn't mean that such life didn't exist in the past and may not exist now. Missions to Mars have found evidence that the planet once had a great deal of water as well as elements considered essential for life. It seems possible that billions of years ago, microbes could have lived on Mars—and may still be living today beneath the planet's surface. Scientists are also looking at the possibility of life on Europa, one of Jupiter's moons, and Titan and Enceladus, two of Saturn's moons. These all seem to have ingredients necessary for life.**

# PLANET EARTH

# SEASONS

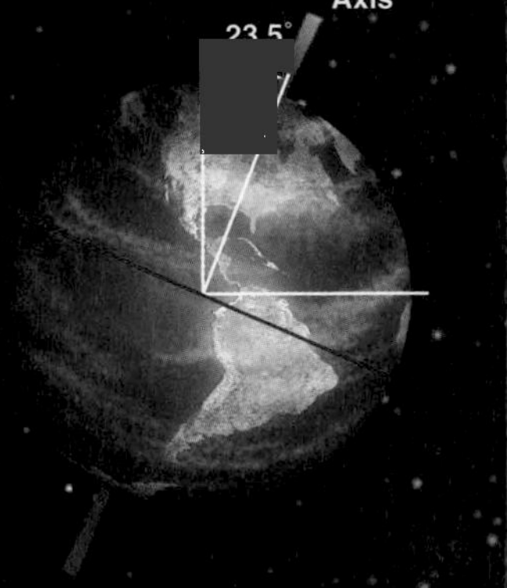

Earth spins on its axis of rotation. That's how we get day and night. But Earth's axis isn't straight up and down. It is tilted about 23½ degrees. Because of this tilt, different parts of the globe get different amounts of sunlight during the year as Earth orbits the Sun. This is why we have seasons.



## SPRING

At the vernal equinox (around March 21), daylight is 12 hours long throughout the world because Earth is not tilted toward or away from the Sun. Days continue to get longer and the sunlight gets more direct in the Northern Hemisphere during spring.

## WINTER

Winter begins at the winter solstice (around December 21) in the Northern Hemisphere (north of the equator, where we live). Our hemisphere is tilted away from the Sun, so the Sun's rays reach us less directly. While days get longer during winter, they are still shorter than in spring and summer, so it's cold. Everything is reversed in the Southern Hemisphere, where it's summer!

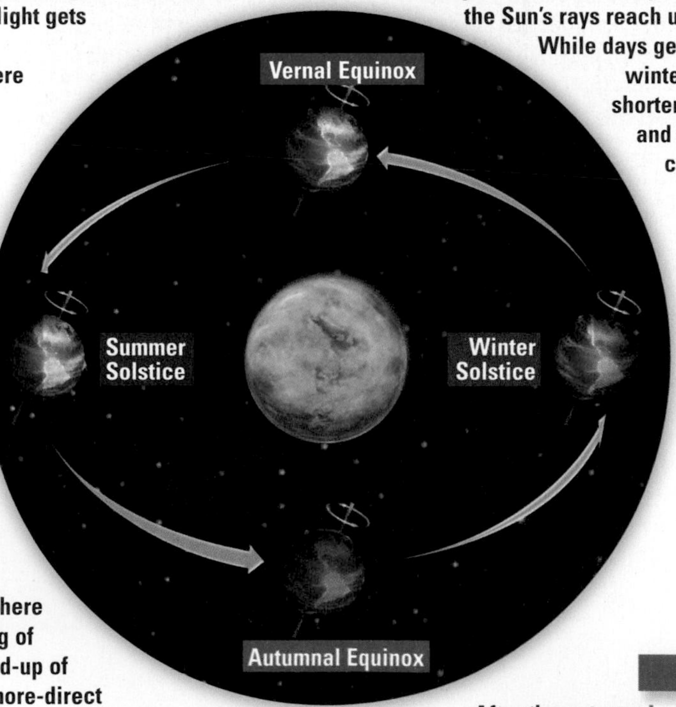

## SUMMER

The summer solstice (around June 21) marks the longest day of the year in the Northern Hemisphere and the beginning of summer. The build-up of heat caused by more-direct sunlight during the long late spring and early summer days in the Northern Hemisphere makes summer our warmest season.

## FALL

After the autumnal equinox (around September 21) the Northern Hemisphere tilts away from the Sun; sunlight is less direct and lasts less than 12 hours. The hemisphere cools off as winter approaches.

# THE MOON

The Moon is about 238,900 miles from Earth. It is 2,160 miles in diameter and has almost no atmosphere. The dusty surface is covered with craters. The Moon takes the same time to rotate on its axis as it does to orbit Earth (27 days, 7 hours, 43 minutes). This is why one side of the Moon is always facing Earth. The Moon has no light of its own but reflects light from the Sun. The lighted part of the Moon that we see changes in a regular cycle, waxing (growing) and waning (shrinking). It takes the Moon about 29½ days to go through all the "phases" in this cycle. This is called a lunar month.

## PHASES OF THE MOON

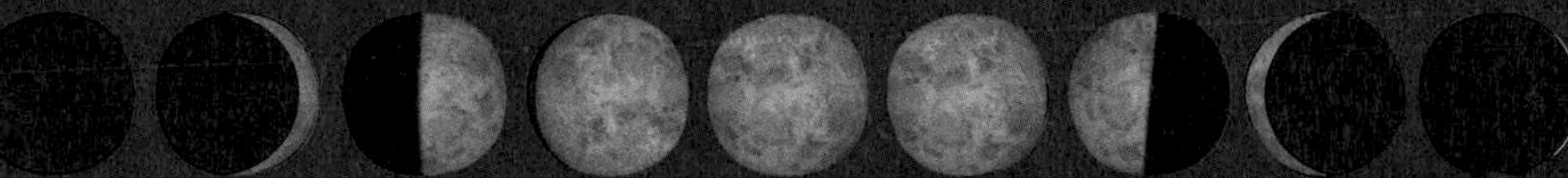

New Moon | Waxing Crescent | First Quarter | Waxing Gibbous | Full Moon | Waning Gibbous | Last Quarter | Waning Crescent | New Moon

# MOON Q&A

**Does the Moon have volcanoes?**
There are no active volcanoes on the Moon's surface today, but for billions of years, the Moon's surface had many such volcanoes. For reasons that are not known, the near side of the Moon had more of this activity. In addition, evidence collected by NASA's GRAIL mission, begun in 2011, indicated that there are volcanic structures beneath the Moon's surface. Today, there may also be liquid magma deep inside the Moon. But it is thought to be too dense to come to the surface.

**How did the Moon form?**
There are different theories about the Moon's formation. According to one theory, a protoplanet—a young planet that had not yet fully formed—may have collided with Earth more than 4 billion years ago. The collision produced debris that eventually came together, as a result of gravitational forces, to form the Moon.

**What is going on to explore the Moon?**
Countries such as the U.S., China, Russia, and India plan to use unmanned spacecraft to explore the Moon in coming years. In October 2010, China put *Chang'e-2* (named for a mythical moon goddess) into orbit around the Moon. After completing its main mission there, it was sent into deep space. *Chang'e-3*, expected to launch in late 2013, will try to place a rover on the lunar surface. In late 2011, the U.S. launched two spacecraft in the GRAIL mission, to learn about the Moon's inner structure by studying its gravity. Once they had completed their mission, the two craft made a controlled descent and crashed into the Moon in December 2012. NASA expected to launch LADEE (Lunar Atmospheric and Dust Environment Explorer) sometime in 2013 to study the Moon's atmosphere.

# SOME UNMANNED MISSIONS IN THE **SOLAR SYSTEM**

**LAUNCH DATE**

| Launch date |  |
|---|---|
| 1959 | **Luna 2** First spacecraft to hit the surface of the Moon |
| 1962 | **Mariner 2** First successful flyby of Venus |
| 1964 | **Mariner 4** First probe to reach Mars, 1965 |
| 1972 | **Pioneer 10** First probe to reach Jupiter, 1973 |
| 1973 | **Mariner 10** First probe to reach Mercury, 1974 |
| 1975 | **Viking 1 and 2** Landed on Mars in 1976 → |
| 1977 | **Voyager 2** Reached Jupiter in 1979, Saturn in 1981, Uranus in 1986, Neptune in 1989 |
| 1989 | **Magellan** Orbited Venus and mapped its surface |
| 1989 | **Galileo** Reached Jupiter in 1995 |
| 1997 | **Cassini** Reached Saturn in June 2004 |
| 2003 | **Mars rovers Spirit and Opportunity** Landed on Mars in early 2004 |
| 2004 | **Messenger** Flew past Mercury, 2008 and 2009, and entered into orbit around the planet in 2011. Sent back first up-close data since 1975 |
| 2006 | **New Horizons** Due to reach Pluto in 2015 |
| 2007 | **Phoenix** Landed in 2008 to search for signs that Mars once held life |
| 2007 | **Dawn** Reached asteroid Vesta in July 2011; due to reach Ceres in 2015 → |
| 2009 | **LCROSS** Slammed into the Moon, kicking up debris for study. Scientists detected signs of water |
| 2011 | **Mars rover Curiosity** Landed in August 2012. Sent back evidence that Mars may once have supported microbial life |
| 2012 | **Dragon** First privately owned (by the SpaceX company) spacecraft to journey to the International Space Station |

*Viking 1*

# MILESTONES IN HUMAN SPACEFLIGHT

The U.S. formed NASA in 1958. It was in response to the Soviet Union's launching of the first artificial satellite *Sputnik I* on October 4, 1957. Since then, more than 525 astronauts have made trips into space to conduct research, visit orbiting space stations, and explore the Moon. Below are some of the biggest moments in human spaceflight.

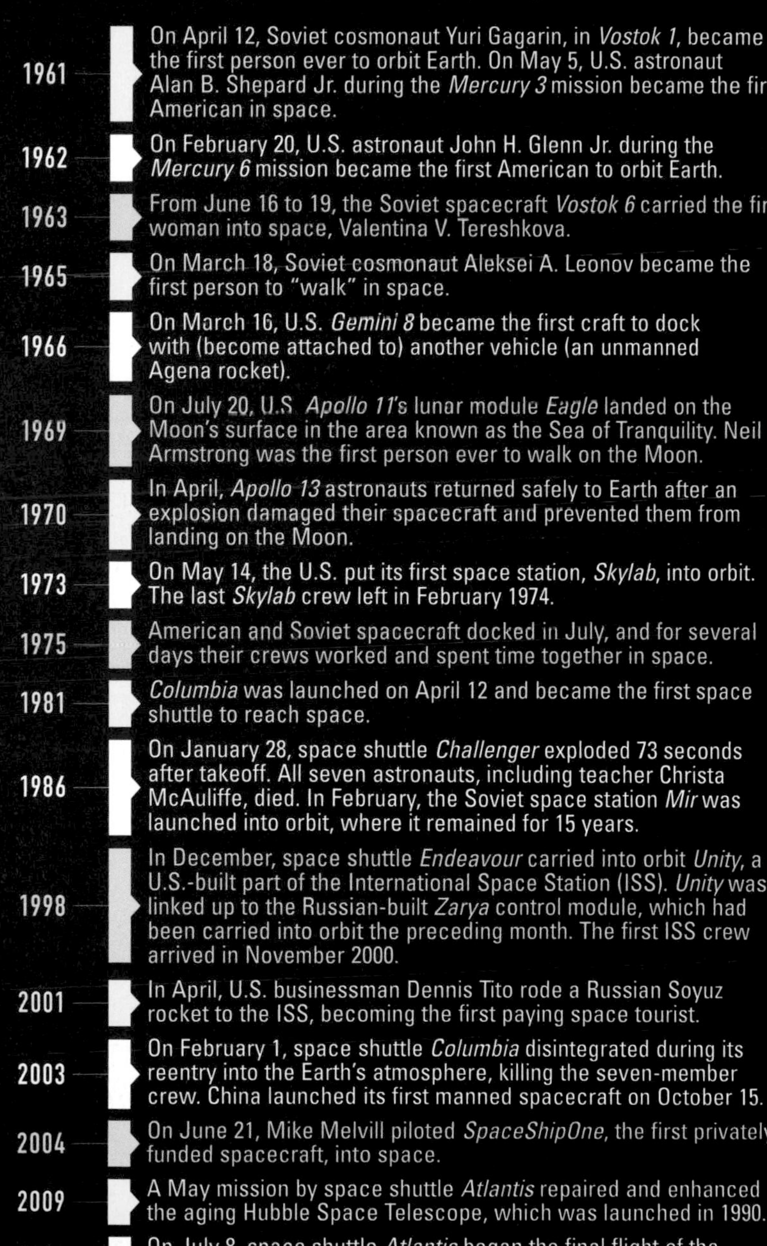

**1961** On April 12, Soviet cosmonaut Yuri Gagarin, in *Vostok 1*, became the first person ever to orbit Earth. On May 5, U.S. astronaut Alan B. Shepard Jr. during the *Mercury 3* mission became the first American in space.

**1962** On February 20, U.S. astronaut John H. Glenn Jr. during the *Mercury 6* mission became the first American to orbit Earth.

**1963** From June 16 to 19, the Soviet spacecraft *Vostok 6* carried the first woman into space, Valentina V. Tereshkova.

**1965** On March 18, Soviet cosmonaut Aleksei A. Leonov became the first person to "walk" in space.

**1966** On March 16, U.S. *Gemini 8* became the first craft to dock with (become attached to) another vehicle (an unmanned Agena rocket).

**1969** On July 20, U.S. *Apollo 11*'s lunar module *Eagle* landed on the Moon's surface in the area known as the Sea of Tranquility. Neil Armstrong was the first person ever to walk on the Moon.

**1970** In April, *Apollo 13* astronauts returned safely to Earth after an explosion damaged their spacecraft and prevented them from landing on the Moon.

**1973** On May 14, the U.S. put its first space station, *Skylab*, into orbit. The last *Skylab* crew left in February 1974.

**1975** American and Soviet spacecraft docked in July, and for several days their crews worked and spent time together in space.

**1981** *Columbia* was launched on April 12 and became the first space shuttle to reach space.

**1986** On January 28, space shuttle *Challenger* exploded 73 seconds after takeoff. All seven astronauts, including teacher Christa McAuliffe, died. In February, the Soviet space station *Mir* was launched into orbit, where it remained for 15 years.

**1998** In December, space shuttle *Endeavour* carried into orbit *Unity*, a U.S.-built part of the International Space Station (ISS). *Unity* was linked up to the Russian-built *Zarya* control module, which had been carried into orbit the preceding month. The first ISS crew arrived in November 2000.

**2001** In April, U.S. businessman Dennis Tito rode a Russian Soyuz rocket to the ISS, becoming the first paying space tourist.

**2003** On February 1, space shuttle *Columbia* disintegrated during its reentry into the Earth's atmosphere, killing the seven-member crew. China launched its first manned spacecraft on October 15.

**2004** On June 21, Mike Melvill piloted *SpaceShipOne*, the first privately funded spacecraft, into space.

**2009** A May mission by space shuttle *Atlantis* repaired and enhanced the aging Hubble Space Telescope, which was launched in 1990.

**2011** On July 8, space shuttle *Atlantis* began the final flight of the shuttle program; *Atlantis* landed July 21.

# WHAT'S IN SPACE BESIDES PLANETS?

↑ **A GALAXY** is a group of billions of stars held close together by gravity. The universe may have more than 100 billion galaxies! The one we live in is called the Milky Way.

**NEBULA** is the name astronomers give to any fuzzy patch in the sky, even galaxies and star clusters. Planetary nebulas come from the late stages of some stars, while star clusters and galaxies are groups of stars. Emission nebulas, reflection nebulas, and dark dust clouds are regions of gas and dust that may be hundreds of light-years wide and are often birthplaces of stars.

**BLACK HOLE** is the name given to a region in space with gravity so strong that nothing can get out—not even light. Many black holes are probably formed when giant stars at least 20 times as massive as our Sun burn up their fuel and collapse, creating very dense cores. Scientists think bigger, "supermassive" black holes may form from the collapse of many stars, or from the merging of smaller black holes, in the centers of galaxies. Black holes can't be seen, because they do not give off light. Astronomers watch for signs, such as effects on the orbits of nearby stars or X-ray bursts from matter being sucked into the black hole.

**SATELLITES** are objects that move in an orbit around a planet. Moons are natural satellites. Artificial satellites, launched into orbit by humans, are used as space stations and observatories. They are also used to take pictures of Earth's surface and to transmit communications signals.

**ASTEROIDS** are solid chunks of rock or metal that range in size from small boulders to hundreds of miles across. Some asteroids orbit other asteroids. Hundreds of thousands of asteroids orbit the Sun in the main asteroid belt between Mars and Jupiter.

**METEOROIDS** are small pieces of stone or metal. Most meteoroids are fragments from comets or asteroids that broke off from crashes in space with other objects. A few are actually chunks that blew off the Moon or Mars after an asteroid hit. When a meteoroid enters Earth's atmosphere, it usually burns up completely. This streak of light is called a **meteor**, or **shooting star**. If a piece of a meteoroid manages to land on Earth, it is called a **meteorite**.

**COMETS** are chunks of ice, → dust, and rock that orbit the Sun. They form long tails as they move nearer to the Sun. They also become brighter when close to the Sun. One of the most well-known is Halley's Comet. It can be seen about every 76 years and will appear again in the year 2061.

# SPACE NEWS 2014

## BEING AWARE OF ASTEROIDS OUT THERE

A meteoroid measuring 60 feet in diameter exploded over Russia on February 15, 2013, shattering windows as a shock wave hit the small city of Chelyabinsk. The same day, by coincidence, a much larger asteroid came within 17,200 miles of Earth. Scientists were aware of the asteroid's approach, but the Chelyabinsk meteoroid caught them by surprise.

The event brought attention to efforts to develop better means of detecting nearby space objects. One such effort, the B612 Foundation, plans to build a space telescope called Sentinel to scan the skies for asteroids in our part of the solar system. NASA's ground-based telescopes currently look for large asteroids and have detected 10,000 so far. None are believed to be a threat to Earth, but it's thought that there are many more such near-Earth objects out there.

***Two planets discovered by Kepler, compared to Venus and Earth***

## EARTH-SIZED PLANETS

At one time, scientists thought that planets the size of Earth were somewhat rare, but now—using evidence from NASA's Kepler telescope—they think that such planets may be fairly common. A team of astronomers announced that there may be 17 billion Earth-sized planets in the Milky Way. However, most are very close to their stars, so they could not support life as we know it. Meanwhile, a different group of astronomers, also using information gathered from Kepler, looked at Earth-sized planets orbiting red dwarf stars, which are cool with low mass. They estimated that of the 75 billion red dwarfs, 6 percent—or 4.5 billion—might have Earth-sized planets. Since these stars are cooler, there's a greater likelihood the planets might have liquid water, which is considered essential for life.

## HUMAN TRIPS TO MARS

NASA has no plans to send humans to Mars anytime soon, but some private businesspeople are thinking otherwise. One is Dennis Tito, who became the first "space tourist" in 2001, when he rode a Russian rocket to the International Space Station. Tito's organization, Inspiration Mars, plans to send a man and a woman on a 501-day, round-trip flyby mission to Mars in 2018. They would come within 100 miles of the Martian surface. A more ambitious effort is Mars One, founded by Dutch engineer Bas Lansdorp. His ultimate goal is to send a four-person crew to Mars in 2023 to establish a permanent human settlement. They would be followed by a second crew of four in 2025. The astronauts—who would never return to Earth—would be chosen and trained during a reality TV show broadcast around the world over the course of several years.

# SPORTS

→Which U.S. athlete won six medals at the 2012 Summer Olympics? PAGE 219

**You don't have to serve like Serena Williams or swim like Michael Phelps to enjoy playing sports. Indoors or out, there are plenty of ways to have fun and get a workout.**

## FAVORITE SPORTS*

**In the U.S., these are the most popular sports played by high school students.**

### BOYS

| Rank/Sport | Athletes |
|---|---|
| 1. Football | 1,095,993 |
| 2. Track and Field | 575,628 |
| 3. Basketball | 535,289 |
| 4. Baseball | 474,219 |
| 5. Soccer | 411,757 |
| 6. Wrestling | 272,149 |
| 7. Cross Country | 248,494 |
| 8. Tennis | 159,800 |
| 9. Golf | 152,725 |
| 10. Swimming and Diving | 133,823 |

### GIRLS

| Rank/Sport | Athletes |
|---|---|
| 1. Track and Field | 468,747 |
| 2. Basketball | 435,885 |
| 3. Volleyball | 418,903 |
| 4. Soccer | 370,975 |
| 5. Softball (Fast Pitch) | 367,023 |
| 6. Cross Country | 212,262 |
| 7. Tennis | 180,870 |
| 8. Swimming and Diving | 160,456 |
| 9. Competitive Spirit Squads | 108,307 |
| 10. Lacrosse | 74,993 |

Source: National Federation of State High School Associations

*In 2011–2012

## Riding the Waves

Riding breaking waves as they move to shore is called surfing. It's usually done standing on a surfboard, and the goal is to remain upright on the board, riding a wave, for as long as you can and with as much flair as possible. A very skilled surfer is able to travel inside the curl of a wave. One of the world's fastest-growing water sports is stand-up paddle surfing, or boarding, in which boarders use a paddle to maneuver on the water. All surfing requires balance, strength, and excellent swimming skills.

**Find out more about competitive surfing at www.isasurf.org**

# GLOBAL GAMES

**Football, baseball, and auto racing are among the most popular professional sports in the U.S. But around the world, soccer (called football in other countries) rules. What other sports do kids in other countries love to watch and play? Here are a few of them.**

**Badminton** In the sport of badminton, players use racquets to hit a shuttlecock (often called a birdie in the U.S.) back and forth over a net on a court. Badminton can be played indoors or outdoors, but official competitions are held indoors to minimize the effects of wind. At the highest levels of play, the game is extremely fast-paced. Badminton has been a medal sport at the Summer Olympics since 1992.

**Karate** Karate is a martial, or fighting, art in which the legs and arms strike, kick, and block opponents. This art of self-defense requires concentration, coordination, flexibility, and strength. The karate student, or *karate-ka*, practices set detailed movements called *katas* in a gym called a *dojo*. Karate, which developed over centuries in East Asia, likely started in places where weapons were outlawed. Karate was introduced to the U.S. in the early 1950s. People of all ages around the world now practice karate, with different colored belts for varying levels of expertise.

**Rugby** Rugby is similar to football but with a bigger ball and much less protective equipment. Teams score a try (similar to a touchdown) by crossing the goal line with the ball. They also score by kicking the ball through goalposts. Players cannot pass the ball forward—only backward or sideways. They advance the ball mainly by running with it while trying to avoid being tackled by defenders. The two main types are rugby union, with 15 players on a team, and rugby league, with 13 players on a team. Rugby sevens, a variation of rugby union featuring seven-player teams, will debut as an Olympic sport in 2016.

## Who Am I ?

I was born in 1962 in Maryland and played college football in Massachusetts. Not quite 5 feet 10 inches (short for a quarterback), I won the Heisman Trophy in 1984. Then I played in the U.S. Football League, the National Football League, and the Canadian Football League, where I won six MVP awards. I retired at the age of 43, with 14,715 passing yards and 86 touchdowns in the NFL. But I am probably best known for a single throw I made as a Boston College senior the day after Thanksgiving in 1984. The televised Orange Bowl game against the University of Miami had been a well-matched fight, but we were behind. Trailing by four points with only six seconds to go, I took the snap, dropped back, scrambled for a few seconds, and throwing into a strong headwind, fired the ball 60 yards into the hands of wide receiver Gerard Phelan to give us the win!

Answer: Doug Flutie

# The OLYMPIC GAMES

The first Olympics were held in Greece in 776 B.C. They featured one event—a footrace. For more than 1,000 years, the Olympic Games were held every four years. The first modern Games were held in Athens, Greece, in 1896. Since then, the Summer Olympics have taken place every four years at a different location. (The Games were canceled due to world wars in 1916, 1940, and 1944.)

## 2012 SUMMER OLYMPICS

*Opening Ceremony in London*

London, England, hosted the 30th Summer Olympics from July 27 to August 12, 2012. More than 10,500 athletes from 204 countries or territories participated in 302 medal events across 26 sports. The Olympic Park in East London covered 1 square mile and featured nine different venues, including a newly built 80,000-seat Olympic Stadium. Many events were held at other locations, including Wembley Stadium, where the U.S. women's soccer team won gold against Japan, and the All-England Club in Wimbledon, where Britain's Andy Murray defeated Roger Federer of Switzerland to win the gold medal in men's singles tennis. Many memorable Olympic moments took place at the London Aquatics Center, where Michael Phelps, Missy Franklin, Ryan Lochte, and Allison Schmitt helped the U.S. win 31 medals, 16 of which were gold, in swimming.

### London 2012 Medal Count

A total of 85 countries won at least one medal in London. The U.S. led all nations in both gold medals and total medals won. Here are the top-10 medal-winning nations.

| Country | Gold | Silver | Bronze | Total |
|---|---|---|---|---|
| United States | 46 | 29 | 29 | 104 |
| China | 38 | 27 | 23 | 88 |
| Russia | 24 | 26 | 32 | 82 |
| Great Britain | 29 | 17 | 19 | 65 |
| Germany | 11 | 19 | 14 | 44 |
| Japan | 7 | 14 | 17 | 38 |
| Australia | 7 | 16 | 12 | 35 |
| France | 11 | 11 | 12 | 34 |
| South Korea | 13 | 8 | 7 | 28 |
| Italy | 8 | 9 | 11 | 28 |

# Olympic All-Stars

Here are just a few of the athletes who provided exciting moments at the 2012 Olympics.

**Michael Phelps**, in 2012, became the most decorated → Olympian in any sport. He got off to a slow start when he failed to qualify for his first Olympic event, the 400-meter individual medley. By the close of the games, however, Phelps had earned six medals, including four gold, to bring his record-setting career totals to 22 medals, 18 of which are gold. When he won the 200-meter individual medley in London, Phelps became the first male swimmer to claim gold in the same individual event at three consecutive Olympics. After the games, the 27-year-old from Maryland announced his retirement from competitive swimming.

←Although **Gabrielle Douglas**, known as Gabby, was just 16 years old at her first Olympics in 2012, the gymnast from Virginia wowed the world by winning the prestigious women's individual all-around gold medal. This medal requires high scores in all four women's events: vault, uneven bars, balance beam, and floor exercise. Douglas and teammates Jordyn Wieber, Aly Raisman, McKayla Maroney, and Kyla Ross also earned a team gold for the U.S. As the first African American to win the all-around gold, Douglas serves as a role model to many. She was also the first American gymnast to win gold in team and individual all-around events.

It was hard for anyone watching the 2012 Olympics → not to be electrified by the speed of the aptly named runner **Usain Bolt**. Many people call the Jamaican sprinter, who holds the world record in the 100-meter dash, the fastest man in the world. In 2012, Bolt repeated his 2008 gold-winning performances in the 100 meters, 200 meters, and 4x100 meter relay.

**Did You KNOW?**

**At the 2012 Summer Olympics, the U.S. continued its golden streak in both the men's and the women's basketball competitions. The men's team, stocked with NBA stars such as veteran LeBron James and 19-year-old rookie Anthony Davis, beat Spain 107-100 in the gold-medal game. The U.S. women, with WNBA players Diana Taurasi and Tamika Catchings, trounced France 86-50 for their fifth Olympic gold in a row.**

# FUTURE OLYMPICS

**2014 Winter Olympics | Sochi, Russia | February 7-23, 2014**

Sochi, a city on the coast of the Black Sea in southern Russia, will host the 2014 Winter Olympics. For these Games, the IOC voted to add 12 new events. They include a figure skating team event, a luge team relay, a biathlon mixed relay, and women's ski jumping as well as men's and women's medal competitions in slopestyle skiing, slopestyle snowboarding, snowboarding parallel special slalom, and halfpipe skiing.

**2016 Summer Olympics | Rio de Janeiro, Brazil | August 5-21, 2016**

Rio de Janeiro, Brazil, will host the 2016 Summer Games. They will be the first ever held in South America. The Games will include at least two new sports: golf and rugby sevens.

**2018 Winter Olympics | Pyeongchang, South Korea | February 9-25, 2018**

The IOC voted to make South Korea a Winter Olympics host nation for the first time.

## Russia Readies for 2014

More than 3,000 athletes are set to compete in 98 events across 15 different sports at the 22nd Olympic Winter Games. Preparing the Russian resort of Sochi to host the 2014 Olympics has been a huge—and expensive—undertaking. Organizers are constructing almost all the required facilities from scratch, including a 40,000-seat Olympic stadium, a 30-mile highway, a seaside park, a mountain park, and a high-speed train line between the parks with the capacity to transport more than 86,000 people a day. In addition to being Russia's first Winter Games, the Sochi Olympics, with a price tag of more than $50 billion, are likely to be history's most expensive.

**Did You KNOW?**

**The first Winter Olympics were held in Chamonix, France, in 1924. Sixteen countries were represented by 258 athletes. Only 11 were women. Originally, the winter and summer games were both held every four years during the same year. Starting in 1994, the schedule changed, and now the winter and summer games alternate every two years.**

## Winter Youth Olympic Games

The first-ever Winter Youth Olympic Games took place in 2012 in and around the Austrian city of Innsbruck. The International Olympic Committee (IOC) holds the Youth Olympic Games every two years, alternating between summer and winter events. The next Summer Youth Olympic Games will be held August 16-28, 2014, in Nanjing, China.

# PARALYMPICS

**The Paralympic Games are the official Olympic Games for athletes with physical, mental, or sensory disabilities. The Games got their start in 1948, when Sir Ludwig Guttman organized a competition in England for World War II veterans with spinal-cord injuries. When athletes from the Netherlands joined in 1952, the movement went international.**

Olympic-style competition began in Rome in 1960, and the first Winter Paralympics were held in Sweden in 1976. Since 1988, the Paralympics have been held just after the Winter and Summer Olympic competitions. Following the 2012 Summer Olympics, more than 4,000 athletes from 166 countries took part in the Paralympic Games at the London Olympic venues. Athletes from around the world are scheduled to compete in the 2014 Winter Paralympic Games in Sochi, Russia.

## OFFICIAL PARALYMPIC SPORTS

**Summer:** archery, boccia, canoe, cycling, equestrian, goalball, judo, powerlifting, rowing, sailing, shooting, sitting volleyball, soccer (5-a-side and 7-a-side), swimming, table tennis, track and field, triathlon, wheelchair basketball, wheelchair dance, wheelchair fencing, wheelchair rugby, wheelchair tennis

**Winter:** alpine skiing, biathlon, cross-country skiing, ice sledge hockey, wheelchair curling

**Find out more at www.paralympic.org**

# SPECIAL OLYMPICS

**The Special Olympics is the world's largest program of sports training and athletic competition for children and adults with intellectual disabilities. Founded in 1968, Special Olympics has offices in all 50 states, Washington, D.C., and throughout the world. The organization offers training and competition to about 3.4 million athletes in more than 170 countries.**

**Special Olympics holds World Games every two years. These alternate between summer and winter sports. The last World Winter Games were held in 2013 in Pyeongchang, South Korea. The next World Summer Games are planned for 2015 in Los Angeles, California.**

**Volunteer or find out more at www.specialolympics.org**

# Auto Racing

## NASCAR

**Bill France founded the National Association for Stock Car Auto Racing (NASCAR) in 1947. Stock cars look a lot like the cars that are "in stock" at a car dealership. In 1949, Red Byron won the first NASCAR championship as the top driver of the season. Since 2008, the championship has been known as the Sprint Cup. Races in the Sprint Cup series include the Daytona 500 and the Brickyard 400.**

*Brad Keselowski*

## NASCAR CHAMPIONS

| Year | Winner | Year | Winner | Year | Winner |
|---|---|---|---|---|---|
| 1986 | Dale Earnhardt Sr. | 1995 | Jeff Gordon | 2004 | Kurt Busch |
| 1987 | Dale Earnhardt Sr. | 1996 | Terry Labonte | 2005 | Tony Stewart |
| 1988 | Bill Elliott | 1997 | Jeff Gordon | 2006 | Jimmie Johnson |
| 1989 | Rusty Wallace | 1998 | Jeff Gordon | 2007 | Jimmie Johnson |
| 1990 | Dale Earnhardt Sr. | 1999 | Dale Jarrett | 2008 | Jimmie Johnson |
| 1991 | Dale Earnhardt Sr. | 2000 | Bobby Labonte | 2009 | Jimmie Johnson |
| 1992 | Alan Kulwicki | 2001 | Jeff Gordon | 2010 | Jimmie Johnson |
| 1993 | Dale Earnhardt Sr. | 2002 | Tony Stewart | 2011 | Tony Stewart |
| 1994 | Dale Earnhardt Sr. | 2003 | Matt Kenseth | 2012 | Brad Keselowski |

## DAYTONA 500

*Jimmie Johnson*

**In 1959, the first Daytona 500 auto race was held at the new Daytona International Speedway. More than 50 years later, the Daytona 500 remains one of the top races in the NASCAR season. The youngest driver to capture the Daytona 500 was Trevor Bayne, who won the race a day after celebrating his 20th birthday in 2011.**

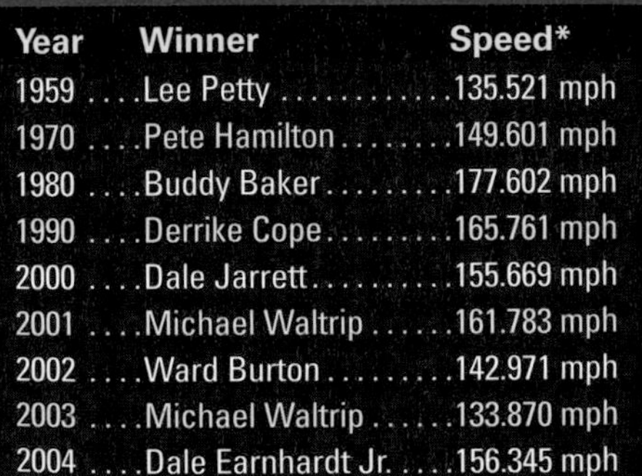

| Year | Winner | Speed* | Year | Winner | Speed* |
|---|---|---|---|---|---|
| 1959 | Lee Petty | 135.521 mph | 2005 | Jeff Gordon | 135.173 mph |
| 1970 | Pete Hamilton | 149.601 mph | 2006 | Jimmie Johnson | 142.667 mph |
| 1980 | Buddy Baker | 177.602 mph | 2007 | Kevin Harvick | 149.335 mph |
| 1990 | Derrike Cope | 165.761 mph | 2008 | Ryan Newman | 152.672 mph |
| 2000 | Dale Jarrett | 155.669 mph | 2009 | Matt Kenseth | 132.816 mph |
| 2001 | Michael Waltrip | 161.783 mph | 2010 | Jamie McMurray | 137.284 mph |
| 2002 | Ward Burton | 142.971 mph | 2011 | Trevor Bayne | 130.326 mph |
| 2003 | Michael Waltrip | 133.870 mph | 2012 | Matt Kenseth | 140.256 mph |
| 2004 | Dale Earnhardt Jr. | 156.345 mph | 2013 | Jimmie Johnson | 159.250 mph |

*Average lap speed

# INDIANAPOLIS 500

The Indianapolis 500 is the biggest event in open-wheel racing. Open-wheel cars have narrow bodies and big uncovered tires. The first Indy 500 was held in 1911.

| Year | Winner | Speed* |
|---|---|---|
| 1911 | Ray Harroun | 74.602 mph |
| 1920 | Gaston Chevrolet | 88.618 mph |
| 1930 | Billy Arnold | 100.448 mph |
| 1940 | Wilbur Shaw | 114.277 mph |
| 1950 | Johnnie Parsons | 124.002 mph |
| 1960 | Jim Rathmann | 138.767 mph |
| 1970 | Al Unser | 155.749 mph |
| 1980 | Johnny Rutherford | 142.862 mph |
| 1990 | Arie Luyendyk | 185.981 mph |
| 2000 | Juan Montoya | 167.607 mph |
| 2001 | Helio Castroneves | 131.294 mph |
| 2002 | Helio Castroneves | 166.499 mph |
| 2003 | Gil de Ferran | 156.291 mph |
| 2004 | Buddy Rice | 138.518 mph |
| 2005 | Dan Wheldon | 157.603 mph |
| 2006 | Sam Hornish Jr. | 157.085 mph |
| 2007 | Dario Franchitti | 151.774 mph |
| 2008 | Scott Dixon | 143.567 mph |
| 2009 | Helio Castroneves | 150.318 mph |
| 2010 | Dario Franchitti | 161.623 mph |
| 2011 | Dan Wheldon | 170.265 mph |
| 2012 | Dario Franchitti | 167.734 mph |
| 2013 | Tony Kanaan ↓ | 187.433 mph** |

*Average lap speed **Race record

# NEED FOR SPEED

**North American race-car fans feed their need for speed mostly with NASCAR and Indy events. Around the world, however, other types of auto races are also popular.**

**Formula One** racing has a large international following. Formula One cars have a single seat and open wheels. A Formula One championship race is usually called a Grand Prix (pronounced *grahn pree*), a French term that means "grand prize." In 2013, Grand Prix races were scheduled for Japan, Brazil, India, the U.S., and several European countries. The most famous Formula One race in Europe is the Grand Prix de Monaco in Monte Carlo.

**Rallying** is also popular worldwide. Rally cars, which resemble → road cars, generally have full-size seats and covered wheels. Rally races are run, rain or shine, on many different types of roads, sometimes alongside regular traffic. Typically, a rally is divided into several stages, with their own start times. The International Automobile Federation conducts an annual World Championship Rally series. Most of the events in this series take place in Europe, but the 2013 calendar also featured rallies in Argentina, Mexico, and Australia.

**In drag racing, two specially prepared vehicles, beginning from a standing start, race side by side on a straight 1/4-mile course. The winner continues to race against other competitors until only one remains as the champion. Find out more at www.nhra.com**

# BASEBALL

The first known game of baseball with rules similar to those of the modern game was played at Elysian Fields in Hoboken, New Jersey, on June 19, 1846. The current National League (NL) was formed in 1876. The American League (AL) was established in 1901. Since the early 1900s, the champions of the NL and AL have met in the World Series.

## NO-HITTERS AND A GIANT WIN

Baseball fans saw a total of seven games in 2012 in which no batter on one team got a hit. Philip Humber of the Chicago White Sox pitched the season's first no-hitter on April 21 with a perfect game—only the 21st in Major League history. The San Francisco Giants' Matt Cain and Felix Hernandez of the Seattle Mariners threw the season's other two perfect games.

In the 2012 World Series, the Giants swept the Detroit Tigers in four games to win their second championship in three years. Pablo Sandoval of the Giants, who batted .500 with 4 runs batted in (RBIs), was named the World Series MVP.

Miguel Cabrera

## CLAIMING THE CROWN

Even though he went hitless in his final game of the 2012 regular season, it was a good day for Detroit Tigers slugger Miguel Cabrera. Leading the American League with a .330 batting average, 44 home runs, and 139 RBIs, Cabrera made history by claiming the Triple Crown. The 29-year-old third baseman was only the 15th player ever to win the Triple Crown. He was the first player to do it in 45 years—since Carl Yastrzemski of the Boston Red Sox batted .326 with 44 home runs and 121 RBIs in 1967. For his outstanding season, Cabrera was named the 2012 AL MVP.

## 2012 AWARD WINNERS

**MVP**
AL: Miguel Cabrera, Detroit Tigers
NL: Buster Posey, San Francisco Giants

**CY YOUNG** (top pitcher)
AL: David Price, Tampa Bay Rays
NL: R. A. Dickey, New York Mets

**ROOKIE OF THE YEAR**
AL: Mike Trout, Los Angeles Angels
NL: Bryce Harper, Washington Nationals

**Little League Baseball and Softball is one of the largest youth sports programs in the world. It began in 1939 in Williamsport, Pennsylvania, with 30 boys playing on three teams. Today, more than 2.4 million boys and girls ages 4 to 18 play on Little League baseball and softball teams in more than 100 countries. Find out more at www.littleleague.org**

# MODERN MAJOR LEAGUE RECORDS*

## BATTERS

### Most Home Runs

Career: 762, Barry Bonds (1986–2007)
Season: 73, Barry Bonds (2001)
Game: 4, by 15 different players

### Most Hits

Career: 4,256, Pete Rose (1963–86)
Season: 262, **Ichiro Suzuki** (2004)
Game: 7, Rennie Stennett (1975)

### Most Stolen Bases

Career: 1,406, Rickey Henderson (1979–2003)
Season: 130, Rickey Henderson (1982)
Game: 6, by four different players

## PITCHERS

### Most Strikeouts

Career: 5,714, Nolan Ryan (1966–93)
Season: 383, Nolan Ryan (1973)
Game: 20, Roger Clemens (1986, 1996); Kerry Wood (1998)

### Most Wins

Career: 511, Cy Young (1890–1911)
Season: 41, Jack Chesbro (1904)

### Most Saves

Career: 608, **Mariano Rivera** (1990–2012)
Season: 62, **Francisco Rodriguez** (2008)

*Records set in seasons from 1901 through 2012. Players in **bold** played in 2012. Single-game records are for nine-inning games only.

# ALL-STAR ANNIVERSARY

*Cal Ripken Jr.*

The year 2013 marked the 80th anniversary of Major League Baseball's first All-Star game, played on July 6, 1933, at Comiskey Park in Chicago as part of the 1933 World's Fair. Fans were enthusiastic about that first game between teams made up of the best American and National League players. So the contest became an annual event. Over the years, there have been many memorable All-Star performances. In 1934, New York Giants pitcher Carl Hubbell struck out five consecutive future Hall of Famers, including Babe Ruth. Ted Williams hit the first All-Star game walk-off home run in 1941, the same year he went on to hit .406 for the season. In 2001, Hall of Fame shortstop Cal Ripken Jr. knocked a solo home run to left field and earned the All-Star MVP award in his 19th and last All-Star game. Since 2003, the winning league in the All-Star game wins home-field advantage for its team in the World Series.

# BASEBALL HALL OF FAME

In 2013, for the first time since 1996, no new members were elected to the National Baseball Hall of Fame and Museum in Cooperstown, New York. The current number of elected Hall of Famers is 300. Of that total, 208 were elected based on their big-league playing careers. Another 35 were Negro leaguers, who played pro baseball at a time when African Americans were barred from playing alongside white ballplayers in the American and National leagues. The Hall of Fame also includes baseball executives, team managers, and umpires.

**Find out more about baseball's legends at www.baseballhall.org**

**In the 2013 season, the AL and NL each had the same number of teams—15. The Houston Astros switched from the National to the American League to end years of imbalance. Each league had three divisions with five teams apiece. The odd number of teams in each league meant more interleague games.**

# BASKETBALL

Dr. James Naismith

Dr. James Naismith invented basketball in Springfield, Massachusetts, in 1891. He used peach baskets as hoops. At first, each team had nine players instead of five. Big-time pro basketball started in the late 1940s, when the National Basketball Association (NBA) was formed. The Women's National Basketball Association (WNBA) began play in 1997.

## The Heat Are Hot Again

In the 2012–2013 NBA regular season, the Miami Heat, last year's NBA champs, had the best record (66-16). For the fourth time in five years, LeBron James of the Heat was named the regular season MVP. The Finals pitted Heat stars James, Dwyane Wade, and Chris Bosh against the older trio of Tony Parker, Tim Duncan, and Manu Ginobili of the San Antonio Spurs. In a thrilling seven-game series, the Heat came out on top. James, who scored 37 points and grabbed 12 rebounds in the deciding game, was named the Finals MVP for the second year in a row.

*LeBron James (6)* →

# HALL OF FAME

The Naismith Memorial Basketball Hall of Fame in Springfield, Massachusetts, honors great players, coaches, and others who have had a big impact on the game. The 2013 inductees included nine-time NBA All-Star Gary Payton, seven-time NCAA Final Four coach Rick Pitino, five-time WNBA All-Star Dawn Staley, and three-time National Coach of the Year Sylvia Hatchell.

**Find out more about the legends of basketball at www.hoophall.com**

*Gary Payton (20)*

**Did You KNOW?**

**The Los Angeles Clippers' power forward Blake Griffin (32) is one of the NBA's most talented—and well paid—stars. The number-one NBA draft pick in 2009, the Oklahoma native was named Rookie of the Year in 2011. In 2013, when Griffin was selected for the All-Star team for the second straight time, the honor also triggered a clause in his new contract that could earn him more than $15 million in extra compensation.**

## NBA Season Leaders*

| Statistic | Number | Player | Team |
|---|---|---|---|
| **Points per Game** | 28.7 | Carmelo Anthony | New York Knicks |
| **Rebounds per Game** | 12.4 | Dwight Howard | Los Angeles Lakers |
| **Blocks per Game** | 3.03 | Serge Ibaka | Oklahoma City Thunder |
| **Field Goal Average**** | .643 | DeAndre Jordan | Los Angeles Clippers |
| **Steals per Game** | 2.41 | Chris Paul | Los Angeles Clippers |
| **Free Throw Average**** | .905 | Kevin Durant | Oklahoma City Thunder |
| **3-Point Field Goal Average**** | .461 | Jose Calderon | Detroit Pistons |

*2012–2013 season. **Among players with 100 or more attempts.

## Some All-Time NBA Records*

### POINTS
**Career:** 38,387, Kareem Abdul-Jabbar (1969–1989)

**Season:** 4,029, Wilt Chamberlain (1961–1962)

**Game:** 100, Wilt Chamberlain (1962)

### ASSISTS
**Career:** 15,806, John Stockton (1984–2003)

**Season:** 1,164, John Stockton (1990–1991)

**Game:** 30, Scott Skiles (1990)

### REBOUNDS
**Career:** 23,924, Wilt Chamberlain (1959–1973)

**Season:** 2,149, Wilt Chamberlain (1960–1961)

**Game:** 55, Wilt Chamberlain (1960)

### 3-POINTERS
**Career:** 2,857, **Ray Allen** (1996–2013)

**Season:** 272, **Stephen Curry** (2012–2013)

**Game:** 12, **Kobe Bryant** (2003); Donyell Marshall (2005)

*Through the 2012–2013 season. Players in **bold** played in 2012–2013.

# The WNBA

After a regular season record of 22 wins and 12 losses, the Indiana Fever was in second place in the Eastern Conference behind the Connecticut Sun. In the conference finals, however, Indiana defeated Connecticut 2 games to 1. The 2012 WNBA Finals pitted the defending champions, the Minnesota Lynx, against the Fever. On October 21, 2012, at Bankers Life Fieldhouse in Indianapolis, Fever star Tamika Catchings scored 25 points, helping her team to an 87-78 victory over the Lynx in the deciding Game 4. It was the Fever's first WNBA title.

The 2012 WNBA Finals MVP was Catchings, who also won her third Olympic gold medal with the U.S. national team in London in 2012. Despite a hearing impairment affecting both ears, Catchings has risen to the top of her game. The former Tennessee Lady Vol was the WNBA's Rookie of the Year in 2002. Catchings has been named a WNBA All-Star seven times.

*Tamika Catchings*

# COLLEGE BASKETBALL

The men's National Collegiate Athletic Association (NCAA) Tournament began in 1939. Today, it is a spectacular 68-team extravaganza known as March Madness. Games on the Final Four weekend, when the semifinals and finals are played, are watched by millions of viewers. The Women's NCAA Tournament began in 1982 and has soared in popularity.

## THE 2013 NCAA TOURNAMENTS

### Louisville on Top

Peyton Siva (center)

The favored #1-seed Louisville Cardinals won their third men's NCAA college basketball championship in 2013. Louisville defeated the #4-seed Michigan Wolverines, 82-76, in the championship game, played at the Georgia Dome in Atlanta, on April 8. It was a come-from-behind victory for the Cardinals, who trailed by as much as 12 points in the first half. Coached by Rick Pitino and led by Peyton Siva and Luke Hancock, who together scored almost half the team's points, Louisville outlasted the young Michigan team and its 2013 Consensus All-American player Trey Burke. Hancock was named the Most Outstanding Player of the Final Four.

### UConn Women Win

The University of Connecticut women capped a strong tournament by defeating Louisville, 93-60, for their eighth national title. Senior Kelly Faris finished with 16 points, nine rebounds, and six assists. But it was freshman Breanna Stewart who earned Most Outstanding Player of the Final Four honors. In the championship game, Stewart scored 18 of her 23 points in a dazzling first half. The win also tied UConn coach Geno Auriemma with University of Tennessee coach Pat Summitt, who retired from active coaching in 2012, for most championship titles.

## PITINO PREVAILS

April 8, 2013, was a remarkable day for Louisville coach Rick Pitino. Just hours after learning that he had been elected to the Basketball Hall of Fame, the seven-time NCAA Final Four coach cut down the nets with his players to celebrate Louisville's tournament victory. With the win, the 60-year-old former NBA coach became the first NCAA Division I coach to lead two different universities to victory. His other win was with the University of Kentucky, in 1996. As an NBA coach, Pitino led the New York Knicks in 1987–1989 and the Boston Celtics in 1997–2001.

# COLLEGE FOOTBALL

**Football began as a college sport in the 1800s. In 1998, the National Collegiate Athletic Association (NCAA) introduced the Bowl Championship Series (BCS), which pits many of the top-ranked college football teams against each other to determine a national champion.**

## A Crimson Tide Sweeps Over Notre Dame

The Crimson Tide of the University of Alabama won the Bowl Championship Series title game on January 7, 2013, overwhelming the Notre Dame Fighting Irish, 42-14. The game was played at the Sun Life Stadium in Miami, Florida. Defending champ Alabama was heavily favored to win, and the victory made up for the lone blemish on the team's 13-1 regular-season record, a 29-24 loss to Texas A&M in November 2012. In the title game, by the time Notre Dame scored in the third quarter, Alabama was ahead by 35. The two title-game MVPs both played for Alabama: running back Eddie Lacy on offense and inside linebacker C. J. Mosley on defense.

C. J. Mosley

## More 2013 Bowls!

Here are the results of other major bowl games played in January 2013.

| Game | Location | Score |
|---|---|---|
| Rose Bowl | Pasadena, CA | Stanford 20, Wisconsin 14 |
| Sugar Bowl | New Orleans, LA | Louisville 33, Florida 23 |
| Fiesta Bowl | Glendale, AZ | Oregon 33, Kansas State 17 |
| Orange Bowl | Miami, FL | Florida State 31, Northern Illinois 10 |

## HEISMAN TROPHY

**Texas A&M quarterback Johnny Manziel won the Heisman Trophy in December 2012 as the year's outstanding player in college football. The first freshman ever to win the Heisman, Manziel led the Aggies to a 10-2 regular-season record and a win in the Cotton Bowl against Oklahoma (41-13).**

# ALL-TIME DIVISION I NCAA LEADERS*

## RUSHING

### YARDS

**Career:** 6,559, Adrian Peterson, Georgia Southern (1998–2001)
**Season:** 2,628, Barry Sanders, Okla. St. (1988)
**Game:** 406, LaDainian Tomlinson, TCU (1999)

### TOUCHDOWNS

**Career:** 84, Adrian Peterson, Georgia Southern (1998–2001)
**Season:** 37, Barry Sanders, Okla. St. (1988)

## PASSING

### YARDS

**Career:** 19,217, Case Keenum, Houston (2006–2011)
**Season:** 5,833, B. J. Symons, Texas Tech (2003)
**Game:** 716, David Klingler, Houston (1990)

### TOUCHDOWNS

**Career:** 155, Case Keenum, Houston (2006–2011)
**Season:** 58, Colt Brennan, Hawaii (2006)

*Through the 2012 season

# NATIONAL FOOTBALL LEAGUE

The professional league that became the modern National Football League (NFL) started in 1920. The rival American Football League began in 1960. The two leagues played the first Super Bowl in 1967. In 1970, the leagues merged to become the NFL as we know it today.

## A SUPER GAME

In Super Bowl XLVII on February 3, 2013, the Baltimore Ravens defeated the San Francisco 49ers, 34-31, at Mercedes-Benz Superdome in New Orleans, Louisiana. What looked like a one-sided Ravens win turned into a thriller after a power outage halted play for a half-hour in the third quarter. Led by quarterback Joe Flacco, Baltimore was up 28-6 at that point. But when play resumed, 49ers quarterback Colin Kaepernick brought his team almost—but not quite all the way—back. The two Super Bowl teams were coached by brothers: John Harbaugh for Baltimore and Jim Harbaugh for San Francisco. On the field, Ravens wide receiver Jacoby Jones scored on a 108-yard kickoff return (that set an NFL postseason record) and a 56-yard touchdown catch. Flacco, who completed 22 of 33 passes for 287 yards and three touchdowns, was named the Super Bowl MVP.

*Jacoby Jones*

## A LUCK-Y ROOKIE YEAR!

At Stanford, quarterback Andrew Luck was a two-time Pac-12 Offensive Player of the Year. In the April 2012 NFL Draft, he was selected as first overall pick by the Indianapolis Colts. A few months later, that looked like a good choice. In his first NFL season, Luck set rookie records in 2012 for most passing yards in a single game (433) and in a season (4,374). He was the second rookie, after the Carolina Panthers' Cam Newton in 2011, to pass for more than 4,000 yards.

*Andrew Luck*

| 2012 NFL Leaders |
|---|
| **Rushing Yards:** 2,097, Adrian Peterson, Minnesota Vikings |
| **Receptions:** 122, Calvin Johnson, Detroit Lions |
| **Receiving Yards:** 1,964, Calvin Johnson, Detroit Lions |
| **Touchdown Receptions:** 14, James Jones, Green Bay Packers |
| **Passing Yards:** 5,177, Drew Brees, New Orleans Saints |
| **Touchdown Passes:** 43, Drew Brees, New Orleans Saints |
| **Points Scored:** 153, Stephen Gostkowski, New England Patriots |
| **Interceptions:** 9, Tim Jennings, Chicago Bears |
| **Sacks:** 20.5, J. J. Watt, Houston Texans |

*Adrian Peterson*

# NFL All-Time Record Holders*

### RUSHING YARDS

Career: 18,355, Emmitt Smith (1990–2004)
Season: 2,105, Eric Dickerson (1984)
Game: 296, **Adrian Peterson** (2007)

### RECEIVING

Career receptions:
1,549, Jerry Rice (1985–2004)
Career yardage:
22,895, Jerry Rice (1985–2004)
Game yardage:
336, Willie "Flipper" Anderson (1989)

*Through the 2012 season. Players in **bold** played in 2012.

### PASSING

Career completions:
6,300, Brett Favre (1991–2010)
Career touchdowns passing:
508, Brett Favre (1991–2010)
Season completions:
468, **Drew Brees** (2011)
Season touchdowns passing:
50, **Tom Brady** (2007)

### POINTS SCORED

Career: 2,544, Morten Andersen (1982–2004, 2006–2007)
Season: 186, LaDainian Tomlinson (2006)
Game: 40, Ernie Nevers (1929)

# FISHER GOES FIRST

The 78th annual NFL Draft was held April 25-27, 2013, in New York City. The Kansas City Chiefs, in a surprising first pick, opted for Central Michigan offensive tackle Eric Fisher. Many predicted that second overall pick Luke Joeckel of Texas A&M, also an offensive tackle, would take the number-one spot.

NFL teams have been holding a draft to select top college players since 1936. That year, with the first pick in NFL Draft history, the Philadelphia Eagles selected Jay Berwanger of the University of Chicago. Over the years, many future NFL superstars were taken first overall in the draft. That list includes Peyton Manning (1998) and Eli Manning (2004), as well as Hall of Fame quarterbacks Terry Bradshaw (1970), John Elway (1983), and Troy Aikman (1989). Many high draft picks have had short NFL careers, however. And many players selected in late rounds became stars. The New England Patriots' star quarterback Tom Brady was the 199th overall pick in 2000.

# PRO FOOTBALL HALL OF FAME

The Pro Football Hall of Fame in Canton, Ohio, was founded in 1963 to honor outstanding players, coaches, and contributors to the NFL. New members announced in February 2013 included Bill Parcells, winner of two Super Bowls with the Giants and the only coach to lead four teams to the playoffs; Minnesota Viking Cris Carter, with the ninth-highest receiving yards total in NFL history (13,899); and defensive tackle Warren Sapp, who collected 96.5 career sacks. Other members of the Class of 2013 were guard/tackle Larry Allen, offensive tackle Jonathan Ogden, defensive tackle Curley Culp, and linebacker Dave Robinson.

**Learn more about football's biggest names at www.profootballhof.com**

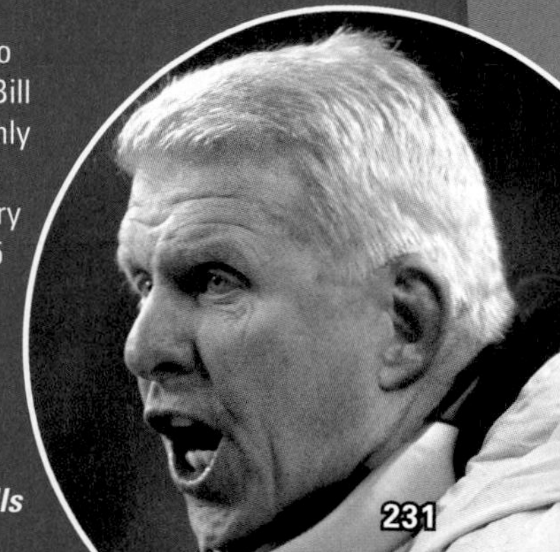
*Bill Parcells*

# GOLF

Golf began in Scotland as early as the 1400s. The first golf course in the U.S. opened in 1888 in Yonkers, New York. The sport has grown to include both men's and women's pro tours.

The **men's tour** in the U.S. is run by the Professional Golfers' Association (PGA). The four major championships (with the year first played) are:
British Open (1860)
U.S. Open (1895)
PGA Championship (1916)
Masters Tournament (1934)

The **women's tour** in the U.S. is guided by the Ladies Professional Golf Association (LPGA). The four major championships are:
U.S. Women's Open (1946)
LPGA Championship (1955)
Kraft Nabisco Championship (1972)
Ricoh Women's British Open (1976)

## The All-Time "Major" Players

**These pro golfers have won the most major championships through April 2013.**

**MEN**
1. Jack Nicklaus, 18
2. Tiger Woods, 14
3. Walter Hagen, 11
4. Ben Hogan, 9
   Gary Player, 9

**WOMEN**
1. Patty Berg, 15
2. Mickey Wright, 13
3. Louise Suggs, 11
4. Babe Didrikson Zaharias, 10
   Annika Sorenstam, 10

**Did You KNOW?**

**↑ Inbee Park of South Korea, the number-one ranked woman golfer in the world in early 2013, is the youngest player to ever capture the U.S. Women's Open. She was 19 years old when she won the tournament in 2008.**

## GREAT SCOTT!

Adam Scott →

**The historic Masters Tournament, played at the Augusta National Golf Club in Georgia, is probably the most famous major pro golf championship in the world. Since 1949, every Masters champion has been awarded an honorary green jacket. In 2013, for the first time in history, an Australian, Adam Scott, earned the right to wear the famous garment by sinking his third-straight long putt of the final day to defeat the 2009 champ Angel Cabrera of Argentina.**

# GYMNASTICS

Gymnastics as a sport goes back to ancient Egypt. But it was only in the early 1800s that the modern-day sport became popular in Europe. Gymnastics became an Olympic sport in 1896, and the first World Gymnastic Championships were held in Belgium in 1903. This international event is run annually except years in which the Summer Olympic Games are held. The next World Gymnastic Championships are set to take place in Antwerp, Belgium, on September 30-October 6, 2013.

Artistic gymnastics is the most popular form of gymnastics. Men compete in the high bar, parallel bars, rings, vault, pommel horse, floor exercise, individual all-around, and team events, while women compete in the uneven parallel bars, vault, balance beam, floor exercise, individual all-around, and team events. Only women compete in rhythmic gymnastics, which includes the rope, hoop, ball, clubs, ribbon, and all-around events.

# ICE HOCKEY

Ice hockey began in Canada in the mid-1800s. The National Hockey League (NHL) was formed in 1917. Today the NHL has 30 teams. In the 2012–2013 season, there were 23 U.S. teams and 7 Canadian teams.



### A SHORT SEASON ENDS WITH A BLACKHAWK WIN

The 2012–2013 NHL regular season had a delayed start, running January 19-April 28, 2013. A labor dispute reduced the number of games from 82 to 48. In the sixth game of the 2013 Stanley Cup Finals, the Chicago Blackhawks scored twice in the last 76 seconds to beat the Boston Bruins, 3-2, and win the series, 4 games to 2. It was Chicago's fifth Stanley Cup title.

### STANLEY CUP CHAMPIONS

| SEASON | WINNER | RUNNER-UP |
|---|---|---|
| 2000–2001 | Colorado Avalanche | New Jersey Devils |
| 2001–2002 | Detroit Red Wings | Carolina Hurricanes |
| 2002–2003 | New Jersey Devils | Anaheim Mighty Ducks |
| 2003–2004 | Tampa Bay Lightning | Calgary Flames |
| 2004–2005 | Season canceled | |
| 2005–2006 | Carolina Hurricanes | Edmonton Oilers |
| 2006–2007 | Anaheim Ducks | Ottawa Senators |
| 2007–2008 | Detroit Red Wings | Pittsburgh Penguins |
| 2008–2009 | Pittsburgh Penguins | Detroit Red Wings |
| 2009–2010 | Chicago Blackhawks | Philadelphia Flyers |
| 2010–2011 | Boston Bruins | Vancouver Canucks |
| 2011–2012 | Los Angeles Kings | New Jersey Devils |
| 2012–2013 | Chicago Blackhawks | Boston Bruins |

### 2012-2013 NHL League Leaders

**Points:** 60, Martin St. Louis, Tampa Bay Lightning

**Goals:** 32, Alex Ovechkin, Washington Capitals

**Assists:** 43, Martin St. Louis, Tampa Bay Lightning

**Save Percentage:** .941, Craig Anderson, Ottawa Senators

**Wins:** Niklas Backstrom, 24, Minnesota Wild
Henrik Lundqvist, 24, New York Rangers
Antti Miemi, 24, San Jose Sharks

Alex Ovechkin

## HALL OF FAME

Located in Toronto, Ontario, Canada, the Hockey Hall of Fame honors former players, referees, and other people who have contributed to the game. There are also exhibits celebrating the history of ice hockey and the NHL.

**Learn more at www.hhof.com**

### SOME ALL-TIME NHL RECORDS*

**GOALS SCORED**

**Career:** 894, Wayne Gretzky (1979–1999)

**Season:** 92, Wayne Gretzky (1981–1982)

**Game:** 7, Joe Malone (1920)

**GOALIE WINS**

**Career:** 669, **Martin Brodeur** (1992–2013)

**Season:** 48, **Martin Brodeur** (2006–2007)

**POINTS**

**Career:** 2,857, Wayne Gretzky (1979–1999)

**Season:** 215, Wayne Gretzky (1985–1986)

**Game:** 10, Darryl Sittler (1976)

**GOALIE SHUTOUTS**

**Career:** 120, **Martin Brodeur** (1992–2013)

**Season:** 22, George Hainsworth (1928–1929)

*Through the 2012–2013 season. Players in **bold** played in 2012–2013.

# SKIING

Tina Maze

## World Cup Record Setter

Slovenian alpine skier Tina Maze dominated the 2012–2013 season in a way not seen since the World Cup began in 1967. In March 2013, her 11th World Cup victory of the season, in giant slalom, earned the 29-year-old a record-breaking total of 2,414 points and the women's overall title. Maze also won the women's giant slalom and super-G World Cup titles. She is one of only three women to have won events in one season in all five disciplines, including slalom, downhill, and combined (downhill and slalom).

On the men's side, Austria's Marcel Hirscher earned the World Cup overall title in 2012–2103 with 1,535 points. Ted Ligety of the U.S. placed third in the season standings with a career-best total of 1,022. He also won the men's giant slalom title.

# SOCCER

## World Cup

**The men's FIFA World Cup, held every four years, is one of the most popular sporting events in the world. The FIFA Women's World Cup is also held every four years, one year after the men's tournament.**

### Brazil Prepares for 2014

Brazil will host the 2014 FIFA men's World Cup, scheduled for June 12-July 13, 2014. As host nation, Brazil has an automatic spot in the draw. More than 200 teams from the six regional FIFA confederations compete for the remaining 31 berths. The world's best players are expected to take part in the next World Cup, including 2012 FIFA Player of the Year Lionel Messi of Argentina.

**Men's World Cup**

| Year | Winner |
|---|---|
| 1930 | Uruguay |
| 1934 | Italy |
| 1938 | Italy |
| 1942 | not held |
| 1946 | not held |
| 1950 | Uruguay |
| 1954 | West Germany |
| 1958 | Brazil |
| 1962 | Brazil |
| 1966 | England |
| 1970 | Brazil |
| 1974 | West Germany |
| 1978 | Argentina |
| 1982 | Italy |
| 1986 | Argentina |
| 1990 | West Germany |
| 1994 | Brazil |
| 1998 | France |
| 2002 | Brazil |
| 2006 | Italy |
| 2010 | Spain |

**Women's World Cup**

| Year | Winner |
|---|---|
| 1991 | U.S. |
| 1995 | Norway |
| 1999 | U.S. |
| 2003 | Germany |
| 2007 | Germany |
| 2011 | Japan |

Lionel Messi

### Looking Ahead

After the 2014 FIFA World Cup, future men's World Cups will be hosted by Russia (2018) and Qatar (2022). The next women's World Cup will be held in Canada in 2015.

## Major League Soccer

In a repeat of 2011, the 2012 season ended with the Los Angeles Galaxy beating the Houston Dynamo for the MLS Cup. The final score, 3-1, included two converted penalty kicks from U.S. veteran Landon Donovan and Irish striker Robbie Keane and a header from center back Omar Gonzalez, who was named the MLS Cup's Most Valuable Player. The regular-season MVP honor went to San Jose Earthquake and U.S. national team striker Chris Wondolowski. With 27 goals, "Wondo" was the league's top scorer in 2012.

Omar Gonzalez (right)

## National Women's Soccer League (NWSL)

Alex Morgan (13)

Winning gold in London's 2012 Olympics was the highlight of the year for U.S. women's national team players. Back in the U.S., however, there was no professional league for them. (The WPS, or Women's Professional Soccer, folded in 2012.) To build a reliable league for high-level play and talent development, U.S. Soccer, the Canadian Soccer Association, and the Mexican Football Federation agreed to subsidize their national players—24 from the U.S. and 16 each from Canada and Mexico—in a new league: the NWSL. The eight founding clubs were the Boston Breakers, Chicago Red Stars, FC Kansas City, Portland Thorns FC, Seattle Reign FC, Sky Blue FC (New York/New Jersey), Washington Spirit, and Western New York Flash. College and supplement drafts filled out the rosters. League play began in April 2013. Gold medalists from the 2012 Olympics competed professionally in Western New York (Abby Wambach and Carli Lloyd), Boston (Sydney Leroux), and Portland (Alex Morgan).

**Did You KNOW?**

**The U.S. Youth Soccer Association began in 1974 with 100,000 players. Today, more than 3 million young soccer enthusiasts from ages 5 to 19 are registered to participate. U.S. Youth Soccer seeks to inspire a lifelong passion for the game while promoting physical, emotional, and intellectual growth in its participants. Find out more at www.usyouthsoccer.org**

# TENNIS

Modern tennis began in 1873. The first championships were held in Wimbledon, near London, England, four years later. Today, the four most important tournaments, or Grand Slam events, for men and women are the Australian Open, the French Open, the All-England (Wimbledon) Championships, and the U.S. Open.

## ALL-TIME GRAND SLAM SINGLES WINS

| MEN | Australian | French | Wimbledon | U.S. | Total |
|---|---|---|---|---|---|
| **Roger Federer** (b. 1981) | 4 | 1 | 7 | 5 | 17 |
| Pete Sampras (b. 1971) | 2 | 0 | 7 | 5 | 14 |
| Roy Emerson (b. 1936) | 6 | 2 | 2 | 2 | 12 |
| **Rafael Nadal** (b. 1986) | 1 | 8 | 2 | 1 | 12 |
| Bjorn Borg (b. 1956) | 0 | 6 | 5 | 0 | 11 |
| Rod Laver (b. 1938) | 3 | 2 | 4 | 2 | 11 |

| WOMEN | Australian | French | Wimbledon | U.S. | Total |
|---|---|---|---|---|---|
| Margaret Smith Court (b. 1942) | 11 | 5 | 3 | 5 | 24 |
| Steffi Graf (b. 1969) | 4 | 6 | 7 | 5 | 22 |
| Helen Wills Moody (1905–1998) | * | 4 | 8 | 7 | 19 |
| Chris Evert (b. 1954) | 2 | 7 | 3 | 6 | 18 |
| Martina Navratilova (b. 1956) | 3 | 2 | 9 | 4 | 18 |
| **Serena Williams** (b. 1981) | 5 | 2 | 5 | 4 | 16 |

*Never played in tournament. Athletes in **bold** competed in 2013. Wins through June 2013.

## SMASHING TENNIS

In the summer of 2012, U.S. superstar Serena Williams dominated women's tennis. Her winning streak began with an impressive victory over Poland's Agnieszka Radwanska for a fifth Wimbledon singles title. Williams returned to the All-England Club to participate in the 2012 Summer Olympics, winning gold medals in women's singles and doubles. Then, she captured the U.S. Open singles title, beating Victoria Azarenka of Belarus. At the start of 2013, however, the 31-year-old was upset in three sets by rising U.S. player Sloane Stephens in the Australian Open quarterfinals. It was Azarenka who ultimately triumphed at the tournament, defeating Li Na of China. At the 2013 French Open, Williams was back on top. She overpowered Russia's Maria Sharapova (6-4, 6-4) in the final to earn her 16th Grand Slam singles title.

Serena Williams

On the men's side, in a dramatic 2012 Wimbledon final, Swiss legend Roger Federer dashed the hopes of British fans everywhere by beating hometown favorite Andy Murray (4-6, 7-5, 6-3, 6-4). It was Federer's seventh Wimbledon singles title—and his 17th Grand Slam win. Murray overcame the heartbreaking loss, however, by defeating Federer in straight sets at the 2012 Olympics to win a gold medal. At the 2012 U.S. Open, Murray again came out on top, this time against Serbian Novak Djokovic. At the start of 2013, Djokovic beat Spain's Rafael Nadal at the Australian Open. Nadal responded by capturing a record eighth French Open crown, defeating Djokovic in the semifinals and fellow countryman David Ferrer in the final (6-3, 6-2, 6-3).

## Wimbledon Singles Champions

| Year | Men | Women |
|---|---|---|
| 2000 | Pete Sampras | Venus Williams |
| 2001 | Goran Ivanisevic | Venus Williams |
| 2002 | Lleyton Hewitt | Serena Williams |
| 2003 | Roger Federer | Serena Williams |
| 2004 | Roger Federer | Maria Sharapova |
| 2005 | Roger Federer | Venus Williams |
| 2006 | Roger Federer | Amelie Mauresmo |
| 2007 | Roger Federer | Venus Williams |
| 2008 | Rafael Nadal | Venus Williams |
| 2009 | Roger Federer | Serena Williams |
| 2010 | Rafael Nadal | Serena Williams |
| 2011 | Novak Djokovic | Petra Kvitova |
| 2012 | Roger Federer | Serena Williams |

## U.S. Open Singles Champions

| Year | Men | Women |
|---|---|---|
| 2000 | Marat Safin | Venus Williams |
| 2001 | Lleyton Hewitt | Venus Williams |
| 2002 | Pete Sampras | Serena Williams |
| 2003 | Andy Roddick | Justine Henin-Hardenne |
| 2004 | Roger Federer | Svetlana Kuznetsova |
| 2005 | Roger Federer | Kim Clijsters |
| 2006 | Roger Federer | Maria Sharapova |
| 2007 | Roger Federer | Justine Henin |
| 2008 | Roger Federer | Serena Williams |
| 2009 | J. M. del Potro | Kim Clijsters |
| 2010 | Rafael Nadal | Kim Clijsters |
| 2011 | Novak Djokovic | Samantha Stosur |
| 2012 | Andy Murray | Serena Williams |

## Davis Cup

The Davis Cup is an international team tennis competition for men. It began in 1900 as a contest between just the U.S. and Great Britain called the International Lawn Tennis Challenge. Now more than 130 countries take part. National teams face off in a best-of-five series of singles and doubles matches to determine who advances. Over the years, the U.S. has won the most Davis Cup championships (32), followed by Australia (28), France and Great Britain (9 each), and Sweden (7).

Novak Djokovic

**Did You KNOW?** Since 1955, the International Tennis Hall of Fame in Newport, Rhode Island, has honored 224 of the game's legends from 19 different countries. Players honored in 2012 included U.S. teen star Jennifer Capriati, French Open winner Gustavo Kuerten of Brazil, and three-time U.S. Paralympic medalist Randy Snow. Find out more at www.tennisfame.com

# X GAMES

ESPN held the first X Games (originally called the Extreme Games) in 1995. The first Winter X Games followed two years later. Considered the Olympics of action sports, the X Games showcase fearless athletes who are always looking for new ways to go higher and faster and invent more exciting tricks.

*Kelly Clark*

## WINTER X GAMES

The Winter X Games feature events in snowboarding, skiing, and snowmobiling. The 17th Winter X Games took place in Aspen, Colorado, January 24-27, 2013. Snowboarder Shaun White earned his 13th gold medal at the Winter X Games, and Kelly Clark's performance in the women's Super Pipe won her a third gold in a row. The death of snowmobiler Caleb Moore after crashing during an X Games final raised questions about the future of the dangerous sport.

*Jagger Eaton*

## SUMMER X GAMES

The Summer X Games feature events in Moto X (motocross), BMX, skateboarding, and rally car racing. In 2012, 11-year-old skateboarder Jagger Eaton became the youngest athlete ever to compete at the X Games. The 19th Summer X Games then were set to be held in and around downtown Los Angeles, August 1-4, 2013. After more than 10 years in Los Angeles, the Summer X Games will then move to another U.S. host city in 2014. Possible locations include Chicago, Illinois; Detroit, Michigan; Austin, Texas; and Charlotte, North Carolina.

**Find out more about extreme sports at espn.go.com/action**

## ALL-TIME X GAMES GOLD MEDALISTS

Here are the X Games competitors who have won the most events at the annual action sports championships.

| WINTER X GAMES | | |
|---|---|---|
| **Competitor** | **Sport(s)** | **Medals*** |
| **Shaun White** | snowboarding | 13 |
| Tanner Hall | skiing | 7 |
| **Tucker Hibbert** | snowmobiling | 7 |
| **Nate Holland** | snowboarding | 7 |
| Lindsey Jacobellis | snowboarding | 7 |

*Through 2013. Athletes in **bold** competed in 2013 X Games.

| SUMMER X GAMES | | |
|---|---|---|
| **Competitor** | **Sport(s)** | **Medals*** |
| Dave Mirra | BMX, rally car | 14 |
| **Travis Pastrana** | motocross, rally car | 11 |
| **Jamie Bestwick** | BMX | 10 |
| Tony Hawk | skateboarding | 10 |
| **Bob Burnquist** | skateboarding | 9 |

*Through 2012. Athletes in **bold** competed in 2012 X Games.

# SPORTS PUZZLES



## SPORTS STAR Challenge

Find the names of the following people discussed in the Sports section. The names are all hidden in the puzzle. The letters of the names may run up, down, forward, backward, or diagonally. Two names may share the same letter.

| NAMES TO FIND | |
|---|---|
| Bolt | Luck |
| Cabrera | Maze |
| Cal | Messi |
| Doug | Phelps |
| Griffin | Park |
| Jones | Serena |

| | | | | | | | | | |
|---|---|---|---|---|---|---|---|---|---|
| G | S | B | O | L | T | O | P | M | U |
| R | E | N | O | A | F | K | R | A | P |
| I | N | S | D | C | Z | C | W | Z | H |
| F | O | E | Y | O | P | U | I | E | E |
| F | J | R | Z | X | U | L | Q | S | L |
| I | M | E | S | S | I | G | K | T | P |
| N | O | N | J | E | F | N | G | O | S |
| F | C | A | B | R | E | R | A | V | D |
| N | D | K | S | O | W | A | Y | L | N |

# MATCH IT!

**Match the sporting term with the related sport.**

### Sporting Terms

1. A super pipe ◯
2. A touchdown ◯
3. A striker ◯
4. A rebound ◯
5. A try ◯
6. The individual medley ◯
7. A serve ◯
8. A dojo ◯

### Sports

**a** Soccer
**b** Basketball
**c** Karate
**d** Football
**e** Snowboarding
**f** Tennis
**g** Rugby
**h** Swimming

ANSWERS ON PAGES 334-336.

# TECHNOLOGY & COMPUTERS

→What are QR codes? PAGE 242

## COMPUTER HIGHLIGHTS TIMELINE

**100 B.C.** The Antikythera Mechanism, which used gears to predict the positions of astronomical bodies, was built by the ancient Greeks. It was the first known mechanical computer.

**1623** Wilhelm Schickard invented the first machine that could automatically add, subtract, multiply, and divide. He called it a "calculating clock."

**1946** The first electronic, programmable, general-purpose computer was invented. It was called ENIAC, for "Electronic Numerical Integrator and Computer."→

**1967** The Advanced Research Projects Agency (ARPA) allotted money toward creating a computer network. It became ARPAnet, which evolved into the Internet.

**1971** The "floppy disk" was introduced by IBM as a means of affordable portable storage.

**1975** Bill Gates and Paul Allen founded Microsoft. Later came the first version of Windows.

**1990** The World Wide Web was first launched by British physicist Tim Berners-Lee.

**1996** Google, the Internet's most popular search engine, began as a graduate student project at Stanford University called BackRub.

**2004** Facebook, the popular social networking site, was launched by Harvard University student Mark Zuckerberg.

**2006** Twitter, a Web service letting people send or post short messages, was founded.

**2010** Apple introduced the iPad, a tablet computer.

**2011** Annual sales of smartphones exceeded personal computer sales for the first time.

**2012** With the Internet fast running out of addresses, the World IPv6 Launch saw many Internet-related companies begin to permanently support the IPv6 protocol, allowing up to 340 trillion trillion trillion addresses.

**Did You KNOW?**

**Linux, an open-source operating system introduced by Finnish college student Linus Torvalds in 1991, is used in PCs, video game consoles, servers, and supercomputers. The popular Android operating system for mobile devices is based on it.**

# Playing It Safe ONLINE

Social networking websites can be a lot of fun. But they can also be a source of problems. To be on the safe side, you should always keep an eye out for risks.

**Protect against cyberbullying.** Cyberbullying refers to emails or posts sent over the Internet that are intended to embarrass or hurt another person. These posts often spread lies or tell secrets the victim shared in confidence. If you are a victim of a cyberbully, save the posts or emails and show them to an adult you trust. Often the person behind the bullying can be found. To help keep cyberbullying from spreading, refuse to pass along bullying emails about someone else, express disapproval of cyberbullying messages, and report them to an adult.

**Be careful about what personal information you make public.** Carefully guard your password, birthday, address, phone number, and other personal information.

**Take advantage of the website's security features.** Pick a unique, hard-to-guess password. Keep your profile viewable only by friends. If the website allows your username to be different from your real name, make sure yours is different—and does not include personal information, such as your age or town.

**Beware of viruses.** Antivirus software may not recognize new viruses. For this reason, it is important to think twice before downloading an app or any other file from a source that you don't know or don't have reason to trust.

# STORED IN THE CLOUD

One of the fastest-growing technology innovations is **cloud computing**. Basically, with cloud computing, software you use and files you keep aren't stored on your computer's hard drive. Instead, they are on the computers of a company that provides cloud computing services. You access them via the Internet. Cloud computing can have several advantages.

→ **What you can do is not limited by what software your computer has or how much speed and power it has.** Even if you don't have a video-editing program, through a service provider you can edit videos—whether for a school project or just for fun.

→ **What you save is not limited by how much storage space your computer has.** Many companies allow people to store photos, music, movies, e-books, and other large files in the cloud.

→ **When you can use software and stored files is not limited by where you are.** Even if you're away from your own computer, as long as you have access to the Internet, you can use programs and retrieve files.

Cloud computing has some possible problems. Some people are concerned about the security of information that is stored in the cloud. And if your service provider has a service interruption, or your Internet connection is lost, then you can't get to software or stored files until the problem is fixed.

Still, many experts think cloud computing will become more widespread as time goes by. Even NASA uses the cloud computing services of companies like Microsoft and Google for data storage and complex calculations.

**Did You KNOW?** **In 2012, the Oak Ridge National Laboratory's Titan earned the title of world's fastest computer. It can do up to 27 thousand trillion calculations a second.**

# How SMART Are SMARTPHONES?

**Today's smartphones are tiny compared to the first cell phones, but they can do much more, and their abilities are growing. Here are some things people can do with their smartphones.**

## Find Where You Are ▷

- Most smartphones offer **GPS** (Global Positioning System), a satellite-based navigation system that can help you find your way. Smartphone GPS apps may offer maps, up-to-date traffic information, and locations of key places of interest.

## Tell the Phone What to Do ▷

- **Speech recognition** is another feature of some smartphones. Special software converts spoken sounds into electric signals, which are then translated into written words or into commands that tell the phone to do something—for example, "Call Mary" or "Open Angry Birds."

## Take a Cue from QR Codes ▷

- Use your phone's camera to scan a **QR code** (QR stands for Quick Response). These generally square-shaped codes can be found on signs, ads, products, and other things. Unlike traditional barcodes, which can hold only up to 20 digits, QR codes can hold nearly 4,300 characters (or more than 7,000 numbers). A QR code might carry a text message for your phone to scan and display. It might hold a telephone number for your phone to dial, or the address of a website for your phone to connect to. Or it might contain an email message, ready for sending by your phone–such as a request for more information.

## Pay for Things ▷

- Some phones serve as **mobile wallets**, used to pay for purchases in stores, train stations, and so on. One type uses a short-range radio technology called NFC, which stands for Near-Field Communication. Swiping or tapping the phone at a reader device at the place of purchase lets you connect with that device and make the payment. The money may come from a credit-card or bank account. It might be subtracted from a prepaid card, such as a gift card, stored in the phone's memory.
- Another purchase method uses a QR code or barcode. The code may be displayed on the phone and read by a device at the store, or it may appear on the product and be scanned with the phone's camera. If you decide to make the transaction, the right amount of money is taken from your account.

**The first commercial portable cell phone, the Motorola DynaTAC 8000X, introduced in 1983, was 13 inches long, weighed 28 ounces, and cost $3,995. It let you talk for half an hour and took 10 hours to recharge.**

→ ON THE JOB ←

# Digital Editorial Manager



Digital editorial managers lead teams of workers who write in content-management systems. The information a team writes appears on websites for desktops and mobile or tablet devices. The manager makes sure the information is accurate, clear, and a great user experience—even if you only have a tiny space to read it on a cell phone. **Anna Goldrein,** an editorial manager at Google, agreed to talk to *The World Almanac for Kids* about her work.

**What do you do in a typical day?** My department puts together information about places around the world. We try to help people who search on Google to make better decisions about which restaurants and attractions they visit. I might work on my own for a few hours, perhaps thinking of new ways to train writers, but a lot of the time I solve problems with software engineers, like how to make their systems easier for our writers to use.

**What interests and strengths of yours make this job right for you?** Growing up, I always loved reading books—any book that I could find in our house in Liverpool, England. I also liked the sound of different languages, and my brother and I even made up a "secret" language (a handful of words, in fact) my parents couldn't understand. Later, I learned to speak French, and I studied and worked in Paris. I traveled to many other countries in Europe and Asia, and I wrote about my experiences for websites, newspapers, and magazines. So now my love of language, travel, and helping people learn more about familiar and faraway places makes this job right for me.

**What kind of education or training did you need to get in order to do your job?** I have a bachelor's degree in French and a Master of Philosophy in 17th-century French fairy tales, and I've worked in content-management systems for over ten years. My education has helped me to analyze and solve problems, and to realize how important stories are to understanding the world.

**What do you like best about your job? What is most challenging?** I get the chance to work with bright and interesting coworkers, and to have a real impact on millions of people who see our content when they do Google searches. It's hard to keep pace with Google's new ideas and products, but I feel lucky to learn new things all the time. It's like being in school.

# TRANSPORTATION

→When did the Panama Canal open? PAGE 247

## GETTING FROM THERE TO HERE

## A SHORT HISTORY OF TRANSPORTATION

**5000 B.C.** People harness **animal power.** Oxen and donkeys carry heavy loads.

**3500 B.C.** Egyptians create the first **sailboat.** Before this, people made rafts or canoes and paddled them with poles or their hands.

**3500 B.C.** In Mesopotamia (modern-day Iraq), vehicles with **wheels** are invented. But the first wheels are made of heavy wood, and the roads are terrible.

**A.D. 800** Fast, shallow-draft **longships** make Vikings a powerful force in Europe from 800 to 1100.

**983** First **locks** to raise water level are built on China's Grand Canal. By 1400, a 1,500-mile water highway system is developed.

**Around 1000** Using **magnetic compasses,** Chinese are able to sail long distances in flat-bottomed ships called junks.

**1450s** Portuguese build **fast ships** with three masts. These, plus the compass, lead to an age of exploration.

**1660s** **Horse-drawn stagecoaches** begin running in France. They stop at "stages" to switch horses and passengers—the first mass transit system.

**1681** France's 150-mile **Canal du Midi** connects the Atlantic Ocean with the Mediterranean Sea.

**1832** The first U.S. **horse-drawn streetcar** is driven up and down the Bowery in New York City.

**1783** In Paris, the Montgolfier brothers fly the first **hot air balloon.**

**1769** James Watt patents the first highly efficient **steam engine.**

**1839** Kirkpatrick Macmillan of Scotland invents the first **pedaled bicycle.**

**1825** The 363-mile **Erie Canal** connects the Hudson River with Lake Erie, opening up the U.S. frontier and making New York City the nation's top port.

**1730s** **Stagecoach service** begins in the U.S.

**1830** **Inter-city passenger rail service** begins in England. Trains are powered by a steam engine built by George Stephenson. They go about 24 miles per hour.

**1807** Robert Fulton patents a highly efficient **steamboat.**

**1869** **Transcontinental railroad** is completed at Promontory Point, Utah. The Suez Canal in Egypt opens, saving ships a long trip around Africa.

**1862** Etienne Lenoir of Belgium builds the **first car** with an internal-combustion engine.

**1887** First practical electric street railway system opens in the U.S. in Richmond, Virginia. Suburbs soon grow around cities as **trolley** systems let people live farther away from the workplace.

**1908** Henry Ford builds the first **Model T**, a practical car for the general public.

**1860s** **Paddle-wheel** steamboats dominate U.S. river travel.

**1863** Using steam locomotives, the **London subway** (known as the "tube") opens.

**1873** San Francisco's **cable car** system begins service.

**1897** The first U.S. **subway service** begins in Boston. New York City follows in 1904.

**1903** At Kitty Hawk, North Carolina, the Wright brothers fly the first powered **heavier-than-air machine**.

**1939**
The first practical **helicopter** and **first jet plane** are invented. The jet flies up to 434 mph. (Jet passenger service begins in 1952.)

**1969**
U.S. astronauts aboard ***Apollo 11*** land on the Moon.

**2012**
China begins service on the world's **longest high-speed rail line**. The train, which travels at a top speed of more than 185 mph, covers the 1,200-mile distance between Beijing and Guangzhou in 8 hours.

**1914**
The 50-mile **Panama Canal** opens, saving ships a nearly 6,000-mile trip around South America.

**1927**
Charles A. Lindbergh makes the first **nonstop solo flight** across the Atlantic, flying from Long Island, New York, to Paris, France, in 33 hours, 30 minutes.

**1964**
Shinkansen "**bullet train**" service (124 mph) begins in Japan.

**1981**
The first **space shuttle** is launched on April 12, 1981.

**1994**
Trains cross under the English Channel in the new **Channel Tunnel**, or "Chunnel."

# TRAVEL

→Which national park contains the deepest lake in the United States? PAGE 250

Hundreds of years ago, brave voyagers set out to explore new places. Their travels took them far, sometimes by foot and sometimes by ship. Many scaled tall mountains and crossed vast oceans. Sometimes, they weren't quite sure where they were headed.

People still like to travel today, but they often do so for fun. And unlike in the days of exploration, modern travelers usually know where they are headed. Whether they go by car, train, bus, ship, or plane, people still enjoy traveling and exploring new places.

## Most Visited Countries*

1. **France**
2. United States
3. China
4. Spain
5. Italy
6. Turkey
7. United Kingdom
8. Germany
9. Malaysia
10. Mexico

*2011

## Most Visited U.S. Tourist Sites*

1. **Times Square, New York, NY**
2. Central Park, New York, NY
3. Union Station, Washington, D.C.
4. Las Vegas Strip, Las Vegas, NV
5. Grand Central Terminal, New York, NY
6. Magic Kingdom, Walt Disney World, Lake Buena Vista, FL
7. Disneyland, Anaheim, CA
8. (tie) Golden Gate Bridge, San Francisco, CA; Faneuil Hall, Boston, MA
10. (tie) Golden Gate National Recreation Area, San Francisco, CA; Balboa Park, San Diego, CA

*2011

## Most Visited Amusement Parks*

1. **Magic Kingdom, Walt Disney World (Lake Buena Vista, FL), 17.1 million visitors**
2. Disneyland (Anaheim, CA), 16.1 million visitors
3. Tokyo Disneyland (Japan), 13.9 million visitors
4. Tokyo Disney Sea (Japan), 11.9 million visitors
5. Disneyland Park, Disneyland Paris (France), 10.9 million visitors

*2011

*Las Vegas Strip*

# Amusement Parks

The first amusement parks appeared in Europe more than 400 years ago. Attractions included flower gardens and a few simple rides. Today's amusement parks are much more impressive, with super-fast roller coasters, parades, shows, and other attractions. Here's a look at some of the most popular amusement parks in the U.S.

## Fabulous Park Facts

**Biggest Park:** Walt Disney World, Lake Buena Vista, Florida, 30,080 acres

**Most Rides:** 72, Cedar Point, Sandusky, Ohio

**Most Roller Coasters:** 17, Six Flags Magic Mountain, Valencia, California

**Fastest Roller Coaster:** 128 mph, Kingda Ka, Six Flags Great Adventure, Jackson, New Jersey

**Tallest Roller Coaster:** 456 feet, Kingda Ka, Six Flags Great Adventure, Jackson, New Jersey

### Walt Disney World/Magic Kingdom (Lake Buena Vista, Florida)

Fantasyland in the Magic Kingdom recently got the largest expansion in the park's history, nearly doubling in size. New attractions include Ariel's Grotto, featuring *The Little Mermaid*, and Enchanted Tales With Belle, where visitors re-create the story of *Beauty and the Beast*. Visitors can also enjoy Storybook Circus, which features a new version of the popular Dumbo ride and a water play area.

### Universal Studios Florida/Islands of Adventure (Orlando, Florida)

Universal Studios opened in 1990, and visitors have been "riding the movies" there ever since. Rides, shows, and many other attractions feature favorite movie and TV characters. A popular attraction, The Wizarding World of Harry Potter, has three rides, as well as shops and restaurants.

### Cedar Point (Sandusky, Ohio)

One of the oldest amusement parks in the U.S., Cedar Point (on Lake Erie) opened in 1870. The most exciting new ride today is the GateKeeper. The longest winged roller coaster in the world, it also has the longest drop of any winged coaster at 164 feet. Cedar Point has plenty of other attractions, like maXair, which spins and swings 140 feet above the ground. ↓

**Did You KNOW?**

**The Cyclone roller coaster in Luna Park, in New York City's Coney Island, is one of the most famous coasters in the world. Made almost entirely of wood, it opened in 1927 and was named a National Historic Landmark in 1991. Riders go up and down a series of steep peaks and drops, reaching a height of 85 feet, then plunging at a speed of 60 miles per hour.**

# NATIONAL PARKS

The world's first national park was Yellowstone, established in 1872. Today in the U.S., there are 58 national parks, including parks in the Virgin Islands, Guam, Puerto Rico, and American Samoa. The National Park Service manages 398 units in all, including national monuments, memorials, battlefields, military parks, historic parks, historic sites, lakeshores, seashores, recreation areas, scenic rivers and trails, wilderness areas, and the White House—more than 84 million acres in all! For more information, go to: www.nps.gov/parks.html

## CRATER LAKE NATIONAL PARK

OR

This park of 183,000 acres, established in 1902 in southwestern Oregon, is home to spectacular Crater Lake, which at 1,958 feet is the deepest lake in the United States and one of the deepest in the world. The lake was created by the eruption of a volcano, Mount Mazama, more than 7,000 years ago. Surrounding glaciers filled the caldera (the volcano's basin) with clear blue water. The lake is not all there is to see. The park boasts 680 plant species, 74 types of mammals, and 158 kinds of birds. Since snow generally falls from October to June, cross-country skiing and snowshoeing are among the most popular pastimes.

## GRAND CANYON NATIONAL PARK

AZ

This national park, established in 1919, has one of the world's most spectacular landscapes, covering more than a million acres in northwestern Arizona. The canyon is 6,000 feet deep at its deepest point and 15 miles wide at its widest. Its 277-mile-long walls display a cross section of Earth's crust from as far back as 2 billion years ago. The Colorado River—which carved out the giant canyon—still runs through the park, which is a valuable wildlife preserve. The pine and fir forests, painted deserts, plateaus, caves, and sandstone canyons offer a wide range of habitats.

## GREAT SMOKY MOUNTAINS NATIONAL PARK

TN NC

This park, on the border between North Carolina and Tennessee, attracts 9 million visitors each year, making it the most visited national park in the country. Its 800-square-mile area, in the southern Appalachians, is home to more than 17,000 species. These include 200 types of birds and 65 species of mammals, such as white-tailed deer, elk, and black bears. There are also more than 1,600 types of flowering plants. Visitors can enjoy bicycling, hiking, camping, fishing, horseback riding—and brilliant fall foliage.

## EVERGLADES NATIONAL PARK

FL

Located in southern Florida, the Everglades is the largest subtropical wilderness in the U.S. More than 1.5 million acres of this wilderness are now protected in Everglades National Park. More than 350 species of birds, 40 species of mammals, and 50 kinds of reptiles live in the park's varied ecosystems, which include swamps, saw grass prairies, and mangrove forests. The park's different habitats allow a huge variety of life forms to thrive. As you move from place to place, you may see all kinds of animals, from tiny frogs to free-roaming alligators and crocodiles, graceful herons, and lots of snakes. You can visit a mahogany forest and pine forests, and you can walk along raised boardwalks to get beautiful views of miles of swaying saw grass marshes full of wildlife.

## YELLOWSTONE NATIONAL PARK

MT
ID
WY

Located mostly in northwestern Wyoming and partly in eastern Idaho and southwestern Montana, Yellowstone is known for its 10,000 hot springs and geysers—more than anyplace else in the world. Old Faithful, the most famous geyser, erupts for about four minutes every one to two hours, shooting 3,700-8,400 gallons of hot water as high as 185 feet. Other geysers include the Giant, which shoots a column of hot water 200 feet high, and the Giantess, which erupts for over four hours at a time, but only about two times per year. There are grizzly bears, wolves, elk, moose, buffalo, deer, beavers, coyotes, antelopes, and 330 species of birds.

# SOME MUST-SEE MUSEUMS

As you travel to new places, you can learn a lot—and have a lot of fun—by visiting local museums. Some museums have exhibits about space, the history of life on Earth, and other areas of science. Some display great art. Some focus on American history. And there are museums about almost any subject you can imagine. Here is a small sampling of some of the leading museums in the United States.

√ The **EXPLORATORIUM**, in San Francisco, California, weaves together science and art to encourage experimentation, curiosity, and creativity. The museum moved to a new, larger space on the San Francisco waterfront in April 2013. Hundreds of interactive exhibits there let visitors touch a tornado, use a joystick to land a lunar spacecraft, and dig through a pile of decay to feel the heat generated when organisms decompose.

For more information, see: **www.exploratorium.edu**

√ The **NATIONAL MUSEUM OF AMERICAN HISTORY,** in Washington, D.C., celebrates the richness of U.S. history. Exhibits include historic cars, First Ladies' gowns, and the flag that inspired "The Star-Spangled Banner." Visitors can also see such popular culture items as a Kermit the Frog puppet and Dorothy's ruby slippers from *The Wizard of Oz*.

For more information, see: **americanhistory.si.edu**

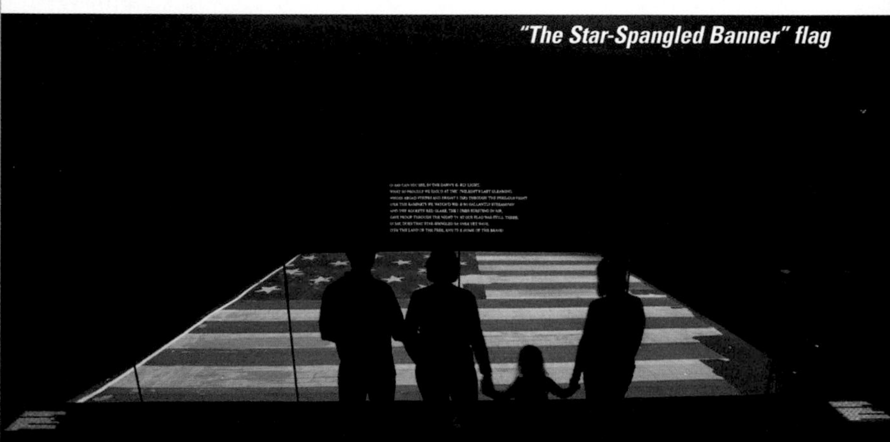

***"The Star-Spangled Banner" flag***

√ The **METROPOLITAN MUSEUM OF ART**, in New York City, is among the largest museums of fine art in the world. Its collection covers art from all parts of the world and includes works by the most important artists in history. The Met also has collections of furniture from past centuries, medieval arms and armor, and a beautiful, peaceful Chinese garden.

For more information, see: **www.metmuseum.org**

ON THE JOB

# Director of Travel Marketing

When people want to travel, they often do research on different places to help them decide where they want to go. **Lisa Hasenbalg** is the director of arts and culture marketing for the San Francisco Travel Association, letting people know about the city. She agreed to talk to *The World Almanac for Kids* about her work.

**What do you do in a typical day?** I work with museums, performing arts companies, and cultural events in San Francisco to find out what fun activities are happening, and then I promote those events to visitors. Each month, I pick out events to feature on our website, Facebook, Twitter, and also in visitor guides. As part of a big team, I work to find travel writers all over the world to feature our events and get people excited to visit San Francisco. We also create advertisements for billboards, websites, and magazines in other cities.

**What interests and strengths of yours make this job right for you?** Having a love of art and being a very curious person is a key part of why I enjoy my job. Knowledge of how the tourism and hospitality business works helps. It's also good to be able to manage multiple projects at the same time.

**What kind of education or training did you need to get in order to do your job?** After attending college, I worked for a major retailer in management for several years and was trained to manage people and run a business. By working hard and volunteering, I was advanced into the marketing division where I learned how to promote a business. I use those same skills to promote the arts and culture of a city.

**What do you like best about your job? What is most challenging?** Working with interesting and artistic people! It's important to be familiar with the events I promote so I'm lucky to be able to attend many performances and visit museums throughout the year. With literally thousands of things to do, it's hard to pick the few you are able to feature.

# UNITED STATES

→When did women gain the right to vote? PAGE 257

## FACTS & FIGURES

AREA 50 States and Washington, D.C.

| | |
|---|---|
| LAND | 3,531,905 square miles |
| WATER | 264,837 square miles |
| TOTAL | 3,796,742 square miles |

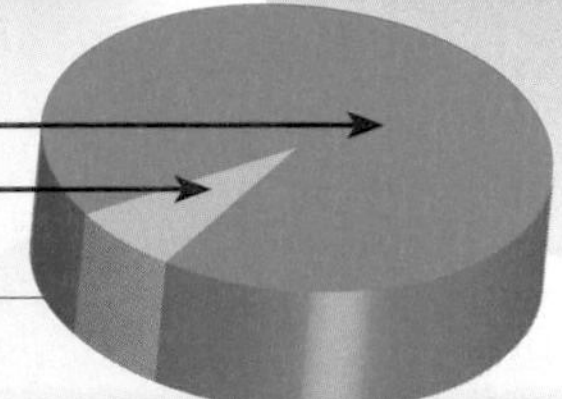

POPULATION (JULY 2013 ESTIMATE): 316,668,567

CAPITAL: WASHINGTON, D.C.

## LARGEST, HIGHEST, AND OTHER STATISTICS

| | |
|---|---|
| **Largest state:** | Alaska (665,384 square miles) |
| **Smallest state:** | Rhode Island (1,545 square miles) |
| **Northernmost city:** | Barrow, Alaska (71°17′ north latitude) |
| **Southernmost city:** | Hilo, Hawaii (19°44′ north latitude) |
| **Easternmost city:** | Eastport, Maine (66°59′ west longitude) |
| **Westernmost city:** | Adak Station, Alaska (173°11′ east longitude) |
| **Highest settlement:** | Tordal Estates, Colorado (10,653 feet) |
| **Lowest settlement:** | Bombay Beach, California (223 feet below sea level) |
| **Oldest national park:** | Yellowstone National Park (Idaho, Montana, Wyoming), 2,219,791 acres, established 1872 |
| **Largest national park:** | Wrangell-St. Elias, Alaska (8,323,147 acres) |
| **Highest mountain:** | Mount McKinley (Denali), Alaska (20,320 feet) → |
| **Lowest point:** | Death Valley, California (282 feet below sea level) |
| **Longest river system:** | Mississippi-Missouri-Red Rock (3,710 miles) |
| **Deepest lake:** | Crater Lake, Oregon (1,958 feet) |
| **Tallest building:** | (as of early 2013) Willis Tower, Chicago, Illinois (1,450 feet) |
| **Tallest structure:** | TV tower, Blanchard, North Dakota (2,063 feet) |
| **Longest bridge span:** | Verrazano-Narrows Bridge, New York (4,260 feet) |
| **Highest bridge:** | Royal Gorge, Colorado (1,053 feet above water) |

**English is the language most commonly spoken in the United States. However, according to the U.S. Census Bureau, almost 400 other languages are spoken by some Americans.**

# SYMBOLS OF THE UNITED STATES

## THE GREAT SEAL

The Great Seal of the United States shows an American bald eagle with a ribbon in its mouth bearing the Latin words *e pluribus unum* (out of many, one). In its talons are the arrows of war and an olive branch of peace. On the back of the Great Seal is an unfinished pyramid with an eye (the eye of Providence) above it. The seal was approved by Congress on June 20, 1782.

## THE FLAG

The flag of the United States has 50 stars (one for each state) and 13 stripes (one for each of the original 13 states). It is unofficially called the "Stars and Stripes."

The first U.S. flag was commissioned by the Second Continental Congress in 1777 but did not exist until 1783, after the American Revolution. Historians are not certain who designed the Stars and Stripes. Many different flags are believed to have been used during the American Revolution.

The flag of 1777 was used until 1795. In that year, Congress passed an act ordering that a new flag have 15 stripes, alternate red and white, and 15 stars on a blue field. In 1818, Congress directed that the flag have 13 stripes and that a new star be added for each new state of the Union. The last star was added in 1960 for the state of Hawaii.

There are many customs for flying the flag and treating it with respect. For example, it should not touch the floor and no other flag should be flown above it, except for the UN flag at UN headquarters. When the flag is raised or lowered, when it passes in a parade, or during the Pledge of Allegiance, people should face it and stand at attention. Those in military uniform should salute. Others should put their right hand over their heart. The flag is flown at half-staff as a sign of mourning.

## PLEDGE OF ALLEGIANCE TO THE FLAG

"I pledge allegiance to the flag of the United States of America and to the republic for which it stands, one nation under God, indivisible, with liberty and justice for all."

## THE NATIONAL ANTHEM

"The Star-Spangled Banner" was a poem written in 1814 by Francis Scott Key after he watched British ships bombard Fort McHenry, Maryland, during the War of 1812. It became the National Anthem by an act of Congress in 1931. The music to "The Star-Spangled Banner" was originally a tune called "Anacreon in Heaven."

# THE U.S. CONSTITUTION

## The Foundation of American Government

The Constitution is the document that created the present government of the United States. It was written in 1787 and went into effect in 1789. It establishes the three branches of the U.S. government—the legislative (Congress), the executive (headed by the president), and the judicial (the Supreme Court and other federal courts). The first 10 amendments to the Constitution (the **Bill of Rights**) explain the basic rights of all American citizens.

**You can find the Constitution online at: www.archives.gov/exhibits/charters/constitution.html**

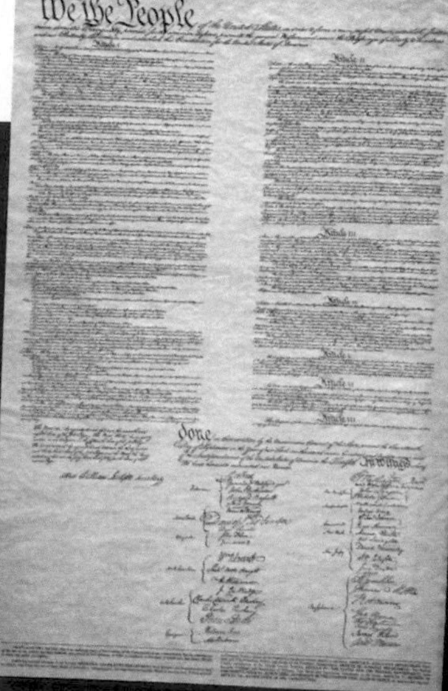

## The Preamble to the Constitution

**The Constitution begins with a short statement called the Preamble. The Preamble states that the government of the United States was established by the people.**

*"We the people of the United States, in order to form a more perfect union, establish justice, insure domestic tranquility, provide for the common defense, promote the general welfare, and secure the blessings of liberty to ourselves and our posterity, do ordain and establish this Constitution for the United States of America."*

## THE ARTICLES

**The original Constitution contained seven articles. The first three articles of the Constitution establish the three branches of the U.S. government.**

**Article 1, Legislative Branch** Creates the Senate and House of Representatives and describes their functions and powers.

**Article 2, Executive Branch** Creates the office of the President and the Electoral College and lists their powers and responsibilities.

**Article 3, Judicial Branch** Creates the Supreme Court and gives Congress the power to create lower courts. The powers of the courts and certain crimes are defined.

**Article 4, The States** Discusses the relationship of the states to one another and to the citizens. Defines the states' powers.

**Article 5, Amending the Constitution** Describes how the Constitution can be amended (changed).

**Article 6, Federal Law** Makes the Constitution the supreme law of the land over state laws and constitutions.

**Article 7, Ratifying the Constitution** Establishes how to ratify (approve) the Constitution.

# AMENDMENTS TO THE CONSTITUTION

The writers of the Constitution understood that it might need to be amended, or changed, in the future, but they wanted to be careful and made it hard to change. Article 5 describes how the Constitution can be amended.

In order to take effect, an amendment must be approved by a two-thirds majority in both the House of Representatives and the Senate. It must then be approved (ratified) by three-fourths of the states (38 states). So far, there have been 27 amendments. One of them (the 18th, ratified in 1919) banned the manufacture or sale of liquor. It was canceled by the 21st Amendment, in 1933.

## The Bill of Rights: The First Ten Amendments

**The first ten amendments were adopted in 1791 and contain the basic freedoms Americans enjoy as a people. These amendments are known as the Bill of Rights.**

1. **Guarantees freedom of religion, speech, and the press.**
2. **Guarantees the right to have firearms.**
3. **Guarantees that soldiers cannot be lodged in private homes unless the owner agrees.**
4. **Protects people from being searched or having property searched or taken away by the government without reason.**
5. **Protects rights of people on trial for crimes.**
6. **Guarantees people accused of crimes the right to a speedy public trial by jury.**
7. **Guarantees the right to a trial by jury for other kinds of cases.**
8. **Prohibits "cruel and unusual punishments."**
9. **Says specific rights listed in the Constitution do not take away rights that may not be listed.**
10. **Establishes that any powers not given specifically to the federal government belong to states or the people.**

## OTHER IMPORTANT AMENDMENTS

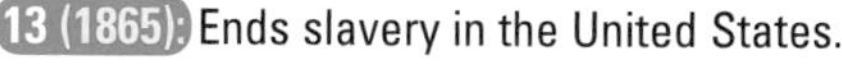

**13 (1865):** Ends slavery in the United States.

**14 (1868):** Bars states from denying rights to citizens; guarantees equal protection under the law for all citizens.

**15 (1870):** Guarantees that a person cannot be denied the right to vote because of race or color.

**19 (1920):** Gives women the right to vote.

**22 (1951):** Limits the president to two four-year terms of office.

**24 (1964):** Outlaws the poll tax (a tax people had to pay before they could vote) in federal elections. (The poll tax had been used to keep African Americans in the South from voting.)

**25 (1967):** Specifies presidential succession; also gives the president the power to appoint a new vice president if one dies or leaves office during a term.

**26 (1971):** Lowers the voting age to 18 from 21.

# THE LEGISLATIVE BRANCH

## CONGRESS

Congress is the legislative branch of the federal government. Congress's major responsibility is to pass the laws that govern the country and determine how money collected in taxes is spent. Congress consists of two parts—the Senate and the House of Representatives.

## THE SENATE

The Senate has 100 members, two from each state. The Constitution says that the Senate will have equal representation (the same number of representatives) from each state. Thus, small states have the same number of senators as large states. Senators are elected for six-year terms. There is no limit on the number of terms a senator can serve.

The Senate also has the responsibility of approving people the president appoints for certain jobs: for example, cabinet members and Supreme Court justices. The Senate must approve all treaties by at least a two-thirds vote. It also has the responsibility under the Constitution of putting on trial high-ranking federal officials who have been impeached (accused of wrongdoing) by the House of Representatives.

For more information, see: **www.senate.gov**

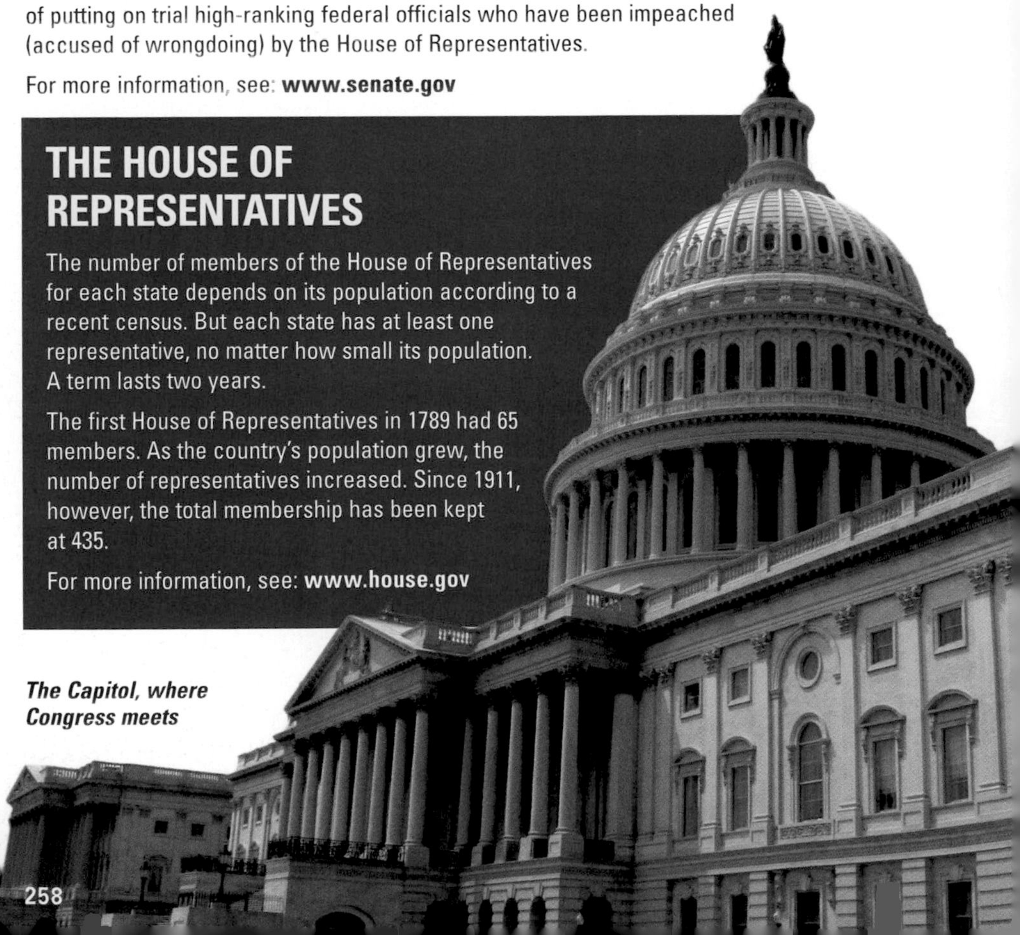

## THE HOUSE OF REPRESENTATIVES

The number of members of the House of Representatives for each state depends on its population according to a recent census. But each state has at least one representative, no matter how small its population. A term lasts two years.

The first House of Representatives in 1789 had 65 members. As the country's population grew, the number of representatives increased. Since 1911, however, the total membership has been kept at 435.

For more information, see: **www.house.gov**

***The Capitol, where Congress meets***

## The House of Representatives, by State

**As a result of the 2010 Census, some states gained or lost House members (or "seats"), starting in 2013, because of population changes. The table shows how many seats each state gained or lost.**

| State | Seats 2013 | Seats 2003–2012 | Change in Seats |
|---|---|---|---|
| Alabama | 7 | 7 | 0 |
| Alaska | 1 | 1 | 0 |
| Arizona | 9 | 8 | +1 |
| Arkansas | 4 | 4 | 0 |
| California | 53 | 53 | 0 |
| Colorado | 7 | 7 | 0 |
| Connecticut | 5 | 5 | 0 |
| Delaware | 1 | 1 | 0 |
| Florida | 27 | 25 | +2 |
| Georgia | 14 | 13 | +1 |
| Hawaii | 2 | 2 | 0 |
| Idaho | 2 | 2 | 0 |
| Illinois | 18 | 19 | –1 |
| Indiana | 9 | 9 | 0 |
| Iowa | 4 | 5 | –1 |
| Kansas | 4 | 4 | 0 |
| Kentucky | 6 | 6 | 0 |
| Louisiana | 6 | 7 | –1 |
| Maine | 2 | 2 | 0 |
| Maryland | 8 | 8 | 0 |
| Massachusetts | 9 | 10 | –1 |
| Michigan | 14 | 15 | –1 |
| Minnesota | 8 | 8 | 0 |
| Mississippi | 4 | 4 | 0 |
| Missouri | 8 | 9 | –1 |
| Montana | 1 | 1 | 0 |
| Nebraska | 3 | 3 | 0 |
| Nevada | 4 | 3 | +1 |
| New Hampshire | 2 | 2 | 0 |
| New Jersey | 12 | 13 | –1 |
| New Mexico | 3 | 3 | 0 |
| New York | 27 | 29 | –2 |
| North Carolina | 13 | 13 | 0 |
| North Dakota | 1 | 1 | 0 |
| Ohio | 16 | 18 | –2 |
| Oklahoma | 5 | 5 | 0 |
| Oregon | 5 | 5 | 0 |
| Pennsylvania | 18 | 19 | –1 |
| Rhode Island | 2 | 2 | 0 |
| South Carolina | 7 | 6 | +1 |
| South Dakota | 1 | 1 | 0 |
| Tennessee | 9 | 9 | 0 |
| Texas | 36 | 32 | +4 |
| Utah | 4 | 3 | +1 |
| Vermont | 1 | 1 | 0 |
| Virginia | 11 | 11 | 0 |
| Washington | 10 | 9 | +1 |
| West Virginia | 3 | 3 | 0 |
| Wisconsin | 8 | 8 | 0 |
| Wyoming | 1 | 1 | 0 |

**Washington, D.C., Puerto Rico, American Samoa, Guam, the Northern Mariana Islands, and the Virgin Islands each has one nonvoting member of the House of Representatives.**

## *How a Bill Becomes a Law*

A proposed law is called a bill. To become a law, a bill must first be approved by both houses, or chambers, of Congress. Most kinds of bills can start in either chamber.

Let's assume that a bill starts in the House of Representatives. It is introduced by one or more members and then assigned to one of the many House committees, where it is studied and possibly changed. The committee may get advice from outside experts and hold public hearings, or meetings, on the proposal. Then the committee votes on the bill. If a majority of the committee members support the bill, it goes to the full House. The House will then debate the bill, perhaps make changes to it, and then vote on the bill. If a majority of the full House votes for the bill, it is approved. It then goes to the Senate, where the process is repeated.

If the two chambers approve different versions of the same bill, usually a committee made up of members from the House and the Senate tries to work out the disagreements and come up with one revised bill. If both chambers of Congress pass this new version, the bill goes to the president. The president can either sign the bill, making it a law, or veto it (turn it down). If the president vetoes the bill, it can still become law if it is passed again by a two-thirds majority in both chambers of Congress.

# THE EXECUTIVE BRANCH

The **executive branch** of the federal government is headed by the president, who enforces the laws passed by Congress and is commander in chief of the U.S. armed forces. It also includes the vice president, people who work for the president or vice president, the major departments of the government, and special agencies. The **cabinet** is made up of the vice president, heads of major departments, and other officials. It meets when the president chooses. The chart at right shows cabinet departments in the order in which they were created.

**President**

**Vice President**

## Cabinet Departments

1 State
2 Treasury
3 Defense
4 Justice
5 Interior
6 Agriculture
7 Commerce
8 Labor
9 Health and Human Services
10 Housing and Urban Development
11 Transportation
12 Energy
13 Education
14 Veterans Affairs
15 Homeland Security

## Who Can Be President?

To be eligible to serve as president, a person must be a native-born U.S. citizen, must be at least 35 years old, and must have been a resident of the United States for at least 14 years.

## How Long Does the President Serve?

The president serves a four-year term, starting on January 20. No president can be elected more than twice, or more than once if he or she had served two years as president filling out the term of a president who left office.

## What Happens If the President Dies in Office?

If the president dies in office or cannot complete the term, the vice president becomes president. If the president is temporarily unable to perform his or her duties, the vice president can become acting president.

**The White House has a website. It is: www.whitehouse.gov**

**You can use the contact form on the website to send email to the president.**

## Voter Turnout in Presidential Elections, 1976–2012

Percent of eligible voters who actually voted.

| Year | Percent | Year | Percent |
|---|---|---|---|
| 1976 | 55.0% | 1996 | 51.4% |
| 1980 | 54.7% | 2000 | 54.2% |
| 1984 | 55.9% | 2004 | 60.4% |
| 1988 | 53.0% | 2008 | 62.3% |
| 1992 | 58.0% | 2012 | 58.2% |

# THE JUDICIAL BRANCH

Above are the nine justices who were on the Supreme Court in the 2012–2013 term (October 2012 to June 2013). The justices are (standing from left to right) Sonia Sotomayor, Stephen Breyer, Samuel Alito, and Elena Kagan; (seated from left to right) Clarence Thomas, Antonin Scalia, Chief Justice John Roberts, Anthony Kennedy, and Ruth Bader Ginsburg.

## THE SUPREME COURT

The highest court in the United States is the Supreme Court. It has nine justices who are appointed for life by the president with the approval of the Senate. Eight of the nine members are called associate justices. The ninth is the Chief Justice, who presides over the Court's meetings.

### What Does the Supreme Court Do?

The Supreme Court's major responsibilities are to judge cases that involve reviewing federal laws, actions of the president, treaties of the United States, and laws passed by state governments to be sure they do not conflict with the U.S. Constitution. If the Supreme Court finds that a law or action violates the Constitution, the law is struck down or the action is reversed.

### The Supreme Court's Decision Is Final.

Most cases must go through other state courts or federal courts before they reach the Supreme Court. The Supreme Court is the final court for a case, and the justices generally can decide which cases they will review. After the Supreme Court hears a case, it may agree or disagree with the decision by a lower court. Each justice has one vote, and the majority rules. When the Supreme Court makes a ruling, its decision is final, so each of the justices has a very important job.

# PRESIDENT of the UNITED STATES

As the nation's chief executive, the president has one of the hardest jobs in the world and can have a big impact on people's lives.

## What Does the President Do?

Here are some of the roles the president has, under the U.S. Constitution.

- ★ Suggest measures for Congress to pass.
- ★ Approve or veto (reject) bills that are passed by Congress.
- ★ Act as the commander-in-chief of the U.S. armed forces.
- ★ Make treaties, or agreements, with other countries, subject to approval by the Senate.
- ★ Appoint justices to the U.S. Supreme Court and many other judges and federal officials.

Many people work in the executive branch of government, and the president's responsibilities have grown over the years. But it is still up to the legislative branch (Congress) to make the laws and the judicial branch (federal courts) to decide what the Constitution allows. Each branch checks, or limits, the powers of the other branches. This system of "checks and balances" helps to prevent any one branch from becoming too powerful.

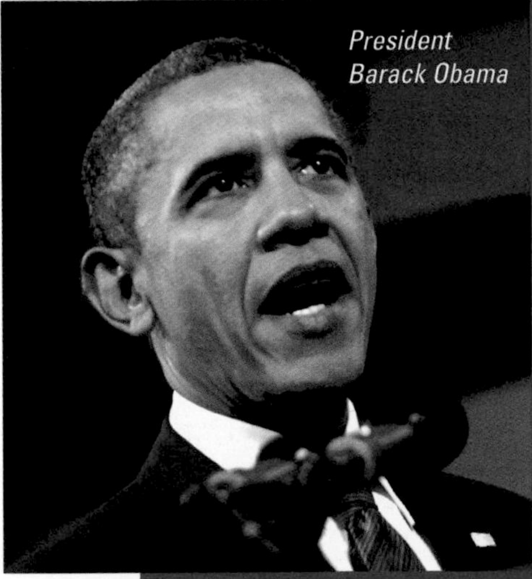

*President Barack Obama*

## What Does the Vice President Do?

According to the Constitution, the vice president has only two major duties. First, the vice president takes over if the president dies, resigns, or is removed from office. Second, the vice president presides over the Senate and can cast the deciding vote in case of a tie.

John Adams, the first vice president, called his job "the most insignificant office that ever the imagination of man contrived."

However, in recent times, the vice president has usually been given other important duties by the president.

*Vice President Joe Biden*

# PRESIDENTIAL FACTS and FIRSTS

**There have been 43 different presidents from George Washington to Barack Obama. (However, Obama is counted as the 44th president. This is because Grover Cleveland served two terms that were not in a row. He is counted as both the 22nd and the 24th president.) Presidents have been distinctive in many ways. Here are a few.**

★ Tallest President: Abraham Lincoln (6 feet, 4 inches)

★ Shortest President: James Madison (5 feet, 4 inches)

★ Heaviest President: William Howard Taft (332 pounds in 1911)

★ Oldest to Become President: Ronald Reagan (69 years old when he took office in 1981)

★ Youngest to Become President: Theodore Roosevelt (42 years old when he was sworn in after William McKinley was assassinated in 1901)

★ Youngest to Get Elected: John F. Kennedy (43 years old when he won the November 1960 election)

★ First President to Live in the White House: John Adams (moved in when the building was completed in 1800)

★ First President to be Photographed in Office: James K. Polk, in 1849

★ First President to Have a Phone in the White House: Rutherford B. Hayes, in 1879

★ First President to Go to a Foreign Country While in Office: Theodore Roosevelt (visited the Panama Canal site in 1906)

★ First President to Give a Press Conference on TV: John F. Kennedy, in 1961

★ First President to Hold an Internet Chat: Bill Clinton, in 1999

★ Only President Who Never Married: James Buchanan

★ Only President to Get Married in the White House: Grover Cleveland, to Frances Folsom in 1886.

★ Only Divorced President: Ronald Reagan

★ Only African American President: Barack Obama

★ Only Catholic President: John F. Kennedy

★ Only Known Left-Handed Presidents: James Garfield, Herbert Hoover, Harry Truman, Gerald Ford, Ronald Reagan, George H. W. Bush, Bill Clinton, Barack Obama

Did You KNOW?

**Though he has been described as left-handed, President Garfield could do many things with either hand. He liked to amuse friends by writing in Latin with one hand while at the same time writing in Greek with the other.**

# ELECTING a PRESIDENT

**WHO ELECTS THE PRESIDENT?**

The president is actually elected by a group of "electors" known as the Electoral College. Members of this group from each state meet in December in their state capitals to cast their votes.

**BUT I THOUGHT ELECTION DAY WAS IN NOVEMBER!**

It is, but on Election Day voters don't directly vote for president. Instead, they vote for a group of presidential electors who have pledged to support whichever candidate wins that state's popular vote.

**WHAT'S THE TOTAL NUMBER OF ELECTORAL VOTES?**

There are 538 total votes. A presidential candidate must win at least 270 of those (a majority).

**HOW MANY ELECTORAL VOTES DOES EACH STATE GET?**

Each state gets one vote for each of its two senators and one for each of its members in the House of Representatives. Also, Washington, D.C., has three electoral votes.

**WHAT IF NO CANDIDATE GETS A MAJORITY OF ELECTORAL VOTES?**

Then the election is decided by the U.S. House of Representatives. That's what happened after the 1800 and 1824 elections.

**CAN A CANDIDATE WHO DIDN'T GET THE MOST VOTES ON ELECTION DAY STILL WIN A MAJORITY OF ELECTORAL VOTES?**

Yes. That happened in the 1876, 1888, and 2000 elections.

## Who CAN Vote?

**Voting rules vary from state to state, but they must agree with the Constitution. No state can deny the right to vote because of a person's race or gender, or because of age if the voter is at least 18 years old.**

**All voters must be U.S citizens, and in some states people convicted of serious crimes cannot vote. In most states, voters must already be registered, or signed up to vote in elections, before Election Day. However, under a 1993 federal law, states have taken steps to allow people to register in many different locations or by mail.**

## Who DOES Vote?

**Voter turnout is highest in presidential elections, but even then, many people who *can* vote do not do so. In the 2012 election, only about 58 percent of those eligible to vote ended up voting. This was down from 62 percent in 2008, but up from 54 percent in 2000.**

**Sometimes only a few votes can make a big difference. In 2000, for example, George W. Bush defeated Al Gore in Florida by only 537 votes and became president!**

# RACE FOR THE WHITE HOUSE 2012

**On November 6, 2012, President Barack Obama, a Democrat, won a second term in the White House, defeating his Republican opponent, former Massachusetts Governor Mitt Romney.**

- The president carried 26 states and the District of Columbia, to get 332 electoral votes, 62 more than he needed. He won 51 percent of the popular vote.
- Obama won all the states in the Northeast, all the West Coast states except Alaska, and almost all states in the Upper Midwest. Romney took most states in the South and West.
- Nine out of ten African Americans and seven out of ten Hispanic Americans who voted cast their ballots for Obama. He also did better than Romney among young people and among women.
- In the fall campaign, Romney blamed Obama for the country's high unemployment rate. Obama argued that the economy was improving under his leadership, after a recession that began under former President George W. Bush, a Republican.
- Both parties had picked their candidates for president and vice president at national conventions in late summer 2012. Obama and his running mate, Vice President Joe Biden, had no serious opposition. On the Republican side, Romney first had to defeat a large field of rivals in primaries and caucuses (political gatherings) around the country. His running mate was Representative Paul Ryan of Wisconsin.

## Electoral College Results, 2012

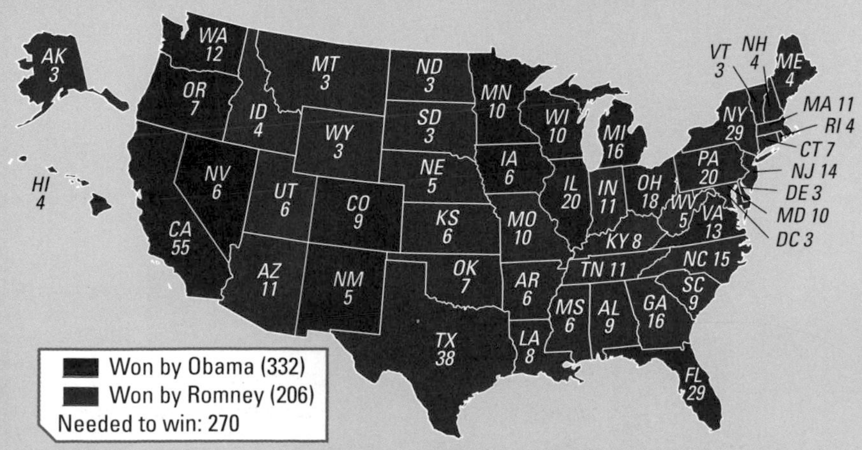

# Facts about the PRESIDENTS

## 1 GEORGE WASHINGTON
independent, 1789–1797

**Born:** Feb. 22, 1732, at Wakefield, Westmoreland County, Virginia

**Married:** Martha Dandridge Custis (1731–1802); no children

**Died:** Dec. 14, 1799; buried at Mount Vernon, Virginia

**Vice President:** John Adams (1789–1797)

## 2 JOHN ADAMS
Federalist Party, 1797–1801

**Born:** Oct. 30, 1735, in Braintree (now Quincy), Massachusetts

**Married:** Abigail Smith (1744–1818); 3 sons, 2 daughters

**Died:** July 4, 1826; buried in Quincy, Massachusetts

**Vice President:** Thomas Jefferson (1797–1801)

## 3 THOMAS JEFFERSON
Democratic-Republican Party, 1801–1809

**Born:** Apr. 13, 1743, at Shadwell, Albemarle County, Virginia

**Married:** Martha Wayles Skelton (1748–1782); 1 son, 5 daughters

**Died:** July 4, 1826; buried at Monticello, Virginia

**Vice President:** Aaron Burr (1801–1805), George Clinton (1805–1809)

## 4 JAMES MADISON
Democratic-Republican Party, 1809–1817

**Born:** Mar. 16, 1751, at Port Conway, King George County, Virginia

**Married:** Dolley Payne Todd (1768–1849); no children

**Died:** June 28, 1836; buried at Montpelier Station, Virginia

**Vice President:** George Clinton (1809–1813), Elbridge Gerry (1813–1817)

## 5 JAMES MONROE
Democratic-Republican Party, 1817–1825

**Born:** Apr. 28, 1758, in Westmoreland County, Virginia

**Married:** Elizabeth Kortright (1768–1830); 1 son, 2 daughters

**Died:** July 4, 1831; buried in Richmond, Virginia

**Vice President:** Daniel D. Tompkins (1817–1825)

## 6 JOHN QUINCY ADAMS
Democratic-Republican Party, 1825–1829

**Born:** July 11, 1767, in Braintree (now Quincy), Massachusetts

**Married:** Louisa Catherine Johnson (1775–1852); 3 sons, 1 daughter

**Died:** Feb. 23, 1848; buried in Quincy, Massachusetts

**Vice President:** John C. Calhoun (1825–1829)

## 7 ANDREW JACKSON
Democratic Party, 1829–1837

**Born:** Mar. 15, 1767, in Waxhaw, South Carolina

**Married:** Rachel Donelson Robards (1767–1828); 1 son (adopted)

**Died:** June 8, 1845; buried in Nashville, Tennessee

**Vice President:** John C. Calhoun (1829–1833), Martin Van Buren (1833–1837)

## 8 MARTIN VAN BUREN
Democratic Party, 1837–1841

**Born:** Dec. 5, 1782, at Kinderhook, New York

**Married:** Hannah Hoes (1783–1819); 4 sons

**Died:** July 24, 1862; buried at Kinderhook, New York

**Vice President:** Richard M. Johnson (1837–1841)

## 9 WILLIAM HENRY HARRISON
Whig Party, 1841

**Born:** Feb. 9, 1773, at Berkeley, Charles City County, Virginia

**Married:** Anna Symmes (1775–1864); 6 sons, 4 daughters

**Died:** Apr. 4, 1841; buried in North Bend, Ohio

**Vice President:** John Tyler (1841)

## 10 JOHN TYLER
Whig Party, 1841–1845

**Born:** Mar. 29, 1790, in Greenway, Charles City County, Virginia

**Married:** Letitia Christian (1790–1842); 3 sons, 5 daughters. Julia Gardiner (1820–1889); 5 sons, 2 daughters

**Died:** Jan. 18, 1862; buried in Richmond, Virginia

**Vice President:** none

## 11 JAMES KNOX POLK
Democratic Party, 1845–1849

**Born:** Nov. 2, 1795, in Mecklenburg County, North Carolina

**Married:** Sarah Childress (1803–1891); no children

**Died:** June 15, 1849; buried in Nashville, Tennessee

**Vice President:** George M. Dallas (1845–1849)

## 12 ZACHARY TAYLOR
Whig Party, 1849–1850

**Born:** Nov. 24, 1784, in Orange County, Virginia

**Married:** Margaret Smith (1788–1852); 1 son, 5 daughters

**Died:** July 9, 1850; buried in Louisville, Kentucky

**Vice President:** Millard Fillmore (1849–1850)

## 13 MILLARD FILLMORE
Whig Party, 1850–1853

**Born:** Jan. 7, 1800, in Cayuga County, New York

**Married:** Abigail Powers (1798–1853); 1 son, 1 daughter. Caroline Carmichael McIntosh (1813–1881); no children

**Died:** Mar. 8, 1874; buried in Buffalo, New York

**Vice President:** none

## 14 FRANKLIN PIERCE
Democratic Party, 1853–1857

**Born:** Nov. 23, 1804, in Hillsboro, New Hampshire

**Married:** Jane Means Appleton (1806–1863); 3 sons

**Died:** Oct. 8, 1869; buried in Concord, New Hampshire

**Vice President:** William R. King (1853–1857)

## 15 JAMES BUCHANAN
Democratic Party, 1857–1861

**Born:** Apr. 23, 1791, Cove Gap, near Mercersburg, Pennsylvania

**Married:** Never

**Died:** June 1, 1868, buried in Lancaster, Pennsylvania

**Vice President:** John C. Breckinridge (1857–1861)

## 16 ABRAHAM LINCOLN
Republican Party, 1861–1865

**Born:** Feb. 12, 1809, in Hardin County, Kentucky

**Married:** Mary Todd (1818–1882); 4 sons

**Died:** Apr. 15, 1865; buried in Springfield, Illinois

**Vice President:** Hannibal Hamlin (1861–1865), Andrew Johnson (1865)

## 17 ANDREW JOHNSON
Democratic Party, 1865–1869

**Born:** Dec. 29, 1808, in Raleigh, North Carolina

**Married:** Eliza McCardle (1810–1876); 3 sons, 2 daughters

**Died:** July 31, 1875; buried in Greeneville, Tennessee

**Vice President:** none

## 18 ULYSSES S. GRANT
Republican Party, 1869–1877

**Born:** Apr. 27, 1822, in Point Pleasant, Ohio

**Married:** Julia Dent (1826–1902); 3 sons, 1 daughter

**Died:** July 23, 1885; buried in New York City

**Vice President:** Schuyler Colfax (1869–1873), Henry Wilson (1873–1877)

## 19 RUTHERFORD B. HAYES
Republican Party, 1877–1881

**Born:** Oct. 4, 1822, in Delaware, Ohio

**Married:** Lucy Ware Webb (1831–1889); 7 sons, 1 daughter

**Died:** Jan. 17, 1893; buried in Fremont, Ohio

**Vice President:** William A. Wheeler (1877–1881)

## 20 JAMES A. GARFIELD
Republican Party, 1881

**Born:** Nov. 19, 1831, in Orange, Cuyahoga County, Ohio

**Married:** Lucretia Rudolph (1832–1918); 5 sons, 2 daughters

**Died:** Sept. 19, 1881; buried in Cleveland, Ohio

**Vice President:** Chester A. Arthur (1881)

## 21 CHESTER A. ARTHUR
Republican Party, 1881–1885

**Born:** Oct. 5, 1829, in Fairfield, Vermont

**Married:** Ellen Lewis Herndon (1837–1880); 2 sons, 1 daughter

**Died:** Nov. 18, 1886; buried in Albany, New York

**Vice President:** none

## 22 GROVER CLEVELAND
Democratic Party, 1885–1889

**Born:** Mar. 18, 1837, in Caldwell, New Jersey

**Married:** Frances Folsom (1864–1947); 2 sons, 3 daughters

**Died:** June 24, 1908; buried in Princeton, New Jersey

**Vice President:** Thomas A. Hendricks (1885–1889)

## 23 BENJAMIN HARRISON
Republican Party, 1889–1893

**Born:** Aug. 20, 1833, in North Bend, Ohio

**Married:** Caroline Lavinia Scott (1832–1892); 1 son, 1 daughter. Mary Scott Lord Dimmick (1858–1948); 1 daughter

**Died:** Mar. 13, 1901; buried in Indianapolis, Indiana

**Vice President:** Levi Morton (1889–1893)

## 24 GROVER CLEVELAND See 22, above
Democratic Party, 1893–1897

**Vice President:** Adlai E. Stevenson (1893–1897)

## 25 WILLIAM MCKINLEY
Republican Party, 1897–1901

**Born:** Jan. 29, 1843, in Niles, Ohio

**Married:** Ida Saxton (1847–1907); 2 daughters

**Died:** Sept. 14, 1901; buried in Canton, Ohio

**Vice President:** Garret A. Hobart (1897–1901), Theodore Roosevelt (1901)

## 26 THEODORE ROOSEVELT
Republican Party, 1901–1909

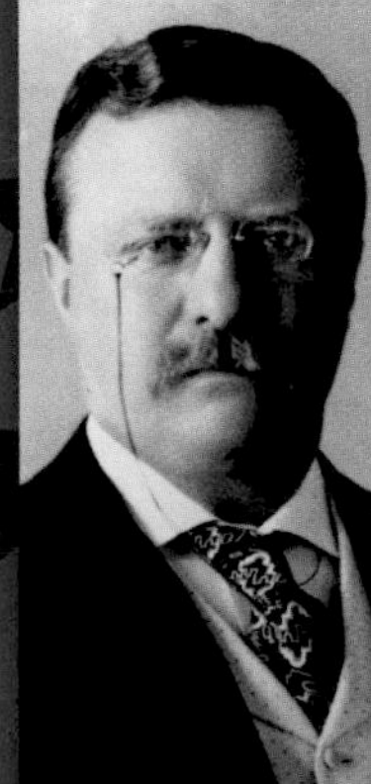

**Born:** Oct. 27, 1858, in New York City

**Married:** Alice Hathaway Lee (1861–1884); 1 daughter. Edith Kermit Carow (1861–1948); 4 sons, 1 daughter

**Died:** Jan. 6, 1919; buried in Oyster Bay, New York

**Vice President:** none 1901–1905, Charles W. Fairbanks (1905–1909)

## 27 WILLIAM HOWARD TAFT
Republican Party, 1909–1913

**Born:** Sept. 15, 1857, in Cincinnati, Ohio

**Married:** Helen Herron (1861–1943); 2 sons, 1 daughter

**Died:** Mar. 8, 1930; buried in Arlington National Cemetery, Virginia

**Vice President:** James S. Sherman (1909–1913)

## 28 WOODROW WILSON
Democratic Party, 1913–1921

**Born:** Dec. 28, 1856, in Staunton, Virginia

**Married:** Ellen Louise Axson (1860–1914); 3 daughters.
Edith Bolling Galt (1872–1961); no children

**Died:** Feb. 3, 1924; buried in Washington, D.C.

**Vice President:** Thomas R. Marshall (1913–1921)

## 29 WARREN G. HARDING
Republican Party, 1921–1923

**Born:** Nov. 2, 1865, near Corsica (now Blooming Grove), Ohio

**Married:** Florence Kling De Wolfe (1860–1924); no children

**Died:** Aug. 2, 1923; buried in Marion, Ohio

**Vice President:** Calvin Coolidge (1921–1923)

## 30 CALVIN COOLIDGE
Republican Party, 1923–1929

**Born:** July 4, 1872, in Plymouth, Vermont

**Married:** Grace Anna Goodhue (1879–1957); 2 sons

**Died:** Jan. 5, 1933; buried in Plymouth, Vermont

**Vice President:** none 1923–1925, Charles G. Dawes (1925–1929)

## 31 HERBERT C. HOOVER
Republican Party, 1929–1933

**Born:** Aug. 10, 1874, in West Branch, Iowa

**Married:** Lou Henry (1875–1944); 2 sons

**Died:** Oct. 20, 1964; buried in West Branch, Iowa

**Vice President:** Charles Curtis (1929–1933)

## 32 FRANKLIN DELANO ROOSEVELT
Democratic Party, 1933–1945

**Born:** Jan. 30, 1882, in Hyde Park, New York

**Married:** Anna Eleanor Roosevelt (1884–1962); 4 sons, 1 daughter

**Died:** Apr. 12, 1945; buried in Hyde Park, New York

**Vice President:** John N. Garner (1933–1941), Henry A. Wallace (1941–1945), Harry S. Truman (1945)

## 33 HARRY S. TRUMAN
Democratic Party, 1945–1953

**Born:** May 8, 1884, in Lamar, Missouri

**Married:** Elizabeth Virginia "Bess" Wallace (1885–1982); 1 daughter

**Died:** Dec. 26, 1972; buried in Independence, Missouri

**Vice President:** none 1945–1949, Alben W. Barkley (1949–1953)

## 34 DWIGHT D. EISENHOWER
Republican Party, 1953–1961

**Born:** Oct. 14, 1890, in Denison, Texas

**Married:** Mary "Mamie" Geneva Doud (1896–1979); 2 sons

**Died:** Mar. 28, 1969; buried in Abilene, Kansas

**Vice President:** Richard M. Nixon (1953–1961)

## 35 JOHN FITZGERALD KENNEDY
Democratic Party, 1961–1963

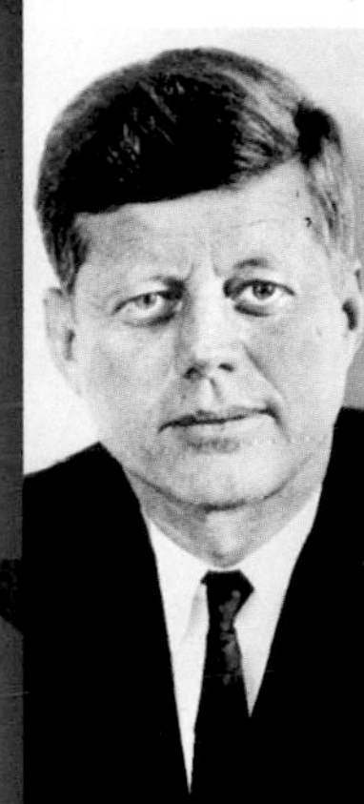

**Born:** May 29, 1917, in Brookline, Massachusetts

**Married:** Jacqueline Lee Bouvier (1929–1994); 2 sons, 1 daughter

**Died:** Nov. 22, 1963; buried in Arlington National Cemetery, Virginia

**Vice President:** Lyndon Baines Johnson (1961–1963)

## 36 LYNDON BAINES JOHNSON
Democratic Party, 1963–1969

**Born:** Aug. 27, 1908, near Stonewall, Texas

**Married:** Claudia "Lady Bird" Alta Taylor (1912–2007); 2 daughters

**Died:** Jan. 22, 1973; buried in Johnson City, Texas

**Vice President:** none 1963–1965, Hubert H. Humphrey (1965–1969)

## 37 RICHARD MILHOUS NIXON
Republican Party, 1969–1974

**Born:** Jan. 9, 1913, in Yorba Linda, California

**Married:** Thelma "Pat" Ryan (1912–1993); 2 daughters

**Died:** Apr. 22, 1994; buried in Yorba Linda, California

**Vice President:** Spiro T. Agnew (1969–1973), Gerald R. Ford (1973–1974)

## 38 GERALD R. FORD
Republican Party, 1974–1977

**Born:** July 14, 1913, in Omaha, Nebraska

**Married:** Elizabeth "Betty" Bloomer (1918–2011); 3 sons, 1 daughter

**Died:** Dec. 26, 2006; buried in Grand Rapids, Michigan

**Vice President:** Nelson A. Rockefeller (1974–1977)

## 39 JIMMY (JAMES EARL) CARTER
Democratic Party, 1977–1981

**Born:** Oct. 1, 1924, in Plains, Georgia

**Married:** Rosalynn Smith (b. 1927); 3 sons, 1 daughter

**Vice President:** Walter F. Mondale (1977–1981)

## 40 RONALD REAGAN
Republican Party, 1981–1989

**Born:** Feb. 6, 1911, in Tampico, Illinois

**Married:** Jane Wyman (1914–2007); 1 son, 1 daughter. Nancy Davis (b. 1923); 1 son, 1 daughter

**Died:** June 5, 2004; buried in Simi Valley, California

**Vice President:** George H. W. Bush (1981–1989)

## 41 GEORGE H. W. BUSH
Republican Party, 1989–1993

**Born:** June 12, 1924, in Milton, Massachusetts

**Married:** Barbara Pierce (b. 1925); 4 sons, 2 daughters

**Vice President:** Dan Quayle (1989–1993)

## 42 BILL (WILLIAM JEFFERSON) CLINTON
Democratic Party, 1993–2001

**Born:** Aug. 19, 1946, in Hope, Arkansas

**Married:** Hillary Rodham (b. 1947); 1 daughter

**Vice President:** Al Gore (1993–2001)

## 43 GEORGE W. BUSH
Republican Party, 2001–2009

**Born:** July 6, 1946, in New Haven, Connecticut

**Married:** Laura Welch (b. 1946); 2 daughters

**Vice President:** Dick Cheney (2001–2009)

## 44 BARACK OBAMA
Democratic Party, 2009–

**Born:** August 4, 1961, in Honolulu, Hawaii

**Married:** Michelle Robinson (b. 1964); 2 daughters

**Vice President:** Joe Biden (2009– )

**Did You KNOW?**

**Tens of millions of people around the world watched President Barack Obama's second inauguration in January 2013 on their TVs, computers, tablets, and smartphones. Before the electronic age, President William McKinley's 1897 inauguration was the first to be captured by a motion picture camera. The first televised inauguration was Harry Truman's in 1949, and Bill Clinton's 1997 swearing-in was the first to be streamed live over the Internet.**

# Some Famous *First Ladies*

The term "First Lady" did not come into wide use until after 1849, when President James Madison's wife, Dolley, was referred to by that title at her funeral. But from the nation's beginning, presidents' wives have both assisted their husbands and taken on important roles in their own right. The First Ladies, with their different personalities and interests, have become a part of history. Here is a brief look at a few of them.

**MARTHA CUSTIS WASHINGTON**, wife of the first president, was a wealthy widow when she married George Washington. During the American Revolution, she helped manage Mount Vernon, their Virginia plantation, but also spent time with her husband at his military headquarters. When he became president, they moved to New York and then Philadelphia, the nation's first capitals. She was the only First Lady who never got to live in the White House.

**SARAH POLK**, wife of James K. Polk, was greatly involved in her husband's political career. In the White House, she acted as his private secretary and adviser, and she controlled who got to see him. She had strict views, and there was no dancing or heavy drinking at social functions. He died soon after leaving office, but she lived on for 42 years, always dressed in black.

**LUCY WEBB HAYES**, wife of Rutherford B. Hayes, was the first First Lady to have graduated from college. A popular figure, she visited disabled soldiers and gave large sums of money to the poor. Because alcohol was banned at the White House for most of her time there, she got the nickname "Lemonade Lucy."

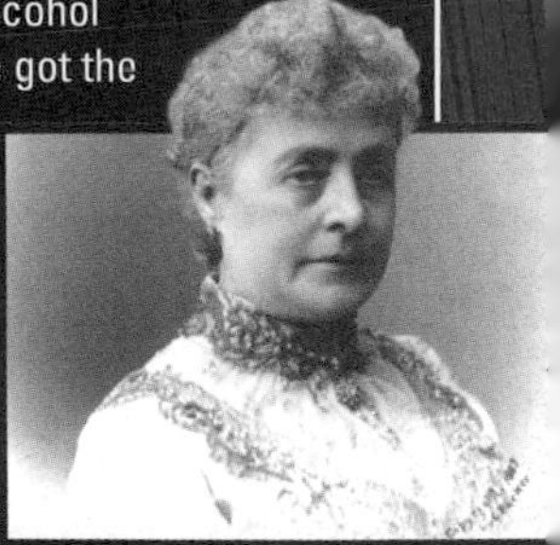

**CAROLINE HARRISON**, wife of Benjamin Harrison, was a book lover and amateur painter all her life and played the piano. She gave elegant receptions as First Lady and had the first White House Christmas tree put up. She pressed for women to be admitted to Johns Hopkins Medical School and was active in many other causes.

**EDITH CAREW ROOSEVELT**, second wife of Theodore Roosevelt, gave birth to five children. As First Lady, she oversaw the building of a new West Wing, leaving more space in the White House for her big family. She had the public rooms decorated in a dignified style, hired a social secretary, and organized the wedding of her lively stepdaughter, called "Princess Alice" by the press.

**ELEANOR ROOSEVELT**, wife of Franklin D. Roosevelt, supported the New Deal policies of her husband and was a strong advocate for civil rights. She had a lifelong career as a writer and champion of causes she believed in. After her husband's death in 1945, she served as a delegate to the United Nations.

**MAMIE EISENHOWER**, wife of Dwight Eisenhower, lived in more than 30 different places, in the U.S. and abroad, during her husband's Army career. She campaigned with him when he ran for president in 1952. As First Lady, she helped make pink a popular color of the 1950s. She enjoyed decorating the White House for special occasions and was hostess to a record number of foreign leaders.

**ROSALYNN CARTER**, wife of Jimmy Carter, was Georgia's first lady when he was governor of that state and traveled independently to campaign for his election as president in 1976. As the nation's First Lady, she stressed the cause of access to mental health care. After leaving the White House, she took an active role at the Carter Center in Atlanta, founded to promote world peace and human rights.

**MICHELLE OBAMA**, wife of Barack Obama, met her husband when both were working as lawyers in Chicago. They were married in 1992 and have two daughters, Malia, born in 1998, and Sasha, born in 2001. As First Lady, she has focused especially on the needs of children, including good eating habits and strong physical education programs in schools.

# WHITE HOUSE Pets

**The White House has been home to many animals, beginning with John Adams's favorite horse, Cleopatra. Here are some other famous White House pets.**

*The Clinton family cat, Socks*

- John Quincy Adams had an alligator that sometimes hung out in the East Room.
- The Lincolns had a variety of animals, including cats, dogs, goats, and a white rabbit.
- Theodore Roosevelt's family had a badger and a macaw, along with horses, dogs, cats, snakes, guinea pigs, and even bears.
- The Coolidge family kept a small zoo that included lion cubs, a bobcat, a pygmy hippo, and a raccoon that got walked on a leash.
- Franklin D. Roosevelt's Scottish terrier, Fala, was often seen with FDR at the White House and went with the president on many trips.
- Millie, a springer spaniel owned by Barbara and George H. W. Bush, was the make-believe writer of a book published by the First Lady.
- The Clintons had a cat named Socks and a chocolate Labrador retriever named Buddy.
- The Obama family has a Portuguese water dog, Bo.

*Franklin D. Roosevelt's dog, Fala*

# American Indians

**People may have arrived in the Americas more than 15,000 years ago, most likely from northeast Asia. Although the American Indian population decreased significantly through the 17th, 18th, and 19th centuries from disease and war, there are still hundreds of tribes, or nations, each with unique languages and traditions.**

## WHAT CAME FROM AMERICAN INDIANS?

### GAMES AND SPORTS

Many of today's games and sports came from practices and inventions of American Indians or other native peoples. The game of lacrosse began as an ancient Indian event called *baggataway*. Algonquian Indians in the northeastern U.S. used birchbark canoes for fishing and travel. The toboggan started out as an American Indian bark-and-skin runnerless sled to move heavy objects over snow or ice. In the far north, the Inuit wore snowshoes strung with caribou skin to walk on deep, soft snow. Many people today canoe, toboggan, or travel on snowshoes just for fun.

### ORAL TRADITION

Oral tradition is the cultural knowledge that one generation passes down to the next by telling stories. Today's literature owes much to the oral traditions of American Indian and Eskimo peoples. Storytelling has been a part of these cultures for centuries. Modern-day authors such as Louise Erdrich, an award-winning novelist who is part Chippewa, and Joseph Bruchac, an Abenaki who writes for children, draw on these folktales, also called myths, for inspiration in their own writing.

*Louise Erdrich*

### NAVAJO (DINE) WAR CODE

With almost 300,000 members, the Navajo make up the largest American Indian group in the U.S. The Dine (dee-NAY), as they call themselves, belong to clans in which members trace descent through the mother. Many Dine still speak a highly descriptive and unique language called Athapaskan. This language, which almost no non-Navajo knew, became the basis for a code used by U.S. forces in World War II. Navajo "code talkers" served in combat zones, sending and receiving top-secret messages in this code, which was never cracked.

# NORTH AMERICAN INDIANS TIMELINE

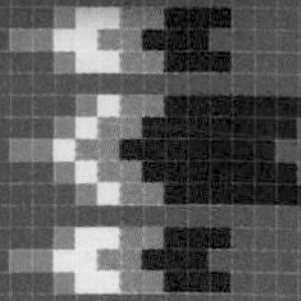

For events before 1492, see page 279.

| | |
|---|---|
| 1492 | Christopher Columbus made contact with Taino tribes on the island he named Hispaniola. |
| c. 1600 | Five tribes—the Mohawk, Oneida, Onondaga, Cayuga, and Seneca—formed the Iroquois Confederacy in the Northeast. |
| 1637 | Settlers in Connecticut defeated Pequot Indians in the Pequot War. |
| 1754–1763 | Many American Indians fought in the French and Indian War. |
| 1804–1806 | Sacagawea served as an interpreter and guide for Lewis and Clark. |
| 1827 | Cherokee tribes in today's Georgia formed the Cherokee Nation. |
| 1830 | The Indian Removal Act forced tribes to move so that U.S. citizens could settle certain areas of land. |
| 1834 | Congress created the Indian Territory for tribes removed from their lands. It covered present-day Oklahoma, Kansas, and Nebraska. |
| 1835–1842 | Seminoles battled U.S. troops in the Second Seminole War. They lost the conflict and their homeland in Florida. |
| 1838–1839 | The U.S. government forced Cherokees to move to Indian Territory. Thousands died during the so-called Trail of Tears. |
| 1876 | Sioux and Cheyenne Indians defeated troops led by U.S. colonel George Armstrong Custer in the Battle of the Little Bighorn. |
| 1877 | After the U.S. government tried to remove his people to Idaho, Chief Joseph led a Nez Percé retreat to Canada but surrendered before reaching the border. |
| 1890 | U.S. soldiers massacred more than 200 Sioux, including unarmed women and children, in the Battle of Wounded Knee, the last major conflict between U.S. troops and American Indians. |
| 1912 | Jim Thorpe, an American Indian, won the decathalon and the pentathalon in the 1912 Olympic Games. |
| 1924 | Congress granted all American Indians U.S. citizenship. |
| 1929 | Charles Curtis, a member of the Kaw Nation, became the first American of Indian ancestry elected vice president of the U.S. |
| 1934 | Congress passed the Indian Reorganization Act to increase tribal self-government. |
| 1968 | The American Indian Movement, a civil rights organization, was founded. |
| 1985 | Wilma Mankiller became the first female Cherokee Nation chief. |
| 2004 | The National Museum of the American Indian opened in Washington, D.C. → |
| 2012 | The U.S. Mint released the 2012 Native American dollar coin. |

# MAJOR CULTURAL AREAS OF NATIVE NORTH AMERICANS

Climate and geography influenced the culture of the people who lived in different regions. On the plains, for example, people depended on the great herds of buffalo for food. For the Aleut and Inuit in the far north, seals and whales were an important food source. There are more than 560 tribes officially recognized by the U.S. government today. Below are some of the major cultural areas of North American Indians and other native peoples.

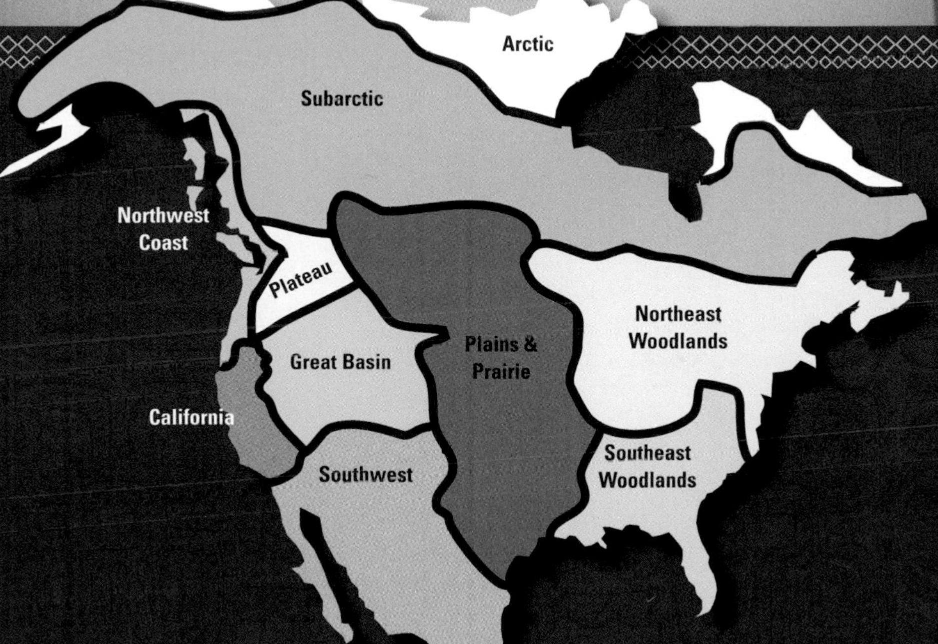


**NORTHEAST WOODLANDS** The Illinois, Iroquois (Mohawk, Onondaga, Cayuga, Oneida, Seneca, and Tuscarora), Lenape, Menominee, Micmac, Narragansett, Potawatomi, Shawnee

**SOUTHEAST WOODLANDS** The Cherokee, Chickasaw, Choctaw, Creek, Seminole

**PLAINS & PRAIRIE** The Arapaho, Blackfoot, Cheyenne, Comanche, Hidatsa, Kaw, Mandan, Sioux

**SOUTHWEST** The Apache, Navajo, Havasupai, Mojave, Pima, Pueblo (Hopi, Isleta, Laguna, Zuñi)

**GREAT BASIN** The Paiute, Shoshoni, Ute

**CALIFORNIA** The Klamath, Maidu, Miwok, Modoc, Patwin, Pomo, Wintun, Yurok

**PLATEAU** The Cayuse, Nez Percé, Okanagon, Salish, Spokan, Umatilla, Walla Walla, Yakima

**NORTHWEST COAST** The Chinook, Haida, Kwakiutl, Makah, Nootka, Salish, Tillamook, Tlingit, Tsimshian

**SUBARCTIC** The Beaver, Chipewyan, Chippewa, Cree, Ingalik, Kaska, Kutchin, Montagnais, Naskapi, Tanana

**ARCTIC** The Aleut, Inuit, and Yuit

# FACTS About America's Native Peoples

## U.S. Tribal Lands

The United States has about 56.2 million acres of Indian land areas. Its tribal lands include more than 325 reservations, pueblos, missions, villages, and communities across the country. The largest is the Navajo Nation Reservation in Arizona, New Mexico, and Utah. It covers 16 million acres. The smallest, a cemetery for the Pit River Tribe in California, is 1.32 acres. Not all tribes have a reservation. Some reservations are part of a tribe's original lands. Others were formed after the American Indians were forced off their homelands.

## Whaling Traditions of Alaska Natives

The native peoples of Alaska, called Alaska Natives, have hunted whales for several thousand years. These peoples include the Inuit, or Eskimos, and Aleuts. In the past, Eskimos hunted with harpoons from kayaks. Aleuts, traveling in wooden dugout boats, used spears poisoned with boiled wildflower roots. In keeping with tradition and a respect for the natural world, Alaska Natives used as much of the kill as possible. A captured whale provided meat to eat and oil for fuel and light. The whalebones were valuable for building shelters and creating tools.

Today, the International Whaling Commission allows the native peoples of Alaska to hunt a limited number of whales to meet their cultural and survival needs. In 2012, Alaska Natives were permitted to catch no more than 75 bowhead whales to protect the population of this animal.

## A Native Hawaiian Dance

The original Hawaiians came to the islands from Polynesia in about A.D. 400—traveling north through the Pacific Ocean for 2,000 miles or more. To honor their gods and chiefs, they performed the *hula*. Native Hawaiians dance with hip, arm, and finger movements, accompanied by rhythmic drumming and chants called *mele*. Legend says the goddess Hi'iaka first danced the hula to appease her sister, Pele, the goddess of volcanoes and fire. To today's native Hawaiians, the art form remains an important expression of their culture.

# UNITED STATES HISTORY

**Before 13,000 B.C.**
People called **Paleo-Indians** cross from Siberia to Alaska and begin to move into North America.

**Before 11,000 B.C.**
Paleo-Indians use stone points attached to spears to hunt **mammoths**, giant caribou, and other large animals.

**11,000 B.C.**
Mammoths and other large animals disappear, and Paleo-Indians begin to gather **plants** for food.

**9,500 B.C.–1,000 B.C.**
North American Indians begin using **stone** to grind food and to hunt bison and smaller animals.

**1,000 B.C.–A.D. 1,000**
Woodland Indians, who lived east of the Mississippi River, bury their dead under large **mounds** of earth (which can still be seen today).

**After A.D. 500**
The Ancestral Puebloans in the Southwestern United States live in homes on cliffs, called **cliff dwellings**. These people's pottery and dishes are known for their beautiful patterns.

**After A.D. 700**
Mississippian Indians in the Southeastern United States **develop farms** and continue to build burial mounds.

**700–1492**
Many **different Indian cultures** develop throughout North America. Several million American Indians probably live on the continent by 1492.

# COLONIAL AMERICA AND THE AMERICAN REVOLUTION: 1492–1783

**1492** Christopher **Columbus** sails across the Atlantic Ocean and reaches an island in the Bahamas in the Caribbean Sea.

**1513** Juan **Ponce de León** explores the Florida coast.

**1524** Giovanni da **Verrazano** explores the coast from Carolina north to Nova Scotia, enters New York harbor.

**1540** Francisco Vásquez de **Coronado** explores the Southwest.

**1565** St. Augustine, Florida, the **first permanent town** established by Europeans in the United States, is founded by the Spanish.

**1607** **Jamestown,** Virginia, the first permanent English settlement in North America, is founded by Captain John Smith.

**1609** Henry Hudson sails into **New York Harbor**, explores the Hudson River. Spaniards settle Santa Fe, New Mexico.

**1619** The first African **slaves** are brought to Jamestown. (Slavery is made legal in 1650.)

**1620** **Pilgrims** from England arrive at Plymouth, Massachusetts, on the *Mayflower*.

**1626** Peter Minuit buys **Manhattan** island for the Dutch from Manahata Indians for goods worth $24. The Dutch settlement is named New Amsterdam.

**1630** **Boston** is founded by Massachusetts colonists led by John Winthrop.

## Benjamin Franklin

was an American leader, printer, scientist, and writer. In his magazine ***Poor Richard's Almanack***, Poor Richard was a make-believe person who gave common-sense advice. Many of his sayings are still known, such as: "Early to bed, early to rise, makes a man healthy, wealthy, and wise."

UNITED STATES

**1634** **Maryland** is founded as a Catholic colony, with religious freedom for all granted in 1649.

**1664** The English seize **New Amsterdam** from the Dutch. The city is renamed New York.

**1669** **French settlers** move into Mississippi and Louisiana.

**1732** Benjamin Franklin begins publishing ***Poor Richard's Almanack***.

**1754–1763** **French and Indian War** between Great Britain and France. The French lose their lands in Canada and the Midwest.

**1764-1766** Britain places taxes on sugar and requires colonists to buy stamps to help pay for royal troops. Colonists protest, and the **Stamp Act** is repealed.

**1770** **Boston Massacre:** Demonstrators against British taxes throw rocks at British troops. The troops open fire, killing 7.

**1773** **Boston Tea Party:** British tea is thrown into the harbor to protest a tax on tea.

**1775** **Lexington and Concord** battles begin the American Revolution.

**1776** **The Declaration of Independence** is approved July 4 by the Continental Congress (made up of representatives from the American colonies).

**1781** British General **Charles Cornwallis** surrenders to the Americans at Yorktown, Virginia, ending major fighting in the Revolutionary War. In a 1783 peace treaty, Great Britain officially recognizes American independence.

## Declaration of Independence • July 4, 1776

*"We hold these truths to be self-evident, that all men are created equal, that they are endowed by their Creator with certain unalienable rights, that among these are life, liberty, and the pursuit of happiness."*

# THE NEW NATION

## 1784–1900

**1784** The first successful daily **newspaper** in the U.S., the *Pennsylvania Packet & General Advertiser*, is published.

### Who Attended the Convention?

The **Constitutional Convention** met in Philadelphia in the hot summer of 1787. Most of the great founders of America attended. Among those present were George Washington, James Madison, and John Adams. They met to form a new government that would be strong and, at the same time, protect the liberties that were fought for in the American Revolution. The Constitution they created is still the law of the United States.

**1787** The **Constitutional Convention** meets to write a Constitution for the U.S.

**1789** The new **Constitution** is approved by the states. George Washington is chosen as the first president.

**1800** The federal government moves from Philadelphia to a new capital, **Washington, D.C.**

**1803** The U.S. makes the **Louisiana Purchase** from France. The Purchase doubles the area of the U.S.

**1804–1806** **Lewis and Clark**, with their guide Sacagawea, explore what is now the northwestern United States.

**1812–1815** **War of 1812** with Great Britain: British forces burn the Capitol and White House. Francis Scott Key writes the words to "The Star-Spangled Banner."

**1820** The **Missouri Compromise** bans slavery west of the Mississippi River and north of 36°30′ latitude, except in Missouri.

**1823** The **Monroe Doctrine** warns European countries not to interfere in the Americas.

**1825** The **Erie Canal** opens, linking New York City with the Great Lakes.

**1831** ***The Liberator***, a newspaper opposing slavery, is published in Boston.

**1836** Texans fighting for independence from Mexico are defeated at the **Alamo**.

## Civil War Dead and Wounded

The **Civil War** resulted in the death or wounding of hundreds of thousands of people—perhaps more than three-quarters of a million. Little was known at the time about infections and the spread of diseases. As a result, many soldiers died from illnesses such as influenza and measles. Many also died from infections from battle wounds.

**1838**

Cherokee Indians are forced to move from the Southeast U.S. to Oklahoma, along "The **Trail of Tears**." On the long march, thousands die because of disease and the cold weather.

**1844**

The **first telegraph** line connects Washington, D.C., and Baltimore.

**1846–1848**

**U.S. war with Mexico**: Mexico is defeated, and the United States takes control of the Republic of Texas and of Mexican territories in the West.

**1848**

The discovery of **gold** in California leads to a "rush" of 80,000 people to the West in search of gold.

**1852**

***Uncle Tom's Cabin***, Harriet Beecher Stowe's novel about the suffering of slaves, is published.

**1860**

Abraham **Lincoln** is elected president.

**1861**

The **Civil War** begins when Confederate troops fire on Fort Sumter, South Carolina.

**1863**

President Lincoln issues the **Emancipation Proclamation**, freeing most slaves.

**1865**

The **Civil War** ends as the South surrenders. President Lincoln is assassinated.

**1869**

The **first railroad** connecting the East and West coasts is completed.

**1890**

**Battle of Wounded Knee** is fought in South Dakota—the last major battle between Indians and U.S. troops.

**1898**

**Spanish-American War:** The U.S. defeats Spain, gains control of the Philippines, Puerto Rico, and Guam.

# UNITED STATES
## 1901–Present

### World War I
In **World War I** the United States fought with Great Britain, France, and Russia (the Allies) against Germany and Austria-Hungary. The Allies won the war in 1918.

### World War II
From 1941 to 1945 the United States, joining Britain, the Soviet Union, and other Allied powers, fought the Axis powers, led by Germany, Italy, and Japan, in the deadliest conflict in human history.

**1903**
The United States begins digging the **Panama Canal**. The canal opens in 1914, connecting the Atlantic and Pacific oceans.

**1908**
Henry Ford introduces the **Model T** car, priced at $850.

**1916**
**Jeannette Rankin** of Montana becomes the first woman elected to Congress.

**1917–1918**
The United States joins **World War I** on the side of the Allies against Germany.

**1927**
Charles A. **Lindbergh** becomes the first person to fly alone nonstop across the Atlantic Ocean.

**1929**
A stock market crash marks the beginning of the **Great Depression**.

**1933**
President Franklin D. Roosevelt's **New Deal** increases government help to people hurt by the Depression.

### The Great Depression
The stock market crash of 1929 led to a period of severe hardship for the American people—the **Great Depression**. As many as 25 percent of all workers could not find jobs. The Depression lasted until the early 1940s. It led to a great change in politics. In 1932, Franklin D. Roosevelt, a Democrat, was elected president. He served for 12 years, longer than any other president.

**1941**
Japan attacks **Pearl Harbor**, Hawaii. The United States enters World War II.

**1945**
Germany surrenders in May. The U.S. drops atomic bombs on **Hiroshima** and Nagasaki in August, leading to Japan's surrender and the end of **World War II**.

**1947**
Jackie Robinson becomes the **first black baseball player** in the major leagues when he joins the Brooklyn Dodgers.

**1950–1953**
U.S. armed forces fight in the **Korean War**.

**1954**
The U.S. Supreme Court **forbids racial segregation** in public schools.

**1963**
President John **Kennedy** is assassinated.

**1964**
Congress passes the **Civil Rights Act**, which outlaws discrimination in voting and jobs.

**1965**
The United States sends large numbers of troops to fight in the **Vietnam War**.

**1968**
Civil rights leader **Martin Luther King Jr.** is assassinated. Senator **Robert F. Kennedy** is assassinated.

**1969**
U.S. astronaut Neil Armstrong becomes the **first person** to walk **on the moon**.

**1973**
U.S. participation in the **Vietnam War ends**.

**1974**
President Richard **Nixon resigns** because of the **Watergate** scandal.

**1979**
U.S. **hostages** are taken **in Iran**, beginning a 444-day crisis that ends with their release in 1981.

**1991**
**The Persian Gulf War**: The U.S. and its allies force Iraq to withdraw its troops from Kuwait.

**2001**
Hijacked jets crash into the **World Trade Center**, the **Pentagon**, and a field in Pennsylvania, September 11, killing about 3,000 people.

**2003**
U.S.-led forces invade Iraq and remove dictator **Saddam Hussein**.

**2008**
**Barack Obama** is elected the first African American president.

**2011**
U.S. forces kill **Osama bin Laden**, mastermind of the September 11, 2001, terrorist attacks.

**2013**
Two bombs explode at the **Boston Marathon**, leaving three dead and more than 170 injured.

W. E. B. Du Bois

# AFRICAN AMERICANS: A Time Line

From the era of slavery to the present, African Americans have struggled to obtain freedom and equal opportunity. The timeline below pinpoints many of the key events and personalities that helped shape this long struggle.

**1619** — **First slaves** from Africa are brought to Virginia.

**1831** — Nat Turner starts a **slave revolt** in Virginia that is unsuccessful.

**1856–1857** — **Dred Scott**, a slave, sues to be freed because he had left slave territory, but the Supreme Court denies his claim.

**1861–1865** — The North defeats the South in the brutal Civil War; the **13th Amendment** ends nearly 250 years of slavery. The Ku Klux Klan is founded.

**1865–1877** — Southern blacks play leadership roles in government under **Reconstruction**; the 15th Amendment (1870) gives black men the right to vote.

**1896** — Supreme Court rules in a case called *Plessy v. Ferguson* that racial segregation is legal when facilities are "**separate but equal.**" Discrimination and violence against blacks increase.

**1910** — W. E. B. Du Bois (1868–1963) founds National Association for the Advancement of Colored People (**NAACP**), fighting for equality for blacks.

**1954** — Supreme Court rules in a case called ***Brown v. Board of Education of Topeka*** that school segregation is unconstitutional.

**1955–1965** — Black students, backed by federal troops, enter recently desegregated Central High School in **Little Rock**, Arkansas.

**1957** — **Malcolm X** (1925–1965) emerges as key spokesperson for black nationalism.

**1963** — **Rev. Dr. Martin Luther King, Jr.** (1929–1968) gives his "I Have a Dream" speech at a march that inspires more than 200,000 people in Washington, D.C.—and many others throughout the nation.

**1964** — Sweeping **civil rights bill** banning racial discrimination is signed by President Lyndon Johnson.

**1965** — Martin Luther King leads protest march in **Selma**, Alabama. Blacks riot in **Watts** section of Los Angeles.

**1967** — Gary, Indiana, and Cleveland, Ohio, are first major U.S. cities to elect black mayors. **Thurgood Marshall** (1908–1993) becomes first African American on the U.S. Supreme Court.

**2001** — **Colin Powell** becomes first African American secretary of state.

**2005** — **Condoleezza Rice** becomes first African American woman secretary of state.

**2008** — Barack Obama becomes the **first African American elected president** of the United States.

**2013** — Tim Scott of South Carolina becomes the first **African American U.S. senator** from the South in more than 130 years.

# They Made HISTORY

**People of many different backgrounds have played important roles in the history of the United States.**

**1818–1895** FREDERICK DOUGLASS

escaped from slavery at age 20. In the decades before the Civil War (1861–1865), he had a major influence on the anti-slavery movement through his lectures and writings. He became an adviser to President Abraham Lincoln.

**1838–1917** LILI'UOKALANI

was the last queen of Hawaii. American companies that sold Hawaiian sugarcane wanted the islands to become part of the United States. In 1893, a group of Americans and Europeans forced her from the throne.

**1840–1904** CHIEF JOSEPH

was a leader of the Nez Percé Indians of the Pacific Northwest. The U.S. government ordered the tribe to move to a small reservation, but many refused. Pursued by the U.S. Army, Chief Joseph led his people on a 1,400-mile retreat toward Canada. Trapped just 40 miles from the border, he surrendered, promising, "I will fight no more forever."

**1927–1993** CESAR CHAVEZ,

a Mexican American who was raised in migrant worker camps, started the union known as the United Farm Workers of America in 1966. Along with UFW cofounder **DOLORES HUERTA** (born 1930), he organized boycotts that eventually made growers agree to better conditions for field workers.

**1929–1968** REV. DR. MARTIN LUTHER KING JR.

was the most influential leader of the civil rights movement from the mid-1950s to his assassination in 1968. A believer in peaceful protest, he received the Nobel Peace Prize in 1964. His wife, **CORETTA SCOTT KING** (1927–2006), helped carry on his work.

**1940–1994** WILMA RUDOLPH

was a sickly child who was left handicapped by polio and went through years of therapy. Competing in track events at the 1960 Olympics, she became the first American woman to win three gold medals.

**1954–** SONIA SOTOMAYOR,

who grew up in a public housing project in New York City, went on to graduate from Princeton University and Yale Law School. Experienced as a prosecutor and a judge, she was named to the U.S. Supreme Court in 2009, becoming the court's first Hispanic justice.

**1961–** BARACK OBAMA

is the son of an American mother and a Kenyan father. After serving in the Illinois Senate, he was elected to the U.S. Senate in 2004. From there he launched a successful campaign to win the presidency in 2008. He was reelected in 2012.

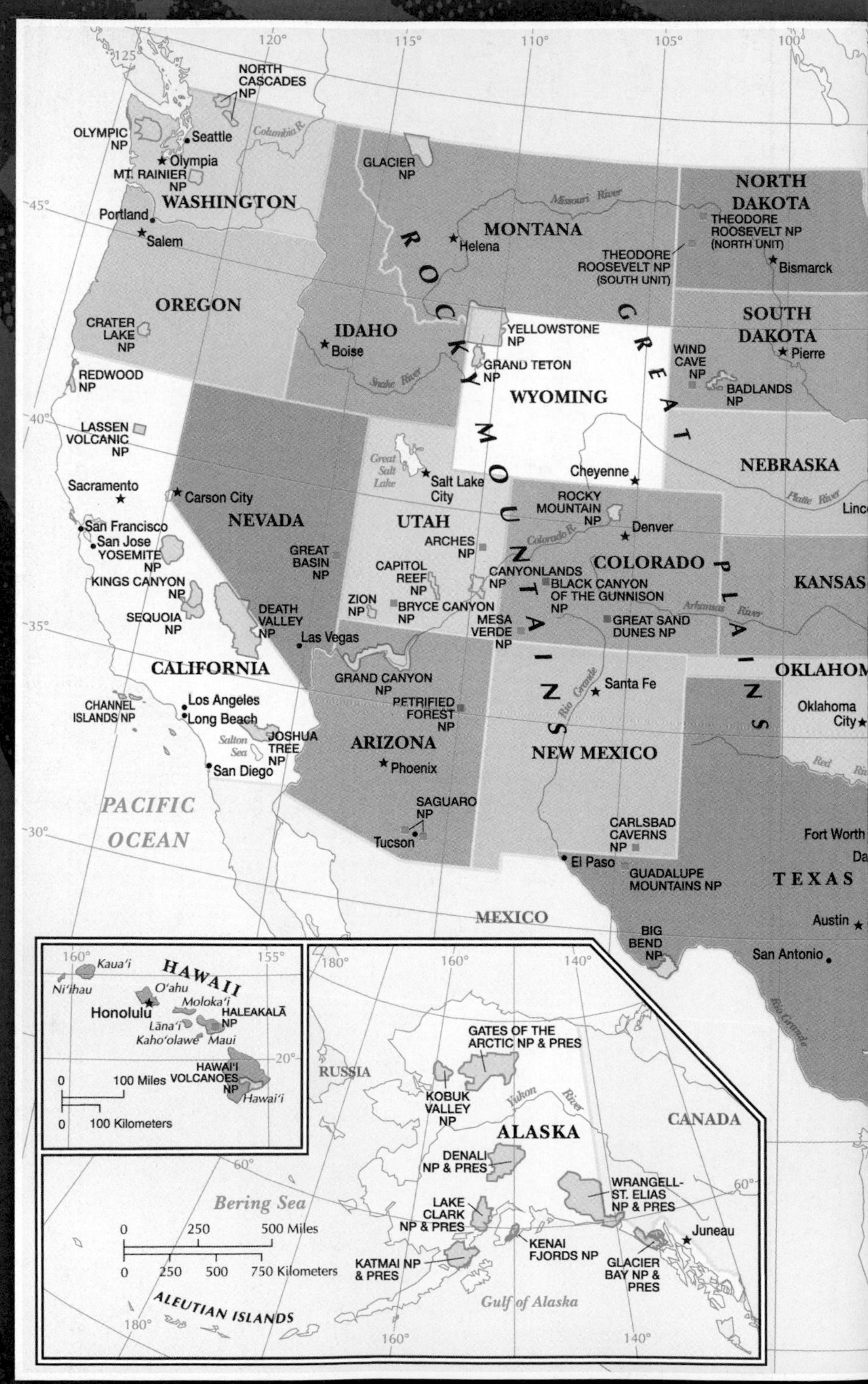
NORTH CASCADES NP
OLYMPIC NP
Seattle
Olympia
MT. RAINIER NP
WASHINGTON
Portland
Salem
OREGON
CRATER LAKE NP
REDWOOD NP
LASSEN VOLCANIC NP
Sacramento
San Francisco
San Jose
YOSEMITE NP
KINGS CANYON NP
SEQUOIA NP
CALIFORNIA
CHANNEL ISLANDS NP
Los Angeles
Long Beach
San Diego
JOSHUA TREE NP
Salton Sea
PACIFIC OCEAN
Columbia R.
GLACIER NP
MONTANA
Helena
Missouri River
IDAHO
Boise
Snake River
ROCKY MOUNTAINS
GREAT PLAINS
YELLOWSTONE NP
GRAND TETON NP
WYOMING
Cheyenne
NEVADA
Carson City
GREAT BASIN NP
DEATH VALLEY NP
Las Vegas
Great Salt Lake
Salt Lake City
UTAH
ARCHES NP
CAPITOL REEF NP
ZION NP
BRYCE CANYON NP
CANYONLANDS NP
ROCKY MOUNTAIN NP
Denver
Colorado R.
COLORADO
BLACK CANYON OF THE GUNNISON NP
MESA VERDE NP
GREAT SAND DUNES NP
Arkansas River
GRAND CANYON NP
PETRIFIED FOREST NP
ARIZONA
Phoenix
SAGUARO NP
Tucson
Santa Fe
Rio Grande
NEW MEXICO
CARLSBAD CAVERNS NP
El Paso
GUADALUPE MOUNTAINS NP
MEXICO
NORTH DAKOTA
THEODORE ROOSEVELT NP (NORTH UNIT)
THEODORE ROOSEVELT NP (SOUTH UNIT)
Bismarck
SOUTH DAKOTA
Pierre
WIND CAVE NP
BADLANDS NP
NEBRASKA
Platte River
KANSAS
OKLAHOMA
Oklahoma City
Red
TEXAS
Fort Worth
Austin
San Antonio
BIG BEND NP
HAWAII
Kaua'i
Ni'ihau
O'ahu
Honolulu
Moloka'i
HALEAKALĀ NP
Lāna'i
Kaho'olawe
Maui
HAWAI'I VOLCANOES NP
Hawai'i
0 100 Miles
0 100 Kilometers
RUSSIA
GATES OF THE ARCTIC NP & PRES
KOBUK VALLEY NP
Yukon River
ALASKA
CANADA
DENALI NP & PRES
Bering Sea
LAKE CLARK NP & PRES
WRANGELL-ST. ELIAS NP & PRES
Juneau
KENAI FJORDS NP
GLACIER BAY NP & PRES
KATMAI NP & PRES
0 250 500 Miles
0 250 500 750 Kilometers
ALEUTIAN ISLANDS
Gulf of Alaska

## THE UNITED STATES

- ⍟ National Capital
- ★ State Capital
- • Other City
- ■ National Park

# How the STATES

**ALABAMA** comes from the name of an Indian tribe, which may mean "gathering thick vegetation."

**ALASKA** comes from *alakshak*, an Aleut word meaning "peninsula" or "land that is not an island."

**ARIZONA** comes from a Pima Indian word meaning "little spring place" or the Aztec word *arizuma,* meaning "silver-bearing."

**ARKANSAS** is a variation of Quapaw, the name of an Indian tribe. Quapaw means "south wind."

**CALIFORNIA** was probably named by Spanish explorers after an imaginary island in a Spanish story.

**COLORADO** comes from a Spanish word meaning "red." It was first given to the Colorado River because of its reddish color.

**CONNECTICUT** comes from an Algonquin Indian word meaning "long river place."

**DELAWARE** is named after Lord De La Warr, the English governor of Virginia in colonial times.

**FLORIDA** was named by the Spanish explorer Ponce de León, who landed there during Easter season, called *pascua florida* ("festival of flowers") in Spanish.

**GEORGIA** was named after King George II of England, who granted the right to create a colony there in 1732.

Waikiki Beach, Hawaii

**HAWAII** probably comes from *Hawaiki,* or *Owhyhee,* the native Polynesian word for "homeland."

**IDAHO**'s name may come from a Kiowa Apache name for the Comanche Indians.

**ILLINOIS** is the French version of *Illini,* an Algonquin Indian word meaning "men" or "warriors."

**INDIANA** means "land of the Indians."

**IOWA** comes from the name of an American Indian tribe that once lived in the region.

Cornfield, Iowa

**KANSAS** comes from a Sioux Indian word that possibly meant "people of the south wind."

**KENTUCKY** may come from an American Indian word that meant "meadowland" or from an Indian word meaning "land of tomorrow."

**LOUISIANA**, which was first settled by French explorers, was named after King Louis XIV of France.

Bayou, Louisiana

**MAINE** means "the mainland." English explorers called it that to distinguish it from islands nearby.

**MARYLAND** was named after Queen Henrietta Maria, wife of King Charles I of England, who granted the right to establish an English colony there.

**MASSACHUSETTS** probably comes from an Indian word that means "large hill place."

**MICHIGAN** comes from the Chippewa Indian words *mici gama,* meaning "great water" (referring to Lake Michigan).

**MINNESOTA** got its name from a Dakota Sioux Indian word meaning "cloudy water" or "sky-tinted water."

**MISSISSIPPI** is probably from Chippewa Indian words meaning "great river" or "gathering of all the waters," or from an Algonquin word, *messipi.*

# Got Their NAMES

**MISSOURI** comes from an Algonquin Indian term meaning "river of the big canoes."

**MONTANA** comes from a Latin or Spanish word meaning "mountainous."

**NEBRASKA** comes from an Omaha or Otos Indian word meaning "flat river" or "broad water," referring to the Platte River.

**NEVADA** means "snow-clad" in Spanish. Spanish explorers gave the name to the Sierra Nevada mountains.

**NEW HAMPSHIRE** was named by an early settler after his home county of Hampshire, in England.

**NEW JERSEY** was named for the English Channel island of Jersey.

Gila River, New Mexico

**NEW MEXICO** comes from the name once given in Mexico to lands north of the Rio Grande river.

**NEW YORK**, first called New Netherland, was renamed for the Duke of York after the English took it from Dutch settlers.

**NORTH CAROLINA**, the northern part of the English colony of Carolana, was named for King Charles I.

**NORTH DAKOTA** comes from a Sioux Indian word meaning "friend" or "ally."

**OHIO** is the Iroquois Indian word for "good river."

**OKLAHOMA** comes from a Choctaw Indian word meaning "red man."

**OREGON** may have come from *Ouaricon-sint,* a name on an old French map that was once given to what is now called the Columbia River.

**PENNSYLVANIA** meaning "Penn's woods," was the name given to the colony founded by William Penn.

**RHODE ISLAND** may have come from the Dutch *Roode Eylandt* ("red island"), or the state may have been named after the Greek island of Rhodes.

**SOUTH CAROLINA**, the southern part of the English colony of Carolana, was named for King Charles I.

**SOUTH DAKOTA** comes from a Sioux Indian word meaning "friend" or "ally."

**TENNESSEE** comes from *Tanasi*, the name of a Cherokee Indian village.

**TEXAS** comes from a word meaning "friends" or "allies," used by the Spanish to describe some of the Indians living there.

**UTAH** comes from the name given to the Ute Indians. The likely meaning is "people of the high land."

**VERMONT** comes from two French words, *vert* meaning "green" and *mont* meaning "mountain."

**VIRGINIA** was named in honor of Queen Elizabeth I of England, who was known as the Virgin Queen because she was never married.

**WASHINGTON** was named after George Washington. It is the only state named after a president.

Mount Rainier, Washington

**WEST VIRGINIA** got its name from the people of western Virginia, who formed their own government during the Civil War.

**WISCONSIN** comes from a Chippewa name that is believed to mean "grassy place."

**WYOMING** comes from Algonquin Indian words that may mean "at the big plains," "large prairie place," or "on the great plain."

# Facts about the STATES

Area includes both land and water; it is given in square miles (sq mi) and square kilometers (sq km). Populations are Census Bureau estimates for 2012 (states) or 2011 (cities). Numbers in parentheses after Population, Area, and Entered Union show the state's rank. The postal abbreviation for each state appears in a circle to the left of the state's population.

## ALABAMA

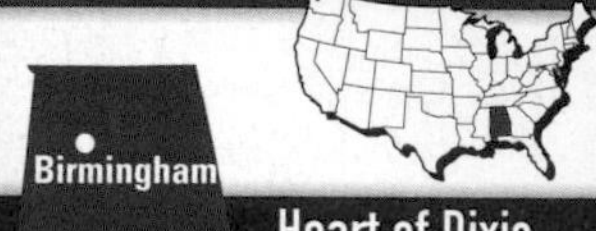

Heart of Dixie, Camellia State

AL **POPULATION:** 4,822,023 (23rd)

**AREA:** 52,420 sq mi (30th) (135,768 sq km)

F Camellia
B Yellowhammer
T Southern longleaf pine
S "Alabama"

**ENTERED UNION:** December 14, 1819 (22nd)

**LARGEST CITIES (WITH POP.):** Birmingham, 212,413; Montgomery, 208,182; Mobile, 194,914; Huntsville, 182,956

✪ Montgomery

P motor vehicles, electronic equipment, metal products, chemicals, paper, food products, clothing, lumber, coal, oil, natural gas, chickens, livestock, eggs, cotton

**Did You KNOW?** In 1881, Booker T. Washington started building what is now Tuskegee University, to educate African Americans, many of them former slaves. George Washington Carver, head of the agriculture department, helped struggling black farmers make the best use of the land to earn a living.

## ALASKA

The Last Frontier State

AK **POPULATION:** 731,449 (47th)

**AREA:** 665,384 sq mi (1st) (1,722,319 sq km)

F Forget-me-not
B Willow ptarmigan
T Sitka spruce
S "Alaska's Flag"

**ENTERED UNION:** January 3, 1959 (49th)

**LARGEST CITIES (WITH POP.):** Anchorage, 295,570; Fairbanks, 32,036; Juneau, 32,164

✪ Juneau

P oil, natural gas, fish, food products, lumber and wood products, greenhouse and nursery products, hay, potatoes, fur

**Did You KNOW?** Alaska has over 3 million lakes bigger than 20 acres in area. The state also has some 10,000 glaciers, one of which is bigger than the state of Rhode Island.

## ARIZONA

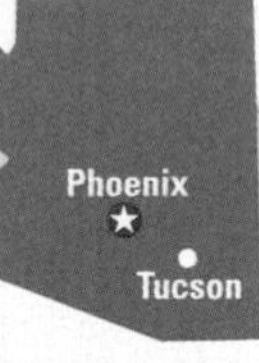


Grand Canyon State

AZ **POPULATION:** 6,553,255 (15th)

**AREA:** 113,990 sq mi (6th) (296,234 sq km)

F Blossom of the Saguaro cactus
B Cactus wren
T Paloverde
S "Arizona"

**ENTERED UNION:** February 14, 1912 (48th)

**LARGEST CITIES (WITH POP.):** Phoenix, 1,469,471; Tucson, 525,796; Mesa, 446,518; Chandler, 240,101; Glendale, 230,482; Scottsdale, 221,020; Gilbert, 211,951

✪ Phoenix

P electronic equipment, transportation and industrial equipment, aerospace products, copper and other minerals, dairy products, lettuce, cattle

**Did You KNOW?** At the Petrified Forest National Park, in northeast Arizona, you can see the remains of fallen trees that have turned into colorful rock over millions of years.

## ARKANSAS

Natural State, Razorback State

**POPULATION:** 2,949,131 (32nd)

**AREA:** 53,179 sq mi (29th) (137,732 sq km)

F Apple blossom
B Mockingbird
T Pine
S "Arkansas"

**ENTERED UNION:** June 15, 1836 (25th)

**LARGEST CITIES (WITH POP.):** Little Rock, 195,314; Fort Smith, 87,152; Fayetteville, 75,102; Springdale, 71,397; Jonesboro, 68,547

★ Little Rock

P food products, transportation and industrial equipment, paper, metal products, lumber and wood products, chickens, soybeans, rice, cotton, natural gas

**Did You KNOW?** In 1906, a farmer named John Huddleston became rich and famous after discovering diamonds beneath his field near Murfreesboro. The site is now a state park—where visitors can look for diamonds.

## CALIFORNIA

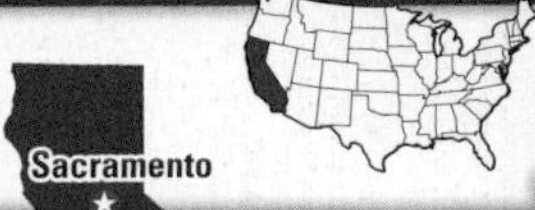



Golden State

CA **POPULATION:** 38,041,430 (1st)

**AREA:** 163,395 sq mi (3rd) (423,967 sq km)

F Golden poppy
B California valley quail
T California redwood
S "I Love You, California"

**ENTERED UNION:** September 9, 1850 (31st)

**LARGEST CITIES (WITH POP.):** Los Angeles, 3,819,702; San Diego, 1,326,179; San Jose, 967,487; San Francisco, 812,826; Fresno, 501,362; Sacramento, 472,178; Long Beach, 465,476; Oakland, 395,817; Bakersfield, 352,428; Anaheim, 341,361; Santa Ana, 329,427; Riverside, 310,651

★ Sacramento

P electronic equipment, oil, transportation and industrial equipment, motion pictures, printed materials, wine, food products, milk, cheese, almonds, grapes, cattle, vegetables

**Did You KNOW?** California boasts both the highest point in the 48 contiguous states (Mount Whitney, at 14,505 feet) and the lowest spot in the nation (Death Valley, at 282 feet below sea level).

## COLORADO

Denver
Colorado Springs

Centennial State

CO **POPULATION:** 5,187,582 (22nd)

**AREA:** 104,094 sq mi (8th) (269,601 sq km)

F Rocky Mountain columbine
B Lark bunting
T Colorado blue spruce
S "Where the Columbines Grow"

**ENTERED UNION:** August 1, 1876 (38th)

**LARGEST CITIES (WITH POP.):** Denver, 619,968; Colorado Springs, 426,388; Aurora, 332,354; Fort Collins, 146,762; Lakewood, 144,406

★ Denver

P electronic equipment, instruments and machinery, food products, metal products, oil, natural gas, coal, cattle, corn

**Did You KNOW?** The small town of Dinosaur, CO, is located near Dinosaur National Monument. Street names in the town include Brontosaurus Boulevard, Tyrannosaurus Trail, Stegosaurus Freeway, and Triceratops Terrace.

**Key:** F Flower B Bird T Tree S Song ★ Capital P Important Products

# CONNECTICUT

Hartford

**Constitution State, Nutmeg State**

**CT POPULATION:** 3,590,347 (29th)

**AREA:** 5,543 sq mi (48th) (14,357 sq km)

- **F** Mountain laurel
- **B** American robin
- **T** White oak
- **S** "Yankee Doodle"

**ENTERED UNION:** January 9, 1788 (5th)

**LARGEST CITIES (WITH POP.):** Bridgeport, 145,638; New Haven, 129,585; Hartford, 124,867; Stamford, 123,868; Waterbury, 110,189; Norwalk, 86,460; Danbury, 81,671

★ Hartford

**P** aircraft parts, helicopters, metals and metal products, electronic equipment, medical instruments, chemicals, greenhouse and nursery products, dairy products, stone

**Did You KNOW?** Famous people who were born in Connecticut include Revolutionary War hero Ethan Allen, banker J. P. Morgan, actresses Katharine Hepburn and Glenn Close, and former President George W. Bush.

# DELAWARE

**First State, Diamond State**

**DE POPULATION:** 917,092 (45th)

**AREA:** 2,489 sq mi (49th) (6,446 sq km)

- **F** Peach blossom
- **B** Blue hen chicken
- **T** American holly
- **S** "Our Delaware"

**ENTERED UNION:** December 7, 1787 (1st)

**LARGEST CITIES (WITH POP.):** Wilmington, 71,305; Dover, 36,560; Newark, 31,618

★ Dover

**P** chemicals, drugs, transportation equipment, food products, chickens

**Did You KNOW?** Pea Patch Island, located in the Delaware River, got its name because people believed a ship carrying peas was wrecked there in the 1700s. Fort Delaware, on the island, was used to hold thousands of Confederate prisoners during the Civil War.

# FLORIDA

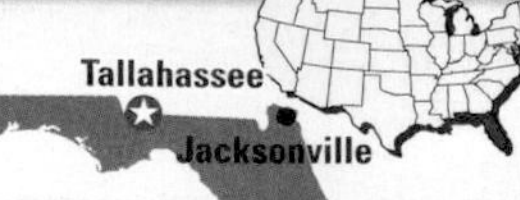

Tallahassee

Jacksonville

Miami

**Sunshine State**

**FL POPULATION:** 19,317,568 (4th)

**AREA:** 65,758 sq mi (22nd) (170,312 sq km)

- **F** Orange blossom
- **B** Mockingbird
- **T** Sabal palmetto palm
- **S** "Old Folks at Home"

**ENTERED UNION:** March 3, 1845 (27th)

**LARGEST CITIES (WITH POP.):** Jacksonville, 827,908; Miami, 408,740; Tampa, 346,037; St. Petersburg, 244,997; Orlando, 243,195; Hialeah, 229,969; Tallahassee, 182,965; Ft. Lauderdale, 168,528; Port St. Lucie, 166,149; Pembroke Pines, 157,594

★ Tallahassee

**P** electronic and transportation equipment, instruments, printed materials, food products, nursery plants, oranges, tomatoes, dairy products, sugar, phosphates, fish

**Did You KNOW?** In 1987, Florida lawmakers named the American alligator as the official state reptile. Alligators are found in canals, lakes, and wetlands throughout Florida. Feeding them is against the law because it may make them lose their fear of humans.

## GEORGIA

Empire State of the South, Peach State

GA **POPULATION:** 9,919,945 (8th)

**AREA:** 59,425 sq mi (24th) (153,910 sq km)

F Cherokee rose
B Brown thrasher
T Live oak
S "Georgia on My Mind"

**ENTERED UNION:** January 2, 1788 (4th)

**LARGEST CITIES (WITH POP.):** Atlanta, 432,427; Augusta, 196,434; Columbus, 194,107; Savannah, 139,491; Athens, 116,084

★ Atlanta

P clothing and textiles, carpets, transportation equipment, food products, paper, chickens, eggs, cotton, peanuts, peaches, clay

**Did You KNOW?** At the Okefenokee National Wildlife Refuge in southern Georgia, visitors can explore forests, marshes, and prairies and see many kinds of animals, including alligators, sandhill cranes, and red-cockaded woodpeckers.

## HAWAII

Aloha State

HI **POPULATION:** 1,392,313 (40th)

**AREA:** 10,932 sq mi (43rd) (28,314 sq km)

F Yellow hibiscus
B Hawaiian goose
T Kukui
S "Hawaii Ponoi"

**ENTERED UNION:** August 21, 1959 (50th)

**LARGEST CITIES (WITH POP.; AS OF 2010 EXCEPT FOR HONOLULU):** Honolulu, 340,936; East Honolulu, 49,914; Pearl 47,698; Hilo, 43,263; Kailua, 38,635; Waipahu, 38,216; Kaneohe, 34,597

★ Honolulu

P food products, sugar, greenhouse and nursery products, cattle, macadamia nuts, coffee, pineapples, fish, concrete

**Did You KNOW?** The humpback whale is Hawaii's state marine mammal. Each winter, thousands of these whales migrate from the icy waters of the north Pacific to the warm waters off Hawaii, where females give birth and care for their newborns.

## IDAHO

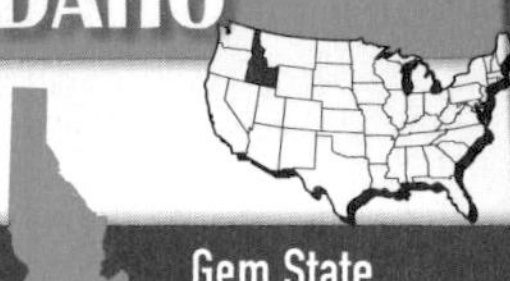


Gem State

ID **POPULATION:** 1,595,728 (39th)

**AREA:** 83,569 sq mi (14th) (216,443 sq km)

F Syringa
B Mountain bluebird
T White pine
S "Here We Have Idaho"

**ENTERED UNION:** July 3, 1890 (43rd)

**LARGEST CITIES (WITH POP.):** Boise, 210,145; Nampa, 82,755; Meridian, 76,750; Idaho Falls, 57,646; Pocatello, 54,810

★ Boise

P electronic products, lumber and wood products, dairy products, food products, cattle, wheat, hay

**Did You KNOW?** The average American eats about 140 pounds of potatoes a year, more than any other food except dairy products. Idaho grows about one-third of the U.S. fall potato crop, more than any other state.

**Key:**    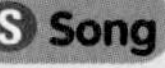  P Important Products

# ILLINOIS

**Prairie State**

IL **POPULATION:** 12,875,255 (5th)

**AREA:** 57,914 sq mi (25th) (149,995 sq km)

- **F** Native violet
- **B** Cardinal
- **T** White oak
- **S** "Illinois"

**ENTERED UNION:** December 3, 1818 (21st)

**LARGEST CITIES (WITH POP.):** Chicago, 2,707,120; Aurora, 199,672; Rockford, 152,222; Joliet, 147,433; Naperville, 142,773; Springfield, 117,076; Peoria, 115,234; Elgin, 109,104

✪ Springfield

**P** industrial machinery, metals and metal products, coal, electronic equipment, food products, corn, soybeans, hogs

**Did You KNOW?** In the city of Lincoln, Illinois, there is a statue of a watermelon. It commemorates the day in 1853 when Abraham Lincoln came there. It was the first place that was ever named after him with his permission. He christened the new town with watermelon juice and gave watermelons to people in the crowd.

# INDIANA

**Hoosier State**

IN **POPULATION:** 6,537,334 (16th)

**AREA:** 36,420 sq mi (38th) (94,326 sq km)

- **F** Peony
- **B** Cardinal
- **T** Tulip poplar
- **S** "On the Banks of the Wabash, Far Away"

**ENTERED UNION:** December 11, 1816 (19th)

**LARGEST CITIES (WITH POP.):** Indianapolis, 827,609; Fort Wayne, 255,824; Evansville, 117,825; South Bend, 101,081; Bloomington, 81,381; Hammond, 80,757; Gary, 80,221

✪ Indianapolis

**P** motor vehicles and parts, electronic equipment, iron and steel, coal, metal products, drugs, corn, soybeans, hogs, coal

**Did You KNOW?** The Lost River in southern Indiana got its name because it "disappears" for part of its course. Actually, the river drops below the surface and flows underground for several miles. Then, it re-emerges and flows aboveground again.

# IOWA

Des Moines

**Hawkeye State**

IA **POPULATION:** 3,074,186 (30th)

**AREA:** 56,273 sq mi (26th) (145,746 sq km)

- **F** Wild rose
- **B** Eastern goldfinch
- **T** Oak
- **S** "The Song of Iowa"

**ENTERED UNION:** December 28, 1846 (29th)

**LARGEST CITIES (WITH POP.):** Des Moines, 206,599; Cedar Rapids, 127,905; Davenport, 100,802; Sioux City, 82,967

✪ Des Moines

**P** corn, soybeans, hogs, cattle, food products, industrial machinery

**Did You KNOW?** Every year in July, thousands of cyclists, from all 50 states and even from a number of foreign countries, get together for RAGBRAI (the *Register's* Annual Great Bicycle Ride Across Iowa). This seven-day, 460-mile group bike ride is said to be the oldest, largest, and longest bicycle touring event in the world. It was started in 1973 by two reporters for the *Des Moines Register* newspaper.

## KANSAS

Sunflower State

KS **POPULATION:** 2,885,905 (33rd)

**AREA:** 82,278 sq mi (15th) (213,100 sq km)

F Native sunflower
B Western meadowlark
T Cottonwood
S "Home on the Range"

**ENTERED UNION:**
January 29, 1861 (34th)

**LARGEST CITIES (WITH POP.):** Wichita, 384,445; Overland Park, 176,185; Kansas City, 146,453; Topeka, 128,188; Olathe, 127,907

★ Topeka

P aircraft and other transportation equipment, machinery, food products, cattle, corn, wheat, soybeans, oil, natural gas

**Did You KNOW?** Railroads came to Kansas in the late 1860s, turning many communities into "cow towns." Ranchers in Texas organized huge cattle drives to bring their herds north to towns in Kansas with railroad stations. Then, the cattle were shipped by train to markets in the East.

## KENTUCKY

Frankfort
Louisville

Bluegrass State

KY **POPULATION:** 4,380,415 (26th)

**AREA:** 40,408 sq mi (37th) (104,656 sq km)

F Goldenrod
B Cardinal
T Tulip poplar
S "My Old Kentucky Home"

**ENTERED UNION:**
June 1, 1792 (15th)

**LARGEST CITIES (WITH POP.):** Louisville, 602,081; Lexington-Fayette, 301,569; Bowling Green, 58,894; Owensboro, 57,605

★ Frankfort

P coal, machinery, electronic equipment, motor vehicles, horses, chickens, corn, cattle, soybeans, tobacco

**Did You KNOW?** A building located in Kentucky, commonly known as Fort Knox, holds most of the gold owned by the federal government. The gold is kept in a vault behind a locked door that weighs more than 20 tons. No one person knows the whole combination needed to open it.

## LOUISIANA

Baton Rouge
New Orleans

Pelican State

LA **POPULATION:** 4,601,893 (25th)

**AREA:** 52,378 sq mi (31st) (135,659 sq km)

F Magnolia
B Eastern brown pelican
T Cypress
S "Give Me Louisiana"

**ENTERED UNION:**
April 30, 1812 (18th)

**LARGEST CITIES (WITH POP.):** New Orleans, 360,740; Baton Rouge, 230,139; Shreveport, 200,975; Lafayette, 122,130

★ Baton Rouge

P natural gas, oil, chemicals, transportation equipment, paper, food products, sugar, corn, soybeans, rice, fish

**Did You KNOW?** In 1827, students returning to Louisiana from Paris put on costumes and danced in the streets of New Orleans on the last day before the Catholic religious season known as Lent. Special celebrations on that day, called "Fat Tuesday," or "Mardi Gras," had been common in parts of Europe for centuries. Since 1827, Mardi Gras in New Orleans has gotten bigger and bigger.

**Key:** F Flower B Bird T Tree S Song ★ Capital P Important Products

## MAINE

Pine Tree State

ME **POPULATION:** 1,329,192 (41st)

**AREA:** 35,380 sq mi (39th) (91,633 sq km)

F White pine cone and tassel
B Chickadee
T Eastern white pine
S "State of Maine Song"

**ENTERED UNION:** March 15, 1820 (23rd)

**LARGEST CITIES (WITH POP.):** Portland, 66,363; Lewiston, 36,491; Bangor, 33,011

★ Augusta

P paper, ships and boats, plastics, wood and wood products, food products, potatoes, blueberries, dairy products, eggs, fish, shellfish

**Did You KNOW?** Maine is known for its rocky seacoasts, lobsters, and fishing villages, as well as for the forests that blanket 90 percent of the state. Eastport, Maine, is the easternmost city in the lower 48 states. The easternmost point, along the Maine coast, is marked by a lighthouse.

## MARYLAND

Old Line State, Free State

MD **POPULATION:** 5,884,563 (19th)

**AREA:** 12,406 sq mi (42nd) (32,131 sq km)

F Black-eyed susan
B Baltimore oriole
T White oak
S "Maryland, My Maryland"

**ENTERED UNION:** April 28, 1788 (7th)

**LARGEST CITIES (WITH POP.):** Baltimore, 619,493; Frederick, 66,169; Rockville, 62,334; Gaithersburg, 61,045; Bowie, 55,232

★ Annapolis

P food products, electronic equipment, chemicals, instruments, drugs, chickens, greenhouse and nursery products, corn, dairy products, soybeans, stone

**Did You KNOW?** Maryland gets very narrow in part of the northwest. In the area around the town of Hancock there is only about a mile between Pennsylvania to the north and West Virginia to the south.

## MASSACHUSETTS

Boston ★

Bay State, Old Colony

MA **POPULATION:** 6,646,144 (14th)

**AREA:** 10,554 sq mi (44th) (27,336 sq km)

F Mayflower
B Chickadee
T American elm
S "All Hail to Massachusetts"

**ENTERED UNION:** February 6, 1788 (6th)

**LARGEST CITIES (WITH POP.):** Boston, 625,087; Worcester, 181,631; Springfield, 153,155; Lowell, 107,584; Cambridge, 106,038

★ Boston

P electronic equipment, instruments, chemicals, drugs, metal products, fish, chickens, flowers, shrubs, cranberries

**Did You KNOW?** In 1996, Boston cream pie was named as the official state dessert. A high school civics class started the idea. Massachusetts students have also convinced the state legislature to name the ladybug as state insect, the tabby as state cat, and the corn muffin as the official state muffin.

## MICHIGAN

Great Lakes State, Wolverine State

MI **POPULATION:** 9,883,360 (9th)

**AREA:** 96,714 sq mi (11th) (250,487 sq km)

- F Apple blossom
- B Robin
- T White pine
- S "Michigan, My Michigan"

**ENTERED UNION:** January 26, 1837 (26th)

**LARGEST CITIES (WITH POP.):** Detroit, 706,585; Grand Rapids, 189,815; Warren, 134,243; Sterling Heights, 129,880; Ann Arbor, 114,925; Lansing, 114,605; Flint, 101,558

★ Lansing

P automobiles, chemicals, machinery, metal products, furniture, plastic products, iron ore, food products, dairy products, corn, soybeans, blueberries

**Did You KNOW?** When in Michigan, you are never more than 6 miles from a lake and never more than 85 miles from one of the Great Lakes.

## MINNESOTA

North Star State, Gopher State

MN **POPULATION:** 5,379,139 (21st)

**AREA:** 86,936 sq mi (12th) (225,163 sq km)

- F Pink and white lady slipper
- B Common loon
- T Red pine
- S "Hail! Minnesota"

**ENTERED UNION:** May 11, 1858 (32nd)

**LARGEST CITIES (WITH POP.):** Minneapolis, 387,753; St. Paul, 288,448; Rochester, 107,890; Duluth, 86,277; Bloomington, 84,057

★ St. Paul

P food products, electronic products, scientific and medical instruments, iron ore, stone, paper, corn, soybeans, hogs, dairy products, cattle

**Did You KNOW?** The world's largest pelican is more than 15 feet tall. Of course, it's a fake pelican. It stands near a small dam on the Pelican River in downtown Pelican Rapids, Minnesota.

## MISSISSIPPI

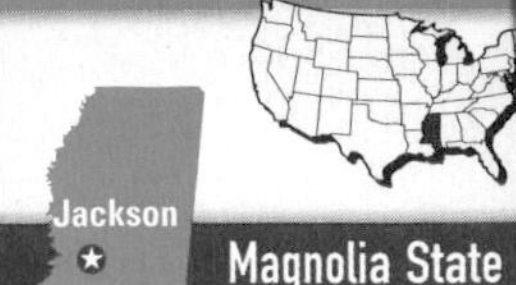

Jackson

Magnolia State

MS **POPULATION:** 2,984,926 (31st)

**AREA:** 48,432 sq mi (32nd) (125,438 sq km)

- F Magnolia
- B Mockingbird
- T Magnolia
- S "Go, Mississippi!"

**ENTERED UNION:** December 10, 1817 (20th)

**LARGEST CITIES (WITH POP.):** Jackson, 175,561; Gulfport, 69,220; Southaven, 49,831; Hattiesburg, 46,626; Biloxi, 44,940

★ Jackson

P transportation equipment, chemicals, furniture, electrical machinery, lumber and wood products, chickens, soybeans, corn, cotton

**Did You KNOW?** The Natchez Trail Parkway is a scenic road that runs 444 miles from Natchez, on the Mississippi River, to Nashville, Tennessee. It follows the route of a famous "trace," or forest trail, that was used in past centuries by American Indians.

**Key:** F Flower B Bird T Tree S Song  Capital P Important Products

# MISSOURI

Kansas City
St. Louis
Jefferson City
Show Me State

MO **POPULATION:** 6,021,988 (18th)

**AREA:** 69,707 sq mi (21st) (180,540 sq km)

F Hawthorn
B Bluebird
T Dogwood
S "Missouri Waltz"

**ENTERED UNION:** August 10, 1821 (24th)

**LARGEST CITIES (WITH POP.):** Kansas City, 463,202; St. Louis, 318,069; Springfield, 160,660; Independence, 117,213; Columbia, 110,438

★ Jefferson City

P motor vehicles, aerospace equipment, chemicals, electrical and electronic equipment, food products, soybeans, corn, cattle, hogs, turkeys, lead

**Did You KNOW?** The town of New Madrid was destroyed by the last of three major earthquakes that shook the central Mississippi valley in 1811 and 1812. They were the biggest known quakes to strike anywhere in the United States east of the Rocky Mountains.

# MONTANA

Helena
Treasure State

MT **POPULATION:** 1,005,141 (44th)

**AREA:** 147,040 sq mi (4th) (380,831 sq km)

F Bitterroot
B Western meadowlark
T Ponderosa pine
S "Montana"

**ENTERED UNION:** November 8, 1889 (41st)

**LARGEST CITIES (WITH POP.):** Billings, 105,636; Missoula, 67,290; Great Falls, 58,950; Bozeman, 37,280; Helena, 28,592

★ Helena

P copper, gold, coal, petroleum products, wood and paper products, food products, wheat, cattle, hay

**Did You KNOW?** The Little Bighorn National Monument, in southeastern Montana, commemorates "Custer's last stand." U.S. Army cavalry troops, under Lt. Col. George Armstrong Custer, were outnumbered and crushed by Sioux and Northern Cheyenne Indians, in a famous 1876 battle on that site.

# NEBRASKA

Omaha
Lincoln
Cornhusker State

NE **POPULATION:** 1,855,525 (37th)

**AREA:** 77,348 sq mi (16th) (200,330 sq km)

F Goldenrod
B Western meadowlark
T Cottonwood
S "Beautiful Nebraska"

**ENTERED UNION:** March 1, 1867 (37th)

**LARGEST CITIES (WITH POP.):** Omaha, 415,068; Lincoln, 262,341; Bellevue, 51,319; Grand Island, 49,239

★ Lincoln

P cattle, corn, soybeans, hogs, wheat, food products, chemicals, machinery

**Did You KNOW?** Actor Marlon Brando, Lakota Indian chief Red Cloud, African-American activist Malcolm X, former Vice President Dick Cheney, and former President Gerald Ford were all born in Nebraska. So was billionaire businessman Warren Buffett, known as the "Oracle of Omaha."

## NEVADA

Carson City
Las Vegas

Sagebrush State, Battle Born State, Silver State

NV **POPULATION:** 2,758,931 (35th)

**AREA:** 110,572 sq mi (7th) (286,380 sq km)

F Sagebrush
B Mountain bluebird
T Single-leaf piñon, bristlecone pine
S "Home Means Nevada"

**ENTERED UNION:** October 31, 1864 (36th)

**LARGEST CITIES (WITH POP.):** Las Vegas, 589,327; Henderson, 260,068; Reno, 227,511; North Las Vegas, 219,020; Sparks, 91,195; Carson City, 55,439

★ Carson City

P gold, silver, cattle, hay, dairy products, food products, plastics, cement, chemicals

**Did You KNOW?** Nevada is the driest state in the nation. On average, it gets only about 7 inches of rain in a typical year. The kangaroo rat, found in southwestern Nevada, can live its whole life without ever drinking a drop of liquid.

## NEW HAMPSHIRE

Granite State

Concord

NH **POPULATION:** 1,320,718 (42nd)

**AREA:** 9,349 sq mi (46th) (24,214 sq km)

F Purple lilac
B Purple finch
T White birch
S "Old New Hampshire"

**ENTERED UNION:** June 21, 1788 (9th)

**LARGEST CITIES (WITH POP.):** Manchester, 109,830; Nashua, 86,704; Concord, 42,733

★ Concord

P electric and electronic equipment, machinery, metal products, plastic products, greenhouse and dairy products, apples, maple syrup and maple sugar

**Did You KNOW?** Mount Washington, in New Hampshire, is the highest mountain in the northeastern United States. Visitors can ride to the top on a cog railway. But it's windy up there! A weather observatory on the mountain once reported a wind speed of 231 miles an hour.

## NEW JERSEY

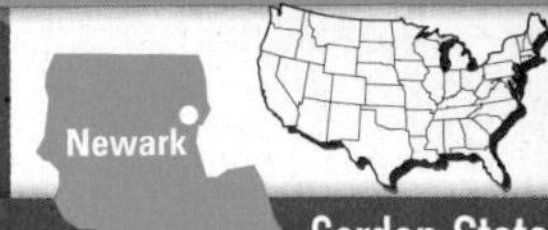

Newark
Trenton

Garden State

NJ **POPULATION:** 8,864,590 (11th)

**AREA:** 8,723 sq mi (47th) (22,591 sq km)

F Purple violet
B Eastern goldfinch
T Red oak
S none

**ENTERED UNION:** December 18, 1787 (3rd)

**LARGEST CITIES (WITH POP.):** Newark, 277,540; Jersey City, 250,323; Paterson, 146,427; Elizabeth, 125,660; Trenton, 84,899; Clifton, 84,269; Camden, 77,283; Union City, 67,187

★ Trenton

P chemicals, drugs and medical equipment, electronic equipment, petroleum products, greenhouse and nursery products, food products, blueberries, horses, corn, peaches, tomatoes

**Did You KNOW?** Next to the Amtrak train tracks in Trenton, you can find what's said to be the world's largest statue of a human tooth. It's a molar about 15 feet tall!

**Key:** F Flower B Bird T Tree S Song ★ Capital P Important Products

# NEW MEXICO

Santa Fe

Albuquerque

Land of Enchantment

NM **POPULATION:** 2,085,538 (36th)

**AREA:** 121,590 sq mi (5th) (314,917 sq km)

F Yucca
B Roadrunner
T Piñon
S "O, Fair New Mexico"

**ENTERED UNION:** January 6, 1912 (47th)

**LARGEST CITIES (WITH POP.):** Albuquerque, 552,804; Las Cruces, 99,665; Rio Rancho, 89,320; Santa Fe, 68,642

★ Santa Fe

P electronic equipment, medical equipment, aircraft, natural gas, oil, copper, potash, uranium, cattle, dairy products, pecans, hay, onions

**Did You KNOW?** Every summer, hundreds of thousands of bats come to stay and give birth to their young at the Bat Cave in Carlsbad Caverns National Park. When weather permits, adult bats fly out at night in huge swarms to search for insects, their main food source. During the day, bat colonies rest, hanging from the ceiling of the dark cave.

# NEW YORK

Albany

Buffalo

New York City

Empire State

NY **POPULATION:** 19,570,261 (3rd)

**AREA:** 54,555 sq mi (27th) (141,297 sq km)

F Rose
B Bluebird
T Sugar maple
S "I Love New York"

**ENTERED UNION:** July 26, 1788 (11th)

**LARGEST CITIES (WITH POP.):** New York, 8,244,910; Buffalo, 261,025; Rochester, 210,855; Yonkers, 197,399; Syracuse, 145,151; Albany, 97,660

★ Albany

P chemicals, drugs, automobile and aircraft parts, electronic equipment, machinery, metal products, books and magazines, dairy products, corn, greenhouse and nursery products, cattle, apples, salt, stone

**Did You KNOW?** What is said to be the world's smallest church sits on a platform in the middle of a pond in Oneida. The church is about 4 feet wide by 7 feet long and can be reached only by boat.

# NORTH CAROLINA

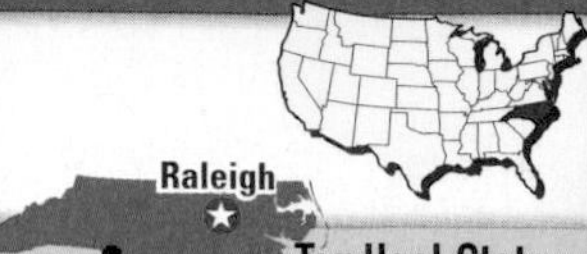

Raleigh

Charlotte

Tar Heel State, Old North State

NC **POPULATION:** 9,752,073 (10th)

**AREA:** 53,819 sq mi (28th) (139,391 sq km)

F Dogwood
B Cardinal
T Pine
S "The Old North State"

**ENTERED UNION:** November 21, 1789 (12th)

**LARGEST CITIES (WITH POP.):** Charlotte, 751,087; Raleigh, 416,468; Greensboro, 273,425; Durham, 233,252; Winston-Salem, 232,385; Fayetteville, 203,945

★ Raleigh

P tobacco and tobacco products, chemicals, drugs, electronic equipment, clothing and textiles, furniture, chickens, hogs, turkeys, greenhouse and nursery products, soybeans, sweet potatoes, cotton, peanuts

**Did You KNOW?** In 1587, a group of 112 English colonists arrived on Roanoke Island off the coast of North Carolina. Their leader, John White, sailed back to England to get more supplies. When he returned in 1590, after many delays, the people were all gone. No one knows what happened to them.

## NORTH DAKOTA

Peace Garden State

ND **POPULATION:** 699,628 (48th)

**AREA:** 70,698 sq mi (19th) (183,108 sq km)

F Wild prairie rose
B Western meadowlark
T American elm
S "North Dakota Hymn"

**ENTERED UNION:** November 2, 1889 (39th)

**LARGEST CITIES (WITH POP.):** Fargo, 107,349; Bismarck, 62,665; Grand Forks, 52,631; Minot, 42,485

★ Bismarck

P oil, farm equipment, transportation equipment, metal products, food products, wheat, soybeans, corn, cattle, canola, sunflowers, sugar beets

**Did You KNOW?** During the 1880s, well before he became president, Theodore Roosevelt traveled to the "badlands" of North Dakota to hunt bison (buffalo). He ended up owning two ranches in this dry, rocky, windswept region. You can see these sites today if you visit Theodore Roosevelt National Park in North Dakota.

## OHIO

Cleveland
Columbus
Cincinnati

Buckeye State

**POPULATION:** 11,544,225 (7th)

**AREA:** 44,826 sq mi (34th) (116,098 sq km)

F Scarlet carnation
B Cardinal
T Buckeye
S "Beautiful Ohio"

**ENTERED UNION:** March 1, 1803 (17th)

**LARGEST CITIES (WITH POP.):** Columbus, 797,434; Cleveland, 393,806; Cincinnati, 296,223; Toledo, 286,038; Akron, 198,402; Dayton, 142,148

★ Columbus

P metals and metal products, transportation equipment, chemicals, machinery, rubber and plastic products, electronic equipment, food products, corn, soybeans, dairy products, hogs, eggs

**Did You KNOW?** Winters can be cold in Ohio. On February 10, 1899, the temperature in Milligan, southeast of Columbus, dropped to 39 degrees below zero—the coldest temperature ever recorded in the state.

## OKLAHOMA

Tulsa
Oklahoma City

Sooner State

OK **POPULATION:** 3,814,820 (28th)

**AREA:** 69,899 sq mi (20th) (181,037 sq km)

F Mistletoe
B Scissor-tailed flycatcher
T Redbud
S "Oklahoma!"

**ENTERED UNION:** November 16, 1907 (46th)

**LARGEST CITIES (WITH POP.):** Oklahoma City, 591,167; Tulsa, 396,466; Norman, 113,273; Broken Arrow, 100,073; Lawton, 98,177

★ Oklahoma City

P natural gas, oil, machinery, motor vehicles, metal products, food products, cattle, hogs, chickens, wheat, dairy products

**Did You KNOW?** At the popular National Cowboy and Western Heritage Museum in Oklahoma City you can visit a replica of an old Western town and see exhibits about cowboy life and the history of the working cowboy.

**Key:** F Flower B Bird T Tree S Song ★ Capital P Important Products

# OREGON

Beaver State

**POPULATION:** 3,899,353 (27th)

**AREA:** 98,379 sq mi (9th) (254,799 sq km)

F Oregon grape
B Western meadowlark
T Douglas fir
S "Oregon, My Oregon"

**ENTERED UNION:** February 14, 1859 (33rd)

**LARGEST CITIES (WITH POP.):** Portland, 593,820; Eugene, 156,929; Salem, 156,244; Gresham, 107,439; Hillsboro, 93,455; Beaverton, 91,625

★ Salem

P electronic products and semiconductors, lumber and wood products, greenhouse and nursery products, cattle, dairy products, wheat, hay, fruits and vegetables

**Did You KNOW?** In 1998, Oregon voters overwhelmingly approved a measure that provided for voting by mail in all elections. Ballots are mailed to all citizens. People usually just mail them back, although they can bring them to a drop-off place if they prefer.

# PENNSYLVANIA

Harrisburg
Pittsburgh
Philadelphia

Keystone State

**POPULATION:** 12,763,536 (6th)

**AREA:** 46,054 sq mi (33rd) (119,280 sq km)

F Mountain laurel
B Ruffed grouse
T Hemlock
S "Pennsylvania"

**ENTERED UNION:** December 12, 1787 (2nd)

**LARGEST CITIES (WITH POP.):** Philadelphia, 1,536,471; Pittsburgh, 307,484; Allentown, 119,141; Erie, 101,807; Reading, 88,414; Upper Darby, 82,795; Scranton, 75,995

★ Harrisburg

P food products, iron and steel, coal, petroleum and metal products, drugs, machinery, transportation equipment, stone and glass products, dairy products, corn, cattle, eggs, mushrooms

**Did You KNOW?** William Penn, the British citizen who founded the Pennsylvania colony in the 1680s, and his wife, Hannah, were made "honorary citizens" of the United States by Congress in 1984. As of 2013, only five other people, including Winston Churchill and Mother Teresa, had received that honor.

# RHODE ISLAND

Providence

Little Rhody, Ocean State

RI **POPULATION:** 1,050,292 (43rd)

**AREA:** 1,545 sq mi (50th) (4,001 sq km)

F Violet
B Rhode Island red
T Red maple
S "Rhode Island"

**ENTERED UNION:** May 29, 1790 (13th)

**LARGEST CITIES (WITH POP.):** Providence, 178,053; Warwick, 82,361; Cranston, 80,392; Pawtucket, 71,153

★ Providence

P metal products, plastics, chemicals, costume jewelry, electronic equipment, greenhouse and nursery products, dairy products, fish

**Did You KNOW?** Rhode Island did not ratify the U.S. Constitution until May 1790, becoming the last of the 13 original colonies to do so. The delay was much criticized, and President George Washington left out Rhode Island when he made a tour of all the other former colonies in 1789.

## SOUTH CAROLINA

Palmetto State

**POPULATION:** 4,723,723 (24th)

**AREA:** 32,020 sq mi (40th) (82,933 sq km)

- F Yellow jessamine
- B Carolina wren
- T Palmetto
- S "Carolina"

**ENTERED UNION:** May 23, 1788 (8th)

**LARGEST CITIES (WITH POP.):** Columbia, 130,591; Charleston, 122,689; North Charleston, 99,727; Mount Pleasant, 69,357; Rock Hill, 67,423

★ Columbia

P chemicals, motor vehicles, plastics, machinery, metal products, chickens, turkeys, greenhouse and nursery products, cotton, cattle, tobacco, cement

**Did You KNOW?** More Revolutionary War battles were fought in South Carolina than in any other state. The famous South Carolina soldier Francis Marion was known as the "Swamp Fox" because he was so successful at leading surprise attacks on British troops and then slipping back into the swamps.

## SOUTH DAKOTA

Pierre

Mt. Rushmore State, Coyote State

**POPULATION:** 833,354 (46th)

**AREA:** 77,116 sq mi (17th) (199,729 sq km)

- F Pasqueflower
- B Chinese ring-necked pheasant
- T Black Hills spruce
- S "Hail, South Dakota"

**ENTERED UNION:** November 2, 1889 (40th)

**LARGEST CITIES (WITH POP.):** Sioux Falls, 156,592; Rapid City, 69,200; Aberdeen, 26,297

★ Pierre

P food products, chemicals, machinery, electrical and electronic equipment, corn, cattle, soybeans, wheat, hogs

**Did You KNOW?** In 1898, South Dakota became the first state to provide for initiative and referendum. This meant that citizens could vote for a new law (bypassing the legislature) or could repeal a law passed by the legislature.

## TENNESSEE

Nashville
Memphis

Volunteer State

**POPULATION:** 6,456,243 (17th)

**AREA:** 42,144 sq mi (36th) (109,153 sq km)

- F Iris, Passionflower
- B Mockingbird
- T Tulip poplar
- S "My Homeland, Tennessee," "When It's Iris Time in Tennessee," "My Tennessee," "Tennessee Waltz," "Rocky Top"

**ENTERED UNION:** June 1, 1796 (16th)

**LARGEST CITIES (WITH POP.):** Memphis, 652,050; Nashville-Davidson, 609,644; Knoxville, 180,761; Chattanooga, 170,136; Clarksville, 136,231; Murfreesboro, 111,327

★ Nashville

P motor vehicles, chemicals, machinery, metal products, electronic equipment, rubber and plastic products, food products, cattle, chickens, corn, cotton, tobacco

**Did You KNOW?** Tennessee was the home state of three presidents, although they were not born there: Andrew Jackson, James K. Polk, and Andrew Johnson.

**Key:** F Flower B Bird T Tree S Song  Capital P Important Products

## TEXAS

Lone Star State

**TX POPULATION:** 26,059,203 (2nd)

**AREA:** 268,596 sq mi (2nd) (695,661 sq km)

F Bluebonnet
B Mockingbird
T Pecan
S "Texas, Our Texas"

**ENTERED UNION:** December 29, 1845 (28th)

**LARGEST CITIES (WITH POP.):** Houston, 2,145,146; San Antonio, 1,359,758; Dallas, 1,223,229; Austin, 820,611; Fort Worth, 758,738; El Paso, 665,568; Arlington, 373,698; Corpus Christi, 307,953; Plano, 269,776; Laredo, 241,935; Lubbock, 233,740; Garland, 231,517; Irving, 220,702; Amarillo, 193,675

✪ Austin

P oil, natural gas, coal, cattle, chemicals and resins, aerospace products, machinery, electrical and electronic equipment, cotton, dairy products, greenhouse and nursery products, fish

**Did You KNOW?** Texas was a separate nation from 1836, when it won its independence from Mexico, until 1845, when it joined the United States.

## UTAH

Salt Lake City

Beehive State

**UT POPULATION:** 2,855,287 (34th)

**AREA:** 84,897 sq mi (13th) (219,882 sq km)

F Sego lily
B Seagull
T Blue spruce
S "Utah, This Is the Place"

**ENTERED UNION:** January 4, 1896 (45th)

**LARGEST CITIES (WITH POP.):** Salt Lake City, 189,889; West Valley City, 131,942; Provo, 115,321; West Jordan, 105,675; Orem, 90,727; Sandy, 89,200; Ogden, 83,949

✪ Salt Lake City

P food products, petroleum products, transportation equipment, medical instruments, electronic equipment, metal products, sporting goods, copper, dairy products, cattle, hay, hogs, wheat

**Did You KNOW?** Some 10,000 years ago, Paleo-Indians (ancestors of today's American Indians) lived in caves near the Great Salt Lake. They hunted mammoths, camels, and giant bison, and they gathered seeds, berries, and plants. The climate was cooler and wetter than it is today.

## VERMONT

Montpelier

Green Mountain State

**VT POPULATION:** 626,011 (49th)

**AREA:** 9,616 sq mi (45th) (24,906 sq km)

F Red clover
B Hermit thrush
T Sugar maple
S "These Green Mountains"

**ENTERED UNION:** March 4, 1791 (14th)

**LARGEST CITIES (WITH POP.):** Burlington, 42,645; South Burlington, 18,017; Rutland, 16,399

✪ Montpelier

P computers and electronic equipment, machinery, furniture, books, dairy products, cattle, hay, hogs, apples, maple syrup

**Did You KNOW?** Many "leaf peepers" from other states and even foreign countries flock to Vermont in the fall foliage season. The amount of color varies from year to year. Sunny days with cool nights help the leaves turn brightest.

## VIRGINIA

Old Dominion

VA **POPULATION:** 8,185,867 (12th)

**AREA:** 42,775 sq mi (35th) (110,787 sq km)

F Dogwood
B Cardinal
T Dogwood
S none

**ENTERED UNION:** June 25, 1788 (10th)

**LARGEST CITIES (WITH POP.):** Virginia Beach, 442,707; Norfolk, 242,628; Chesapeake, 225,050; Arlington, 207,627; Richmond, 205,533; Newport News, 179,611; Alexandria, 144,301; Hampton, 136,401

★ Richmond

P food products, transportation equipment, chemicals, machinery, electronic equipment, coal, chickens, cattle, dairy products, turkeys, tobacco, wood products, furniture

**Did You KNOW?** The world's biggest candy company is based in McLean, Virginia. Mars Incorporated makes Snickers, M&Ms, Milky Way, Twix, Mars bars, and many other candies, along with various other products such as Uncle Ben's rice and Pedigree dog food.

## WASHINGTON

Evergreen State

WA **POPULATION:** 6,897,012 (13th)

**AREA:** 71,298 sq mi (18th) (184,661 sq km)

F Western rhododendron
B Willow goldfinch
T Western hemlock
S "Washington, My Home"

**ENTERED UNION:** November 11, 1889 (42nd)

**LARGEST CITIES (WITH POP.):** Seattle, 620,778; Spokane, 210,103; Tacoma, 200,678; Vancouver, 164,759; Bellevue, 124,798; Kent, 120,916; Everett, 104,295

★ Olympia

P aircraft, electronic products and computer software, lumber and wood products, machinery, metal products, food products, apples, wheat, dairy products, potatoes, fish

**Did You KNOW?** The "pig war" is the name given to an almost-war between the United States and Great Britain, on an island off the Washington coast that both nations claimed. In 1859, an American killed a British-owned pig that got into his garden. Both sides then built up their forces, but the dispute was resolved without bloodshed.

## WEST VIRGINIA

Mountain State

WV **POPULATION:** 1,855,413 (38th)

**AREA:** 24,230 sq mi (41st) (62,756 sq km)

F Big rhododendron
B Cardinal
T Sugar maple
S "The West Virginia Hills"; "This Is My West Virginia"; "West Virginia, My Home Sweet Home"

**ENTERED UNION:** June 20, 1863 (35th)

**LARGEST CITIES (WITH POP.):** Charleston, 51,177; Huntington, 49,253; Parkersburg, 31,557; Morgantown, 30,293; Wheeling, 28,355

★ Charleston

P chemicals, automobile parts, metal products, coal, aluminum, chickens, cattle, turkeys, eggs, dairy products, peaches, tobacco

**Did You KNOW?** West Virginia has a very thin panhandle that extends northward, between Ohio and Pennsylvania. The city of Weirton, in the panhandle, is the only U.S. city that lies entirely in one state while bordering on two others.

**Key:** F Flower B Bird T Tree S Song ★ Capital P Important Products

# WISCONSIN

**POPULATION:** 5,726,398 (20th)

**AREA:** 65,496 sq mi (23rd) (169,635 sq km)

- **F** Wood violet
- **B** Robin
- **T** Sugar maple
- **S** "On, Wisconsin!"

**ENTERED UNION:** May 29, 1848 (30th)

**LARGEST CITIES (WITH POP.):** Milwaukee, 597,867; Madison, 236,901; Green Bay, 105,809; Kenosha, 99,738; Racine, 78,853; Appleton, 73,243; Waukesha, 70,567

**Capital:** Madison

**P** food products, milk, butter, cheese, machinery, transportation equipment, lumber and wood products, electrical and electronic products, plastics, cattle, hay, corn, potatoes

**Did You KNOW?** Architect Frank Lloyd Wright, artist Georgia O'Keeffe, *Little House on the Prairie* author Laura Ingalls Wilder, and Supreme Court Chief Justice William H. Rehnquist were all born in Wisconsin.

# WYOMING

**POPULATION:** 576,412 (50th)

**AREA:** 97,813 sq mi (10th) (253,334 sq km)

- **F** Indian paintbrush
- **B** Western meadowlark
- **T** Plains cottonwood
- **S** "Wyoming"

**ENTERED UNION:** July 10, 1890 (44th)

**LARGEST CITIES (WITH POP.):** Cheyenne, 60,096; Casper, 55,988; Laramie, 31,312; Gillette, 29,389; Rock Springs, 23,229

**Capital:** Cheyenne

**P** oil, natural gas, coal, petroleum and coal products, chemicals, cattle, hay, hogs, sugar beets, corn

**Did You KNOW?** The Green River rendezvous was an annual gathering of fur trappers, traders, and American Indians in Wyoming in the 1820s and 1830s. Mountain men came together to exchange goods and stories, and to relax and socialize after months of isolation in the wilderness.

# COMMONWEALTH OF PUERTO RICO

San Juan

**HISTORY:** Christopher Columbus landed in Puerto Rico in 1493. Puerto Rico was a Spanish colony for centuries, then was ceded (given) to the United States in 1898 after the Spanish-American War. In 1952, still associated with the United States, Puerto Rico became a commonwealth with its own constitution.

**POPULATION:** 3,667,084

**AREA:** 5,325 sq mi (13,791 sq km)

- **F** Maga
- **B** Reinita
- **T** Ceiba

**NATIONAL ANTHEM:** "La Borinqueña"

**LARGEST CITIES (WITH POP.):** San Juan, 389,714; Bayamón, 205,693; Carolina, 175,129; Ponce, 163,727; Caguas, 142,678

**Capital:** San Juan

**P** drugs, medical equipment, electronic equipment, clothing and textiles, dairy products, chickens, cattle, coffee, fruit

**Did You KNOW?** The coqui, a tiny tree frog about 1 inch long, is found only in Puerto Rico. It has become a symbol of the island.

**Key:** F Flower · B Bird · T Tree · S Song · ★ Capital · P Important Products

# WASHINGTON, D.C.

## CAPITAL OF THE UNITED STATES

**POPULATION (2012):** 632,323 **AREA:** 68 sq mi (177 sq km)

**FLOWER:** American beauty rose **BIRD:** Wood thrush

In 1790, Congress agreed to create the District of Columbia, on land taken from Virginia and Maryland, and build a new capital city there. The city was named after George Washington and built on the land that had belonged to Maryland. The Virginia part was later given back. In 1800, Congress moved from Philadelphia into the new Capitol building, and President John Adams moved into the White House.

## SOME PLACES TO SEE

Many of the city's major sights are on or near the **Mall,** a grassy open area that runs from the Capitol to the Potomac River.

**CAPITOL,** which houses the U.S. Congress, stands at the east end of the Mall on Capitol Hill. Its dome can be seen from many parts of the city.

**FRANKLIN DELANO ROOSEVELT MEMORIAL** includes statues of Franklin D. and Eleanor Roosevelt, in a park-like setting near the Potomac River.

**JEFFERSON MEMORIAL,** a circular marble building located near the Potomac River, is modeled after the ancient Roman temple called the Pantheon.

**LINCOLN MEMORIAL**, at the west end of the Mall, features a large, seated statue of Abraham Lincoln. His Gettysburg Address is carved on a nearby wall.

**MARTIN LUTHER KING JR. MEMORIAL,** between the Lincoln and Jefferson memorials, includes a towering statue of King and a granite wall carved with words from his speeches and sermons.

**NATIONAL ARCHIVES,** on Constitution Avenue, holds the Declaration of Independence, Constitution, and Bill of Rights.

**NATIONAL WORLD WAR II MEMORIAL,** located near the Lincoln Memorial, honors the 16 million Americans who served in that war.

**SMITHSONIAN INSTITUTION** has 19 museums, including the National Air and Space Museum and the Museum of Natural History.

**U.S. HOLOCAUST MEMORIAL MUSEUM** describes the Nazis' murder of more than six million Jews and millions of other people from 1933 to 1945.

**VIETNAM VETERANS MEMORIAL** includes a wall with the names of those killed or missing in action during the conflict.

**WASHINGTON MONUMENT** is a white marble pillar, or obelisk, rising to more than 555 feet.

**WHITE HOUSE,** at 1600 Pennsylvania Avenue, has been the home of every U.S. president except George Washington.

**FOR MORE INFORMATION, SEE: www.dc.gov • www.washington.org**

# VOLUNTEERING

→What is a Bag of Hope? PAGE 311

Environmental threats, poverty, natural disasters . . . sometimes the problems of the world seem so large that it's hard to imagine how we can help. But just one person really can make a difference. And people who help others also help themselves! Studies have shown that kids who volunteer perform better in school, are happier, and feel more positive about themselves. Does this win-win situation have you ready to take action? Here's how to get started.

*RESEARCH* Pick an area that interests you, and research different ways you can help. The website **www.dosomething.org** features a great search tool to get you started. First pick a cause—such as the environment, animal welfare, or disaster relief. Then decide whom you want to work with (alone? with your family? with friends?), where you want to help, and how much time you have to volunteer. The search generates a list of action guides that fit your needs.

*ASK AROUND* There's a good chance that different groups in your community already have projects under way—and would welcome another helping hand. Many people volunteer through their **religious community**. Churches, synagogues, and mosques often organize ways to help the needy. Many **schools** also offer opportunities for their students to volunteer. Schools may sponsor plant sales to raise money for a worthy cause or ask students to visit elderly people in a nursing home. Girl Scout councils, county 4-H organizations, American Red Cross chapters, and other **community groups** participate in volunteering projects such as cleaning up a local park or organizing a car wash to raise money for a cause.

*MAKE A CHOICE* Do you want to provide direct services or raise money for your cause? For example, you can read to patients in a children's hospital or hold a bake sale and buy an acre of rain forest with the money you raise.

**Did You KNOW?**

**Not all Americans know that Martin Luther King Jr. Day, the third Monday in January, is also a national day of service, as designated by Congress in 1994. President Barack Obama has used his two inaugurations, which fell on or near the federal holiday, to promote the National Day of Service, calling on people to join him and the First Lady in a day of volunteering. In 2013, citizens in all 50 states delivered meals, planted trees, refurbished schools, and cleared debris after Hurricane Sandy. Find out more at mlkday.gov**

# Volunteering All-Stars



## Believing in Yourself

In sixth grade, Mason Harvey, of Guthrie, Oklahoma, weighed an unhealthy 206 pounds. One day, he told his parents he was "sick and tired of being sick and tired" and began exercising and eating healthier food. By seventh grade, Mason had lost an extraordinary 85 pounds and "felt awesome." Sharing his experience, he hoped, might encourage others. Using his number of lost pounds for inspiration, Mason set a goal to share his story with 85 influential people and get involved in 85 events promoting healthy living. Since then, Mason, now 13, has met First Lady Michelle Obama, been asked to speak about childhood obesity by Oklahoma City's mayor, and planned numerous fitness events. "I am the boy that could barely finish exercise during football," he says, "and now I run 5Ks. Don't let people tell you it can't be done."

## Bags of Hope

Brianna Swinderman, 16, of Rio Rancho, New Mexico, has collected more than 2,000 pieces of luggage but she's not going anywhere. She has been distributing them to foster children and victims of domestic violence in her hometown and Albuquerque. As the daughter of a social worker and the friend of foster kids, Brianna has seen children and families in times of crisis with only garbage bags to carry their things. "This sends a message that they, and their possessions, are trash," Brianna explains. "My hope [with the luggage] is to give hope, dignity, and self-esteem." As part of her campaign Bags of Hope, Brianna has written letters asking for donations, set up a website, presented her idea to business and civic groups, and organized drop-off sites for gently used and new suitcases and duffel bags. Bags of Hope has been so successful that the National Foster Parent Association has asked Brianna to help create a national campaign.

## End to Cyberbullying

Cyberbullying is the electronic posting, often anonymous and often repeated, of mean-spirited messages about someone. It can take place through email, texting, social networks, blogs, and websites. After enduring cyberbullying as an eighth grader, Samuel Lam, now a senior in Old Westbury, New York, resolved to improve the situation. He set up a cyberbullying website with statistics, news, and prevention tips, made school presentations, and used social media to spread his message. Samuel and his friend organized the End to Cyberbullying Organization, which they hoped would encourage global awareness. The campaign, says Samuel, has inspired youth initiatives in various states as well as Great Britain, Australia, and China. Samuel has also worked with a New York state senator on a law to address cyberbullying.

**The Prudential Spirit of Community Awards honor young people for outstanding service. Find out more at spirit.prudential.com**

# WEATHER

→Which state set a new highest temperature record in 2012? PAGE 313

## Weather Forecasting

Rain or shine? Weather scientists called **meteorologists** help forecast the weather for tomorrow or even the week ahead. They are able to do this by studying winds, temperature, and changes in the atmosphere. For example, an area of high pressure usually means dry, calm weather, while an area of low pressure often brings rain, clouds, and wind.

A **front** is a sharp change in air temperature. Storms usually come before a cold front. As a cold front passes through an area, the temperature drops. Light rain might bring a warm front. As a warm front moves in, the air gets warmer.

Around the world, meteorologists use the same set of symbols to show weather conditions (see the table below and the map above). These common symbols let them share weather data.

| Selected Weather Symbols | | |
|---|---|---|
| **Sky Cover** | **Fronts** | **Weather** |
| ○ Clear | ▲▲ Cold front | ▪ Rain; = Fog |
| ◔ Scattered | ●●● Warm front | * Snow; ∞ Haze |
| ● Overcast | Stationary front | Thunderstorm |
| **Wind:** ◎ Calm | — 1-2 knots (1-2 mph) | 3-7 knots (3-8 mph) |
| **L** Low Pressure Center | **H** High Pressure Center | |

- The heat is on! 2012 was the hottest year on record for the U.S. mainland, according to the National Oceanic and Atmospheric Administration (NOAA).
- *Boom!* Lightning is so hot that it causes the air around it to expand, resulting in a loud sound we know as thunder.
- Heat and drought (a long period of dry weather) led to 2012 being the third-worst wildfire year in U.S. history. More than 9 million acres burned—an area larger than the state of Maryland.

**Did You KNOW?** In February 2013, a record-breaking blizzard slammed the northeastern United States. Some parts of Connecticut, Massachusetts, and Rhode Island were buried under more than 3 feet of snow.

# RECORD TEMPERATURES BY STATE (Through May 2013)

Coldest Temperature: Alaska
Hottest Temperature: California

| STATE | Lowest °F | Lowest Latest date | Highest °F | Highest Latest date |
|---|---|---|---|---|
| Alabama | –27 | Jan. 30, 1966 | 112 | Sept. 5, 1925 |
| Alaska | –80 | Jan. 23, 1971 | 100 | June 27, 1915 |
| Arizona | –40 | Jan. 7, 1971 | 128 | July 5, 2007 |
| Arkansas | –29 | Feb. 13, 1905 | 120 | Aug. 10, 1936 |
| California | –45 | Jan. 20, 1937 | 134 | July 10, 1913 |
| Colorado | –61 | Feb. 1, 1985 | 118 | July 11, 1888 |
| Connecticut | –32 | Jan. 22, 1961 | 106 | July 15, 1995 |
| Delaware | –17 | Jan. 17, 1893 | 110 | July 21, 1930 |
| Florida | –2 | Feb. 13, 1899 | 109 | June 29, 1931 |
| Georgia | –17 | Jan. 27, 1940 | 112 | Aug. 20, 1983 |
| Hawaii | 12 | May 17, 1979 | 100 | Apr. 27, 1931 |
| Idaho | –60 | Jan. 18, 1943 | 118 | July 28, 1934 |
| Illinois | –36 | Jan. 5, 1999 | 117 | July 14, 1954 |
| Indiana | –36 | Jan. 19, 1994 | 116 | July 14, 1936 |
| Iowa | –47 | Feb. 3, 1996 | 118 | July 20, 1934 |
| Kansas | –40 | Feb. 13, 1905 | 121 | July 24, 1936 |
| Kentucky | –37 | Jan. 19, 1994 | 114 | July 28, 1930 |
| Louisiana | –16 | Feb. 13, 1899 | 114 | Aug. 10, 1936 |
| Maine | –50 | Jan. 16, 2009 | 105 | July 10, 1911 |
| Maryland | –40 | Jan. 13, 1912 | 109 | July 10, 1936 |
| Massachusetts | –35 | Jan. 12, 1981 | 107 | Aug. 2, 1975 |
| Michigan | –51 | Feb. 9, 1934 | 112 | July 13, 1936 |
| Minnesota | –60 | Feb. 2, 1996 | 114 | July 6, 1936 |
| Mississippi | –19 | Jan. 30, 1966 | 115 | July 29, 1930 |
| Missouri | –40 | Feb. 13, 1905 | 118 | July 14, 1954 |
| Montana | –70 | Jan. 20, 1954 | 117 | July 5, 1937 |
| Nebraska | –47 | Dec. 22, 1989 | 118 | July 24, 1936 |
| Nevada | –50 | Jan. 8, 1937 | 125 | June 29, 1994 |
| New Hampshire | –47 | Jan. 29, 1934 | 106 | July 4, 1911 |
| New Jersey | –34 | Jan. 5, 1904 | 110 | July 10, 1936 |
| New Mexico | –50 | Feb. 1, 1951 | 122 | June 27, 1994 |
| New York | –52 | Feb. 18, 1979 | 108 | July 22, 1926 |
| North Carolina | –34 | Jan. 21, 1985 | 110 | Aug. 21, 1983 |
| North Dakota | –60 | Feb. 15, 1936 | 121 | July 6, 1936 |
| Ohio | –39 | Feb. 10, 1899 | 113 | July 21, 1934 |
| Oklahoma | –31 | Feb. 10, 2011 | 120 | June 27, 1994 |
| Oregon | –54 | Feb. 10, 1933 | 119 | Aug. 10, 1898 |
| Pennsylvania | –42 | Jan. 5, 1904 | 111 | July 10, 1936 |
| Rhode Island | –25 | Feb. 5, 1996 | 104 | Aug. 2, 1975 |
| South Carolina | –19 | Jan. 21, 1985 | 113 | June 29, 2012 |
| South Dakota | –58 | Feb. 17, 1936 | 120 | July 15, 2006 |
| Tennessee | –32 | Dec. 30, 1917 | 113 | Aug. 9, 1930 |
| Texas | –23 | Feb. 8, 1933 | 120 | June 28, 1994 |
| Utah | –69 | Feb. 1, 1985 | 117 | July 5, 1985 |
| Vermont | –50 | Dec. 30, 1933 | 105 | July 4, 1911 |
| Virginia | –30 | Jan. 22, 1985 | 110 | July 15, 1954 |
| Washington | –48 | Dec. 30, 1968 | 118 | Aug. 5, 1961 |
| West Virginia | –37 | Dec. 30, 1917 | 112 | July 10, 1936 |
| Wisconsin | –55 | Feb. 4, 1996 | 114 | July 13, 1936 |
| Wyoming | –66 | Feb. 9, 1933 | 115 | Aug. 8, 1983 |

Source: National Climatic Data Center

Record temperatures may have occurred on earlier dates. Dates listed here are for most recent occurrence of a record temperature.

# WEIGHTS & MEASURES

→Where is the hottest place on Earth? PAGE 315

Metrology isn't the study of weather. (That's meteorology.) It is the science of measurement. Almost everything you use (or eat or drink) is measured—either when it is made or when it's sold. Materials for buildings and parts for machines must be measured carefully so they will fit together. Clothes have sizes so you'll know what to buy. Recipes help you measure the ingredients so your cookies bake properly.

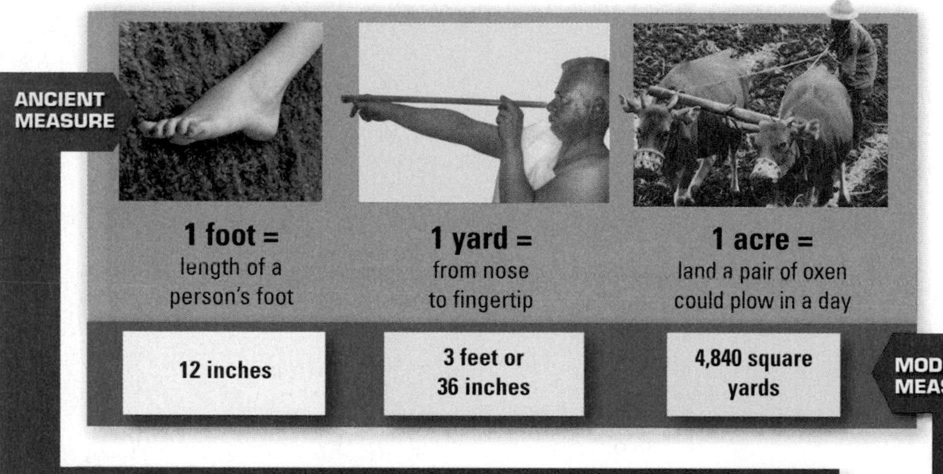


## EARLIEST MEASUREMENTS

The human body was the first "ruler." An "inch" was the width of a thumb; a "hand" was five fingers wide; a "foot" was—you guessed it—the length of a foot! A "cubit" ran from the elbow to the tip of the middle finger (about 20 inches), and a "yard" was roughly the length of a whole arm.

Later, measurements came from daily activities, like plowing a field. A "furlong" was the distance a pair of oxen could plow before stopping to rest (now we say it is about 220 yards). The trouble with these units is that they vary from person to person, place to place, and ox to ox.

## MEASUREMENTS WE USE TODAY

The official system in the U.S. is the customary system (sometimes called the imperial or English system). Scientists and most other countries use the International System of Units (SI, or the metric system). The Weights and Measures Division of the U.S. National Institute of Standards and Technology (NIST) makes sure that a gallon of milk is the same in every state. When the NIST was founded in 1901, the U.S. had as many as eight different "standard" gallons, and there were four different legal measures of a "foot" in Brooklyn, New York, alone.

# TAKING TEMPERATURES

**There are two main systems for measuring temperature.** One is **Fahrenheit** (abbreviated F). The other is **Celsius** (abbreviated C). Another word for Celsius is Centigrade.

Zero degrees (0°) Celsius is equal to 32 degrees (32°) Fahrenheit.

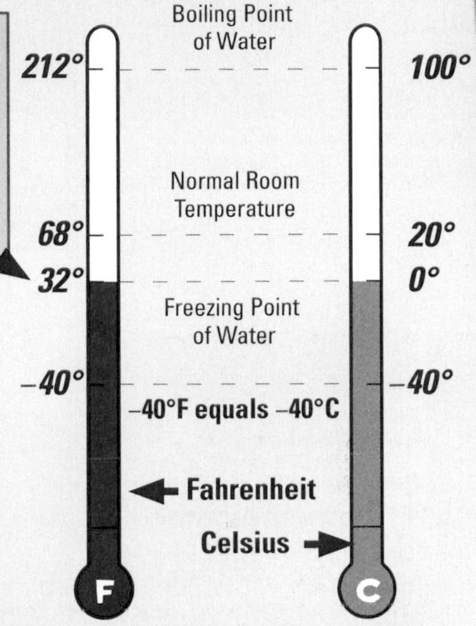


## To convert from Celsius to Fahrenheit:

Multiply by 1.8 and add 32.
(°F = 1.8 × °C + 32)

**Example:** 20°C × 1.8 = 36; 36 + 32 = 68°F

## To convert from Fahrenheit to Celsius:

Subtract 32 and divide by 1.8.

**Example:** 68°F – 32 = 36; 36 ÷ 1.8 = 20°C

## HOTTEST and COLDEST Places in the World

| Continent | Highest Temperature | Lowest Temperature |
|---|---|---|
| AFRICA | Kebili, Tunisia, 131°F (55°C) | Ifrane, Morocco, –11°F (–24°C) |
| ANTARCTICA | Vanda Station, 59°F (15°C) | Vostok, –129°F (–89°C) |
| ASIA | Tirat Tsvi, Israel, 129°F (54°C) | Verkhoyansk, Russia, and Oimekon, Russia, –90°F (–68°C) |
| AUSTRALIA | Oodnadatta, South Australia, 123°F (51°C) | Charlotte Pass, New South Wales, –9°F (–23°C) |
| EUROPE | Athens, Greece, and Elefsina, Greece, 118°F (48°C) | Ust'-Shchugor, Russia, –73°F (–58°C) |
| NORTH AMERICA | Death Valley, California, U.S., 134°F (57°C) | Snag, Yukon, Canada, –81°F (–63°C) |
| SOUTH AMERICA | Rivadavia, Argentina, 120°F (49°C) | Sarmiento, Argentina, –27°F (–33°C) |

Coldest Temperature

Hottest Temperature

**Did You KNOW?**

**El Azizia, Libya, held the world's high-temperature record of 136°F (58°C) for 90 years. In 2012, the World Meteorological Organization (WMO) determined that a measuring error was made. Death Valley, California, now holds the record for the hottest place on Earth.**

## LENGTH

The basic unit of **length** in the U.S. system is the **inch**. Length, width, and thickness all use the inch or larger related units.

1 foot (ft) = 12 inches (in)
1 yard (yd) = 3 feet = 36 inches
1 rod (rd) = 5½ yards
1 furlong (fur) = 40 rods = 220 yards = 660 feet
1 mile (mi) (also called statute mile) = 8 furlongs = 1,760 yards = 5,280 feet
1 nautical mile = 6,076 feet = 1.15 statute miles
1 league = 3 miles

## CAPACITY

Units of **capacity** measure how much of something will fit into a container. **Liquid measure** is used to measure liquids such as water or gasoline. **Dry measure** is used with large amounts of solid materials such as grain or fruit. Although both liquid and dry measures use the terms "pint" and "quart," they mean different amounts and should not be confused.

### Dry Measure

1 quart (qt) = 2 pints (pt)
1 peck (pk) = 8 quarts
1 bushel (bu) = 4 pecks

### Liquid Measure

1 gill = 4 fluid ounces (fl oz)
1 pint (pt) = 4 gills = 16 ounces (oz)
1 quart (qt) = 2 pints = 32 ounces
1 gallon (gal) = 4 quarts = 128 ounces

For measuring most U.S. liquids,
1 barrel (bbl) = 31½ gallons

For measuring oil, 1 barrel = 42 gallons

### Cooking Measurements

The measurements in cooking are based on the **fluid ounce**.
1 teaspoon (tsp) = ⅙ fluid ounce (fl oz)
1 tablespoon (tbsp) = 3 teaspoons = ½ fluid ounce
1 cup = 16 tablespoons = 8 fluid ounces
1 pint = 2 cups
1 quart (qt) = 2 pints (pt)
1 gallon (gal) = 4 quarts

## AREA

**Area** measures a section of a two-dimensional surface like a floor or a piece of paper. Most area measurements are given in **square units**. Land is measured in **acres**.

1 square foot (sq ft) = 144 square inches (sq in)
1 square yard (sq yd) = 9 square feet = 1,296 square inches
1 square rod (sq rd) = 30¼ square yards
1 acre = 160 square rods = 4,840 square yards = 43,560 square feet
1 square mile (sq mi) = 640 acres

## VOLUME

The amount of space taken up by a three-dimensional object (or the amount of space available within an object) is measured in **volume**. Volume is usually expressed in **cubic units**.

1 cubic foot (cu ft) = 12 inches x 12 inches x 12 inches = 1,728 cubic inches (cu in)
1 cubic yard (cu yd) = 27 cubic feet

## DEPTH

Some measurements of length measure ocean depth and distance.

1 fathom = 6 feet (ft)
1 cable = 120 fathoms = 720 feet

## WEIGHT

Although 1 cubic foot of popcorn and 1 cubic foot of rock take up the same amount of space, lifting them isn't the same. We measure heaviness as **weight**. Most objects are measured in **avoirdupois weight** (pronounced a-ver-de-POIZ):

1 dram (dr) = 27.344 grains (gr)
1 ounce (oz) = 16 drams = 437.5 grains
1 pound (lb) = 16 ounces
1 hundredweight (cwt) = 100 pounds
1 (short) ton = 2,000 pounds

# THE METRIC SYSTEM

The metric system was created in France in 1795. Standardized in 1960, the International System of Units is now used in most countries and in scientific works. The system is based on 10, like the decimal counting system. The basic unit for length is the **meter**. The **liter** is a basic unit of volume or capacity, and the **gram** is a basic unit of mass. Related units are made by adding a prefix to the basic unit. The prefixes and their meanings are:

**milli-** = $\frac{1}{1,000}$

**centi-** = $\frac{1}{100}$

**deci-** = $\frac{1}{10}$

**deka-** = 10

**hecto-** = 100

**kilo-** = 1,000

## For Example

millimeter (mm) = $\frac{1}{1,000}$ of a meter

kilometer (km) = 1,000 meters

milligram (mg) = $\frac{1}{1,000}$ of a gram

kilogram (kg) = 1,000 grams

To get a rough idea of measurements in the metric system, it helps to know that a **liter** is a little more than a quart. A **meter** is a little more than a yard. A **kilogram** is a little more than 2 pounds. And a **kilometer** is just over half a mile.

## HOMEWORK TIP → CONVERTING MEASUREMENTS

| If you have: | Multiply by: | To get: | If you have: | Multiply by: | To get: |
|---|---|---|---|---|---|
| **inches** | *2.54* | centimeters | **centimeters** | *0.3937* | inches |
| **inches** | *0.0254* | meters | **centimeters** | *0.0328* | feet |
| **feet** | *30.48* | centimeters | **meters** | *39.3701* | inches |
| **feet** | *0.3048* | meters | **meters** | *3.2808* | feet |
| **yards** | *0.9144* | meters | **meters** | *1.0936* | yards |
| **miles** | *1.6093* | kilometers | **kilometers** | *0.621* | miles |
| **square inches** | *6.4516* | square centimeters | **square centimeters** | *0.155* | square inches |
| **square feet** | *0.0929* | square meters | **square meters** | *10.7639* | square feet |
| **square yards** | *0.8361* | square meters | **square meters** | *1.196* | square yards |
| **acres** | *0.4047* | hectares | **hectares** | *2.471* | acres |
| **cubic inches** | *16.3871* | cubic centimeters | **cubic centimeters** | *0.061* | cubic inches |
| **cubic feet** | *0.0283* | cubic meters | **cubic meters** | *35.3147* | cubic feet |
| **cubic yards** | *0.7646* | cubic meters | **cubic meters** | *1.308* | cubic yards |
| **quarts (liquid)** | *0.9464* | liters | **liters** | *1.0567* | quarts (liquid) |
| **ounces** | *28.3495* | grams | **grams** | *0.0353* | ounces |
| **pounds** | *0.4536* | kilograms | **kilograms** | *2.2046* | pounds |

# WORLD HISTORY

→What was the Silk Road? PAGE 322

Sumerian temple

## THE ANCIENT MIDDLE EAST

← *hieroglyphics*

**4000–3000 B.C.** The world's first cities are built by the Sumerian peoples in Mesopotamia, now southern Iraq. Sumerians develop a kind of writing called **cuneiform**. Egyptians develop a kind of writing called **hieroglyphics**.

**2700 B.C.** Egyptians begin building the great pyramids in the desert.

**1792 B.C.** Some of the first written laws are created in Babylonia. They are called the **Code of Hammurabi**.

**1200 B.C.** Hebrew people settle in Canaan in Palestine after escaping from slavery in Egypt. They are led by the prophet Moses.

**1000 B.C.** King David unites the Hebrews.

**ANCIENT PALESTINE** Palestine is invaded by many different peoples after 1000 B.C., including the Babylonians, Egyptians, Persians, and Romans.

**336 B.C.** Alexander the Great, king of Macedonia, builds an empire from Egypt to India. ↓

**63 B.C.** Roman general Pompey → conquers Palestine and makes it part of the Roman Empire.

**Around 4 B.C.** Jesus Christ, the founder of Christianity, is born in Bethlehem. He is crucified about A.D. 29.

**ISLAM: A RELIGION GROWS IN THE MIDDLE EAST A.D. 610–632** Around 610, the prophet Muhammad starts to proclaim and teach Islam. By the time of his death in 632, Islam is accepted in Arabia as a religion. The religion then spreads from Arabia to all the neighboring regions in the Middle East and North Africa. Its followers are called Muslims.

**THE KORAN**
The holy book of Islam is the Koran. It was related by Muhammad beginning in 611.

**THE SPREAD OF ISLAM**
As Arab armies move across North Africa, Arabic replaces many local languages as an official language. North Africa is still an Arabic-speaking region today, and Islam is the major faith.

**641** Arab Muslims conquer the Persians.

**Early 700s** Islam begins to spread into Spain.

# THE MIDDLE EAST

**THE UMAYYAD AND ABBASID DYNASTIES** The Umayyads (661–750) and the Abbasids (750–1256) are the first two Muslim-led dynasties. Both empires include northern Africa and the Middle East.

**711–732** Umayyads invade Europe but are defeated by Frankish leader Charles Martel in France. This defeat halts the spread of Islam into Western Europe.

**1071** Muslim Turks conquer Jerusalem.

**1095–1291** Europeans try to take back Jerusalem and other parts of the Middle East for Christians during the Crusades.

**1300–1900s** The Ottoman Turks, who are Muslims, create a huge empire, covering the Middle East, North Africa, and part of Eastern Europe. European countries take over portions of it beginning in the 1800s.

**1914–1918** In World War I, the British officer widely known as Lawrence of Arabia → leads an Arab revolt against Turkish rule. After the war, most of the Middle East falls under British or French control.

**1921** Two new Arab kingdoms are created: Transjordan and Iraq.

**1922** Egypt becomes independent from Great Britain.

**1948** The state of Israel is created.

**THE ARAB-ISRAELI WARS** Arab countries near Israel (Egypt, Iraq, Jordan, Lebanon, and Syria) attack the new country in 1948 but fail to destroy it. Israel and its neighbors fight wars again in 1956, 1967, and 1973. Israel wins each war. In the 1967 war, Israel captures the Sinai Peninsula and Gaza from Egypt, the Golan Heights from Syria, and the West Bank from Jordan.

**1979** Egypt and Israel sign a peace treaty. Israel returns the Sinai to Egypt.

**THE MIDDLE EAST AND OIL** Many countries rely on oil imports from the region, which has more than half the world's crude oil reserves.

**1991** The U.S. and its allies go to war with Iraq after Iraq had invaded Kuwait in 1990. Iraq is defeated and forced out of Kuwait.

**2003–2011** The U.S. and its allies invade Iraq in 2003 and remove the regime of dictator Saddam Hussein. The U.S. declares the war officially over in December 2011.

**2011** In what becomes known as the "Arab spring," demonstrations against repressive governments break out in the region, including in Syria, Lebanon, Egypt, Bahrain, and Yemen. Leaders in Egypt and Yemen are overthrown.

**2013** Almost 70 people are killed after Islamic militants attack a gas field in Algeria and take hostages. In Syria, a civil war that began in 2012 results in about 70,000 deaths by early 2013.

*Syrian rebels*

# ANCIENT AFRICA

Niger River

**ANCIENT AFRICA** In ancient times, northern Africa was dominated by the Egyptians, Greeks, and Romans. Ancient Africans south of the Sahara Desert did not have written languages. What we learn about them comes from weapons, tools, and other items from their civilization.

**2000 B.C.** The Nubian Kingdom of Kush, rich with gold, ivory, and jewels, arises south of Egypt. It is a major center of art, learning, and trade until around A.D. 350.

**1000 B.C.** Bantu-speaking people around Cameroon begin an 1,800-year expansion into much of eastern and southern Africa.

**500 B.C.** Carthage, an empire centered in Tunisia, becomes rich and powerful through trading. Its ports span the African coast of the Mediterranean. Rome defeats Carthage and ← Hannibal, its most famous leader, during the second Punic War, from 218 to 201 B.C.

• The Nok in Nigeria are the earliest users of iron for tools and weapons south of the Sahara Desert. They are also known for their terracotta sculptures.

**Around A.D. 100** The Kingdom of Aksum in northern Ethiopia becomes a wealthy trading center on the Red Sea.

**By A.D. 700** Ghana, the first known empire south of the Sahara Desert, takes power through trade around the upper Senegal and Niger Rivers. Its Mande people control the trade in gold from nearby mines to Arabs in the north.

**By 900** Arab Muslim merchants bring Islam to the Bantu speakers along the east coast of Africa, creating the Swahili language and culture. Traders in Kenya and Tanzania export ivory, slaves, perfumes, and gold to Asia.

**1054–1145** Islamic Berbers unite into the Almoravid Kingdom centered at Marrakech, Morocco. They spread into Ghana and southern Spain.

**1230–1400s** A Mande prince named Sundiata (the "Lion King") forms the Mali Kingdom where Ghana once stood. Timbuktu becomes its main city.

**TIMBUKTU** Located on the trade routes between North Africa and West Africa, Timbuktu was one of the wealthiest cities in Africa in the 1300s, as well as a center for scholarship. Gold, ivory, cloth, salt, and slaves were all traded in Timbuktu.

**1250–1400s** Great Zimbabwe becomes the largest settlement (12,000-20,000 Bantu-speaking people) in southern Africa.

**1464–1591** As Mali loses power, Songhai rises to become the third and final great empire of western Africa.

**1481** Portugal sets up the first permanent European trading post south of the Sahara Desert at Elmina, Ghana. Slaves, in addition to gold and ivory, are soon exported.

**1483–1665** Kongo, the most powerful kingdom on central Africa's west coast, provides thousands of slaves each year for Portugal. Portugal's colony Angola overtakes the Kongo in 1665.

# AFRICA

**1650–1810** Slave trading peaks across the "Slave Coast" from eastern Ghana to western Nigeria as African states sell tens of thousands of captured foes each year to European traders.

**THE AFRICAN SLAVE TRADE**
African slaves are taken to the Caribbean to harvest sugar on European plantations and then taken to South America and the United States. The ships from Africa are overcrowded and diseased. About 20% of the slaves die during the long journey.

**1652** The Dutch East India Company sets up a supply camp in southern Africa at the Cape of Good Hope (later Cape Town). Dutch settlers and French Protestants (Huguenots) establish Cape Colony. Their descendants are known as the Boers or Afrikaners.

**1803** Denmark is the first European country to ban slave trading. Britain follows in 1807, the U.S. in 1808. Most European nations ban the trade by 1820, but illegal trading continues for decades.

**1814** Britain purchases the Dutch South African colony at Cape Town. British colonists arrive after 1820.

**1835–1843** The "Great Trek" (march) of the Boers away from British Cape Town takes place.

**1884–1885** European nations meet in Berlin and agree to divide control of Africa. The "Scramble for Africa" lasts until World War I.

**1899–1902** Great Britain and the Boers fight in South Africa in the Boer War. The Boers accept British rule but are allowed a role in government.

**1948** The white Afrikaner-dominated South African government creates the policy of apartheid ("apartness"), the total separation of races. Blacks are banned from many public places.

**1957** Ghana gains independence from Britain, becoming the first territory in Africa below the Sahara to regain freedom from European rule. Over the next 20 years, the rest of Africa gains independence.

**1990–1994** South Africa abolishes apartheid. In 1994, Nelson Mandela becomes South Africa's first black president.

**1994** Members of Rwanda's Hutu majority launch a genocide against the country's Tutsi minority, killing about 800,000 people.

**1998–2004** Fighting in the Democratic Republic of the Congo involves nine nations. About 4 million people die.

**2006** Ellen Johnson Sirleaf becomes president of Liberia and Africa's first elected female leader.

**2011** South Sudan becomes Africa's newest independent nation, on July 9. Protesters in Tunisia overthrow that country's longtime dictator. In Libya, rebels helped by Western governments overthrow dictator Muammar al-Qaddafi. Ellen Johnson Sirleaf and another Liberian leader share the Nobel Peace Prize.

**2012** In a terrorist attack in the city of Benghazi, the U.S. ambassador to Libya and three other Americans are killed.

**2013** French troops help push back Islamic militants who had taken control of large areas of northern Mali. Some ancient manuscripts are destroyed while militants occupy Timbuktu.

*French troops in Mali*

# ANCIENT ASIA

*Taj Mahal*

**3500 B.C.** People settle in the Indus River Valley of India and Pakistan and the Yellow River Valley of China.

**Around 1523 B.C.** Shang peoples in China build walled towns and use a kind of writing based on pictures. This writing develops into the writing Chinese people use today.

**Around 1050 B.C.** Zhou peoples in China overthrow the Shang and control large territories.

**563 B.C.** Siddhartha Gautama is born in India. He becomes known as the Buddha—the "Enlightened One"—and is the founder of the Buddhist religion (Buddhism).→

**551 B.C.** The Chinese philosopher Confucius is born. His teachings—especially rules about how people should treat each other—spread throughout China and are still followed.

*Confucius*

**320–232 B.C.**

- Northern India is united under the emperor Chandragupta Maurya.
- Asoka, emperor of India, sends Buddhist missionaries throughout southern Asia to spread the Buddhist religion.

**221 B.C.** The Chinese begin building the Great Wall. Its main section is more than 2,000 miles long and is meant to keep invading peoples out.

**202 B.C.** The Han people of China win control of all of China.

**A.D. 320** The Gupta Empire controls northern India. The Guptas, who are Hindus, drive the Buddhist religion out of India. They are well known for their many advances in mathematics and medicine.

**618** The Tang dynasty begins in China. The Tang dynasty is well known for music, poetry, and painting. China exports silk and porcelains as far away as Africa.

**THE SILK ROAD** Around 100 B.C., only the Chinese know how to make silk. To get this light, comfortable material, Europeans send fortunes in glass, gold, jade, and other items to China. The exchanges between Europeans and Chinese create one of the greatest trading routes in history—the Silk Road. Chinese inventions such as paper and gunpowder are also spread via the Silk Road. Europeans find out how to make silk around A.D. 500, but trade continues until about 1400.

**960** The Northern Sung dynasty in China makes advances in banking and paper money. China's population of 50 million doubles over 200 years, thanks to improved ways of farming that lead to greater food production.

# ASIA

← **1000** The Samurai, a warrior people, become powerful in Japan. They live by a code of honor known as *Bushido*.

**1180** The Khmer Empire in Cambodia becomes widely known for its beautiful temples.

**1206** The Mongol leader Genghis Khan creates an empire that stretches from China to India, Russia, and Eastern Europe.

**1264** Kublai Khan, grandson of Genghis Khan, rules China as emperor from his new capital at Beijing.

**1368** The Ming dynasty comes to power in China and drives out the Mongols.

**1526** The Mughal Empire in India begins under Babur. The Mughals are Muslims who invade and conquer India. They make major changes in government and culture. Mughal rulers also build architectural masterpieces such as the Taj Mahal.

**1644** The Ming dynasty in China is overthrown by the Manchu peoples.

**1839** The Opium War takes place in China between the Chinese and the British. The British and other Western powers want to control trade in Asia. The Chinese want the British to stop selling opium to the Chinese. Britain wins the war in 1842.

**1858** The French begin to take control of Indochina (Southeast Asia).

**JAPANESE EXPANSION** In the 1930s, Japan begins to invade some of its neighbors. In 1941, the United States and Japan go to war after Japan attacks the U.S. Navy base at Pearl Harbor, Hawaii.

**1945** Japan is defeated in World War II after the U.S. drops atomic bombs on the Japanese cities of Hiroshima and Nagasaki.

**1947** India and Pakistan become independent from Great Britain.

**1949** China comes under the rule of the Communists led by Mao Zedong.

**1950–1953** **THE KOREAN WAR** Communist North Korea invades South Korea. The U.S. and allies fight the invasion. China sides with North Korea. The fighting ends in a truce in 1953.

**1954–1975** **THE VIETNAM WAR** The French are defeated in Indochina in 1954 by Vietnamese nationalists. The U.S. sends troops in 1965 to help South Vietnam fight against the Communists in the North, led by Ho Chi Minh. → The U.S. withdraws in 1973. In 1975, South Vietnam is taken over by North Vietnam.

**1989** Chinese students protest for democracy, but the protests are crushed by the army in Beijing's Tiananmen Square.

**1997** Britain returns Hong Kong to China.

**2004** A powerful earthquake in the Indian Ocean in December sets off huge waves (tsunamis) that kill almost 228,000 people in Indonesia, Sri Lanka, and other countries.

**THE U.S. IN AFGHANISTAN** U.S.-led military action overthrows the Taliban regime in Afghanistan in 2001 and seeks to root out terrorists there. In 2009 and 2010, the United States sends additional troops to fight the Taliban, which had regained strength. The U.S. announces plans to remove its troops by 2014.

**2011** A massive earthquake and tsunami in March cause widespread destruction and thousands of deaths in northeastern Japan. In North Korea, longtime dictator Kim Jong Il dies and is replaced by his son, Kim Jong Un.

*Hong Kong, China*

# ANCIENT EUROPE

Roman aqueduct in France

**4000 B.C.** People in Europe start building monuments out of large stones called megaliths, such as Stonehenge in England.

**2500 B.C.–1200 B.C.**
**The Minoans and the Mycenaeans**
- People on the island of Crete (Minoans) in the Mediterranean Sea build great palaces and become sailors and traders.
- People from Mycenae invade Crete and destroy the power of the Minoans.

**THE TROJAN WAR** The Trojan War is a conflict between invading Greeks and the people of Troas (Troy) in southwestern Turkey around 1200 B.C. Although little is known today about the real war, according to legend, a group of Greek soldiers hides inside a huge wooden horse. The horse is pulled into the city of Troy. Then the soldiers jump out and conquer Troy.

**900–600 B.C.** Celtic peoples in Northern Europe settle on farms and in villages and learn to mine for iron ore.

**600 B.C.** Etruscan peoples take over most of Italy. They build many cities and become traders.

Trojan horse

## SOME ACHIEVEMENTS OF THE GREEKS

The early Greeks are responsible for:
- the first governments elected by the people.
- great poets such as Homer, who composed the *Iliad* and the *Odyssey*,
- great thinkers such as Socrates, Plato, and Aristotle,
- great architecture, including the Parthenon on the Acropolis in Athens.

**431 B.C.** The Peloponnesian Wars begin between the Greek cities of Athens and Sparta. The wars end in 404 B.C. when Sparta wins.

**338 B.C.** King Philip II of Macedonia in northern Greece conquers all of Greece.

**336 B.C.** Philip's son Alexander the Great becomes king. He creates an empire from the Mediterranean Sea to India. For the next 300 years, Greek culture dominates this area.

**264 B.C.–A.D. 476** **THE ROMAN EMPIRE** The city of Rome in Italy begins to expand and capture surrounding lands. The Romans gradually build a great empire and control all of the Mediterranean region. At its height, the Roman Empire includes Western Europe, Greece, Egypt, and much of the Middle East.

## ROMAN ACHIEVEMENTS

- Roman law; many of our laws are based on Roman law.
- Great roads to connect their huge empire; the Appian Way, south of Rome, is a Roman road that is still in use today.
- Aqueducts to bring water to large cities.
- Great sculpture; Roman statues can still be seen in Europe.
- Great architecture, some of which still stands. →
- Great writers, such as the poet Virgil, who wrote the *Aeneid*.

Pantheon, Rome

**49 B.C.** A civil war breaks out that destroys Rome's republican form of government.

**45 B.C.** Julius Caesar becomes the sole ruler of Rome but is murdered one year later by rivals.

**27 B.C.** Octavian becomes the first emperor of Rome. He takes the name Augustus. ↓

**THE CHRISTIAN FAITH** Christians believe that Jesus Christ is the Son of God. The history and beliefs of Christianity are found in the New Testament of the Bible. Christianity spreads slowly throughout the Roman Empire. The Romans try to stop the new religion, and they persecute Christians. Over time, however, more and more Romans become Christian.

**A.D. 43** Rome invades and begins the conquest of Britain.

**A.D. 313** The Roman Emperor Constantine gives full rights to Christians. He eventually becomes a Christian himself.

**THE BYZANTINE EMPIRE,** centered in modern-day Turkey, is the eastern half of the old Roman Empire. Byzantine rulers extend their power into western Europe. Constantinople (now Istanbul, Turkey) becomes the capital of the Byzantine Empire in A.D. 330.

**410** The Visigoths and other barbarian tribes from northern Europe invade the Roman Empire and begin to take over its lands.

**476** The last Roman emperor, Romulus Augustus, is overthrown.

**768** Charlemagne becomes king of the Franks in northern Europe. He rules a kingdom that includes most of France, Germany, and northern Italy. →

**Around 800** During the Middle Ages, feudalism becomes important in Europe. Poor farmers, called serfs, are allowed to farm a lord's land in return for certain services to the lord.

**896** Magyar peoples found Hungary.

**800s–900s** Viking warriors and traders from Scandinavia begin to move into the British Isles, France, and parts of the Mediterranean.

**962** Saxon ruler Otto I is crowned Holy Roman Emperor by the pope.

**989** The Russian state of Kiev becomes Christian.

*Serfs in the Middle Ages*

**1066** William of Normandy, a Frenchman, invades England and makes himself king. He is known as William the Conqueror.

**1095–1291 THE ← CRUSADES** Christian leaders send a series of armies to try to capture Jerusalem from the Muslims. The Christians do not succeed, but trade increases between the Middle East and Europe.

**1215** The Magna Carta is agreed to by King John of England and the nobility. The king agrees that he does not have absolute power. The document is a major step toward democracy.

**1290** The Ottoman Empire begins. It is controlled by Turkish Muslims who conquer lands in the eastern Mediterranean and the Middle East.

**1337** The Hundred Years' War begins in Europe between France and England. The war lasts until 1453 when France wins.

**1348** The bubonic plague (Black Death) begins in Europe. As much as one-third of the whole population of Europe dies from this disease.

**1453** The Ottoman Turks capture the city of Constantinople and rename it Istanbul.

**1517 THE REFORMATION** The Protestant Reformation splits European Christians apart. It starts when German priest Martin Luther breaks away from the Roman Catholic pope.

**1520–1566** Under Sultan Suleiman I, known as The Magnificent, the Ottoman Turks expand their empire in Eastern Europe, Asia, and North Africa.

**1534** King Henry VIII of England breaks away from the Roman Catholic church. He names himself head of the English (Anglican) Church. →

**1558** The reign of King Henry's daughter Elizabeth I begins in England.

**1588** The Spanish Armada (fleet of warships) is defeated by the English Navy as Spain tries to invade England.

**1618** Much of Europe is destroyed in the Thirty Years' War, which ends in 1648.

**1642** The English Civil War begins. King Charles I fights against the forces of the Parliament. The king is defeated and is executed in 1649. His son, Charles II, returns as king in 1660.

**1762** Catherine the Great becomes Empress of Russia. She extends the Russian Empire.

**1789 THE FRENCH REVOLUTION** The French Revolution begins. It brings a temporary end to royal rule in France. During the revolution, dictators take control, and many people die on the guillotine. King Louis XVI and Queen Marie Antoinette are executed in 1793.

**1799** Napoleon Bonaparte, an army officer, becomes dictator of France. Under his rule, France conquers most of Europe by 1812.

**1815** Napoleon's forces are defeated by the British and German armies at Waterloo (in Belgium). Napoleon is exiled to a remote island and dies there in 1821.

**1848** Revolutions break out in countries of Europe. People force their rulers to make more democratic changes.

**1914–1918 WORLD WAR I IN EUROPE** At the start of World War I in Europe, Germany, Austria-Hungary, and the Ottoman Empire (the Central Powers) oppose Britain, France, Italy, and Russia (the Allies). The United States joins the war on the Allied side in 1917. The Allies win in 1918.

**1917** Tsar Nicholas II is overthrown in the Russian Revolution. He and members of his family are executed in 1918. The Bolsheviks (Communists) under Vladimir Lenin take control. Millions are starved, sent to labor camps, or executed under Joseph Stalin (1929–1953).

**1933** Adolf Hitler becomes dictator of Germany. Before his rule ends in 1945, Hitler's Nazis kill millions of Jews and other people in the Holocaust.

**1939–1945 WORLD WAR II IN EUROPE** Axis powers Germany and Italy are defeated by the Allies—Great Britain, the Soviet Union, the U.S., and others.

*Allied Commander Dwight Eisenhower*

**1990s** Communist governments in Eastern Europe are overthrown. Germany is reunited. The Soviet Union breaks up.

**2013** Five years after a major financial crisis, European economies remain weak.

# AUSTRALIA AND OCEANIA

**Around 58,000 B.C.** The first people to live in Australia, now known as Aborigines, reach the continent, after traveling by boat from Southeast Asia.

**Around 28,000 B.C.** Polynesians begin migrating east from Asia. During the next 25,000 years, they establish settlements on many islands of the South Pacific.

**Around A.D. 800** The Maori, a Polynesian people, become the first humans to settle New Zealand.

**1606** Dutch sea captain Willem Jansz explores part of the northern Australian coast and is believed to be the first European to set foot in Australia.

**1770** Captain James Cook explores the east coast of Australia and claims the area for Great Britain.

**1788 BRITISH SETTLEMENT OF AUSTRALIA** Under a British policy to send convicted criminals to Australia, the first English settlers arrive on January 26, 1788, at what is now Sydney Harbor. By the time the "transportation" policy ends in 1868, 160,000 convicts have come to Australia.

**1790s** The first free British settlers arrive in Australia.

**1830** The British claim and settle the entire continent.

**1840** British colonial settlement of New Zealand begins.

**1901** Australia becomes independent on January 1. It continues to recognize the British monarch as head of state.

**1907** New Zealand becomes a self-governing dominion. It achieves full independence 40 years later.

**1967** In a national referendum, Australians vote to change parts of the constitution that discriminated against Aborigines.

**2012** The first U.S. Marines arrive in Australia under a new military agreement.

*Sydney, Australia*

# The AMERICAS

*Pyramid at Teotihuacán*

**10,000–8000 B.C.** People in North and South America gather plants for food and hunt animals using stone-pointed spears.

**Around 3000 B.C.** People in Central America begin farming, growing corn and beans for food.

**1500 B.C.** Mayan people in Central America begin to live in small villages.

**500 B.C.** People in North America begin to hunt buffalo to use for meat and for clothing.

**100 B.C.** The city of Teotihuacán is founded in Mexico. It becomes the center of a huge empire extending from central Mexico to Guatemala. Teotihuacán contains many large pyramids and temples.

**A.D. 150** Mayan people in Guatemala build many centers for religious ceremonies. They create a calendar and learn mathematics and astronomy.

**900** Toltec warriors in Mexico begin to invade lands of Mayan people. Mayans leave their old cities and move to the Yucatan Peninsula of Mexico.

**1000** Native Americans in the southwestern United States begin to live in settlements called pueblos. They learn to farm.

**1325** Mexican Indians known as Aztecs create the huge city of Tenochtitlán and rule a large empire in Mexico. They are warriors who practice human sacrifice.

**1492** Christopher Columbus sails from Europe across the Atlantic Ocean and lands in the Bahamas, in the Caribbean Sea. This marks the first step toward the founding of European settlements in the Americas.

**1500** Portuguese explorers reach Brazil and claim it for Portugal.

**1519** Spanish conqueror Hernán Cortés travels into the Aztec Empire in search of gold. The Aztecs are defeated in 1521, and Spain takes control of Mexico.

**WHY DID THE SPANISH WIN?** How did the Spanish defeat the powerful Aztec Empire? One reason is that the Spanish had better weapons. Another is that many Aztecs died from diseases brought to the New World by the Spanish. Also, many neighboring Indians hated the Aztecs as conquerors and helped the Spanish.

**1532–1535** Spanish conqueror Francisco Pizarro defeats the Inca Empire based in Peru. →

**1534** Jacques Cartier of France explores Canada.

**1583** The first English colony in Canada is set up in Newfoundland.

**1607** English colonists led by Captain John Smith settle in Jamestown, Virginia.

**1619** The first African slaves arrive in English-controlled America.

**1682** The French explorer René-Robert Cavelier, sieur de La Salle, sails down the Mississippi River to the Gulf of Mexico.

*Christopher Columbus*

**EUROPEAN COLONIES** By 1700, most of the Americas are under European control.

**Spain:** Florida, southwestern United States, Mexico, Central America, western South America

**Portugal:** eastern South America

**France:** central United States, parts of Canada

**England:** eastern U.S., parts of Canada

**Holland:** West Indies, eastern South America

**1756–1763** France loses its lands in eastern North America to Britain in the French and Indian War. ↓

**1775–1783 AMERICAN REVOLUTION** The American Revolution begins in 1775 when the first shot is fired in Lexington, Massachusetts. The thirteen British colonies that become the United States officially gain independence in 1783.

**SIMÓN BOLÍVAR: LIBERATOR OF SOUTH AMERICA**
In 1810, Simón Bolívar begins a revolt against Spain. As a result of his leadership, nine South American countries gain their independence by the 1820s.

**1821** After an 11-year revolt against colonial rule, Mexico wins its independence from Spain.

**1882** Brazil gains its independence from Portugal.

**1846–1848 MEXICAN-AMERICAN WAR** In 1846, Mexico and the United States go to war. Mexico loses most of the Southwest and California to the U.S.

**1867** Canadian provinces are united as the Dominion of Canada.

**1898 SPANISH-AMERICAN WAR** Spain and the U.S. fight a brief war in 1898. Spain loses its colonies Cuba, Puerto Rico, and the Philippines.

**1911** A revolution in Mexico that began in 1910 overthrows Porfirio Díaz. ↓

**1959** Fidel Castro becomes president of Cuba, which becomes a Communist country allied with the Soviet Union.

**1962** U.S. President John F. Kennedy forces the Soviet Union to withdraw missiles it had installed in Cuba.

**1994** The North American Free Trade Agreement (NAFTA) increases trade between the U.S., Canada, and Mexico.

**2001** On September 11, Muslim terrorists crash planes into U.S. targets, killing about 3,000 people.

**2009** Barack Obama becomes the first African American president of the U.S.

**2010** More than 300,000 people are killed in a devastating earthquake in Haiti.

**2013** Cardinal Jorge Mario Bergoglio, archbishop of Buenos Aires, Argentina, is elected pope and takes the name Francis. He is the first leader of the Roman Catholic Church to come from Latin America.

# THEN & NOW 2014

## 10 YEARS AGO—2004

***THEN:*** An underwater earthquake in the Indian Ocean causes a tsunami that kills more than 225,000 people in Southeast Asia.

**NOW:** Tsunami warning centers have been established in Indonesia, Australia, and New Zealand. Centers in the Caribbean and Mediterranean seas are planned.

***THEN:*** George W. Bush, 43rd U.S. president, wins a second term, defeating U.S. senator John Kerry of Massachusetts in the national presidential election.

**NOW:** Dedicated in 2013, the George W. Bush Presidential Library and Museum in Dallas, Texas, is open to the public.

## 50 YEARS AGO—1964

***THEN:*** The Summer Olympics, held in Tokyo, Japan, are Asia's first Olympic Games.

**NOW:** Sochi, Russia, is set to host the 2014 Winter Olympics. They will be the first Russian-hosted Winter Games.

←***THEN:*** After "I Want to Hold Your Hand" hits number one on the U.S. charts, the British rock group The Beatles performs live for the first time on American TV on the popular variety program *The Ed Sullivan Show.*

**NOW:** The Beatles remain the best-selling band ever, with more than 1 billion recordings sold.

## 100 YEARS AGO—1914

***THEN:*** World War I begins—an international conflict between the Central Powers (mainly Germany, Austria-Hungary, and Turkey) and the Allied Powers (mainly France, Britain, Russia, Italy, Japan, and as of 1917, the U.S.).

**NOW:** The European Union (EU) is an economic and political confederation of more than two dozen nations working together for growth and peace. It was awarded the Nobel Peace Prize in 2012.

***THEN:*** The Panama Canal, one of the world's greatest engineering projects, opens officially, connecting the Pacific and Atlantic oceans.

**NOW:** An expansion of the Panama Canal doubling its shipping capacity is scheduled for completion in 2015.

# THEN & NOW 2015



## 10 YEARS AGO—2005

***THEN:*** Hurricane Katrina strikes the southeastern U.S., killing more than 1,800 people and causing more damage than any other natural disaster in the country's history. Many levees and flood walls fail, flooding about 80 percent of New Orleans, Louisiana.

**NOW:** Rebuilding and recovery efforts have brought old and new residents, as well as tourists, to New Orleans. It is now one of the fastest-growing large cities in the U.S.

***THEN:*** Three former employees of the U.S. e-commerce company PayPal register the YouTube website. Its first video is an 18-second clip of a man standing in front of elephants at the San Diego Zoo.

**NOW:** Every minute, 72 hours of video are uploaded to YouTube in more than 60 languages and in 57 countries. More than 1 billion unique users visit the site every month.

## 50 YEARS AGO—1965

***THEN:*** The 19-year-old United Nations Children's Fund, or UNICEF, is awarded the Nobel Peace Prize for providing aid to "all children without any distinction of race, creed, nationality, or political conviction."

**NOW:** UNICEF provides health care and immunizations, clean water and sanitation, nutrition, education, and emergency relief to children in more than 190 countries and territories around the world.

***THEN:*** A major escalation in the Vietnam War takes places when about 200,000 U.S. combat troops are sent to support South Vietnam in a conflict with the communist government of North Vietnam and its South Vietnamese allies, known as the Viet Cong.

**NOW:** The reunified country of Vietnam is a major U.S. trading partner, with total trade of $25 billion a year, and is a tourist destination for many Americans.

## 100 YEARS AGO—1915

***THEN:*** Alexander Graham Bell and Thomas A. Watson conduct the first transcontinental telephone call. From New York, Bell calls his former assistant in San Francisco, California, and says, "Mr. Watson, come here, I want to talk to you."

**NOW:** About 87 percent of U.S. adults own a cell phone. Almost half of the country's adults own a smartphone, which allows users to access the Internet.

***THEN:*** The Ford Motor Company builds its one-millionth car, the popular Model T.

**NOW:** The Flat Rock Assembly Plant in Michigan celebrates → the production of its one-millionth Ford Mustang, 49 years after the car's debut in 1964.

# WOMEN IN History

## 624?–705 WU ZETIAN

Only woman emperor of China. She was born into a noble family and married an emperor. After her husband became seriously ill, she took over running the government. When her husband died, his son became emperor. She overthrew him, however, and also his brother and became emperor in her own name. As emperor, she brought in scholars to help run the government and lowered taxes.

## 1533–1603 QUEEN ELIZABETH I

One of the greatest rulers of England. She was the daughter of King Henry VIII. Elizabeth ruled for 45 years, until her death. She built England into a world power, especially after her navy's victory in 1588 over the Spanish Armada, an invasion fleet sent by Spain. Elizabeth never married. She used the possibility of marriage to increase her political power.

## 1717–1780 MARIA THERESA

Empress of Austria-Hungary for 40 years who ruled over much of Eastern Europe as well as other areas. When she came to the throne, many regions refused to accept a woman as ruler, which led to a nine-year war. As empress, Maria Theresa was a strong leader who put in place many educational reforms and encouraged the growth of commerce and industry. Among her 16 children was Marie Antoinette, who as queen of France was guillotined during the French Revolution.

## 1775–1817 JANE AUSTEN

English author whose works remain as popular today as when they were written 200 years ago. Her six novels focus on the daily lives of families in small, rural villages and gently mock social conventions. Austen began writing stories as a young child. As an adult, she traveled very little and disliked large cities. Four of her books, including her most famous, *Pride and Prejudice*, were published in her lifetime (without her name on them, since it was not acceptable for a woman to be an author). All her books have been made into movies, some many times.

## 1820–1913 HARRIET TUBMAN

Abolitionist leader in the United States before the Civil War. Born a slave, Tubman escaped to Pennsylvania in 1849. She became a "conductor" on the Underground Railroad, which helped escaping slaves. Risking her life, she made 19 trips back to the South to lead slaves to freedom.

## 1821–1910 ELIZABETH BLACKWELL

First woman to receive a degree from a medical school in the U.S. At first she couldn't find a medical school that would accept her, but finally she did—and she graduated first in her class. She later trained nurses and founded a hospital and a medical school for women.

## 1871–1945 EMILY CARR

Canadian writer and artist, best known for paintings set in her home province of British Columbia. After studying in France, she returned home and traveled around painting pictures of native culture, such as totem poles. Her goal was to preserve a record of a culture in danger of disappearing. In her 50s, she began painting canvases of the area's rugged landscapes, focusing on scenes of forests and beaches. As her health worsened, she began writing short stories about native life in British Columbia. She won several literary awards for her work.

## 1907–1964 RACHEL CARSON

American scientist and author. She is often credited with launching the modern environmental movement with the publication of her book *Silent Spring* (1962), about the dangers of pesticides. (The book brought her much criticism from the chemical industry.) Carson worked for many years as a scientist with the U.S. Fish and Wildlife Service.

## 1917–1984 INDIRA GANDHI

India's powerful prime minister from 1966 to 1977 and again from 1980 to 1984. The daughter of Jawaharlal Nehru, the first prime minister of India after independence, she helped India modernize and grow into a world power. She negotiated a peace with rival Pakistan, reduced food shortages, and developed a nuclear weapon. However, she also took on unpopular dictatorial powers and was defeated for reelection in 1977. She returned to power in 1980, but four years later, she was assassinated.

## 1921–2006 BETTY FRIEDAN

American leader of the women's movement that began in the 1960s. A graduate of Smith College and a psychologist, Friedan gave up her career after having children to stay home with them. Bored and frustrated, she surveyed other Smith graduates. Her study developed into *The Feminine Mystique* (1963), which urged women to pursue careers. She cofounded the National Organization for Women and remained an activist all her life, working for equal rights for women.

## 1938– ELLEN JOHNSON SIRLEAF

Liberian political leader who became the first woman elected to head the government of an African country. After attending college in the U.S., she returned home and became a government official. Twice she was forced to leave Liberia because of political unrest, and once she was imprisoned. She successfully ran for president in 2005 and was reelected in 2011. Also in 2011, she won a Nobel Peace Prize for her work to ensure women's safety and promote women's rights in Africa.

## 1945– AUNG SAN SUU KYI

Burmese political activist and winner of the Nobel Peace Prize (1991). Suu Kyi's father is considered the founder of modern Burma, now called Myanmar. Suu Kyi opposed the country's military government and became a leader of the pro-democracy movement. She spent many years under house arrest but was released in 2010. She was elected to Parliament in 2012 and leads the opposition.

# ANSWERS

## Animals Word Scramble p. 31

koala
rhinoceros
opossum
guinea pig
chimpanzee
chipmunk

## Celebrity Crossword Puzzle p. 43

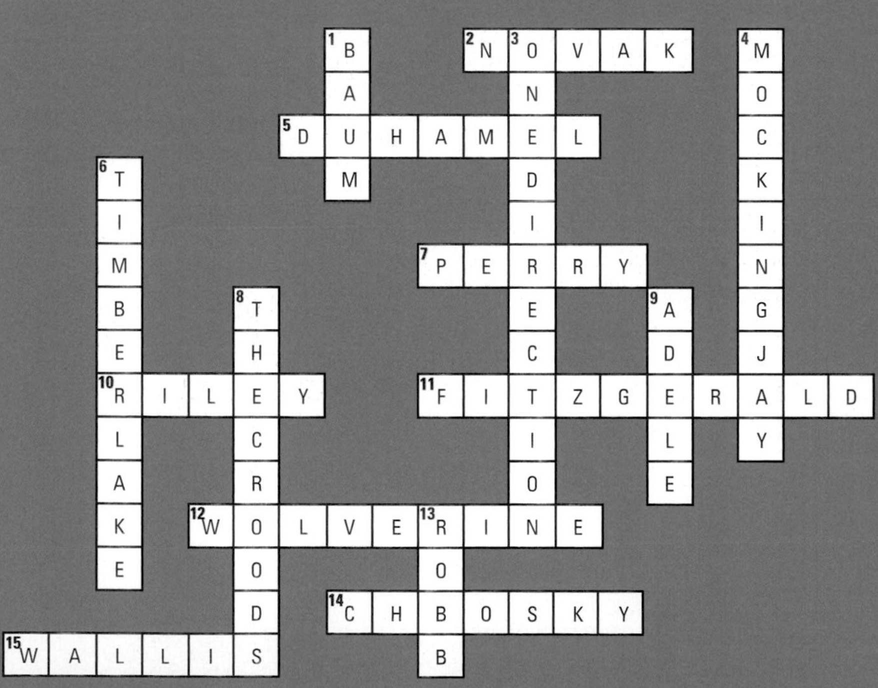


## Building Quiz p. 54

Elephant Building
Hagia Sophia
Eiffel Tower
The Shard →
Alhambra Palace
Basket House

## Saying It Right! p. 110

Jonah = noun
carefully = adverb
washed = verb
his = pronoun
dirty = adjective
dishes = noun

## Movies & TV Word Search p. 131

| G | T | H | E | V | O | I | C | E | P | F | J | D | Y | H |
|---|---|---|---|---|---|---|---|---|---|---|---|---|---|---|
| D | R | R | A | F | N | K | G | G | D | P | Z | R | A | S |
| J | O | A | I | V | Z | Q | N | D | W | M | T | A | J | Q |
| E | V | H | V | K | A | Y | R | N | D | H | P | K | G | J |
| R | H | J | S | I | H | T | E | C | E | I | S | E | N | J |
| H | R | F | R | U | T | M | A | A | C | Z | I | A | I | S |
| E | S | N | C | B | R | Y | V | R | F | W | Y | N | K | L |
| S | Q | X | T | G | Y | E | F | S | Q | E | P | D | C | P |
| P | H | M | S | C | N | R | M | A | F | C | M | J | O | I |
| X | F | T | T | G | F | Y | B | I | L | T | S | O | M | H |
| T | Q | L | E | Y | M | R | U | O | T | L | U | S | Q | O |
| Q | S | R | S | F | N | T | P | N | R | G | S | H | D | C |
| L | S | O | M | E | N | G | N | I | D | N | I | F | E | E |
| L | B | N | B | N | Z | N | T | S | B | S | E | B | M | X |
| M | S | Y | H | Q | Z | U | G | R | O | I | T | U | M | B |

## Roman Numerals p. 179

Super Bowl XLVII was the 47th Super Bowl.
2013 = MMXIII
34-31 = XXXIV-XXXI

## Homework Tip: Decimals to Fractions p. 180

0.3 = 3/10    0.75 = 3/4    0.6 = 3/5

## Numbers Brain Teasers! p. 181

**Number Facts:** 476 – 7 + 430 – 2 + 123 – 20 – 1,000 = 0

**Secret Message:** "The way up is the way down" (a saying by the Greek philosopher Heraclitus)

**Missing Numbers:**

| A | | | | B | | | C | | | D | | |
|---|---|---|---|---|---|---|---|---|---|---|---|---|
| 1 | 4 | 9 | 16 | 2 | 3 | 5 | 45 | 9 | 72 | 19 | 9 | 33 |
| 25 | 36 | 49 | 64 | 7 | 11 | 13 | 69 | 15 | 78 | 90 | 0 | 80 |
| 81 | 100 | 121 | 144 | 17 | 19 | 23 | 20 | 2 | 11 | 14 | 4 | 22 |

In Group A, the numbers are 1 x 1, 2 x 2, and so forth. Group B consists of the first 9 prime numbers. In Group C, each number in the middle is the sum of the digits in the numbers on either side; so, 2 in the bottom row is the sum of 2 + 0 and also 1 + 1. In Group D, each number in the middle is the product of the digits in the numbers on either side; for example, 9 x 0 and 8 x 0 both equal 0.

**A Little Logic:**

1. 3 socks
2. 4 socks

If you pick one more sock than the number of colors, you can be sure of getting a pair.

## Sports Star Challenge p. 239

| | | | | | | | | | |
|---|---|---|---|---|---|---|---|---|---|
| G | S | B | O | L | T | O | P | M | U |
| R | E | N | O | A | F | K | R | A | P |
| I | N | S | D | C | Z | C | W | Z | H |
| F | O | E | Y | O | P | U | I | E | E |
| F | J | R | Z | X | U | L | Q | S | L |
| I | M | E | S | S | I | G | K | T | P |
| N | O | N | J | E | F | N | G | O | S |
| F | C | A | B | R | E | R | A | V | D |
| N | D | K | S | O | W | A | Y | L | N |

## Match It! p. 239

1. (e) 2. (d) 3. (a) 4. (b) 5. (g) 6. (h) 7. (f) 8. (c)

# INDEX

Note: Words in **boldface** refer to key content sections. Page numbers in **boldface** refer to maps.

## A

## D



## E

# F



# G

# J



# K



# L

## M

## Q



## R

## S

# PHOTO CREDITS





**FRONT COVER: Newscom:** Jim Rassol/MCT (James); Bob Daemmrich/Polaris (Douglas); PhotoPQR/Le Parisien (One Direction). **Shutterstock:** toucan, flags, Taj Mahal, smartphone. **BACK COVER: AP Images:** Charles Skyes/Invision (Swift). **Newscom:** infch-02/INF/photo.com (Smith). **Shutterstock:** Zendaya, tarsier, One World Trade Center. **INTERIOR: Alamy:** Aerial Archives, 74 (The Geysers); David R. Frazier/Photolibrary, Inc., 3, 52 (Basket building); epa european pressphoto agency b.v., 7 (Yousafzai); Jake Lyell, 183 (W. African family); Juniors Bildarchiv GmbH, 199 (firefly); Mary Evans Picture Library, 137 (Jason), 245 (bicycle); National Geographic Image Collection, 276 (Am. Indian Museum); North Wind Picture Archives, 68 (Pompeii), 281 (Battle of Lexington), 283 (Gold Rush), 325 (Middle Ages peasants), 329 (French and Indian War); Photo Resource Hawaii, 278 (Hula); Prisma Archivo, 326 (Crusades); The Print Collector, 87 (hennin); Tom Wallace/*Minneapolis Star Tribune*/ZUMAPRESS, 187 (Hmong); www.BibleLandPictures.com, 125 (Lydian coin). **AP Images:** 9 (King), 31 (elephant tusks), 323 (Ho Chi-Minh), 330 (The Beatles); Abdullah al-Yassin, 319 (Syria); Autostock/Nigel Kinrade, 222 (Keselowski); Bettmann/Corbis, 122 (Vietnam War), 204 (Mayer), 226 (Naismith), 247 (Sikorsky), 263 (Reagan), 333 (Gandhi); Cal Sport Media, 235 (Morgan); Charles Dharapak, 265 (Romney and Obama); Charles Krupa, 3, 312 (2013 blizzard); Chelyabinsk.ru/Yekaterina Pustynnikova, 215 (meteoroid); Dan Hallman/Invision, 3, 86 (Mars); David Drapkin, 230 (Luck); David J. Phillip, 232 (Scott); *Detroit News*/John T. Greilick, 331 (Mustang); DreamWorks Animation, 15 (*The Croods*); Eduardo Di Baia, 234 (Messi); Elaine Thompson, 4, 224 (Cabrera), 230 (Jones); Evan Agostini, 88 (Lauren); Gregory Bull, 219 (Douglas); Hussein Malla, 6 (Syria); Imaginechina, 5, 247 (high speed train); John Bazemore, 228 (Pitino); John Marshall/Invision for Parkwood Entertainment, 16 (Beyoncé); John Swart, 217 (Flutie); Julio Cortez, 69 (rollercoaster); Kevin P. Casey/file, 231 (Parcells); Kevin Terrell, 18 (Flacco), 226 (Griffin); Keystone/Peter Schneider, 234 (Maze); Kyodo, 77 (Prius); Larry Papke, 22 (Johnson); Lionel Cironneau, 237 (Djokovic); LM Otero, 232 (Inbee); *L'Osservatore Romano*, 6 (Pope Francis); Marcy Nighswander, 274 (Socks); Matt Ludtke, 230 (Peterson); Michael Dwyer, 9 (Boston bombing); NBC, Brownie Harris/File, 10 (*Revolution*); Nick Wass, 233 (Ovechkin); Nomaan Merchant, 64 (Arledge); North Wind Picture Archives, 279 (Dutch New York); *The Oklahoman*, Paul Hellstern, 8 (tornado); Paul Connors, 226 (Payton); *The Press of Atlantic City*/Michael Ein, 118 (Hurricane Sandy); PRNewsFoto/Forevermark, 128 (Wallis); Ray Tang/Rex Features, 35 (Villareal); Rex Features, 3, 112 (Google Glass), 14 (*The Great Gatsby*), 262 (Obama); Scott Kirkland, 124 (Parker); Seonggwang Kim for Special Olympics, 221 (Special Olympics); Sherwin Crasto, 188 (Mother Teresa); SIPA, 188 (Schweitzer); Steve Helber, 262 (Biden); Tomasso DeRosa, 231 (Fisher); *The Tribune* (of San Luis Obispo)/Joe Johnston, 64 (fingerprint dusting); Wilfredo Lee, 226 (James), 236 (Williams). **Bridgeman Art Library:** Metropolitan Museum of Art, New York, USA/Giraudon, 35 (Vermeer). **Timothy Bryk:** 314 (1 yard). **Joe Burgess:** 291 (New Mexico). **Candlewick:** 44 (cover: *This Is Not My Hat*. Copyright © 2012 by Jon Klassen. Reproduced by permission of the publisher, Candlewick Press, Inc., Somerville, MA). **Phillip Capper:** 168 (Port Levy). **The Jimmy Carter Library & Museum:** 274 (Carter). **Courtesy of Louise Casey:** 91 (Casey). **Courtesy of Cedar Point:** 249, 352 (maXair). **Centers for Disease Control and Prevention:** Janice Haney Carr, 203 (bacteria). **Central Intelligence Agency:** 172 (Slovakia), 174 (Switzerland).

**Dtwographics Photography:** 65 (Burgess). **Dwight D. Eisenhower Presidential Library & Museum:** 274 (Eisenhower). **Exploratorium:** Photo by Amy Snyder/© Exploratorium/Exploratorium.edu, 252 (Exploratorium). **Flickr:** jonjanego, 95 (Zheng He). **Getty Images:** Adam Taylor/ABC, 134 (*Dancing With the Stars*); Al Bello, 219 (Phelps); Alberto E. Rodriguez, 4, 130 (*The Hunger Games* actors); Alfred Eisenstaedt/Time Life Pictures, 333 (Carson); Araya Diaz for TechCrunch, 124 (Moskovitz); Archive Photos, 38 (Bach), 280 (Minuit), 281 (French and Indian War), 319 (Lawrence); Bachrach, 45 (White); Bertrand Rindoff Petroff, 124 (Bettencourt); Bloomberg, 40 (Kahlo); Bob Levey, 21 (Texas vs. Houston); Bryn Lennon, 219 (Bolt); Chip Somodevilla, 261 (Supreme Court); Chris Graythen, 18 (Stewart), 223 (Kanaan); Chris Steppig-Pool, 221 (Hancock), 228 (Siva); Christopher Furlong, 195 (Pope Francis); Claus Andersen, 235 (Gonzalez); Dan Levine/AFP, 225 (Ripken); Dana Nalbandian for Free the Children, 129 (Novak); David Gray/ABC, 11 (*Once Upon a Time*); David McNew, 80 (shopping bag); De Agostini, 87 (wigs); Dean Mouhtaropoulos, 221 (Paralympics); Dennis Hallinan/Archive Photos, 91 (*Pac-Man*); Evin Mazur/WireImage, 4, 133 (Perry); FilmMagic, 45 (Meyer); Frederic J. Brown/AFP, 264 (polling station); Heinz Kluetmeier/*Sports Illustrated*, 218 (2012 Olympic Games); Hulton Archive, 41 (Gandhi), 274 (Fala), 284 (WWI); Hulton Fine Art Collection, 332 (Wu Zetian); Hulton Royals Collection, 325 (Charlemagne); International Olympic Committee, 220 (Youth Olympics); Jacques Demarthon, 217 (karate); Jeff Kravitz/FilmMagic, 17 (Swift), 132 (LL Cool J); John Harrelson/NASCAR, 19 (Johnson); Julian Finney, 20 (Wambach); Justin Sullivan, 242 (Google map app); Kevin Mazur/WireImage, 16 (Timberlake); Kevin Winter, 17 (fun.); 134 (*American Idol*); Kevork Djansezian, 91 (Sony PS Vita); Leon Neal/AFP, 220 (Sochi); Luciana Whitaker/LatinContent, 278 (Alaska); Mark Davis/KCA2013, 189 (Patrick); Mark Davis/WireImage, 4, 132 (Adele); Massimo Bettio, 223 (rallying); *McClatchy-Tribune*, 190 (Spelling Bee); Michael Bezjian/WireImage, 86 (skinny jeans); Michael Hickey, 227 (Catchings); National Football League, 38 (Flacco); Oli Scarff, 50 (The Shard); Peter Adams, 195 (Hindu festival); Peter Kramer/NBC/NBC NewsWire, 133 (One Direction); Popperfoto, 285 (Nixon), 326 (Henry VIII); Richard Bord, 238 (Clark); Romeo Gacad/AFP, 60 (Eid Al-Fitr); Ronald C. Modra/Sports Imagery, 20 (Lacy); Ronald Martinez, 229 (Mosley); Sadatsugu Tomizawa/AFP, 67 (tsunami); Sattish Bate/*Hindustan Times*, 135 (Bollywood dancers); Sean Gallup, 193 (rabbi); Sonja Flemming/CBS, 10 (*The Big Bang Theory*); Stan Honda/AFP, 76 (bike sharing); Superstock, 3, 35 (Cassatt), 282 (Erie Canal); Thomas Bregardis/AFP, 74 (Rance Tidal Power Station); Tibrina Hobson/WireImage, 86 (maxi dress); Tim Rue/Bloomberg, 77 (hydrogen car); Time & Life Pictures, 41 (Curie), 287 (Chavez); Tony Karumba/AFP, 139 (Somalia); Tyler Golden/NBC/NBCU Photo Bank, 131 (*The Voice*); Ulf Andersen, 275 (Erdrich); WireImage, 39 (Panjabi), 88 (Wang). **Glow Images:** HBSS/Corbis, 81 (girl with water); Tetra, 100 (vaccination). **Groundwood Books:** 47, (cover: *Sita's Ramayana*, by Samhita Arni). **HarperCollins Children's Books:** 44 (cover: *The One and Only Ivan*, by Katherine Applegate), 47 (cover: *Justin Bieber: First Step 2 Forever: My Story*, by Justin Bieber), 48 (Creech). **Courtesy of Lisa Hasenbalg:** 253. **Hawaii State Archives:** 287 (Lili'uokalani). **Hooda Math LLC:** 179 (screen shot: Hooda Math). **Houghton Mifflin Harcourt Children's Book Group:** 45 (Lowry). **Imangi Studios:** 90 (*Temple Run 2*). © **Infobase Learning:** 47 (cover: *The World Almanac for Kids 2014*), 84 (Amazon Rain Forest Destruction), 202 (animal cell, plant cell), 242 (QR-code). **International Astronomical Union:** Martin Kornmesser, 206 (sun and planets). **King:** 3, 90 (*Candy Crush Saga*). **Courtesy of Richard King:** 205. **Russell Knightly Media:** 203 (mimivirus). **Knopf Books for Young Readers:** 44 (cover: *Wonder* by R. J. Palacio). **LaLonnie Lehman:** 89 (Doss). **Library of Congress:** 263 (Lincoln), 266-272 (U.S Presidents: Washington-Clinton, unless otherwise noted); LC-USZC4-10986, 3, 71 (*Lusitania*); LC-D41-24, 66 (1906 earthquake); LC-USZ62-101298, 87 (corset); LC-USZC4-2070, 94 (da Gama); LC-USZ62-48300, 112 (Benz automobile); LC-DIG-cwpb-03540, 120 (Grant); LC-USZC4-2912, 120 (American Revolution); LC-USZC4-6893, 120 (War of 1812); LC-USZC4-2678, 120 (Spanish-American War); LC-USZ62-52389, 197 (Darwin); LC-D4-22602, 245 (steamboat); LC-USZ62-43058, 245 (balloon); LC-USZ62-47579, 245 (horse car); LC-DIG-highsm-11904, 246 (cable car); LC-USZ62-21222, 246 (Model T); LC-USZ62-6166A, 246 (Wright flyer); LC-USZ62-7992, 263 (Cleveland); LC-USZC2-3273, 273 (Washington); LC-USZ62-25792, 273 (Hayes); LC-USZ62-73641, 273 (Harrison); LC-USZ62-17631, 273 (Roosevelt); LC-DIG-highsm-13647, 280 (de Leon); LC-H8-CT-C01-063-E, 281 (Declaration of Independence); LC-USZC2-3796, 282 (War of 1812); LC-DIG-stereo-1s00612, 283 (train); LC-DIG-hec-18526, 284 (Rankin); LC-USZ62-16767, 286 (Du Bois); LC-DIG-ppmsca-15836, 321 (slaves); LC-USZC4-8655, 323 (samurai); LC-USZ62-25600,

327 (Eisenhower); LC-DIG-pga-00710, 328 (Columbus); LC-USZ62-89439, 328 (Pizarro); LC-USZ62-100275, 329 (Diaz); LC-USZ62-7816, 332 (Tubman). **Mars One:** 215. **Jon Martin:** 243 (Anna Martin). **Ad Meskens:** 309 (*Spirit of St. Louis*). **National Aeronautics and Space Administration:** 4, 212 (*Viking 1*), 95 (Ride), 207 (Sun), 285 (man on the Moon), 353 (Sun); Ames/JPL-Caltech, 215 (Earth-sized planets); ESA and the Hubble Heritage Team STScI/AURA), 214 (galaxy); JPL, 211 (Moon); JPL/GSFC/Ames, 207 (Saturn rings); PL-Caltech/UCLA/McREL, 212 (*Dawn*); Johnson Space Center (NASA-JSC), 247 (shuttle). **National Archives:** Army Signal Corps Collection, 121 (D-Day); ARC Identifier 530748, 121 (WWI tanks); 256 (U.S. Constitution); 268 (Grant). **National Geographic:** Mark Thiessen, 113 (*The Deep Challenger*). **National Park Service:** 251 (Great Smoky Mountains National Park). **National Science Foundation:** 214 (comet). **New Hampshire Historical Society:** 268 (Pierce).. **Newscom:** akg-images, 48 (monk); Andre Jenny Stock Connection Worldwide, 278 (totem pole); Billy Farrell/BFAnyc/Sipa USA, 88 (Gevinson); Eric Feferberg/AFP/Getty Images, 321 (Mali); JKG/ZOJ WENN Photos, 238 (Eaton); Marvel Studios, 12 (*Iron Man 3*); Michael Holahan/ZUMA Press, 58 (St. Patrick's Day); Michael Kappeler/dpa/picture-alliance, 242 (MyWallet); OddLott Entertainment, 13 (*The Way, Way Back*); Paramount Pictures, 3, 14 (*Star Trek Into Darkness*); Pedro Saura/AFP/Getty Images, 34 (cave painting); Picture History, 283 (Trail of Tears); Pixar Animation Studios/Walt Disney Pictures/Album, 12 (*Monsters University*); Roth Films/Walt Disney Pictures, 13 (*Oz: The Great and Powerful*); ZUMA Press, 52 (Crooked House), 124 (Helú).**Courtesy of Vivian Ng:** 33. **National Oceanic and Atmospheric Administration:** 70 (tornado). **National Snow and Ice Data Center:** Ted Scambos, 353 (Antarctica). **Nuclear Regulatory Commission:** 72 (nuclear power plant). **Raymond Ostertag:** 53 (Tikal). **Vincent Pampillonia:** 107 (Clemente). **Penguin Group:** Diane H. Reilly, 45 (Lupica). **Penguin Young Reader's Group:** 46 (cover: *Al Capone Does My Shirts*, By Jennifer Choldenko). **Photofest:** ABC, 11 (*The Neighbors*); NBC, 87 (*Miami Vice*); Paramount Pictures, 129 (*Captain America*); Summit Entertainment, 130 (*The Perks of Being a Wallflower*); Twentieth Century Fox Film Corporation, 15 (*The Wolverine*); Walt Disney Studios Motion Pictures, 130 (*Oz: The Great and Powerful*), 189 (*Brave*). **Pinnacle Foods, Inc.:** 112 (Birdseye). **James K. Polk Memorial Association, Columbia, Tennessee:** 273 (Polk). **Prudential Spirit of Community Awards:** 311 (Harvey, Swinderman, and Lam). **Reuters:** KCNA, 7 (North Korea); Max Rossi, 240 (woman checking smartphone). **Franklin D. Roosevelt Library:** 273 (Roosevelt). **Courtesy of Dr. Jodi Rowley, Australian Museum:** 22 (Helen's Flying Frog). **Scholastic, Inc.:** 45 (Collins), 46 (covers: *Storm Runners: Wind* by Roland Smith; *The 39 Clues, Book One: The Maze of Bones*, by Rick Riordan; *13 Gifts*, by Wendy Mass). **David Shankbone:** 51 (Chrysler Building). **Courtesy of ShurTech Brands, LLC:** 191 (Duck Tape prom). **Smithsonian Institution's National Museum of American History:** 252 ("The Star Spangled Banner" flag). **Thinkstock:** Brand X Pictures, 60 (teen science experiment); Fuse, 3, 83 (picking up recycling); iStockphoto, 80 (students leaving school), 81 (LED light), 101 (boy playing soccer), 244 (three-masted ship); Lite Productions, 4, 186 (family); Photodisc, 3, 102 (boy drinking milk); Photos.com, 204 (Copernicus), 281 (Franklin). **Edward A. Thomas:** 318 (hieroglyphics). **Toronto Zoo:** 25 (ferret). **U.S. Army:** 240 (ENIAC); Spc. April Stewart, 318 (Ziggurat of Ur). **U.S. Coast Guard:** Petty Officer 2nd Class Kyle Niem, 331 (Hurricane Katrina). **U.S. Department of Agriculture:** 102 (USDA food plate). **U.S. Department of Defense:** 4, 121 (Persian Gulf War); Erin A. Kirk-Cuomo, 122 (Iraq War). **U.S. Department of State:** 41 (Kerry), 333 (Johnson Sirleaf). **U.S. Department of the Treasury:** U.S. Treasury Bureau of Engraving and Printing, 4, 126 (new $100 bill), 127 (front of $1 bill). **U.S. Fish and Wildlife Service:** Rabon David, 353 (turtle). **U.S. Mint:** 126 (quarters). **U.S. Navy:** 59, Aviation Ordnanceman 2nd Class Charles Reeves (veterans parade); Photographer's Mate 2nd Class Jim Watson, 285 (September 11, 2001). **U.S. Supreme Court:** 39 (Sotomayor). **University of Alcalá:** 270 (Coolidge). **University of Oklahoma Libraries:** Courtesy History of Science Collections, 203 (van Leeuwenhoek). **USA Today Sports:** Kyle Terada, 19 (James). **Oliver Vass:** 155 (Botswana). **Visuals Unlimited, Inc.:** Wim van Egmond, 203 (amoeba). **walterdeanmyers.net:** 45 (Myers). **The White House:** 8 (Obama inauguration 2013), 271 (Eisenhower), 272 (George W. Bush, Obama), 274 (Obama); Pete Souza, 122 (Karzai meeting); Lawrence Jackson, 258 (Congress speech). **James Willis:** 52 (new library in Alexandria, Egypt). **Works Progress Administration:** Federal Art Project, 35

**THE WORLD ALMANAC® FOR KIDS 2014**

# #1 *for* Facts *and* Fun

**Amazing facts fill every page of *The World Almanac for Kids*. Here are just a few...**

What movie won the Academy Award in 2013 for best animated feature film? see page 189

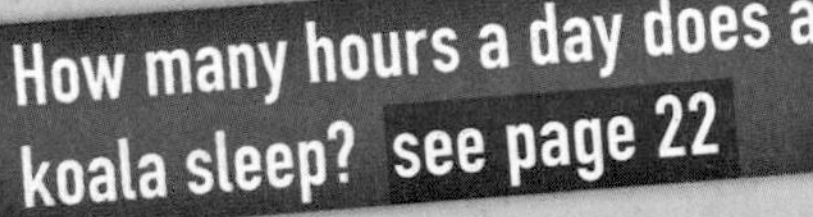


Which planet in our solar system has the most moons? see page 207

What percentage of Americans own tablet computers? see page 49

What U.S. theme park has the most rides? see page 249

Where is the world's largest indoor desert? see page 25

Who was the only woman to rule China? see page 332

What does the prefix *giga* mean in gigabyte? see page 178